PRAISE FOR
THE BIG BOOK OF SMALL PYTHON I

T0076385

"I've always been impressed by the variety of simple, but interesting and fun, projects Al can come up with and this collection takes that to the next level. . . . Even experienced coders are likely to be pulled into browsing through the wide variety that Al has put into this book."

—Naomi Ceder, Fellow of the
Python Software Foundation

"Al Sweigart presents fun programs, inspiring learners to tweak them. That's how I learned to program: tinkering with examples from books and magazines. It works!"

—Luciano Ramalho, Technical
Principal at ThoughtWorks and
author of *Fluent Python*

"Whether you're new to Python or want to exercise your coding brain, I recommend *The Big Book of Small Python Projects* to spark your thinking. Both the 'big' and the 'small' in the title are accurate. There are a lot of projects in this book, but most code takes up only a page or two. That makes it a fun reference book to get you into the flow or kick off a session in your terminal."

—Adam DuVander, Founder,
EveryDeveloper

"This book is excellent for beginners to Python and a great reference book for programmers who are well versed in programming. I'm happy to give this book 5 out of 5 stars!"

—Greg Walters, Full Circle Magazine

"Both informative and entertaining."

—Sumana Bhattacharya,
Analytics Insight

"Will not disappoint . . . After coding a few Python projects from this book, you will definitely start to learn some cool tricks and coding styles that you will start to incorporate into your own projects."

—Seraph VI, The Code Crypt

THE BIG BOOK OF SMALL PYTHON PROJECTS

81 Easy Practice Programs

Al Sweigart

no starch press

San Francisco

Printed in the United States of America

Third printing

26 25 24 23 22   3 4 5 6 7

ISBN-13: 978-1-7185-0124-9 (print)
ISBN-13: 978-1-7185-0125-6 (ebook)

Publisher: William Pollock
Production Manager: Rachel Monaghan
Production Editor: Paula Williamson
Developmental Editor: Frances Saux
Technical Reviewer: Sarah Kuchinsky
Cover and Interior Design: Octopod Studios
Cover Illustrator: Josh Ellingson
Copyeditor: Bart Reed
Compositor: Maureen Forys, Happenstance Type-O-Rama
Proofreader: Scout Festa

For information on distribution, bulk sales, corporate sales, or translations, please contact No Starch Press, Inc. directly at info@nostarch.com or:

No Starch Press, Inc.
245 8th Street, San Francisco, CA 94103
phone: 1.415.863.9900
www.nostarch.com

Library of Congress Control Number: 2021936413

About the Author

Al Sweigart is a software developer, author, and Fellow of the Python Software Foundation. He was previously the education director at Oakland, California's video game museum, The Museum of Art and Digital Entertainment. He has written several programming books, including *Automate the Boring Stuff with Python* and *Invent Your Own Computer Games with Python*. His books are freely available under a Creative Commons license at his website *https://inventwithpython.com*. His cat Zophie loves eating nori seaweed snacks.

About the Technical Reviewer

Sarah Kuchinsky, MS, is a corporate trainer and consultant. She uses Python for a variety of applications, including health systems modeling, game development, and task automation. Sarah is a co-founder of the North Bay Python conference, tutorials chair for PyCon US, and lead organizer for PyLadies Silicon Valley. She holds degrees in Management Science & Engineering and Mathematics.

CONTENTS IN DETAIL

INTRODUCTION

Programming was so easy when it was just
following `print('Hello, world!')` tutorials.
Perhaps you've followed a well-structured
book or online course for beginners, worked
through the exercises, and nodded along with its technical jargon that you (mostly) understood. However,
when it came time to leave the nest to write your own
programs, maybe you found it hard to fly on your own. You found yourself
staring at a blank editor window and unsure of how to get started writing
Python programs of your own.

The problem is that following a tutorial is great for learning concepts,
but that isn't necessarily the same thing as learning to create original programs from scratch. The common advice given at this stage is to examine
the source code of open source software or to work on your own projects,
but open source projects aren't always well documented or especially accessible to newcomers. And while it's motivating to work on your own project,
you're left completely without guidance or structure.

This book provides you with practice examples of how programming concepts are applied, with a collection of over 80 games, simulations, and digital art programs. These aren't code snippets; they're full, runnable Python programs. You can copy their code to become familiar with how they work, experiment with your own changes, and then attempt to re-create them on your own as practice. After a while, you'll start to get ideas for your own programs and, more importantly, know how to go about creating them.

How to Design Small Programs

Programming has proven to be a powerful skill, creating billion-dollar tech companies and amazing technological advances. It's easy to want to aim high with your own software creations, but biting off more than you can chew can leave you with half-finished programs and frustration. However, you don't need to be a computer genius to code fun and creative programs.

The Python programs in this book follow several design principles to aid new programmers in understanding their source code:

Small   Most of these programs are limited to 256 lines of code and are often significantly shorter. This size limit makes them easier to comprehend. The choice of 256 is arbitrary, but 256 is also 2^8, and powers of 2 are lucky programmer numbers.

Text based   Text is simpler than graphics. Since the source code and program output are both text, it's easy to trace the cause and effect between print('Thanks for playing!') in the code and Thanks for playing! appearing on the screen.

No installation needed   Each program is self-contained in a single Python source file with the *.py* file extension, like *tictactoe.py*. You don't need to run an installer program, and you can easily post these programs online to share with others.

Numerous   There are 81 programs in this book. Between board games, card games, digital artwork, simulations, mathematical puzzles, mazes, and humor programs, you're bound to find many things you'll love.

Simple   The programs have been written to be easy to understand by beginners. Whenever I had to choose between writing code using sophisticated, high-performance algorithms or writing plain, straightforward code, I've chosen the latter every time.

The text-based programs may seem old school, but this style of programming cuts out the distractions and potholes that downloading graphics, installing additional libraries, and managing project folders bring. Instead, you can just focus on the code.

Who Is This Book For?

This book is written for two groups of people. The people in the first group are those who have already learned the basics of Python and programming but are still unsure of how to write programs on their own. They may feel that programming hasn't "clicked" for them. They may be able to solve the practice exercises from their tutorials but still struggle to picture what a complete program "looks like." By first copying and then later re-creating the games in this book, they'll be exposed to how the programming concepts they've learned are assembled into a variety of real programs.

The people in the second group are those who are new to programming but are excited and a bit adventurous. They want to dive right in and get started making games, simulations, and number-crunching programs right away. They're fine with copying the code and learning along the way. Or perhaps they already know how to program in another language but are new to Python. While it's no substitute for a complete introductory Python course, this book contains a brief introduction to Python basics and how to use the debugger to examine the inner workings of a program as it runs.

Experienced programmers might have fun with the programs in this book as well, but keep in mind that this book was written for beginners.

About This Book

While the bulk of this book is dedicated to the featured programs, there are also extra resources with general programming and Python information. Here's what's contained in this book:

Projects The 81 projects are too numerous to list here, but each one is a self-contained mini-chapter that includes the project's name, a description, a sample run of the program's output, and the source code of the program. There are also suggestions for experimental edits you can make to the code to customize the program.

Appendix A: Tag Index Lists all of the projects categorized by their project tags.

Appendix B: Character Map A list of character codes for symbols such as hearts, lines, arrows, and blocks that your programs can print.

How to Learn from the Programs in This Book

This book doesn't teach Python or programming concepts like a traditional tutorial. It has a learn-by-doing approach, where you're encouraged to manually copy the programs, play with them, and inspect their inner workings by running them under a debugger.

The point of this book isn't to give a detailed explanation of programming language syntax, but to show solid examples of programs that perform an actual activity, whether it's a card game, an animation, or exploration of a mathematical puzzle. As such, I recommend the following steps:

1. Download the program and run it to see what the program does for yourself.

2. Starting from a blank file, copy the code of the game from this book by manually typing it yourself. (Don't use copy and paste!)

3. Run the program again, and go back and fix any typos or bugs you may have introduced.

4. Run the program under a debugger, so you can carefully execute each line of code one at a time to understand what it does.

5. Find the comments marked with (!) to find code that you can modify and then see how this affects the program the next time you run it.

6. Finally, try to re-create the program yourself from scratch. It doesn't have to be an exact copy; you can put your own spin on the program.

When copying the code from this book, you don't necessarily have to type the comments (the text at the end of a line following the # symbol), as these are notes for human programmers and are ignored by Python. However, try to write your Python code on the same line numbers as the programs in this book to make comparison between the two easier. If you have trouble finding typos in your program, you can compare your code to the code in this book with the online diff tool at *https://inventwithpython.com/bigbookpython/diff/*.

Each program has been given a set of tags to describe it, such as **board game**, **simulation**, **artistic**, and **two-player**. An explanation of each of these tags and a cross-index of tags and projects can be found in Appendix A. The projects are listed in alphabetical order, however.

Downloading and Installing Python

Python is the name of both the programming language and the interpreter software that runs your Python code. The Python software is completely free to download and use. You can check if you already have Python installed from a command line window. On Windows, open the Command Prompt program and then enter `py --version`. If you see output like the following, then Python is installed:

```
C:\Users\Al>py --version
Python 3.9.1
```

On macOS and Linux, open the Terminal program and then enter `python3 --version`. If you see output like the following, then Python is installed:

```
$ python3 --version
Python 3.9.1
```

This book uses Python version 3. Several backward-incompatible changes were made between Python 2 and 3, and the programs in this book require at least Python version 3.1.1 (released in 2009) to run. If you see an error message telling you that Python cannot be found or the version reports Python 2, you can download the latest Python installer for your operating system from *https://python.org/*. If you're having trouble installing Python, you can find more instructions at *https://installpython3.com/*.

Downloading and Installing the Mu Editor

While the Python software runs your program, you'll type the Python code into a text editor or integrated development environment (IDE) application. I recommend using Mu Editor for your IDE if you are a beginner because it's simple and doesn't distract you with an overwhelming number of advanced options.

Open *https://codewith.mu/* in your browser. On Windows and macOS, download the installer for your operating system and then run it by double-clicking the installer file. If you are on macOS, running the installer opens a window where you must drag the Mu icon to the Applications folder icon to continue the installation. If you are on Ubuntu, you'll need to install Mu as a Python package. In that case, open a new Terminal window and run `pip3 install mu-editor` to install and `mu-editor` to run it. Click the **Instructions** button in the Python Package section of the download page for full instruction details.

Running the Mu Editor

Once it's installed, let's start Mu:

- On Windows 7 or later, click the **Start** icon in the lower-left corner of your screen, enter `mu` in the search box, and select **Mu** when it appears.
- On macOS, open the Finder window, click **Applications**, and then click **mu-editor**.
- On Ubuntu, press CTRL-ALT-T to open a Terminal window and then enter `python3 -m mu`.

The first time Mu runs, a Select Mode window appears with the following options: Adafruit CircuitPython, BBC micro:bit, Pygame Zero, and Python 3. Select Python 3. You can always change the mode later by clicking the **Mode** button at the top of the editor window.

You'll be able to enter the code into Mu's main window and then save, open, and run your files from the buttons at the top.

Running IDLE and Other Editors

You can use any number of editors for writing Python code. The Integrated Development and Learning Environment (IDLE) software installs along with Python, and it can serve as a second editor if for some reason you can't get Mu installed or working. Let's start IDLE now:

- On Windows 7 or later, click the **Start** icon in the lower-left corner of your screen, enter `idle` in the search box, and select **IDLE (Python GUI)**.

- On macOS, open the Finder window and click **Applications ▸ Python 3.9 ▸ IDLE**.
- On Ubuntu, select **Applications ▸ Accessories ▸ Terminal** and then enter `idle3`. (You may also be able to click **Applications** at the top of the screen, select **Programming**, and then click **IDLE 3**.)
- On the Raspberry Pi, click the Raspberry Pi menu button in the top-left corner; then click **Programming** and **Python 3 (IDLE)**. You can also select **Thonny Python IDE** from under the **Programming** menu.

There are several other free editors you can use to enter and run Python code, such as:

- Thonny, a Python IDE for beginners, at *https://thonny.org/*.
- PyCharm Community Edition, a Python IDE used by professional developers, at *https://www.jetbrains.com/pycharm/*.

Installing Python Modules

Most of the programs in this book only require the Python Standard Library, which is installed automatically with Python. However, some programs require third-party modules such as `pyperclip`, `bext`, `playsound`, and `pyttsx3`. All of these can be installed at once by installing the `bigbookpython` module.

For the Mu Editor, you must install the 1.1.0-alpha version (or later). As of 2020, you can find this version at the top of the download page at *https://codewith.mu/en/download* under the "Try the Alpha of the Next Version of Mu" section. After installation, click the gear icon in the lower-left corner of the window to bring up the Mu Administration window. Select the **Third Party Packages** tab, enter `bigbookpython` into the text field, and click **Ok**. This installs all of the third-party modules used by the programs in this book.

For the Visual Studio Code or IDLE editor, open the editor and run the following Python code from the interactive shell:

```
>>> import os, sys
>>> os.system(sys.executable + ' -m pip install --user bigbookpython')
0
```

The number 0 appears after the second instruction if everything worked correctly. Otherwise, if you see an error message or another number, try running the following instructions, which don't have the --user option:

```
>>> import os, sys
>>> os.system(sys.executable + ' -m pip install bigbookpython')
0
```

No matter which editor you use, you can try running `import pyperclip` or `import bext` to check if the installation worked. If these import instruction don't produce an error message, these modules installed correctly and you'll be able to run the projects in this book that use these modules.

Copying the Code from This Book

Programming is a skill that you improve by programming. Don't just read the code in this book or copy and paste it to your computer. Take the time to enter the code into the editor for yourself. Open a new file in your code editor and enter the code. Pay attention to the line numbers in this book and your editor to make sure you aren't accidentally skipping any lines. **If you encounter errors, use the online diff tool at *https://inventwithpython.com/bigbookpython/diff/* to show you any differences between your code and the code in this book**. To get a better understanding of these programs, try running them under the debugger.

After entering the source code and running it a few times, try making experimental changes to the code. The comments marked with (!) have suggestions for small changes you can make, and each project lists suggestions for larger modifications.

Next, try re-creating the program from scratch without looking at the source code in this book. It doesn't have to be exactly the same as this program; you can invent your own version!

Once you've worked through the programs in this book, you might want to start creating your own. Most modern video games and software applications are complicated, requiring teams of programmers, artists, and designers to create. However, many board, card, and paper-and-pencil games are often simple enough to re-create as a program. Many of these fall under the category of "abstract strategy games." You can find a list of them at *https://en.wikipedia.org/wiki/List_of_abstract_strategy_games*.

Running Programs from the Terminal

The programming projects in this book that use the `bext` module have colorful text for their output. However, these colors won't appear when you run them from Mu, IDLE, or other editors. These programs should be run from a *terminal*, also called *command line*, window. On Windows, run the Command Prompt program from the Start menu. On macOS, run Terminal from Spotlight. On Ubuntu Linux, run Terminal from Ubuntu Dash or press CTRL-ALT-T.

When the terminal window appears, you should change the current directory to the folder with your *.py* files with the `cd` (change directory) command. (*Directory* is another term for folder.) For example, if I were on Windows and saved my Python programs to the *C:\Users\Al* folder, I would enter the following line.

```
C:\>cd C:\Users\Al

C:\Users\Al>
```

Then, to run Python programs, enter python *yourProgram.py* on Windows or python3 *yourProgram.py* on macOS and Linux, replacing *yourProgram.py* with the name of your Python program:

```
C:\Users\Al>python guess.py
Guess the Number, by Al Sweigart al@inventwithpython.com

I am thinking of a number between 1 and 100.
You have 10 guesses left. Take a guess.
--snip--
```

You can terminate programs run from the terminal by pressing CTRL-C rather than close the terminal window itself.

Running Programs from a Phone or Tablet

Ideally you'll have a laptop or desktop computer with a full keyboard to write code, as tapping on a phone or even tablet keyboard can be tedious. While there are no established Python interpreters for Android or iOS, there are websites that host online Python interactive shells you can use from a web browser. These will also work for laptops and desktops, in case you're an instructor who doesn't have account permission to install new software on your classroom's computers.

The websites *https://repl.it/languages/Python3/* and *https://www.pythonany where.com/* have Python interpreters that are free to use in your web browser. These websites will work with most of the projects in this book. However, they won't work with programs that make use of third-party modules, such as bext, pyperclip, pyttsx3, and playsound. They also won't work with programs that need to read or write files with the open() function. If you see these terms in the program's code, the program won't work in these online Python interpreters. However, the majority of programs in this book will work just fine.

How to Get Help

Unless you can hire a private tutor or have a programmer friend who can answer your programming questions, you'll need to rely on yourself to find answers to your questions. Fortunately, your questions have almost certainly been asked before. Being able to find answers on your own is an important skill for programmers to learn.

Don't feel discouraged if you find yourself constantly looking up answers to your programming questions online. You may feel like it's "cheating" to check online instead of memorizing everything about programming from the start, but as long as you're learning, it's not cheating. Even professional software developers search the internet on a daily basis. In this section, you'll learn how to ask smart questions and search for answers on the internet.

When your program tries to carry out an invalid instruction, it displays an error message called a traceback. The traceback tells you what kind of error occurred and which line of code the error occurred on. Here's an example of a program that had an error while calculating how many slices of pizza each person should get:

```
Traceback (most recent call last):
  File "pizza.py", line 5, in <module>
    print('Each person gets', (slices / people), ' slices of pizza.')
ZeroDivisionError: division by zero
```

From this traceback, you might not realize that the problem is that the people variable is set to 0, and so the expression slices / people caused a zero-divide error. Error messages are often so short they're not even full sentences. Since programmers encounter them regularly, they're intended as reminders rather than full explanations. If you're encountering an error message for the first time, copying and pasting it into an internet search often returns a detailed explanation of what the error means and what its likely causes are.

If you're unable to find the solution to your problem by searching the internet, you can post your question to an online forum or email someone. To make this process as efficient as possible, ask specific, well-stated questions. This means providing full source code and error message details, explaining what you've already tried, and telling your helper what operating system and version of Python you're using. Not only will the posted answers solve your problem, but they can help future programmers who have your same question and find your post.

Typing Code

You don't have to be able to type fast to be a programmer, but it helps. While many people take a "hunt and peck" approach to typing, a faster typing speed can make programming less of a chore. As you work through the programs in this book, you'll want your eyes on the code and not on your keyboard.

There are free websites for learning how to type, such as *https://typing club.com/* or *https://www.typing.com/*. A good typing program will display a keyboard and transparent hands on the screen so you can practice without the bad habit of looking down at the keyboard to find keys. Like every skill, typing is a matter of practice, and writing code can provide you with plenty of opportunities to type.

Keyboard shortcuts allow you to perform actions in a fraction of the time it takes to move the mouse to a menu and perform the action. A shortcut is often written like "CTRL-C," which means pressing down one of the two CTRL keys on either side of the keyboard and then pressing the C key. It does not mean pressing the CTRL key once, followed by pressing the C key.

You can discover the common shortcuts, such as CTRL-S to save and CTRL-C to copy, by using the mouse to open the menu bar at the top of the application (in Windows and Linux) or top of the screen (in macOS). It's well worth the time to learn and use these keyboard shortcuts.

Other shortcuts are not so obvious. For example, ALT-TAB on Windows and Linux and COMMAND-TAB on macOS allow you to switch focus to another application's window. You can hold the ALT or COMMAND key down and repeatedly press TAB to select a specific window to switch to.

Copying and Pasting

The *clipboard* is a feature of your operating system that can temporarily store data for pasting. While this data can be text, images, files, or other types of information, we'll be dealing with text data in this section. *Copying* text places a copy of the currently selected text onto the clipboard. *Pasting* text enters the text on the clipboard into wherever the text cursor currently is, as though you had instantly typed it yourself. Copying and pasting text frees you from having to retype text that already exists on your computer, whether it's a single line or hundreds of pages.

To copy and paste text, first select, or *highlight*, the text to copy. You can do this by holding down the primary mouse button (which is the left button, if the mouse is set for right-handed users) and dragging over the text to select it. However, holding down the SHIFT key and moving the cursor with the keyboard shortcuts is often faster and more precise. Many applications allow you to double-click a word to immediately select the entire word. You can also often triple-click to immediately select an entire line or paragraph.

The next step is to press CTRL-C on Windows or COMMAND-C on macOS to copy the selected text to the clipboard. The clipboard can only hold one selection of text, so copying text replaces anything that was previously on the clipboard.

Finally, move the cursor to where you want the text to appear and press CTRL-V on Windows or COMMAND-V on macOS to paste the text. You can paste as many times as you want; the text remains on the clipboard until you copy new text to replace it.

Finding and Replacing Text

Dan Russell, a search anthropologist at Google, explained in a 2011 *Atlantic* article that when he studied people's computer usage habits, 90 percent of them didn't know they could press CTRL-F (on Windows and Linux) or COMMAND-F (on macOS) to search for words in their applications. This is an incredibly useful feature, not just in code editors, but in word processors, web browsers, spreadsheet applications, and almost every kind of program that displays text. You can press CTRL-F to bring up a Find window to enter a word to find in the program. Often the F3 key will repeat this search to highlight the next occurrence of the word. This feature can save you an extraordinary amount of time compared to manually scrolling through your document to find a word.

Editors also have a find-and-replace feature, which is often assigned the CTRL-H or COMMAND-H shortcut. This allows you to locate occurrences of one bit of text and replace it with another. This is useful if you want to rename a variable or function. However, you need to be careful using the find-and-replace feature because you could unintentionally replace text that matched your find criteria by coincidence.

The Debugger

A debugger is a tool that runs programs one line at a time and lets you inspect the current state of the program's variables. It's a valuable tool for tracking down bugs. This section will explain the features of the Mu Editor's debugger. Don't worry; every debugger will have these same features, even if the user interface looks different.

To start a program in the debugger, use the Debug menu item in your IDE instead of the Run menu item. The debugger will start in a paused state on the first line of your program. All debuggers have the following buttons: Continue, Step In, Step Over, Step Out, and Stop.

Clicking the Continue button causes the program to execute normally until it terminates or reaches a breakpoint. (I describe breakpoints later in this section.) If you are done debugging and want the program to continue normally, click the Continue button.

Clicking the Step In button causes the debugger to execute the next line of code and then pause again. If the next line of code is a function call, the debugger will "step into" that function and jump to the first line of code of that function.

Clicking the Step Over button executes the next line of code, similar to the Step In button. However, if the next line of code is a function call, the Step Over button will "step over" the code in the function. The function's code executes at full speed, and the debugger will pause as soon as the function call returns. Using the Step Over button is more common than using the Step In button.

Clicking the Step Out button causes the debugger to execute lines of code at full speed until it returns from the current function. If you have stepped into a function call with the Step In button and now simply want to keep executing instructions until you get back out, click the Step Out button to "step out" of the current function call.

If you want to stop debugging entirely and not bother to continue executing the rest of the program, click the Stop button. The Stop button immediately terminates the program.

You can set a *breakpoint* on a particular line and let the program run at normal speed until it reaches the breakpoint line. At that point, the debugger pauses to let you inspect the variables and lets you resume stepping through individual lines of code. In most IDEs, you can set a breakpoint by double-clicking the line numbers on the left side of the window.

The values currently stored in the program's variables are displayed somewhere in the debugging window in every debugger. However, one common method of debugging your programs is *print debugging*: adding print() calls to display the values of variables and then rerunning your program. While simple and convenient, this approach to debugging can often be slower than using a debugger. With print debugging, you must add the print() calls, rerun your program, and then remove the print() calls later. However, after rerunning the program, you'll often find that you need to add more print() calls to see the values of other variables. This means you need to rerun the program yet again, and this run could reveal that you need another round of adding print() calls, and so on. Also, it's common to forget some of the print() calls you've added, requiring an additional round of deleting print() calls. Print debugging is straightforward for simple bugs, but using an actual debugger can save you time in the long run.

Summary

Programming is a fun, creative skill to develop. Whether you've mastered the basics of Python syntax or simply want to dive into some real Python programs, the projects in this book will spark new ideas for what's possible with as little as a few pages of code.

The best way to work through these programs isn't to merely read their code or copy and paste it to your computer. Take the time to manually type the code from this book into your editor to develop the muscle memory of writing code. This also slows you down so you can consider each line as you type, instead of merely skimming it over with your eyes. Look up any instructions you don't recognize using an internet search engine, or experiment with them in the interactive shell.

Finally, take it upon yourself to re-create the program from scratch and then modify it with features of your own. These exercises give you a solid foundation for how programming concepts are applied to create actual, runnable programs. And most of all, don't forget to have fun!

#1

BAGELS

In Bagels, a deductive logic game, you must guess a secret three-digit number based on clues. The game offers one of the following hints in response to your guess: "Pico" when your guess has a correct digit in the wrong place, "Fermi" when your guess has a correct digit in the correct place, and "Bagels" if your guess has no correct digits. You have 10 tries to guess the secret number.

The Program in Action

When you run *bagels.py*, the output will look like this:

```
Bagels, a deductive logic game.
By Al Sweigart al@inventwithpython.com

I am thinking of a 3-digit number. Try to guess what it is.
Here are some clues:
When I say:    That means:
  Pico         One digit is correct but in the wrong position.
  Fermi        One digit is correct and in the right position.
  Bagels       No digit is correct.
I have thought up a number.
 You have 10 guesses to get it.
Guess #1:
> 123
Pico
Guess #2:
> 456
Bagels
Guess #3:
> 178
Pico Pico
--snip--
Guess #7:
> 791
Fermi Fermi
Guess #8:
> 701
You got it!
Do you want to play again? (yes or no)
> no
Thanks for playing!
```

How It Works

Keep in mind that this program uses not integer values but rather string values that contain numeric digits. For example, '426' is a different value than 426. We need to do this because we are performing string comparisons with the secret number, not math operations. Remember that '0' can be a leading digit: the string '026' is different from '26', but the integer 026 is the same as 26.

```
1. """Bagels, by Al Sweigart al@inventwithpython.com
2. A deductive logic game where you must guess a number based on clues.
3. View this code at https://nostarch.com/big-book-small-python-projects
4. A version of this game is featured in the book "Invent Your Own
5. Computer Games with Python" https://nostarch.com/inventwithpython
6. Tags: short, game, puzzle"""
7.
8. import random
9.
```

```
10. NUM_DIGITS = 3  # (!) Try setting this to 1 or 10.
11. MAX_GUESSES = 10  # (!) Try setting this to 1 or 100.
12.
13.
14. def main():
15.     print('''Bagels, a deductive logic game.
16. By Al Sweigart al@inventwithpython.com
17.
18. I am thinking of a {}-digit number with no repeated digits.
19. Try to guess what it is. Here are some clues:
20. When I say:    That means:
21.   Pico         One digit is correct but in the wrong position.
22.   Fermi        One digit is correct and in the right position.
23.   Bagels       No digit is correct.
24.
25. For example, if the secret number was 248 and your guess was 843, the
26. clues would be Fermi Pico.'''.format(NUM_DIGITS))
27.
28.     while True:  # Main game loop.
29.         # This stores the secret number the player needs to guess:
30.         secretNum = getSecretNum()
31.         print('I have thought up a number.')
32.         print(' You have {} guesses to get it.'.format(MAX_GUESSES))
33.
34.         numGuesses = 1
35.         while numGuesses <= MAX_GUESSES:
36.             guess = ''
37.             # Keep looping until they enter a valid guess:
38.             while len(guess) != NUM_DIGITS or not guess.isdecimal():
39.                 print('Guess #{}: '.format(numGuesses))
40.                 guess = input('> ')
41.
42.             clues = getClues(guess, secretNum)
43.             print(clues)
44.             numGuesses += 1
45.
46.             if guess == secretNum:
47.                 break  # They're correct, so break out of this loop.
48.             if numGuesses > MAX_GUESSES:
49.                 print('You ran out of guesses.')
50.                 print('The answer was {}.'.format(secretNum))
51.
52.         # Ask player if they want to play again.
53.         print('Do you want to play again? (yes or no)')
54.         if not input('> ').lower().startswith('y'):
55.             break
56.     print('Thanks for playing!')
57.
58.
59. def getSecretNum():
60.     """Returns a string made up of NUM_DIGITS unique random digits."""
61.     numbers = list('0123456789')  # Create a list of digits 0 to 9.
62.     random.shuffle(numbers)  # Shuffle them into random order.
63.
64.     # Get the first NUM_DIGITS digits in the list for the secret number:
```

```
65.       secretNum = ''
66.       for i in range(NUM_DIGITS):
67.           secretNum += str(numbers[i])
68.       return secretNum
69.
70.
71. def getClues(guess, secretNum):
72.       """Returns a string with the pico, fermi, bagels clues for a guess
73.       and secret number pair."""
74.       if guess == secretNum:
75.           return 'You got it!'
76.
77.       clues = []
78.
79.       for i in range(len(guess)):
80.           if guess[i] == secretNum[i]:
81.               # A correct digit is in the correct place.
82.               clues.append('Fermi')
83.           elif guess[i] in secretNum:
84.               # A correct digit is in the incorrect place.
85.               clues.append('Pico')
86.       if len(clues) == 0:
87.           return 'Bagels'  # There are no correct digits at all.
88.       else:
89.           # Sort the clues into alphabetical order so their original order
90.           # doesn't give information away.
91.           clues.sort()
92.           # Make a single string from the list of string clues.
93.           return ' '.join(clues)
94.
95.
96. # If the program is run (instead of imported), run the game:
97. if __name__ == '__main__':
98.       main()
```

After entering the source code and running it a few times, try making experimental changes to it. The comments marked with (!) have suggestions for small changes you can make. On your own, you can also try to figure out how to do the following:

- Change the number of digits for the secret number by changing NUM_DIGITS.
- Change the number of guesses the player gets by changing MAX_GUESSES.
- Try to create a version with letters as well as digits in the secret number.

Exploring the Program

Try to find the answers to the following questions. Experiment with some modifications to the code and rerun the program to see what effect the changes have.

1. What happens when you change the NUM_DIGITS constant?

2. What happens when you change the MAX_GUESSES constant?

3. What happens if you set NUM_DIGITS to a number larger than 10?

4. What happens if you replace secretNum = getSecretNum() on line 30 with secretNum = '123'?

5. What error message do you get if you delete or comment out numGuesses = 1 on line 34?

6. What happens if you delete or comment out random.shuffle(numbers) on line 62?

7. What happens if you delete or comment out if guess == secretNum: on line 74 and return 'You got it!' on line 75?

8. What happens if you comment out numGuesses += 1 on line 44?

#2

BIRTHDAY PARADOX

The Birthday Paradox, also called the Birthday Problem, is the surprisingly high probability that two people will have the same birthday even in a small group of people. In a group of 70 people, there's a 99.9 percent chance of two people having a matching birthday. But even in a group as small as 23 people, there's a 50 percent chance of a matching birthday. This program performs several probability experiments to determine the percentages for groups of different sizes. We call these types of experiments, in which we conduct multiple random trials to understand the likely outcomes, Monte Carlo experiments.

You can find out more about the Birthday Paradox at *https://en.wikipedia .org/wiki/Birthday_problem*.

The Program in Action

When you run *birthdayparadox.py*, the output will look like this:

```
Birthday Paradox, by Al Sweigart al@inventwithpython.com
--snip--
How many birthdays shall I generate? (Max 100)
> 23

Here are 23 birthdays:
Oct 9, Sep 1, May 28, Jul 29, Feb 17, Jan 8, Aug 18, Feb 19, Dec 1, Jan 22,
May 16, Sep 25, Oct 6, May 6, May 26, Oct 11, Dec 19, Jun 28, Jul 29, Dec 6,
Nov 26, Aug 18, Mar 18

In this simulation, multiple people have a birthday on Jul 29

Generating 23 random birthdays 100,000 times...
Press Enter to begin...
Let's run another 100,000 simulations.
0 simulations run...
10000 simulations run...
--snip--
90000 simulations run...
100000 simulations run.
Out of 100,000 simulations of 23 people, there was a
matching birthday in that group 50955 times. This means
that 23 people have a 50.95 % chance of
having a matching birthday in their group.
That's probably more than you would think!
```

How It Works

Running 100,000 simulations can take a while, which is why lines 95 and 96 report that another 10,000 simulations have finished. This feedback can assure the user that the program hasn't frozen. Notice that some of the integers, like 10_000 on line 95 and 100_000 on lines 93 and 103, have underscores. These underscores have no special meaning, but Python allows them so that programmers can make integer values easier to read. In other words, it's easier to read "one hundred thousand" from 100_000 than from 100000.

```
 1. """Birthday Paradox Simulation, by Al Sweigart al@inventwithpython.com
 2. Explore the surprising probabilities of the "Birthday Paradox".
 3. More info at https://en.wikipedia.org/wiki/Birthday_problem
 4. View this code at https://nostarch.com/big-book-small-python-projects
 5. Tags: short, math, simulation"""
 6.
 7. import datetime, random
 8.
 9.
10. def getBirthdays(numberOfBirthdays):
11.     """Returns a list of number random date objects for birthdays."""
12.     birthdays = []
```

```
13.     for i in range(numberOfBirthdays):
14.         # The year is unimportant for our simulation, as long as all
15.         # birthdays have the same year.
16.         startOfYear = datetime.date(2001, 1, 1)
17.
18.         # Get a random day into the year:
19.         randomNumberOfDays = datetime.timedelta(random.randint(0, 364))
20.         birthday = startOfYear + randomNumberOfDays
21.         birthdays.append(birthday)
22.     return birthdays
23.
24.
25. def getMatch(birthdays):
26.     """Returns the date object of a birthday that occurs more than once
27.     in the birthdays list."""
28.     if len(birthdays) == len(set(birthdays)):
29.         return None  # All birthdays are unique, so return None.
30.
31.     # Compare each birthday to every other birthday:
32.     for a, birthdayA in enumerate(birthdays):
33.         for b, birthdayB in enumerate(birthdays[a + 1 :]):
34.             if birthdayA == birthdayB:
35.                 return birthdayA  # Return the matching birthday.
36.
37.
38. # Display the intro:
39. print('''Birthday Paradox, by Al Sweigart al@inventwithpython.com
40.
41. The Birthday Paradox shows us that in a group of N people, the odds
42. that two of them have matching birthdays is surprisingly large.
43. This program does a Monte Carlo simulation (that is, repeated random
44. simulations) to explore this concept.
45.
46. (It's not actually a paradox, it's just a surprising result.)
47. ''')
48.
49. # Set up a tuple of month names in order:
50. MONTHS = ('Jan', 'Feb', 'Mar', 'Apr', 'May', 'Jun',
51.           'Jul', 'Aug', 'Sep', 'Oct', 'Nov', 'Dec')
52.
53. while True:  # Keep asking until the user enters a valid amount.
54.     print('How many birthdays shall I generate? (Max 100)')
55.     response = input('> ')
56.     if response.isdecimal() and (0 < int(response) <= 100):
57.         numBDays = int(response)
58.         break  # User has entered a valid amount.
59. print()
60.
61. # Generate and display the birthdays:
62. print('Here are', numBDays, 'birthdays:')
63. birthdays = getBirthdays(numBDays)
64. for i, birthday in enumerate(birthdays):
65.     if i != 0:
66.         # Display a comma for each birthday after the first birthday.
67.         print(', ', end='')
```

```
68.     monthName = MONTHS[birthday.month - 1]
69.     dateText = '{} {}'.format(monthName, birthday.day)
70.     print(dateText, end='')
71. print()
72. print()
73.
74. # Determine if there are two birthdays that match.
75. match = getMatch(birthdays)
76.
77. # Display the results:
78. print('In this simulation, ', end='')
79. if match != None:
80.     monthName = MONTHS[match.month - 1]
81.     dateText = '{} {}'.format(monthName, match.day)
82.     print('multiple people have a birthday on', dateText)
83. else:
84.     print('there are no matching birthdays.')
85. print()
86.
87. # Run through 100,000 simulations:
88. print('Generating', numBDays, 'random birthdays 100,000 times...')
89. input('Press Enter to begin...')
90.
91. print('Let\'s run another 100,000 simulations.')
92. simMatch = 0  # How many simulations had matching birthdays in them.
93. for i in range(100_000):
94.     # Report on the progress every 10,000 simulations:
95.     if i % 10_000 == 0:
96.         print(i, 'simulations run...')
97.     birthdays = getBirthdays(numBDays)
98.     if getMatch(birthdays) != None:
99.         simMatch = simMatch + 1
100. print('100,000 simulations run.')
101.
102. # Display simulation results:
103. probability = round(simMatch / 100_000 * 100, 2)
104. print('Out of 100,000 simulations of', numBDays, 'people, there was a')
105. print('matching birthday in that group', simMatch, 'times. This means')
106. print('that', numBDays, 'people have a', probability, '% chance of')
107. print('having a matching birthday in their group.')
108. print('That\'s probably more than you would think!')
```

Exploring the Program

Try to find the answers to the following questions. Experiment with some modifications to the code and rerun the program to see what effect the changes have.

1. How are birthdays represented in this program? (Hint: look at line 16.)

2. How could you remove the maximum limit of 100 birthdays the program generates?

3. What error message do you get if you delete or comment out numBDays = int(response) on line 57?

4. How can you make the program display full month names, such as 'January' instead of 'Jan'?

5. How could you make 'X simulations run...' appear every 1,000 simulations instead of every 10,000?

#3

BITMAP MESSAGE

This program uses a multiline string as a *bitmap*, a 2D image with only two possible colors for each pixel, to determine how it should display a message from the user. In this bitmap, space characters represent an empty space, and all other characters are replaced by characters in the user's message. The provided bitmap resembles a world map, but you can change this to any image you'd like. The binary simplicity of the space-or-message-characters system makes it good for beginners. Try experimenting with different messages to see what the results look like!

The Program in Action

When you run *bitmapmessage.py*, the output will look like this:

```
Bitmap Message, by Al Sweigart al@inventwithpython.com
Enter the message to display with the bitmap.
> Hello!

Hello!Hello!Hello!Hello!Hello!Hello!Hello!Hello!Hello!Hello!Hello!He
    lo!Hello!Hello   l !He lo  e      llo!Hello!Hello!Hello!Hello!He
   llo!Hello!Hello!Hello He lo H  l !Hello!Hello!Hello!Hello!Hello H
  el      lo!Hello!Hello!He         lo!Hello!Hello!Hello!Hello!Hel
          o!Hello!Hello            lo  e lo!H ll !Hello!Hello!H l
          !Hello!He               llo!Hel   Hello!Hello!Hell ! e
          Hello!He                ello!Hello!Hello!Hello!Hell  H
  l       H llo! ell              ello!Hello!Hell !Hello  el o
           lo!H  l                ello!Hello!Hell   ell !He  o
            !Hello                llo!Hello!Hel    el   He  o
            !Hello!H               lo!Hello!Hell    l  !H llo
            ello!Hel               Hello!He         H llo Hell
            ello!Hell              ello!H  l        Hell !H l o!
            ello!Hell              ello!H l o           o!H l   H
             lo!Hel                ello! el             o!Hel   H
             lo!He                 llo! e              llo!Hell
             llo!H                 llo!                llo!Hello
             llo!                  ll                   lo!Hell   e
             llo                                         l    e
             ll    l                          H
Hello!Hello!Hello!Hello!Hello!Hello!Hello!Hello!Hello!Hello!Hello!He
```

How It Works

Instead of individually typing each character of the world map pattern, you can copy and paste the whole thing from *https://inventwithpython.com/bitmap world.txt*. A line of 68 periods at the top and bottom of the pattern acts as a ruler to help you align it correctly. However, the program will still work if you make typos in the pattern.

The bitmap.splitlines() method call on line 43 returns a list of strings, each of which is a line in the multiline bitmap string. Using a multiline string makes the bitmap easier to edit into whatever pattern you like. The program fills in any non-space character in the pattern, which is why asterisks, periods, or any other character do the same thing.

The message[i % len(message)] code on line 51 causes the repetition of the text in message. As i increases from 0 to a number larger than len(message), the expression i % len(message) evaluates to 0 again. This causes message[i % len(message)] to repeat the characters in message as i increases.

1. """Bitmap Message, by Al Sweigart al@inventwithpython.com
2. Displays a text message according to the provided bitmap image.
3. View this code at https://nostarch.com/big-book-small-python-projects

```
 4. Tags: tiny, beginner, artistic"""
 5.
 6. import sys
 7.
 8. # (!) Try changing this multiline string to any image you like:
 9.
10. # There are 68 periods along the top and bottom of this string:
11. # (You can also copy and paste this string from
12. # https://inventwithpython.com/bitmapworld.txt)
13. bitmap = """
14. ....................................................................
15.      **************   *  *** **  *        ****************************
16.     ******************* ** ** *  * **************************** *
17.    **       *****************          *****************************
18.             *************         **  * **** **  ************** *
19.             *********           *******    ***************** * *
20.             ********          *************************** *
21.    *        * **** ***        ************** ****** ** *
22.               ****  *         *************** *** *** *
23.               ******          ************** **   ** *
24.               ********          *************   *  ** ***
25.                ********          ********        * *** ****
26.                *********          ******  *        **** ** * **
27.                *********          ****** * *         *** *    *
28.                 ******           ***** **           *****   *
29.                 *****            **** *             ********
30.                 *****            ****               *********
31.                 ****             **                 *******   *
32.                 ***                                      *   *
33.                 **     *                       *
34. ...................................................................."""
35.
36. print('Bitmap Message, by Al Sweigart al@inventwithpython.com')
37. print('Enter the message to display with the bitmap.')
38. message = input('> ')
39. if message == '':
40.     sys.exit()
41.
42. # Loop over each line in the bitmap:
43. for line in bitmap.splitlines():
44.     # Loop over each character in the line:
45.     for i, bit in enumerate(line):
46.         if bit == ' ':
47.             # Print an empty space since there's a space in the bitmap:
48.             print(' ', end='')
49.         else:
50.             # Print a character from the message:
51.             print(message[i % len(message)], end='')
52.     print()  # Print a newline.
```

After entering the source code and running it a few times, try making experimental changes to it. You can change the string in bitmap to create entirely new patterns.

Exploring the Program

Try to find the answers to the following questions. Experiment with some modifications to the code and rerun the program to see what effect the changes have.

1. What happens if the player enters a blank string for the message?
2. Does it matter what the nonspace characters are in the bitmap variable's string?
3. What does the i variable created on line 45 represent?
4. What bug happens if you delete or comment out print() on line 52?

#4

BLACKJACK

Blackjack, also known as 21, is a card game where players try to get as close to 21 points as possible without going over. This program uses images drawn with text characters, called *ASCII art*. American Standard Code for Information Interchange (ASCII) is a mapping of text characters to numeric codes that computers used before Unicode replaced it. The playing cards in this program are an example of ASCII art:

```
 ___     ___
|A  |   |10 |
| ♣ |   | ♦ |
|__A|   |_10|
```

You can find other rules and the history of this card game at *https://en.wikipedia.org/wiki/Blackjack*.

The Program in Action

When you run *blackjack.py*, the output will look like this:

```
Blackjack, by Al Sweigart al@inventwithpython.com

    Rules:
        Try to get as close to 21 without going over.
        Kings, Queens, and Jacks are worth 10 points.
        Aces are worth 1 or 11 points.
        Cards 2 through 10 are worth their face value.
        (H)it to take another card.
        (S)tand to stop taking cards.
        On your first play, you can (D)ouble down to increase your bet
        but must hit exactly one more time before standing.
        In case of a tie, the bet is returned to the player.
        The dealer stops hitting at 17.
Money: 5000
How much do you bet? (1-5000, or QUIT)
> 400
Bet: 400

DEALER: ???

 ___   ___
|## | |2  |
|###| | ♥ |
|_##| |__2|

PLAYER: 17

 ___   ___
|K  | |7  |
| ♠ | | ♦ |
|__K| |__7|


(H)it, (S)tand, (D)ouble down
> h
You drew a 4 of ♦.
--snip--
DEALER: 18

 ___   ___   ___
|K  | |2  | |6  |
| ♦ | | ♥ | | ♠ |
|__K| |__2| |__6|

PLAYER: 21

 ___   ___   ___
|K  | |7  | |4  |
| ♠ | | ♦ | | ♦ |
|__K| |__7| |__4|

You won $400!
--snip-
```

How It Works

The card suit symbols don't exist on your keyboard, which is why we call the chr() function to create them. The integer passed to chr() is called a Unicode *code point*, a unique number that identifies a character according to the Unicode standard. Unicode is often misunderstood. However, Ned Batchelder's 2012 PyCon US talk "Pragmatic Unicode, or How Do I Stop the Pain?" is an excellent introduction to Unicode, and you can find it at *https://youtu.be/sgHbC6udIqc/*. Appendix B gives a full list of Unicode characters you can use in your Python programs.

```python
1. """Blackjack, by Al Sweigart al@inventwithpython.com
2. The classic card game also known as 21. (This version doesn't have
3. splitting or insurance.)
4. More info at: https://en.wikipedia.org/wiki/Blackjack
5. View this code at https://nostarch.com/big-book-small-python-projects
6. Tags: large, game, card game"""
7.
8. import random, sys
9.
10. # Set up the constants:
11. HEARTS   = chr(9829) # Character 9829 is '♥'.
12. DIAMONDS = chr(9830) # Character 9830 is '♦'.
13. SPADES   = chr(9824) # Character 9824 is '♠'.
14. CLUBS    = chr(9827) # Character 9827 is '♣'.
15. # (A list of chr codes is at https://inventwithpython.com/charactermap)
16. BACKSIDE = 'backside'
17.
18.
19. def main():
20.     print('''Blackjack, by Al Sweigart al@inventwithpython.com
21.
22.     Rules:
23.       Try to get as close to 21 without going over.
24.       Kings, Queens, and Jacks are worth 10 points.
25.       Aces are worth 1 or 11 points.
26.       Cards 2 through 10 are worth their face value.
27.       (H)it to take another card.
28.       (S)tand to stop taking cards.
29.       On your first play, you can (D)ouble down to increase your bet
30.       but must hit exactly one more time before standing.
31.       In case of a tie, the bet is returned to the player.
32.       The dealer stops hitting at 17.''')
33.
34.     money = 5000
35.     while True:  # Main game loop.
36.         # Check if the player has run out of money:
37.         if money <= 0:
38.             print("You're broke!")
39.             print("Good thing you weren't playing with real money.")
40.             print('Thanks for playing!')
41.             sys.exit()
42.
43.         # Let the player enter their bet for this round:
```

```
44.          print('Money:', money)
45.          bet = getBet(money)
46.
47.          # Give the dealer and player two cards from the deck each:
48.          deck = getDeck()
49.          dealerHand = [deck.pop(), deck.pop()]
50.          playerHand = [deck.pop(), deck.pop()]
51.
52.          # Handle player actions:
53.          print('Bet:', bet)
54.          while True:  # Keep looping until player stands or busts.
55.              displayHands(playerHand, dealerHand, False)
56.              print()
57.
58.              # Check if the player has bust:
59.              if getHandValue(playerHand) > 21:
60.                  break
61.
62.              # Get the player's move, either H, S, or D:
63.              move = getMove(playerHand, money - bet)
64.
65.              # Handle the player actions:
66.              if move == 'D':
67.                  # Player is doubling down, they can increase their bet:
68.                  additionalBet = getBet(min(bet, (money - bet)))
69.                  bet += additionalBet
70.                  print('Bet increased to {}.'.format(bet))
71.                  print('Bet:', bet)
72.
73.              if move in ('H', 'D'):
74.                  # Hit/doubling down takes another card.
75.                  newCard = deck.pop()
76.                  rank, suit = newCard
77.                  print('You drew a {} of {}.'.format(rank, suit))
78.                  playerHand.append(newCard)
79.
80.                  if getHandValue(playerHand) > 21:
81.                      # The player has busted:
82.                      continue
83.
84.              if move in ('S', 'D'):
85.                  # Stand/doubling down stops the player's turn.
86.                  break
87.
88.          # Handle the dealer's actions:
89.          if getHandValue(playerHand) <= 21:
90.              while getHandValue(dealerHand) < 17:
91.                  # The dealer hits:
92.                  print('Dealer hits...')
93.                  dealerHand.append(deck.pop())
94.                  displayHands(playerHand, dealerHand, False)
95.
96.                  if getHandValue(dealerHand) > 21:
97.                      break  # The dealer has busted.
98.                  input('Press Enter to continue...')
```

```
 99.                print('\n\n')
100.
101.            # Show the final hands:
102.            displayHands(playerHand, dealerHand, True)
103.
104.            playerValue = getHandValue(playerHand)
105.            dealerValue = getHandValue(dealerHand)
106.            # Handle whether the player won, lost, or tied:
107.            if dealerValue > 21:
108.                print('Dealer busts! You win ${}!'.format(bet))
109.                money += bet
110.            elif (playerValue > 21) or (playerValue < dealerValue):
111.                print('You lost!')
112.                money -= bet
113.            elif playerValue > dealerValue:
114.                print('You won ${}!'.format(bet))
115.                money += bet
116.            elif playerValue == dealerValue:
117.                print('It\'s a tie, the bet is returned to you.')
118.
119.            input('Press Enter to continue...')
120.            print('\n\n')
121.
122.
123. def getBet(maxBet):
124.     """Ask the player how much they want to bet for this round."""
125.     while True:  # Keep asking until they enter a valid amount.
126.         print('How much do you bet? (1-{}, or QUIT)'.format(maxBet))
127.         bet = input('> ').upper().strip()
128.         if bet == 'QUIT':
129.             print('Thanks for playing!')
130.             sys.exit()
131.
132.         if not bet.isdecimal():
133.             continue  # If the player didn't enter a number, ask again.
134.
135.         bet = int(bet)
136.         if 1 <= bet <= maxBet:
137.             return bet  # Player entered a valid bet.
138.
139.
140. def getDeck():
141.     """Return a list of (rank, suit) tuples for all 52 cards."""
142.     deck = []
143.     for suit in (HEARTS, DIAMONDS, SPADES, CLUBS):
144.         for rank in range(2, 11):
145.             deck.append((str(rank), suit))  # Add the numbered cards.
146.         for rank in ('J', 'Q', 'K', 'A'):
147.             deck.append((rank, suit))  # Add the face and ace cards.
148.     random.shuffle(deck)
149.     return deck
150.
151.
152. def displayHands(playerHand, dealerHand, showDealerHand):
153.     """Show the player's and dealer's cards. Hide the dealer's first
```

```
154.     card if showDealerHand is False."""
155.     print()
156.     if showDealerHand:
157.         print('DEALER:', getHandValue(dealerHand))
158.         displayCards(dealerHand)
159.     else:
160.         print('DEALER: ???')
161.         # Hide the dealer's first card:
162.         displayCards([BACKSIDE] + dealerHand[1:])
163.
164.     # Show the player's cards:
165.     print('PLAYER:', getHandValue(playerHand))
166.     displayCards(playerHand)
167.
168.
169. def getHandValue(cards):
170.     """Returns the value of the cards. Face cards are worth 10, aces are
171.     worth 11 or 1 (this function picks the most suitable ace value)."""
172.     value = 0
173.     numberOfAces = 0
174.
175.     # Add the value for the non-ace cards:
176.     for card in cards:
177.         rank = card[0]  # card is a tuple like (rank, suit)
178.         if rank == 'A':
179.             numberOfAces += 1
180.         elif rank in ('K', 'Q', 'J'):  # Face cards are worth 10 points.
181.             value += 10
182.         else:
183.             value += int(rank)  # Numbered cards are worth their number.
184.
185.     # Add the value for the aces:
186.     value += numberOfAces  # Add 1 per ace.
187.     for i in range(numberOfAces):
188.         # If another 10 can be added with busting, do so:
189.         if value + 10 <= 21:
190.             value += 10
191.
192.     return value
193.
194.
195. def displayCards(cards):
196.     """Display all the cards in the cards list."""
197.     rows = ['', '', '', '', '']  # The text to display on each row.
198.
199.     for i, card in enumerate(cards):
200.         rows[0] += ' ___  '  # Print the top line of the card.
201.         if card == BACKSIDE:
202.             # Print a card's back:
203.             rows[1] += '|## | '
204.             rows[2] += '|###| '
205.             rows[3] += '|_##| '
206.         else:
207.             # Print the card's front:
208.             rank, suit = card  # The card is a tuple data structure.
```

```
209.                rows[1] += '|{} |  '.format(rank.ljust(2))
210.                rows[2] += '| {} |  '.format(suit)
211.                rows[3] += '|_{}| '.format(rank.rjust(2, '_'))
212.
213.    # Print each row on the screen:
214.    for row in rows:
215.        print(row)
216.
217.
218. def getMove(playerHand, money):
219.     """Asks the player for their move, and returns 'H' for hit, 'S' for
220.     stand, and 'D' for double down."""
221.     while True:  # Keep looping until the player enters a correct move.
222.         # Determine what moves the player can make:
223.         moves = ['(H)it', '(S)tand']
224.
225.         # The player can double down on their first move, which we can
226.         # tell because they'll have exactly two cards:
227.         if len(playerHand) == 2 and money > 0:
228.             moves.append('(D)ouble down')
229.
230.         # Get the player's move:
231.         movePrompt = ', '.join(moves) + '> '
232.         move = input(movePrompt).upper()
233.         if move in ('H', 'S'):
234.             return move  # Player has entered a valid move.
235.         if move == 'D' and '(D)ouble down' in moves:
236.             return move  # Player has entered a valid move.
237.
238.
239. # If the program is run (instead of imported), run the game:
240. if __name__ == '__main__':
241.     main()
```

After entering the source code and running it a few times, try making experimental changes to it. Blackjack has several custom rules that you could implement. For example, if the first two cards have the same value, a player can split them into two hands and wager on them separately. Also, if the player receives a "blackjack" (the ace of spades and a black jack) for their first two cards, the player wins a ten-to-one payout. You can find out more about the game from *https://en.wikipedia.org/wiki/Blackjack*.

Exploring the Program

Try to find the answers to the following questions. Experiment with some modifications to the code and rerun the program to see what effect the changes have.

1. How can you make the player start with a different amount of money?
2. How does the program prevent the player from betting more money than they have?

3. How does the program represent a single card?

4. How does the program represent a hand of cards?

5. What do each of the strings in the rows list (created on line 197) represent?

6. What happens if you delete or comment out random.shuffle(deck) on line 148?

7. What happens if you change money -= bet on line 112 to money += bet?

8. What happens when showDealerHand in the displayHands() function is set to True? What happens when it is False?

#5

BOUNCING DVD LOGO

If you are of a certain age, you'll remember those ancient technological devices called DVD players. When not playing DVDs, they would display a diagonally traveling DVD logo that bounced off the edges of the screen. This program simulates this colorful DVD logo by making it change direction each time it hits an edge. We'll also keep track of how many times a logo hits a corner of the screen. This creates an interesting visual animation to look at, especially for the magical moment when a logo lines up perfectly with a corner.

You can't run this program from your integrated development environment (IDE) or editor because it uses the bext module. Therefore, it must be run from the Command Prompt or Terminal in order to display correctly. You can find more information about the bext module at *https://pypi.org/project/bext/*.

The Program in Action

When you run *bouncingdvd.py*, the output will look like Figure 5-1.

Figure 5-1: The diagonally moving DVD logos of the bouncingdvd.py program

How It Works

You may remember Cartesian coordinates from your math class in school. In programming, the x-coordinate represents an object's horizontal position and the y-coordinate represents its vertical position, just like in mathematics. However, unlike in mathematics, the origin point (0, 0) is in the upper-left corner of the screen, and the y-coordinate increases as you go down. The x-coordinate increases as the object moves right, just like in mathematics. Figure 5-2 shows the coordinate system for your screen.

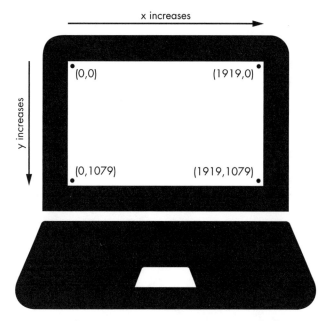

x increases

y increases

(0,0)   (1919,0)

(0,1079)   (1919,1079)

Figure 5-2: The origin point (0, 0) is in the upper left of the screen, while the x- and y-coordinates increase going right and down, respectively.

The bext module's goto() function works the same way: calling bext.goto (0, 0) places the text cursor at the top left of the terminal window. We represent each bouncing DVD logo using a Python dictionary with the keys 'color', 'direction', 'x', and 'y'. The values for the 'x' and 'y' are integers representing the logo's position in the window. Since these values get passed to bext.goto(), increasing them will move the logo right and down, while decreasing them will move the logo left and up.

```
1. """Bouncing DVD Logo, by Al Sweigart al@inventwithpython.com
2. A bouncing DVD logo animation. You have to be "of a certain age" to
3. appreciate this. Press Ctrl-C to stop.
4.
5. NOTE: Do not resize the terminal window while this program is running.
6. View this code at https://nostarch.com/big-book-small-python-projects
7. Tags: short, artistic, bext"""
8.
9. import sys, random, time
10.
11. try:
12.     import bext
13. except ImportError:
14.     print('This program requires the bext module, which you')
15.     print('can install by following the instructions at')
16.     print('https://pypi.org/project/Bext/')
17.     sys.exit()
18.
19. # Set up the constants:
20. WIDTH, HEIGHT = bext.size()
```

```
21. # We can't print to the last column on Windows without it adding a
22. # newline automatically, so reduce the width by one:
23. WIDTH -= 1
24.
25. NUMBER_OF_LOGOS = 5  # (!) Try changing this to 1 or 100.
26. PAUSE_AMOUNT = 0.2  # (!) Try changing this to 1.0 or 0.0.
27. # (!) Try changing this list to fewer colors:
28. COLORS = ['red', 'green', 'yellow', 'blue', 'magenta', 'cyan', 'white']
29.
30. UP_RIGHT    = 'ur'
31. UP_LEFT     = 'ul'
32. DOWN_RIGHT = 'dr'
33. DOWN_LEFT  = 'dl'
34. DIRECTIONS = (UP_RIGHT, UP_LEFT, DOWN_RIGHT, DOWN_LEFT)
35.
36. # Key names for logo dictionaries:
37. COLOR = 'color'
38. X = 'x'
39. Y = 'y'
40. DIR = 'direction'
41.
42.
43. def main():
44.     bext.clear()
45.
46.     # Generate some logos.
47.     logos = []
48.     for i in range(NUMBER_OF_LOGOS):
49.         logos.append({COLOR: random.choice(COLORS),
50.                       X: random.randint(1, WIDTH - 4),
51.                       Y: random.randint(1, HEIGHT - 4),
52.                       DIR: random.choice(DIRECTIONS)})
53.         if logos[-1][X] % 2 == 1:
54.             # Make sure X is even so it can hit the corner.
55.             logos[-1][X] -= 1
56.
57.     cornerBounces = 0  # Count how many times a logo hits a corner.
58.     while True:  # Main program loop.
59.         for logo in logos:  # Handle each logo in the logos list.
60.             # Erase the logo's current location:
61.             bext.goto(logo[X], logo[Y])
62.             print('  ', end='')  # (!) Try commenting this line out.
63.
64.             originalDirection = logo[DIR]
65.
66.             # See if the logo bounces off the corners:
67.             if logo[X] == 0 and logo[Y] == 0:
68.                 logo[DIR] = DOWN_RIGHT
69.                 cornerBounces += 1
70.             elif logo[X] == 0 and logo[Y] == HEIGHT - 1:
71.                 logo[DIR] = UP_RIGHT
72.                 cornerBounces += 1
73.             elif logo[X] == WIDTH - 3 and logo[Y] == 0:
74.                 logo[DIR] = DOWN_LEFT
75.                 cornerBounces += 1
```

```
76.                elif logo[X] == WIDTH - 3 and logo[Y] == HEIGHT - 1:
77.                    logo[DIR] = UP_LEFT
78.                    cornerBounces += 1
79.
80.                # See if the logo bounces off the left edge:
81.                elif logo[X] == 0 and logo[DIR] == UP_LEFT:
82.                    logo[DIR] = UP_RIGHT
83.                elif logo[X] == 0 and logo[DIR] == DOWN_LEFT:
84.                    logo[DIR] = DOWN_RIGHT
85.
86.                # See if the logo bounces off the right edge:
87.                # (WIDTH - 3 because 'DVD' has 3 letters.)
88.                elif logo[X] == WIDTH - 3 and logo[DIR] == UP_RIGHT:
89.                    logo[DIR] = UP_LEFT
90.                elif logo[X] == WIDTH - 3 and logo[DIR] == DOWN_RIGHT:
91.                    logo[DIR] = DOWN_LEFT
92.
93.                # See if the logo bounces off the top edge:
94.                elif logo[Y] == 0 and logo[DIR] == UP_LEFT:
95.                    logo[DIR] = DOWN_LEFT
96.                elif logo[Y] == 0 and logo[DIR] == UP_RIGHT:
97.                    logo[DIR] = DOWN_RIGHT
98.
99.                # See if the logo bounces off the bottom edge:
100.               elif logo[Y] == HEIGHT - 1 and logo[DIR] == DOWN_LEFT:
101.                   logo[DIR] = UP_LEFT
102.               elif logo[Y] == HEIGHT - 1 and logo[DIR] == DOWN_RIGHT:
103.                   logo[DIR] = UP_RIGHT
104.
105.               if logo[DIR] != originalDirection:
106.                   # Change color when the logo bounces:
107.                   logo[COLOR] = random.choice(COLORS)
108.
109.               # Move the logo. (X moves by 2 because the terminal
110.               # characters are twice as tall as they are wide.)
111.               if logo[DIR] == UP_RIGHT:
112.                   logo[X] += 2
113.                   logo[Y] -= 1
114.               elif logo[DIR] == UP_LEFT:
115.                   logo[X] -= 2
116.                   logo[Y] -= 1
117.               elif logo[DIR] == DOWN_RIGHT:
118.                   logo[X] += 2
119.                   logo[Y] += 1
120.               elif logo[DIR] == DOWN_LEFT:
121.                   logo[X] -= 2
122.                   logo[Y] += 1
123.
124.           # Display number of corner bounces:
125.           bext.goto(5, 0)
126.           bext.fg('white')
127.           print('Corner bounces:', cornerBounces, end='')
128.
129.           for logo in logos:
130.               # Draw the logos at their new location:
```

```
131.              bext.goto(logo[X], logo[Y])
132.              bext.fg(logo[COLOR])
133.              print('DVD', end='')
134.
135.          bext.goto(0, 0)
136.
137.          sys.stdout.flush()  # (Required for bext-using programs.)
138.          time.sleep(PAUSE_AMOUNT)
139.
140.
141. # If this program was run (instead of imported), run the game:
142. if __name__ == '__main__':
143.     try:
144.         main()
145.     except KeyboardInterrupt:
146.         print()
147.         print('Bouncing DVD Logo, by Al Sweigart')
148.         sys.exit()  # When Ctrl-C is pressed, end the program.
```

After entering the source code and running it a few times, try making experimental changes to it. The comments marked with (!) have suggestions for small changes you can make. On your own, you can also try to figure out how to do the following:

- Change NUMBER_OF_LOGOS to increase the number of bouncing logos on the screen.
- Change PAUSE_AMOUNT to speed up or slow down the logos.

Exploring the Program

Try to find the answers to the following questions. Experiment with some modifications to the code and rerun the program to see what effect the changes have.

1. What happens if you change WIDTH, HEIGHT = bext.size() on line 20 to WIDTH, HEIGHT = 10, 5?
2. What happens if you replace DIR: random.choice(DIRECTIONS) on line 52 with DIR: DOWN_RIGHT?
3. How can you make the 'Corner bounces:' text not appear on the screen?
4. What error message do you get if you delete or comment out cornerBounces = 0 on line 57?

#6

CAESAR CIPHER

The Caesar cipher is an ancient encryption algorithm used by Julius Caesar. It encrypts letters by shifting them over by a certain number of places in the alphabet. We call the length of shift the *key*. For example, if the key is 3, then *A* becomes *D*, *B* becomes *E*, *C* becomes *F*, and so on. To decrypt the message, you must shift the encrypted letters in the opposite direction. This program lets the user encrypt and decrypt messages according to this algorithm.

In modern times, the Caesar cipher isn't very sophisticated, but that makes it ideal for beginners. The program in Project 7, "Caesar Hacker," can brute-force through all 26 possible keys to decrypt messages, even if you don't know the original key. Also, if you encrypt the message with the key 13, the Caesar cipher becomes identical to Project 61, "ROT 13 Cipher."

Learn more about the Caesar cipher at *https://en.wikipedia.org/wiki/Caesar_cipher*. If you'd like to learn about ciphers and code breaking in general, you can read my book *Cracking Codes with Python* (No Starch Press, 2018; *https://nostarch.com/crackingcodes/*).

The Program in Action

When you run *caesarcipher.py*, the output will look like this:

```
Caesar Cipher, by Al Sweigart al@inventwithpython.com
Do you want to (e)ncrypt or (d)ecrypt?
> e
Please enter the key (0 to 25) to use.
> 4
Enter the message to encrypt.
> Meet me by the rose bushes tonight.
QIIX QI FC XLI VSWI FYWLIW XSRMKLX.
Full encrypted text copied to clipboard.

Caesar Cipher, by Al Sweigart al@inventwithpython.com
Do you want to (e)ncrypt or (d)ecrypt?
> d
Please enter the key (0 to 26) to use.
> 4
Enter the message to decrypt.
> QIIX QI FC XLI VSWI FYWLIW XSRMKLX.
MEET ME BY THE ROSE BUSHES TONIGHT.
Full decrypted text copied to clipboard.
```

How It Works

Like most cipher programs, the Caesar cipher works by translating characters into numbers, performing some math operations on those numbers, and translating the numbers back into text characters. In the context of ciphers, we call these text characters *symbols*. Symbols can include letters, numeric digits, and punctuation marks, each of which gets assigned a unique integer. In the case of the Caesar cipher program, the symbols are all letters, and their integers are their position in the SYMBOLS string: 'ABCDEFGHIJKLMNOPQRSTUVWXYZ'.

```
 1. """Caesar Cipher, by Al Sweigart al@inventwithpython.com
 2. The Caesar cipher is a shift cipher that uses addition and subtraction
 3. to encrypt and decrypt letters.
 4. More info at: https://en.wikipedia.org/wiki/Caesar_cipher
 5. View this code at https://nostarch.com/big-book-small-python-projects
 6. Tags: short, beginner, cryptography, math"""
 7.
 8. try:
 9.     import pyperclip  # pyperclip copies text to the clipboard.
10. except ImportError:
11.     pass  # If pyperclip is not installed, do nothing. It's no big deal.
```

```
12.
13. # Every possible symbol that can be encrypted/decrypted:
14. # (!) You can add numbers and punctuation marks to encrypt those
15. # symbols as well.
16. SYMBOLS = 'ABCDEFGHIJKLMNOPQRSTUVWXYZ'
17.
18. print('Caesar Cipher, by Al Sweigart al@inventwithpython.com')
19. print('The Caesar cipher encrypts letters by shifting them over by a')
20. print('key number. For example, a key of 2 means the letter A is')
21. print('encrypted into C, the letter B encrypted into D, and so on.')
22. print()
23.
24. # Let the user enter if they are encrypting or decrypting:
25. while True:  # Keep asking until the user enters e or d.
26.     print('Do you want to (e)ncrypt or (d)ecrypt?')
27.     response = input('> ').lower()
28.     if response.startswith('e'):
29.         mode = 'encrypt'
30.         break
31.     elif response.startswith('d'):
32.         mode = 'decrypt'
33.         break
34.     print('Please enter the letter e or d.')
35.
36. # Let the user enter the key to use:
37. while True:  # Keep asking until the user enters a valid key.
38.     maxKey = len(SYMBOLS) - 1
39.     print('Please enter the key (0 to {}) to use.'.format(maxKey))
40.     response = input('> ').upper()
41.     if not response.isdecimal():
42.         continue
43.
44.     if 0 <= int(response) < len(SYMBOLS):
45.         key = int(response)
46.         break
47.
48. # Let the user enter the message to encrypt/decrypt:
49. print('Enter the message to {}.'.format(mode))
50. message = input('> ')
51.
52. # Caesar cipher only works on uppercase letters:
53. message = message.upper()
54.
55. # Stores the encrypted/decrypted form of the message:
56. translated = ''
57.
58. # Encrypt/decrypt each symbol in the message:
59. for symbol in message:
60.     if symbol in SYMBOLS:
61.         # Get the encrypted (or decrypted) number for this symbol.
62.         num = SYMBOLS.find(symbol)  # Get the number of the symbol.
63.         if mode == 'encrypt':
64.             num = num + key
65.         elif mode == 'decrypt':
66.             num = num - key
```

```
67.
68.         # Handle the wrap-around if num is larger than the length of
69.         # SYMBOLS or less than 0:
70.         if num >= len(SYMBOLS):
71.             num = num - len(SYMBOLS)
72.         elif num < 0:
73.             num = num + len(SYMBOLS)
74.
75.         # Add encrypted/decrypted number's symbol to translated:
76.         translated = translated + SYMBOLS[num]
77.     else:
78.         # Just add the symbol without encrypting/decrypting:
79.         translated = translated + symbol
80.
81. # Display the encrypted/decrypted string to the screen:
82. print(translated)
83.
84. try:
85.     pyperclip.copy(translated)
86.     print('Full {}ed text copied to clipboard.'.format(mode))
87. except:
88.     pass  # Do nothing if pyperclip wasn't installed.
```

After entering the source code and running it a few times, try making experimental changes to it. The comments marked with (!) have suggestions for small changes you can make. You can expand the encryptable symbols by adding characters to the SYMBOLS string.

Exploring the Program

Try to find the answers to the following questions. Experiment with some modifications to the code and rerun the program to see what effect the changes have.

1. What happens if you change SYMBOLS = 'ABCDEFGHIJKLMNOPQRSTUVWXYZ' on line 16 to SYMBOLS = 'ABC'?

2. What happens when you encrypt a message with key 0?

3. What error message do you get if you delete or comment out translated = '' on line 56?

4. What error message do you get if you delete or comment out key = int(response) on line 45?

5. What happens if you change translated = translated + SYMBOLS[num] on line 76 to translated = translated + symbol?

#7

CAESAR HACKER

This program can hack messages encrypted with the Caesar cipher from Project 6, even if you don't know the key. There are only 26 possible keys for the Caesar cipher, so a computer can easily try all possible decryptions and display the results to the user. In cryptography, we call this technique a *brute-force attack*. If you'd like to learn more about ciphers and code breaking, you can read my book *Cracking Codes with Python* (No Starch Press, 2018; *https://nostarch.com/crackingcodes/*).

The Program in Action

When you run *caesarhacker.py*, the output will look like this:

```
Caesar Cipher Hacker, by Al Sweigart al@inventwithpython.com
Enter the encrypted Caesar cipher message to hack.
> QIIX QI FC XLI VSWI FYWLIW XSRMKLX.
Key #0: QIIX QI FC XLI VSWI FYWLIW XSRMKLX.
Key #1: PHHW PH EB WKH URVH EXVKHV WRQLJKW.
Key #2: OGGV OG DA VJG TQUG DWUJGU VQPKIJV.
Key #3: NFFU NF CZ UIF SPTF CVTIFT UPOJHIU.
Key #4: MEET ME BY THE ROSE BUSHES TONIGHT.
Key #5: LDDS LD AX SGD QNRD ATRGDR SNMHFGS.
Key #6: KCCR KC ZW RFC PMQC ZSQFCQ RMLGEFR.
--snip--
```

How It Works

Note that lines 20 to 36 in this program are nearly identical to lines 55 to 78 in the Caesar cipher program. The hacking program implements the same decryption code, except that it does so in a for loop, which runs the code for every possible key.

Unfortunately, the hacking program isn't sophisticated enough to identify when it has found the correct key. It relies on a human to read the output and identify which decryption produced the original English (or whichever written language was encrypted). Chapter 11 of the book *Cracking Codes with Python* (No Starch Press, 2018) details how you can write Python code to detect English messages.

```python
1. """Caesar Cipher Hacker, by Al Sweigart al@inventwithpython.com
2. This program hacks messages encrypted with the Caesar cipher by doing
3. a brute force attack against every possible key.
4. More info at:
5. https://en.wikipedia.org/wiki/Caesar_cipher#Breaking_the_cipher
6. View this code at https://nostarch.com/big-book-small-python-projects
7. Tags: tiny, beginner, cryptography, math"""
8.
9. print('Caesar Cipher Hacker, by Al Sweigart al@inventwithpython.com')
10.
11. # Let the user specify the message to hack:
12. print('Enter the encrypted Caesar cipher message to hack.')
13. message = input('> ')
14.
15. # Every possible symbol that can be encrypted/decrypted:
16. # (This must match the SYMBOLS used when encrypting the message.)
17. SYMBOLS = 'ABCDEFGHIJKLMNOPQRSTUVWXYZ'
18.
19. for key in range(len(SYMBOLS)):  # Loop through every possible key.
20.     translated = ''
21.
22.     # Decrypt each symbol in the message:
23.     for symbol in message:
```

```
24.         if symbol in SYMBOLS:
25.             num = SYMBOLS.find(symbol)  # Get the number of the symbol.
26.             num = num - key  # Decrypt the number.
27.
28.             # Handle the wrap-around if num is less than 0:
29.             if num < 0:
30.                 num = num + len(SYMBOLS)
31.
32.             # Add decrypted number's symbol to translated:
33.             translated = translated + SYMBOLS[num]
34.         else:
35.             # Just add the symbol without decrypting:
36.             translated = translated + symbol
37.
38.     # Display the key being tested, along with its decrypted text:
39.     print('Key #{}: {}'.format(key, translated))
```

After entering the source code and running it a few times, try making experimental changes to it. Keep in mind that the string stored in the SYMBOLS variable must match the SYMBOLS variable in the Caesar cipher program that produced the encrypted text.

Exploring the Program

Try to find the answers to the following questions. Experiment with some modifications to the code and rerun the program to see what effect the changes have.

1. What error message do you get if you delete or comment out translated = '' on line 20?

2. What happens if you change translated = translated + SYMBOLS[num] on line 33 to translated = translated + symbol?

3. What happens if you enter an unencrypted message into the Caesar cipher hacker program?

#8

CALENDAR MAKER

This program generates printable text files of monthly calendars for the month and year you enter. Dates and calendars are a tricky topic in programming because there are so many different rules for determining the number of days in a month, which years are leap years, and which day of the week a particular date falls on. Fortunately, Python's datetime module handles these details for you. This program focuses on generating the multiline string for the monthly calendar page.

The Program in Action

When you run *calendarmaker.py*, the output will look like this:

```
Calendar Maker, by Al Sweigart al@inventwithpython.com
Enter the year for the calendar:
> 2029
Enter the month for the calendar, 1-12:
> 12
                              December 2029
...Sunday.....Monday....Tuesday...Wednesday...Thursday....Friday....Saturday..
+----------+----------+----------+----------+----------+----------+----------+
|25        |26        |27        |28        |29        |30        |1         |
|          |          |          |          |          |          |          |
|          |          |          |          |          |          |          |
|          |          |          |          |          |          |          |
+----------+----------+----------+----------+----------+----------+----------+
| 2        | 3        | 4        | 5        | 6        | 7        | 8        |
|          |          |          |          |          |          |          |
|          |          |          |          |          |          |          |
|          |          |          |          |          |          |          |
+----------+----------+----------+----------+----------+----------+----------+
| 9        |10        |11        |12        |13        |14        |15        |
|          |          |          |          |          |          |          |
|          |          |          |          |          |          |          |
|          |          |          |          |          |          |          |
+----------+----------+----------+----------+----------+----------+----------+
|16        |17        |18        |19        |20        |21        |22        |
|          |          |          |          |          |          |          |
|          |          |          |          |          |          |          |
|          |          |          |          |          |          |          |
+----------+----------+----------+----------+----------+----------+----------+
|23        |24        |25        |26        |27        |28        |29        |
|          |          |          |          |          |          |          |
|          |          |          |          |          |          |          |
|          |          |          |          |          |          |          |
+----------+----------+----------+----------+----------+----------+----------+
|30        |31        | 1        | 2        | 3        | 4        | 5        |
|          |          |          |          |          |          |          |
|          |          |          |          |          |          |          |
|          |          |          |          |          |          |          |
+----------+----------+----------+----------+----------+----------+----------+

Saved to calendar_2029_12.txt
```

How It Works

Note that the getCalendarFor() function returns a giant multiline string of the calendar for the given month and year. In this function, the calText variable stores this string, which adds the lines, spaces, and dates to it. To track the date, the currentDate variable holds a datetime.date() object, which gets set to the next or previous date by adding or subtracting datetime .timedelta() objects. You can learn about Python's date and time modules by reading Chapter 17 of *Automate the Boring Stuff with Python* at *https://automatetheboringstuff.com/2e/chapter17/*.

```python
1. """Calendar Maker, by Al Sweigart al@inventwithpython.com
2. Create monthly calendars, saved to a text file and fit for printing.
3. View this code at https://nostarch.com/big-book-small-python-projects
4. Tags: short"""
5.
6. import datetime
7.
8. # Set up the constants:
9. DAYS = ('Sunday', 'Monday', 'Tuesday', 'Wednesday', 'Thursday',
10.        'Friday', 'Saturday')
11. MONTHS = ('January', 'February', 'March', 'April', 'May', 'June', 'July',
12.          'August', 'September', 'October', 'November', 'December')
13.
14. print('Calendar Maker, by Al Sweigart al@inventwithpython.com')
15.
16. while True:  # Loop to get a year from the user.
17.     print('Enter the year for the calendar:')
18.     response = input('> ')
19.
20.     if response.isdecimal() and int(response) > 0:
21.         year = int(response)
22.         break
23.
24.     print('Please enter a numeric year, like 2023.')
25.     continue
26.
27. while True:  # Loop to get a month from the user.
28.     print('Enter the month for the calendar, 1-12:')
29.     response = input('> ')
30.
31.     if not response.isdecimal():
32.         print('Please enter a numeric month, like 3 for March.')
33.         continue
34.
35.     month = int(response)
36.     if 1 <= month <= 12:
37.         break
38.
39.     print('Please enter a number from 1 to 12.')
40.
41.
42. def getCalendarFor(year, month):
43.     calText = ''  # calText will contain the string of our calendar.
44.
45.     # Put the month and year at the top of the calendar:
46.     calText += (' ' * 34) + MONTHS[month - 1] + ' ' + str(year) + '\n'
47.
48.     # Add the days of the week labels to the calendar:
49.     # (!) Try changing this to abbreviations: SUN, MON, TUE, etc.
```

```
50.     calText += '...Sunday.....Monday....Tuesday...Wednesday...Thursday....
        Friday....Saturday..\n'
51.
52.     # The horizontal line string that separate weeks:
53.     weekSeparator = ('+----------' * 7) + '+\n'
54.
55.     # The blank rows have ten spaces in between the | day separators:
56.     blankRow = ('|          ' * 7) + '|\n'
57.
58.     # Get the first date in the month. (The datetime module handles all
59.     # the complicated calendar stuff for us here.)
60.     currentDate = datetime.date(year, month, 1)
61.
62.     # Roll back currentDate until it is Sunday. (weekday() returns 6
63.     # for Sunday, not 0.)
64.     while currentDate.weekday() != 6:
65.         currentDate -= datetime.timedelta(days=1)
66.
67.     while True:  # Loop over each week in the month.
68.         calText += weekSeparator
69.
70.         # dayNumberRow is the row with the day number labels:
71.         dayNumberRow = ''
72.         for i in range(7):
73.             dayNumberLabel = str(currentDate.day).rjust(2)
74.             dayNumberRow += '|' + dayNumberLabel + (' ' * 8)
75.             currentDate += datetime.timedelta(days=1) # Go to next day.
76.         dayNumberRow += '|\n'  # Add the vertical line after Saturday.
77.
78.         # Add the day number row and 3 blank rows to the calendar text.
79.         calText += dayNumberRow
80.         for i in range(3):  # (!) Try changing the 4 to a 5 or 10.
81.             calText += blankRow
82.
83.         # Check if we're done with the month:
84.         if currentDate.month != month:
85.             break
86.
87.     # Add the horizontal line at the very bottom of the calendar.
88.     calText += weekSeparator
89.     return calText
90.
91.
92. calText = getCalendarFor(year, month)
93. print(calText)  # Display the calendar.
94.
95. # Save the calendar to a text file:
96. calendarFilename = 'calendar_{}_{}.txt'.format(year, month)
97. with open(calendarFilename, 'w') as fileObj:
98.     fileObj.write(calText)
99.
100. print('Saved to ' + calendarFilename)
```

After you've entered the code and run it a few times, try re-creating this program from scratch without looking at the source code in this book. It doesn't have to be exactly the same as this program; you can invent your own version! On your own, you can also try to figure out how to do the following:

- Add text inside some of the boxes for holidays.
- Add text inside some of the boxes for reoccurring events.
- Print a "mini" calendar that has dates without boxes.

Exploring the Program

Try to find the answers to the following questions. Experiment with some modifications to the code and rerun the program to see what effect the changes have.

1. How can you make the calendar display abbreviated months? For example, show 'Jan' instead of 'January'?
2. What error message do you get if you delete or comment out year = int (response) on line 21?
3. How can you make the calendar not display the days of the week at the top?
4. How can you make the program not save the calendar to a file?
5. What happens if you delete or comment out print(calText) on line 93?

#9

CARROT IN A BOX

This is a simple and silly bluffing game for two human players. Each player has a box. One box has a carrot in it, and each player wants to have the carrot. The first player looks in their box and then tells the second player they either do or don't have the carrot. The second player gets to decide whether to swap boxes or not.

The ASCII art in the code makes typing this program take a while (though copying and pasting the ASCII art can speed up the task), but this project is good for beginners because it is straightforward, with minimal looping and no defined functions.

The Program in Action

When you run *carrotinabox.py*, the output will look like this:

```
Carrot in a Box, by Al Sweigart al@inventwithpython.com
--snip--
Human player 1, enter your name: Alice
Human player 2, enter your name: Bob
HERE ARE TWO BOXES:

  _____    _____
 /         /|  /         /|
+---------+ | +---------+ |
|   RED   | | |  GOLD   | |
|   BOX   | / |   BOX   | /
+---------+/  +---------+/
   Alice         Bob


Alice, you have a RED box in front of you.
Bob, you have a GOLD box in front of you.
Press Enter to continue...
--snip--
When Bob has closed their eyes, press Enter...
Alice here is the inside of your box:

    ___VV___
   |   VV   |
   |   VV   |
   |__||__|
  /   ||  /|   _____
 +---------+ | /         /|
 +---------+ | +---------+ |
 |   RED   | | |  GOLD   | |
 |   BOX   | / |   BOX   | /
 +---------+/  +---------+/
 (carrot!)
    Alice         Bob
Press Enter to continue...
--snip--
```

How It Works

This program relies on the second player closing their eyes so they don't see the contents of the first player's box. In order to keep the second player from seeing the box contents after this step, we need to find a way to clear the screen. Line 83 does this with print('\n' * 100). This prints 100 newline characters, causing the previously printed content to scroll up and out of view. This keeps the second player from accidentally seeing what was only intended for the first player. While the second player could always scroll up to see this text, it'd be obvious to the first player, who's sitting right next to them, that they had done so.

On lines 114, 130, and 142, the spacing of the vertical lines may look incorrect, but the program replaces the curly braces with the string 'RED ' (with a space at the end) or `'GOLD'`. The four characters in these strings will cause the rest of the box's vertical lines to line up with the rest of the ASCII-art image.

```
1. """Carrot in a Box, by Al Sweigart al@inventwithpython.com
2. A silly bluffing game between two human players. Based on the game
3. from the show 8 Out of 10 Cats.
4. View this code at https://nostarch.com/big-book-small-python-projects
5. Tags: large, beginner, game, two-player"""
6.
7. import random
8.
9. print('''Carrot in a Box, by Al Sweigart al@inventwithpython.com
10.
11. This is a bluffing game for two human players. Each player has a box.
12. One box has a carrot in it. To win, you must have the box with the
13. carrot in it.
14.
15. This is a very simple and silly game.
16.
17. The first player looks into their box (the second player must close
18. their eyes during this). The first player then says "There is a carrot
19. in my box" or "There is not a carrot in my box". The second player then
20. gets to decide if they want to swap boxes or not.
21. ''')
22. input('Press Enter to begin...')
23.
24. p1Name = input('Human player 1, enter your name: ')
25. p2Name = input('Human player 2, enter your name: ')
26. playerNames = p1Name[:11].center(11) + '     ' + p2Name[:11].center(11)
27.
28. print('''HERE ARE TWO BOXES:
29.    _____      _____
30.   /         /|    /         /|
31.  +---------+ |   +---------+ |
32.  |   RED   | |   |  GOLD   | |
33.  |   BOX   | /   |   BOX   | /
34.  +---------+/    +---------+/''')
35.
36. print()
37. print(playerNames)
38. print()
39. print(p1Name + ', you have a RED box in front of you.')
40. print(p2Name + ', you have a GOLD box in front of you.')
41. print()
42. print(p1Name + ', you will get to look into your box.')
43. print(p2Name.upper() + ', close your eyes and don\'t look!!!')
44. input('When ' + p2Name + ' has closed their eyes, press Enter...')
45. print()
46.
47. print(p1Name + ' here is the inside of your box:')
48.
49. if random.randint(1, 2) == 1:
50.     carrotInFirstBox = True
```

```
51. else:
52.     carrotInFirstBox = False
53.
54. if carrotInFirstBox:
55.     print('''
56.      ___VV___
57.     |   VV   |
58.     |   VV   |
59.     |__||___|    _____
60.    /   ||  /|   /       /|
61. +---------+ |  +---------+ |
62. |   RED   | |  |  GOLD  | |
63. |   BOX   | /  |   BOX  | /
64. +---------+/   +---------+/
65.  (carrot!)''')
66.     print(playerNames)
67. else:
68.     print('''
69.      _____
70.     |       |
71.     |       |
72.     |_____|    _____
73.    /       /|   /       /|
74. +---------+ |  +---------+ |
75. |   RED   | |  |  GOLD  | |
76. |   BOX   | /  |   BOX  | /
77. +---------+/   +---------+/
78. (no carrot!)''')
79.     print(playerNames)
80.
81. input('Press Enter to continue...')
82.
83. print('\n' * 100)  # Clear the screen by printing several newlines.
84. print(p1Name + ', tell ' + p2Name + ' to open their eyes.')
85. input('Press Enter to continue...')
86.
87. print()
88. print(p1Name + ', say one of the following sentences to ' + p2Name + '.')
89. print('  1) There is a carrot in my box.')
90. print('  2) There is not a carrot in my box.')
91. print()
92. input('Then press Enter to continue...')
93.
94. print()
95. print(p2Name + ', do you want to swap boxes with ' + p1Name + '? YES/NO')
96. while True:
97.     response = input('> ').upper()
98.     if not (response.startswith('Y') or response.startswith('N')):
99.         print(p2Name + ', please enter "YES" or "NO".')
100.    else:
101.        break
102.
103. firstBox = 'RED '  # Note the space after the "D".
```

```python
104. secondBox = 'GOLD'
105.
106. if response.startswith('Y'):
107.     carrotInFirstBox = not carrotInFirstBox
108.     firstBox, secondBox = secondBox, firstBox
109.
110. print('''HERE ARE THE TWO BOXES:
111.    _____      _____
112.   /         /|    /         /|
113. +---------+ |   +---------+ |
114. |   {}    | |   |   {}    | |
115. |   BOX   | /   |   BOX   | /
116. +---------+/    +---------+/'''.format(firstBox, secondBox))
117. print(playerNames)
118.
119. input('Press Enter to reveal the winner...')
120. print()
121.
122. if carrotInFirstBox:
123.     print('''
124.    __VV____        _____
125.   |  VV    |      |         |
126.   |  VV    |      |         |
127.   |__||____|      |_____|
128.   /    ||   /|    /         /|
129. +---------+ |   +---------+ |
130. |   {}    | |   |   {}    | |
131. |   BOX   | /   |   BOX   | /
132. +---------+/    +---------+/'''.format(firstBox, secondBox))
133.
134. else:
135.     print('''
136.    _____        __VV____
137.   |         |      |  VV    |
138.   |         |      |  VV    |
139.   |_____|      |__||____|
140.   /         /|    /    ||   /|
141. +---------+ |   +---------+ |
142. |   {}    | |   |   {}    | |
143. |   BOX   | /   |   BOX   | /
144. +---------+/    +---------+/'''.format(firstBox, secondBox))
145.
146. print(playerNames)
147.
148. # This modification made possible through the 'carrotInFirstBox' variable
149. if carrotInFirstBox:
150.     print(p1Name + ' is the winner!')
151. else:
152.     print(p2Name + ' is the winner!')
153.
154. print('Thanks for playing!')
```

After entering the source code and running it a few times, try making experimental changes to it. On your own, you can also try to figure out how to do the following:

- Change the ASCII art for the boxes and carrots to something more ornate.
- Add a "would you like to play again?" feature that lets the players play again while keeping score.
- Add a third player that the second player must bluff to.

Exploring the Program

Try to find the answers to the following questions. Experiment with some modifications to the code and rerun the program to see what effect the changes have.

1. Note that line 26 has the code p1Name[:11] and p2Name[:11]. Enter a name longer than 11 letters. What do you notice about how the program displays this name?
2. What happens if you omit the space at the end of firstBox = 'RED ' on line 103?
3. What happens if you delete or comment out print('\n' * 100) on line 83?
4. What happens if you delete or comment out the else: on line 100 and break on line 101?

#10

CHO-HAN

 Cho-han is a dice game played in gambling houses of feudal Japan. Two six-sided dice are rolled in a cup, and gamblers must guess if the sum is even (cho) or odd (han). The house takes a small cut of all winnings. The simple random number generation and basic math used to determine odd or even sums make this project especially suitable for beginners. More information about Cho-han can be found at *https://en.wikipedia.org/wiki/ Cho-han*.

The Program in Action

When you run *chohan.py*, the output will look like this:

```
Cho-Han, by Al Sweigart al@inventwithpython.com

In this traditional Japanese dice game, two dice are rolled in a bamboo
cup by the dealer sitting on the floor. The player must guess if the
dice total to an even (cho) or odd (han) number.

You have 5000 mon. How much do you bet? (or QUIT)
> 400
The dealer swirls the cup and you hear the rattle of dice.
The dealer slams the cup on the floor, still covering the
dice and asks for your bet.

    CHO (even) or HAN (odd)?
> cho
The dealer lifts the cup to reveal:
    GO - GO
     5 - 5
You won! You take 800 mon.
The house collects a 40 mon fee.
--snip--
```

How It Works

The random.randint(1, 6) call returns a random integer between 1 and 6, making it ideal for representing a six-sided die roll. However, we also need to display the Japanese words for the numbers one to six. Instead of having an if statement followed by five elif statements, we have a dictionary, stored in JAPANESE_NUMBERS, that maps the integers 1 to 6 to strings of the Japanese words. This is how line 57's JAPANESE_NUMBERS[dice1] and JAPANESE_NUMBERS[dice2] can display the Japanese words for the dice results in just one line of code.

```
 1. """Cho-Han, by Al Sweigart al@inventwithpython.com
 2. The traditional Japanese dice game of even-odd.
 3. View this code at https://nostarch.com/big-book-small-python-projects
 4. Tags: short, beginner, game"""
 5.
 6. import random, sys
 7.
 8. JAPANESE_NUMBERS = {1: 'ICHI', 2: 'NI', 3: 'SAN',
 9.                     4: 'SHI', 5: 'GO', 6: 'ROKU'}
10.
11. print('''Cho-Han, by Al Sweigart al@inventwithpython.com
12.
13. In this traditional Japanese dice game, two dice are rolled in a bamboo
14. cup by the dealer sitting on the floor. The player must guess if the
15. dice total to an even (cho) or odd (han) number.
16. ''')
17.
18. purse = 5000
```

```
19. while True:  # Main game loop.
20.     # Place your bet:
21.     print('You have', purse, 'mon. How much do you bet? (or QUIT)')
22.     while True:
23.         pot = input('> ')
24.         if pot.upper() == 'QUIT':
25.             print('Thanks for playing!')
26.             sys.exit()
27.         elif not pot.isdecimal():
28.             print('Please enter a number.')
29.         elif int(pot) > purse:
30.             print('You do not have enough to make that bet.')
31.         else:
32.             # This is a valid bet.
33.             pot = int(pot)  # Convert pot to an integer.
34.             break  # Exit the loop once a valid bet is placed.
35.
36.     # Roll the dice.
37.     dice1 = random.randint(1, 6)
38.     dice2 = random.randint(1, 6)
39.
40.     print('The dealer swirls the cup and you hear the rattle of dice.')
41.     print('The dealer slams the cup on the floor, still covering the')
42.     print('dice and asks for your bet.')
43.     print()
44.     print('    CHO (even) or HAN (odd)?')
45.
46.     # Let the player bet cho or han:
47.     while True:
48.         bet = input('> ').upper()
49.         if bet != 'CHO' and bet != 'HAN':
50.             print('Please enter either "CHO" or "HAN".')
51.             continue
52.         else:
53.             break
54.
55.     # Reveal the dice results:
56.     print('The dealer lifts the cup to reveal:')
57.     print('  ', JAPANESE_NUMBERS[dice1], '-', JAPANESE_NUMBERS[dice2])
58.     print('    ', dice1, '-', dice2)
59.
60.     # Determine if the player won:
61.     rollIsEven = (dice1 + dice2) % 2 == 0
62.     if rollIsEven:
63.         correctBet = 'CHO'
64.     else:
65.         correctBet = 'HAN'
66.
67.     playerWon = bet == correctBet
68.
69.     # Display the bet results:
70.     if playerWon:
71.         print('You won! You take', pot, 'mon.')
72.         purse = purse + pot  # Add the pot from player's purse.
73.         print('The house collects a', pot // 10, 'mon fee.')
```

```
74.          purse = purse - (pot // 10)  # The house fee is 10%.
75.      else:
76.          purse = purse - pot  # Subtract the pot from player's purse.
77.          print('You lost!')
78.
79.      # Check if the player has run out of money:
80.      if purse == 0:
81.          print('You have run out of money!')
82.          print('Thanks for playing!')
83.          sys.exit()
```

After entering the source code and running it a few times, try making experimental changes to it. On your own, you can also try to figure out how to do the following:

- Implement one of the variations of this game, described in the Wikipedia article, where multiple players bet against each other. Add computer-controlled gamblers with their own purses to play against.
- Add extra bonuses for certain rolls, such as 7 or snake eyes.
- Allow the player to bet on a specific number to get a bonus to their wager.

Exploring the Program

Try to find the answers to the following questions. Experiment with some modifications to the code and rerun the program to see what effect the changes have.

1. How can you make the player start with a different amount of money?
2. How does the program prevent the player from betting more money than they have?
3. How does the program know if the sum of the two dice is even or odd?
4. What happens if you change random.randint(1, 6) on line 37 to random.randint(1, 1)?
5. Does the house still collect a 10 percent fee if you change pot // 10 on line 73 (not line 74) to 0?
6. What happens if you delete or comment out lines 80, 81, 82, and 83?

#11

CLICKBAIT HEADLINE GENERATOR

Our website needs to trick people into looking at advertisements! But coming up with creative, original content is too hard. Luckily, with the clickbait headline generator, we can make a computer come up with millions of outrageous fake headlines. They're all low quality, but readers don't seem to mind. This program generates as many headlines as you need from a Mad Libs–style template.

There's a lot of text in this program for the headline templates, but the code itself is straightforward and suitable for beginners.

The Program in Action

When you run *clickbait.py*, the output will look like this:

```
Clickbait Headline Generator
By Al Sweigart al@inventwithpython.com

Our website needs to trick people into looking at ads!
Enter the number of clickbait headlines to generate:
> 1000
Big Companies Hate Him! See How This New York Cat Invented a Cheaper Robot
What Telephone Psychics Don't Want You To Know About Avocados
You Won't Believe What This North Carolina Shovel Found in Her Workplace
--snip--
14 Reasons Why Parents Are More Interesting Than You Think (Number 1 Will Surprise You!)
What Robots Don't Want You To Know About Cats
This Florida Telephone Psychic Didn't Think Robots Would Take Her Job. She Was Wrong.
```

How It Works

This program has several functions for generating different kinds of click-bait headlines. Each of them gets random words from STATES, NOUNS, PLACES, WHEN, and other lists. The functions then insert these words into a template string with the format() string method before returning this string. This is like a "Mad Libs" activity book, except the computer fills in the blanks, allowing the program to generate thousands of clickbait headlines in seconds.

```
1. """Clickbait Headline Generator, by Al Sweigart al@inventwithpython.com
2. A clickbait headline generator for your soulless content farm website.
3. View this code at https://nostarch.com/big-book-small-python-projects
4. Tags: large, beginner, humor, word"""
5.
6. import random
7.
8. # Set up the constants:
9. OBJECT_PRONOUNS = ['Her', 'Him', 'Them']
10. POSSESIVE_PRONOUNS = ['Her', 'His', 'Their']
11. PERSONAL_PRONOUNS = ['She', 'He', 'They']
12. STATES = ['California', 'Texas', 'Florida', 'New York', 'Pennsylvania',
13.          'Illinois', 'Ohio', 'Georgia', 'North Carolina', 'Michigan']
14. NOUNS = ['Athlete', 'Clown', 'Shovel', 'Paleo Diet', 'Doctor', 'Parent',
15.         'Cat', 'Dog', 'Chicken', 'Robot', 'Video Game', 'Avocado',
16.         'Plastic Straw','Serial Killer', 'Telephone Psychic']
17. PLACES = ['House', 'Attic', 'Bank Deposit Box', 'School', 'Basement',
18.          'Workplace', 'Donut Shop', 'Apocalypse Bunker']
19. WHEN = ['Soon', 'This Year', 'Later Today', 'RIGHT NOW', 'Next Week']
20.
21.
22. def main():
23.     print('Clickbait Headline Generator')
24.     print('By Al Sweigart al@inventwithpython.com')
```

```
25.     print()
26.
27.     print('Our website needs to trick people into looking at ads!')
28.     while True:
29.         print('Enter the number of clickbait headlines to generate:')
30.         response = input('> ')
31.         if not response.isdecimal():
32.             print('Please enter a number.')
33.         else:
34.             numberOfHeadlines = int(response)
35.             break  # Exit the loop once a valid number is entered.
36.
37.     for i in range(numberOfHeadlines):
38.         clickbaitType = random.randint(1, 8)
39.
40.         if clickbaitType == 1:
41.             headline = generateAreMillennialsKillingHeadline()
42.         elif clickbaitType == 2:
43.             headline = generateWhatYouDontKnowHeadline()
44.         elif clickbaitType == 3:
45.             headline = generateBigCompaniesHateHerHeadline()
46.         elif clickbaitType == 4:
47.             headline = generateYouWontBelieveHeadline()
48.         elif clickbaitType == 5:
49.             headline = generateDontWantYouToKnowHeadline()
50.         elif clickbaitType == 6:
51.             headline = generateGiftIdeaHeadline()
52.         elif clickbaitType == 7:
53.             headline = generateReasonsWhyHeadline()
54.         elif clickbaitType == 8:
55.             headline = generateJobAutomatedHeadline()
56.
57.         print(headline)
58.     print()
59.
60.     website = random.choice(['wobsite', 'blag', 'Facebuuk', 'Googles',
61.                              'Facesbook', 'Tweedie', 'Pastagram'])
62.     when = random.choice(WHEN).lower()
63.     print('Post these to our', website, when, 'or you\'re fired!')
64.
65.
66. # Each of these functions returns a different type of headline:
67. def generateAreMillennialsKillingHeadline():
68.     noun = random.choice(NOUNS)
69.     return 'Are Millennials Killing the {} Industry?'.format(noun)
70.
71.
72. def generateWhatYouDontKnowHeadline():
73.     noun = random.choice(NOUNS)
74.     pluralNoun = random.choice(NOUNS) + 's'
75.     when = random.choice(WHEN)
76.     return 'Without This {}, {} Could Kill You {}'.format(noun, pluralNoun, when)
77.
78.
79. def generateBigCompaniesHateHerHeadline():
```

```
80.        pronoun = random.choice(OBJECT_PRONOUNS)
81.        state = random.choice(STATES)
82.        noun1 = random.choice(NOUNS)
83.        noun2 = random.choice(NOUNS)
84.        return 'Big Companies Hate {}! See How This {} {} Invented a Cheaper {}'.
           format(pronoun, state, noun1, noun2)
85.
86.
87. def generateYouWontBelieveHeadline():
88.        state = random.choice(STATES)
89.        noun = random.choice(NOUNS)
90.        pronoun = random.choice(POSSESIVE_PRONOUNS)
91.        place = random.choice(PLACES)
92.        return 'You Won\'t Believe What This {} {} Found in {} {}'.format(state, noun,
           pronoun, place)
93.
94.
95. def generateDontWantYouToKnowHeadline():
96.        pluralNoun1 = random.choice(NOUNS) + 's'
97.        pluralNoun2 = random.choice(NOUNS) + 's'
98.        return 'What {} Don\'t Want You To Know About {}'.format(pluralNoun1, pluralNoun2)
99.
100.
101. def generateGiftIdeaHeadline():
102.       number = random.randint(7, 15)
103.       noun = random.choice(NOUNS)
104.       state = random.choice(STATES)
105.       return '{} Gift Ideas to Give Your {} From {}'.format(number, noun, state)
106.
107.
108. def generateReasonsWhyHeadline():
109.       number1 = random.randint(3, 19)
110.       pluralNoun = random.choice(NOUNS) + 's'
111.       # number2 should be no larger than number1:
112.       number2 = random.randint(1, number1)
113.       return '{} Reasons Why {} Are More Interesting Than You Think (Number {} Will
           Surprise You!)'.format(number1, pluralNoun, number2)
114.
115.
116. def generateJobAutomatedHeadline():
117.       state = random.choice(STATES)
118.       noun = random.choice(NOUNS)
119.
120.       i = random.randint(0, 2)
121.       pronoun1 = POSSESIVE_PRONOUNS[i]
122.       pronoun2 = PERSONAL_PRONOUNS[i]
123.       if pronoun1 == 'Their':
124.           return 'This {} {} Didn\'t Think Robots Would Take {} Job. {} Were
               Wrong.'.format(state, noun, pronoun1, pronoun2)
125.       else:
126.           return 'This {} {} Didn\'t Think Robots Would Take {} Job. {} Was
               Wrong.'.format(state, noun, pronoun1, pronoun2)
127.
128.
```

```
129. # If the program is run (instead of imported), run the game:
130. if __name__ == '__main__':
131.     main()
```

After entering the source code and running it a few times, try making experimental changes to it. On your own, you can also try to figure out how to do the following:

- Add additional types of clickbait headlines.
- Add new categories of words, beyond NOUNS, STATES, and so on.

Exploring the Program

Try to find the answers to the following questions. Experiment with some modifications to the code and rerun the program to see what effect the changes have.

1. What error message do you get if you delete or comment out numberOf Headlines = int(response) on line 34?

2. What error message do you get if you change int(response) to response on line 34?

3. What error message do you get if you change line 19 to WHEN = []?

#12

COLLATZ SEQUENCE

The Collatz sequence, also called the 3n + 1 problem, is the simplest impossible math problem. (But don't worry, the program itself is easy enough for beginners.) From a starting number, n, follow three rules to get the next number in the sequence:

1. If n is even, the next number n is $n / 2$.
2. If n is odd, the next number n is $n * 3 + 1$.
3. If n is 1, stop. Otherwise, repeat.

It is generally thought, but so far not mathematically proven, that every starting number eventually terminates at 1. More information about the Collatz sequence can be found at *https://en.wikipedia.org/wiki/ Collatz_conjecture*.

The Program in Action

When you run *collatz.py*, the output will look like this:

```
Collatz Sequence, or, the 3n + 1 Problem
By Al Sweigart al@inventwithpython.com

The Collatz sequence is a sequence of numbers produced from a starting
number n, following three rules:
--snip--
Enter a starting number (greater than 0) or QUIT:
> 26
26, 13, 40, 20, 10, 5, 16, 8, 4, 2, 1

Collatz Sequence, or, the 3n + 1 Problem
By Al Sweigart al@inventwithpython.com
--snip--
Enter a starting number (greater than 0) or QUIT:
> 27
27, 82, 41, 124, 62, 31, 94, 47, 142, 71, 214, 107, 322, 161, 484, 242, 121,
364, 182, 91, 274, 137, 412, 206, 103, 310, 155, 466, 233, 700, 350, 175, 526,
263, 790, 395, 1186, 593, 1780, 890, 445, 1336, 668, 334, 167, 502, 251, 754,
377, 1132, 566, 283, 850, 425, 1276, 638, 319, 958, 479, 1438, 719, 2158,
1079, 3238, 1619, 4858, 2429, 7288, 3644, 1822, 911, 2734, 1367, 4102, 2051,
6154, 3077, 9232, 4616, 2308, 1154, 577, 1732, 866, 433, 1300, 650, 325, 976,
488, 244, 122, 61, 184, 92, 46, 23, 70, 35, 106, 53, 160, 80, 40, 20, 10, 5,
16, 8, 4, 2, 1
```

How It Works

The % mod operator can help you determine if a number is even or odd.
Remember that this operator is a sort of "remainder" operator. While 23
divided by 7 is 3-remainder-2, 23 mod 7 is simply 2. Even numbers divided
by 2 have no remainder, while odd numbers divided by 2 have a remainder
of 1. When n is even, the condition in if n % 2 == 0: on line 33 evaluates to
True. When n is odd, it evaluates to False.

```
1. """Collatz Sequence, by Al Sweigart al@inventwithpython.com
2. Generates numbers for the Collatz sequence, given a starting number.
3. More info at: https://en.wikipedia.org/wiki/Collatz_conjecture
4. View this code at https://nostarch.com/big-book-small-python-projects
5. Tags: tiny, beginner, math"""
6.
7. import sys, time
8.
9. print('''Collatz Sequence, or, the 3n + 1 Problem
10. By Al Sweigart al@inventwithpython.com
11.
12. The Collatz sequence is a sequence of numbers produced from a starting
13. number n, following three rules:
14.
15. 1) If n is even, the next number n is n / 2.
16. 2) If n is odd, the next number n is n * 3 + 1.
```

```
17. 3) If n is 1, stop. Otherwise, repeat.
18.
19. It is generally thought, but so far not mathematically proven, that
20. every starting number eventually terminates at 1.
21. ''')
22.
23. print('Enter a starting number (greater than 0) or QUIT:')
24. response = input('> ')
25.
26. if not response.isdecimal() or response == '0':
27.     print('You must enter an integer greater than 0.')
28.     sys.exit()
29.
30. n = int(response)
31. print(n, end='', flush=True)
32. while n != 1:
33.     if n % 2 == 0:  # If n is even...
34.         n = n // 2
35.     else:  # Otherwise, n is odd...
36.         n = 3 * n + 1
37.
38.     print(', ' + str(n), end='', flush=True)
39.     time.sleep(0.1)
40. print()
```

Exploring the Program

Try to find the answers to the following questions. Experiment with some modifications to the code and rerun the program to see what effect the changes have.

1. How many numbers are in a Collatz sequence that begins with 32?
2. How many numbers are in a Collatz sequence that begins with 33?
3. Are the Collatz sequences for starting numbers that are powers of two (2, 4, 8, 16, 32, 64, 128, on so on) always composed of only even numbers (aside from the final 1)?
4. What happens when you enter 0 for the starting integer?

#13

CONWAY'S GAME OF LIFE

Conway's Game of Life is a cellular automata simulation that follows simple rules to create interesting patterns. It was invented by mathematician John Conway in 1970 and popularized by Martin Gardner's "Mathematical Games" column in *Scientific American*. Today, it's a favorite among programmers and computer scientists, though it's more an interesting visualization than a true "game." The two-dimensional board has a grid of "cells," each of which follows three simple rules:

- Living cells with two or three neighbors stay alive in the next step of the simulation.
- Dead cells with exactly three neighbors become alive in the next step of the simulation.
- Any other cell dies or stays dead in the next step of the simulation.

The living or dead state of the cells in the next step of the simulation depends entirely on their current state. The cells don't "remember" any older states. There is a large body of research regarding the patterns that these simple rules produce. Tragically, Professor Conway passed away of complications from COVID-19 in April 2020. More information about Conway's Game of Life can be found at *https://en.wikipedia.org/wiki/Conway%27s_Game_of_Life*, and more information about Martin Gardner at *https://en.wikipedia.org/wiki/Martin_Gardner*.

The Program in Action

When you run *conwaysgameoflife.py*, the output will look like this:

```
              0                    0                  00      0 0
0     0    0  0                    0                 0 0000              0 00
00    0  0                         0          0          0               0 0
00        0   0                            00                     00
00        00                             0 0   0                 00
                                         00    0 0               0  00
        000                              00    00                 0
                          0                   0      000       0 0
            00          00 00              00  0
            000            00            0000    0 0
        0     00           0 0        0 00  00 0   0    00
        0 0              0    0          0  00 0  0  000
        0             0000  00           00   0  00000 0
00        0            0    000        0 000     0000        0
```

How It Works

The state of the cells is stored in dictionaries in the `cells` and `nextCells` variables. Both dictionaries have `(x, y)` tuples for keys (where x and y are integers), `'0'` for living cells, and `' '` for dead cells. Lines 40 to 44 are set up to print a representation of these dictionaries onto the screen. The `cells` variable's dictionary represents the current state of the cells, while `nextCells` stores the dictionary for the cells in the next step in the simulation.

```python
 1. """Conway's Game of Life, by Al Sweigart al@inventwithpython.com
 2. The classic cellular automata simulation. Press Ctrl-C to stop.
 3. More info at: https://en.wikipedia.org/wiki/Conway%27s_Game_of_Life
 4. View this code at https://nostarch.com/big-book-small-python-projects
 5. Tags: short, artistic, simulation"""
 6.
 7. import copy, random, sys, time
 8.
 9. # Set up the constants:
10. WIDTH = 79   # The width of the cell grid.
11. HEIGHT = 20  # The height of the cell grid.
12.
13. # (!) Try changing ALIVE to '#' or another character:
```

```
14. ALIVE = 'O'  # The character representing a living cell.
15. # (!) Try changing DEAD to '.' or another character:
16. DEAD = ' '   # The character representing a dead cell.
17.
18. # (!) Try changing ALIVE to '|' and DEAD to '-'.
19.
20. # The cells and nextCells are dictionaries for the state of the game.
21. # Their keys are (x, y) tuples and their values are one of the ALIVE
22. # or DEAD values.
23. nextCells = {}
24. # Put random dead and alive cells into nextCells:
25. for x in range(WIDTH):  # Loop over every possible column.
26.     for y in range(HEIGHT):  # Loop over every possible row.
27.         # 50/50 chance for starting cells being alive or dead.
28.         if random.randint(0, 1) == 0:
29.             nextCells[(x, y)] = ALIVE  # Add a living cell.
30.         else:
31.             nextCells[(x, y)] = DEAD  # Add a dead cell.
32.
33. while True:  # Main program loop.
34.     # Each iteration of this loop is a step of the simulation.
35.
36.     print('\n' * 50)  # Separate each step with newlines.
37.     cells = copy.deepcopy(nextCells)
38.
39.     # Print cells on the screen:
40.     for y in range(HEIGHT):
41.         for x in range(WIDTH):
42.             print(cells[(x, y)], end='')  # Print the # or space.
43.         print()  # Print a newline at the end of the row.
44.     print('Press Ctrl-C to quit.')
45.
46.     # Calculate the next step's cells based on current step's cells:
47.     for x in range(WIDTH):
48.         for y in range(HEIGHT):
49.             # Get the neighboring coordinates of (x, y), even if they
50.             # wrap around the edge:
51.             left  = (x - 1) % WIDTH
52.             right = (x + 1) % WIDTH
53.             above = (y - 1) % HEIGHT
54.             below = (y + 1) % HEIGHT
55.
56.             # Count the number of living neighbors:
57.             numNeighbors = 0
58.             if cells[(left, above)] == ALIVE:
59.                 numNeighbors += 1  # Top-left neighbor is alive.
60.             if cells[(x, above)] == ALIVE:
61.                 numNeighbors += 1  # Top neighbor is alive.
62.             if cells[(right, above)] == ALIVE:
63.                 numNeighbors += 1  # Top-right neighbor is alive.
64.             if cells[(left, y)] == ALIVE:
65.                 numNeighbors += 1  # Left neighbor is alive.
66.             if cells[(right, y)] == ALIVE:
67.                 numNeighbors += 1  # Right neighbor is alive.
68.             if cells[(left, below)] == ALIVE:
```

```
69.                    numNeighbors += 1  # Bottom-left neighbor is alive.
70.                if cells[(x, below)] == ALIVE:
71.                    numNeighbors += 1  # Bottom neighbor is alive.
72.                if cells[(right, below)] == ALIVE:
73.                    numNeighbors += 1  # Bottom-right neighbor is alive.
74.
75.                # Set cell based on Conway's Game of Life rules:
76.                if cells[(x, y)] == ALIVE and (numNeighbors == 2
77.                    or numNeighbors == 3):
78.                        # Living cells with 2 or 3 neighbors stay alive:
79.                        nextCells[(x, y)] = ALIVE
80.                elif cells[(x, y)] == DEAD and numNeighbors == 3:
81.                    # Dead cells with 3 neighbors become alive:
82.                    nextCells[(x, y)] = ALIVE
83.                else:
84.                    # Everything else dies or stays dead:
85.                    nextCells[(x, y)] = DEAD
86.
87.    try:
88.        time.sleep(1)  # Add a 1 second pause to reduce flickering.
89.    except KeyboardInterrupt:
90.        print("Conway's Game of Life")
91.        print('By Al Sweigart al@inventwithpython.com')
92.        sys.exit()  # When Ctrl-C is pressed, end the program.
```

After entering the source code and running it a few times, try making experimental changes to it. The comments marked with (!) have suggestions for small changes you can make. On your own, you can also try to figure out how to do the following:

- Adjust the percentage of cells that start as living, instead of always using 50 percent.
- Add the ability to read in the initial state from a text file, so the user can edit the starting cell states manually.

Exploring the Program

Try to find the answers to the following questions. Experiment with some modifications to the code and rerun the program to see what effect the changes have.

1. What happens when you change WIDTH = 79 on line 10 to WIDTH = 7?
2. What happens if you delete or comment out print('\n' * 50) on line 36?
3. What happens if you change random.randint(0, 1) on line 28 to random .randint(0, 10)?
4. What happens if you change nextCells[(x, y)] = DEAD on line 85 to nextCells[(x, y)] = ALIVE?

#14

COUNTDOWN

This program displays a digital timer that counts down to zero. Rather than render numeric characters directly, the *sevseg.py* module from Project 64, "Seven-Segment Display Module," generates the drawings for each digit. You must create this file before the Countdown program can work. Then, set the countdown timer to any number of seconds, minutes, and hours you like. This program is similar to Project 19, "Digital Clock."

The Program in Action

When you run *countdown.py*, the output will look like this:

```
 _   _   *  _   _   *   _   _ 
| | | |  *  | | | |  *  _| |_|
|_| |_|  *  |_| |_|  *  |_   _|
```

Press Ctrl-C to quit.

How It Works

After running import sevseg, you can call the sevseg.getSevSegStr() function to get a multiline string of the seven segment digits. However, the
Countdown program needs to display a colon made out of asterisks in
between the hours, minutes, and seconds. This requires splitting up the
three lines of the multiline strings for these digits into three separate
strings with the splitlines() method.

```
1. """Countdown, by Al Sweigart al@inventwithpython.com
2. Show a countdown timer animation using a seven-segment display.
3. Press Ctrl-C to stop.
4. More info at https://en.wikipedia.org/wiki/Seven-segment_display
5. Requires sevseg.py to be in the same folder.
6. View this code at https://nostarch.com/big-book-small-python-projects
7. Tags: tiny, artistic"""
8.
9. import sys, time
10. import sevseg  # Imports our sevseg.py program.
11.
12. # (!) Change this to any number of seconds:
13. secondsLeft = 30
14.
15. try:
16.     while True:  # Main program loop.
17.         # Clear the screen by printing several newlines:
18.         print('\n' * 60)
19.
20.         # Get the hours/minutes/seconds from secondsLeft:
21.         # For example: 7265 is 2 hours, 1 minute, 5 seconds.
22.         # So 7265 // 3600 is 2 hours:
23.         hours = str(secondsLeft // 3600)
24.         # And 7265 % 3600 is 65, and 65 // 60 is 1 minute:
25.         minutes = str((secondsLeft % 3600) // 60)
26.         # And 7265 % 60 is 5 seconds:
27.         seconds = str(secondsLeft % 60)
28.
29.         # Get the digit strings from the sevseg module:
30.         hDigits = sevseg.getSevSegStr(hours, 2)
31.         hTopRow, hMiddleRow, hBottomRow = hDigits.splitlines()
32.
33.         mDigits = sevseg.getSevSegStr(minutes, 2)
34.         mTopRow, mMiddleRow, mBottomRow = mDigits.splitlines()
```

```
35.
36.          sDigits = sevseg.getSevSegStr(seconds, 2)
37.          sTopRow, sMiddleRow, sBottomRow = sDigits.splitlines()
38.
39.          # Display the digits:
40.          print(hTopRow    + '     ' + mTopRow    + '     ' + sTopRow)
41.          print(hMiddleRow + '  *  ' + mMiddleRow + '  *  ' + sMiddleRow)
42.          print(hBottomRow + '  *  ' + mBottomRow + '  *  ' + sBottomRow)
43.
44.          if secondsLeft == 0:
45.              print()
46.              print('    * * * * BOOM * * * *')
47.              break
48.
49.          print()
50.          print('Press Ctrl-C to quit.')
51.
52.          time.sleep(1)  # Insert a one-second pause.
53.          secondsLeft -= 1
54. except KeyboardInterrupt:
55.     print('Countdown, by Al Sweigart al@inventwithpython.com')
56.     sys.exit()  # When Ctrl-C is pressed, end the program.)
```

After entering the source code and running it a few times, try making experimental changes to it. On your own, you can also try to figure out how to do the following:

- Prompt the user to enter the starting countdown time.
- Let the user enter a message to display at the end of the countdown.

Exploring the Program

Try to find the answers to the following questions. Experiment with some modifications to the code and rerun the program to see what effect the changes have.

1. What happens if you change secondsLeft = 30 on line 13 to secondsLeft = 30.5?
2. What happens if you change the 2 on lines 30, 33, and 36 to 1?
3. What happens if you change time.sleep(1) on line 52 to time.sleep(0.1)?
4. What happens if you change secondsLeft -= 1 on line 53 to secondsLeft -= 2?
5. What happens if you delete or comment out print('\n' * 60) on line 18?
6. What error message do you get if you delete or comment out import sevseg on line 10?

#15

DEEP CAVE

This program is an animation of a deep cave that descends forever into the earth. Although short, this program takes advantage of the scrolling nature of the computer screen to produce an interesting and unending visualization, proof that it doesn't take much code to produce something fun to watch. This program is similar to Project 58, "Rainbow."

The Program in Action

When you run *deepcave.py*, the output will look like this:

```
Deep Cave, by Al Sweigart al@inventwithpython.com
Press Ctrl-C to stop.
####################            #########################################
####################            #########################################
####################            #########################################
####################            #########################################
####################            #########################################
#####################           ########################################
#####################           ########################################
####################            #########################################
###################             #########################################
--snip--
```

How It Works

This program takes advantage of the fact that printing new lines eventually causes the previous lines to move up the screen. By printing a slightly different gap on each line, the program creates a scrolling animation that looks like the viewer is moving downward.

The number of hashtag characters on the left side is tracked by the leftWidth variable. The number of spaces in the middle is tracked by the gapWidth variable. The number of hashtag characters on the right side is calculated from WIDTH - gapWidth - leftWidth. This ensures that each line is always the same width.

```python
1. """Deep Cave, by Al Sweigart al@inventwithpython.com
2. An animation of a deep cave that goes forever into the earth.
3. View this code at https://nostarch.com/big-book-small-python-projects
4. Tags: tiny, beginner, scrolling, artistic"""
5.
6.
7. import random, sys, time
8.
9. # Set up the constants:
10. WIDTH = 70  # (!) Try changing this to 10 or 30.
11. PAUSE_AMOUNT = 0.05  # (!) Try changing this to 0 or 1.0.
12.
13. print('Deep Cave, by Al Sweigart al@inventwithpython.com')
14. print('Press Ctrl-C to stop.')
15. time.sleep(2)
16.
17. leftWidth = 20
18. gapWidth = 10
19.
20. while True:
21.     # Display the tunnel segment:
22.     rightWidth = WIDTH - gapWidth - leftWidth
23.     print(('#' * leftWidth) + (' ' * gapWidth) + ('#' * rightWidth))
```

```
24.
25.      # Check for Ctrl-C press during the brief pause:
26.      try:
27.          time.sleep(PAUSE_AMOUNT)
28.      except KeyboardInterrupt:
29.          sys.exit()  # When Ctrl-C is pressed, end the program.
30.
31.      # Adjust the left side width:
32.      diceRoll = random.randint(1, 6)
33.      if diceRoll == 1 and leftWidth > 1:
34.          leftWidth = leftWidth - 1  # Decrease left side width.
35.      elif diceRoll == 2 and leftWidth + gapWidth < WIDTH - 1:
36.          leftWidth = leftWidth + 1  # Increase left side width.
37.      else:
38.          pass  # Do nothing; no change in left side width.
39.
40.      # Adjust the gap width:
41.      # (!) Try uncommenting out all of the following code:
42.      #diceRoll = random.randint(1, 6)
43.      #if diceRoll == 1 and gapWidth > 1:
44.      #    gapWidth = gapWidth - 1  # Decrease gap width.
45.      #elif diceRoll == 2 and leftWidth + gapWidth < WIDTH - 1:
46.      #    gapWidth = gapWidth + 1  # Increase gap width.
47.      #else:
48.      #    pass  # Do nothing; no change in gap width.
```

After entering the source code and running it a few times, try making experimental changes to it. The comments marked with (!) have suggestions for small changes you can make.

Exploring the Program

Try to find the answers to the following questions. Experiment with some modifications to the code and rerun the program to see what effect the changes have.

1. What happens if you change (' ' * gapWidth) on line 23 to ('.' * gapWidth)?

2. What happens if you change random.randint(1, 6) on line 32 to random.randint(1, 1)?

3. What happens if you change random.randint(1, 6) on line 32 to random.randint(2, 2)?

4. What error message do you get if you delete or comment out leftWidth = 20 on line 17?

5. What happens if you change WIDTH = 70 on line 10 to WIDTH = -70?

6. What error message do you get if you change PAUSE_AMOUNT = 0.05 on line 11 to PAUSE_AMOUNT = -0.05?

#16

DIAMONDS

This program features a small algorithm for drawing ASCII-art diamonds of various sizes. It contains functions for drawing either an outline or filled-in-style diamond of the size you dictate. These functions are good practice for a beginner; try to understand the pattern behind the diamond drawings as they increase in size.

The Program in Action

When you run *diamonds.py*, the output will look like this:

```
Diamonds, by Al Sweigart al@inventwithpython.com

/\
\/

/\
\/

 /\
/  \
\  /
 \/

 /\
//\\
\\//
 \/

  /\
 /  \
/    \
\    /
 \  /
  \/

  /\
 //\\
///\\\
\\\///
 \\//
  \/
--snip--
```

How It Works

A helpful approach to creating this program yourself is to "draw" diamonds of several sizes in your editor first and then figure out the pattern they follow as the diamond gets bigger. This technique will help you realize that each row of an outline diamond has four parts: the number of leading spaces, the exterior forward slash, the number of interior spaces, and the exterior backslash. Filled diamonds have several interior forward slashes and backslashes rather than interior spaces. Cracking this pattern is how I wrote *diamonds.py*.

```
1. r"""Diamonds, by Al Sweigart al@inventwithpython.com
2. Draws diamonds of various sizes.
3. View this code at https://nostarch.com/big-book-small-python-projects
```

```
 4.                                  /\        /\
 5.                                 /  \      //\\
 6.                      /\        /    \    ///\\\
 7.                     /  \      //\\    /       \   ////\\\\
 8.  /\     /\    /       \ ///\\\    \        /  \\\\////
 9. /  \  //\\  \     /  \\\///   \      /    \\\///
10. \  /  \\//   \    /    \\//     \      /      \\//
11.  \/     \/      \/       \/       \/          \/
12. Tags: tiny, beginner, artistic"""
13.
14. def main():
15.     print('Diamonds, by Al Sweigart al@inventwithpython.com')
16.
17.     # Display diamonds of sizes 0 through 6:
18.     for diamondSize in range(0, 6):
19.         displayOutlineDiamond(diamondSize)
20.         print()  # Print a newline.
21.         displayFilledDiamond(diamondSize)
22.         print()  # Print a newline.
23.
24.
25. def displayOutlineDiamond(size):
26.     # Display the top half of the diamond:
27.     for i in range(size):
28.         print(' ' * (size - i - 1), end='')  # Left side space.
29.         print('/', end='')  # Left side of diamond.
30.         print(' ' * (i * 2), end='')  # Interior of diamond.
31.         print('\\')  # Right side of diamond.
32.
33.     # Display the bottom half of the diamond:
34.     for i in range(size):
35.         print(' ' * i, end='')  # Left side space.
36.         print('\\', end='')  # Left side of diamond.
37.         print(' ' * ((size - i - 1) * 2), end='')  # Interior of diamond.
38.         print('/')  # Right side of diamond.
39.
40.
41. def displayFilledDiamond(size):
42.     # Display the top half of the diamond:
43.     for i in range(size):
44.         print(' ' * (size - i - 1), end='')  # Left side space.
45.         print('/' * (i + 1), end='')  # Left half of diamond.
46.         print('\\' * (i + 1))  # Right half of diamond.
47.
48.     # Display the bottom half of the diamond:
49.     for i in range(size):
50.         print(' ' * i, end='')  # Left side space.
51.         print('\\' * (size - i), end='')  # Left side of diamond.
52.         print('/' * (size - i))  # Right side of diamond.
53.
54.
55. # If this program was run (instead of imported), run the game:
56. if __name__ == '__main__':
57.     main()
```

After entering the source code and running it a few times, try making experimental changes to it. On your own, you can also try to figure out how to do the following:

- Create other shapes: triangles, rectangles, and rhombuses.
- Output the shapes to a text file instead of the screen.

Exploring the Program

Try to find the answers to the following questions. Experiment with some modifications to the code and rerun the program to see what effect the changes have.

1. What happens when you change print('\\') on line 31 to print('@')?
2. What happens when you change print(' ' * (i * 2), end='') on line 30 to print('@' * (i * 2), end='')?
3. What happens when you change range(0, 6) on line 18 to range(0, 30)?
4. What happens when you delete or comment out for i in range(size): on line 34 or on line 49?

#17

DICE MATH

This math quiz program rolls two to six dice whose sides you must add up as quickly as possible. But this program operates as more than just automated flash cards; it draws the faces of the dice to random places on the screen. The ASCII-art aspect adds a fun twist while you practice arithmetic.

The Program in Action

When you run *dicemath.py*, the output will look like this:

```
Dice Math, by Al Sweigart al@inventwithpython.com

Add up the sides of all the dice displayed on the screen. You have
30 seconds to answer as many as possible. You get 4 points for each
correct answer and lose 1 point for each incorrect answer.

Press Enter to begin...
```

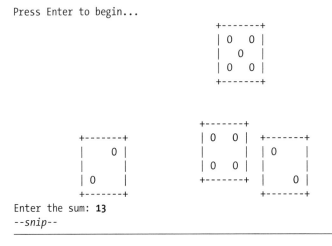

```
Enter the sum: 13
--snip--
```

How It Works

The dice on the screen are represented by a dictionary stored in the canvas variable. In Python, tuples are similar to lists, but their contents cannot be changed. The keys to this dictionary are (x, y) tuples marking the position of a die's top left corner, while the values are one of the "dice tuples" in ALL_DICE. You can see in lines 28 to 80 that each dice tuple contains a list of strings, which graphically represents one possible die face, and an integer of how many pips are on the die face. The program uses this information to display the dice and calculate their sum total.

Lines 174 to 177 render the data in the canvas dictionary on the screen in a manner similar to how Project 13, "Conway's Game of Life," renders cells on the screen.

```
1. """Dice Math, by Al Sweigart al@inventwithpython.com
2. A flash card addition game where you sum the total on random dice rolls.
3. View this code at https://nostarch.com/big-book-small-python-projects
4. Tags: large, artistic, game, math"""
5.
6. import random, time
7.
8. # Set up the constants:
9. DICE_WIDTH = 9
10. DICE_HEIGHT = 5
11. CANVAS_WIDTH = 79
```

```
12. CANVAS_HEIGHT = 24 - 3  # -3 for room to enter the sum at the bottom.
13.
14. # The duration is in seconds:
15. QUIZ_DURATION = 30  # (!) Try changing this to 10 or 60.
16. MIN_DICE = 2  # (!) Try changing this to 1 or 5.
17. MAX_DICE = 6  # (!) Try changing this to 14.
18.
19. # (!) Try changing these to different numbers:
20. REWARD = 4  # (!) Points awarded for correct answers.
21. PENALTY = 1  # (!) Points removed for incorrect answers.
22. # (!) Try setting PENALTY to a negative number to give points for
23. # wrong answers!
24.
25. # The program hangs if all of the dice can't fit on the screen:
26. assert MAX_DICE <= 14
27.
28. D1 = (['+-------+',
29.        '|       |',
30.        '|   O   |',
31.        '|       |',
32.        '+-------+'], 1)
33.
34. D2a = (['+-------+',
35.         '| O     |',
36.         '|       |',
37.         '|     O |',
38.         '+-------+'], 2)
39.
40. D2b = (['+-------+',
41.         '|     O |',
42.         '|       |',
43.         '| O     |',
44.         '+-------+'], 2)
45.
46. D3a = (['+-------+',
47.         '| O     |',
48.         '|   O   |',
49.         '|     O |',
50.         '+-------+'], 3)
51.
52. D3b = (['+-------+',
53.         '|     O |',
54.         '|   O   |',
55.         '| O     |',
56.         '+-------+'], 3)
57.
58. D4 = (['+-------+',
59.        '| O   O |',
60.        '|       |',
61.        '| O   O |',
62.        '+-------+'], 4)
63.
64. D5 = (['+-------+',
65.        '| O   O |',
66.        '|   O   |',
```

```
67.         '| O    O |',
68.         '+-------+'], 5)
69.
70. D6a = (['+-------+',
71.         '| O    O |',
72.         '| O    O |',
73.         '| O    O |',
74.         '+-------+'], 6)
75.
76. D6b = (['+-------+',
77.         '| O O O |',
78.         '|       |',
79.         '| O O O |',
80.         '+-------+'], 6)
81.
83. ALL_DICE = [D1, D2a, D2b, D3a, D3b, D4, D5, D6a, D6b]
83.
84. print('''Dice Math, by Al Sweigart al@inventwithpython.com
85.
86. Add up the sides of all the dice displayed on the screen. You have
87. {} seconds to answer as many as possible. You get {} points for each
88. correct answer and lose {} point for each incorrect answer.
89. '''.format(QUIZ_DURATION, REWARD, PENALTY))
90. input('Press Enter to begin...')
91.
92. # Keep track of how many answers were correct and incorrect:
93. correctAnswers = 0
94. incorrectAnswers = 0
95. startTime = time.time()
96. while time.time() < startTime + QUIZ_DURATION:  # Main game loop.
97.     # Come up with the dice to display:
98.     sumAnswer = 0
99.     diceFaces = []
100.    for i in range(random.randint(MIN_DICE, MAX_DICE)):
101.        die = random.choice(ALL_DICE)
102.        # die[0] contains the list of strings of the die face:
103.        diceFaces.append(die[0])
104.        # die[1] contains the integer number of pips on the face:
105.        sumAnswer += die[1]
106.
107.    # Contains (x, y) tuples of the top-left corner of each die.
108.    topLeftDiceCorners = []
109.
110.    # Figure out where dice should go:
111.    for i in range(len(diceFaces)):
112.        while True:
113.            # Find a random place on the canvas to put the die:
114.            left = random.randint(0, CANVAS_WIDTH  - 1 - DICE_WIDTH)
115.            top  = random.randint(0, CANVAS_HEIGHT - 1 - DICE_HEIGHT)
116.
117.            # Get the x, y coordinates for all four corners:
118.            #      left
119.            #       v
120.            #top > +-------+ ^
121.            #      | O    | |
```

```
122.        #        |   O   | DICE_HEIGHT (5)
123.        #        |     O | |
124.        #        +-------+ v
125.        #        <------->
126.        #         DICE_WIDTH (9)
127.        topLeftX = left
128.        topLeftY = top
129.        topRightX = left + DICE_WIDTH
130.        topRightY = top
131.        bottomLeftX = left
132.        bottomLeftY = top + DICE_HEIGHT
133.        bottomRightX = left + DICE_WIDTH
134.        bottomRightY = top + DICE_HEIGHT
135.
136.        # Check if this die overlaps with previous dice.
137.        overlaps = False
138.        for prevDieLeft, prevDieTop in topLeftDiceCorners:
139.            prevDieRight = prevDieLeft + DICE_WIDTH
140.            prevDieBottom = prevDieTop + DICE_HEIGHT
141.            # Check each corner of this die to see if it is inside
142.            # of the area the previous die:
143.            for cornerX, cornerY in ((topLeftX, topLeftY),
144.                                     (topRightX, topRightY),
145.                                     (bottomLeftX, bottomLeftY),
146.                                     (bottomRightX, bottomRightY)):
147.                if (prevDieLeft <= cornerX < prevDieRight
148.                    and prevDieTop <= cornerY < prevDieBottom):
149.                    overlaps = True
150.        if not overlaps:
151.            # It doesn't overlap, so we can put it here:
152.            topLeftDiceCorners.append((left, top))
153.            break
154.
155.    # Draw the dice on the canvas:
156.
157.    # Keys are (x, y) tuples of ints, values the character at that
158.    # position on the canvas:
159.    canvas = {}
160.    # Loop over each die:
161.    for i, (dieLeft, dieTop) in enumerate(topLeftDiceCorners):
162.        # Loop over each character in the die's face:
163.        dieFace = diceFaces[i]
164.        for dx in range(DICE_WIDTH):
165.            for dy in range(DICE_HEIGHT):
166.                # Copy this character to the correct place on the canvas:
167.                canvasX = dieLeft + dx
168.                canvasY = dieTop + dy
169.                # Note that in dieFace, a list of strings, the x and y
170.                # are swapped:
171.                canvas[(canvasX, canvasY)] = dieFace[dy][dx]
172.
173.    # Display the canvas on the screen:
174.    for cy in range(CANVAS_HEIGHT):
175.        for cx in range(CANVAS_WIDTH):
176.            print(canvas.get((cx, cy), ' '), end='')
```

```
177.        print()  # Print a newline.
178.
179.    # Let the player enter their answer:
180.    response = input('Enter the sum: ').strip()
181.    if response.isdecimal() and int(response) == sumAnswer:
182.        correctAnswers += 1
183.    else:
184.        print('Incorrect, the answer is', sumAnswer)
185.        time.sleep(2)
186.        incorrectAnswers += 1
187.
188. # Display the final score:
189. score = (correctAnswers * REWARD) - (incorrectAnswers * PENALTY)
190. print('Correct:  ', correctAnswers)
191. print('Incorrect:', incorrectAnswers)
192. print('Score:     ', score)
```

After entering the source code and running it a few times, try making experimental changes to it. The comments marked with (!) have suggestions for small changes you can make. On your own, you can also try to figure out how to do the following:

- Redesign the ASCII-art dice faces.
- Add dice faces with seven, eight, or nine pips.

Exploring the Program

Try to find the answers to the following questions. Experiment with some modifications to the code and rerun the program to see what effect the changes have.

1. What happens if you change line 82 to ALL_DICE = [D1]?
2. What happens if you change get((cx, cy), ' ') on line 176 to get((cx, cy), '.')?
3. What happens if you change correctAnswers += 1 on line 182 to correctAnswers += 0?
4. What error message do you get if you delete or comment out correct Answers = 0 on line 93?

18

DICE ROLLER

Dungeons & Dragons and other tabletop role-playing games use special dice that can have 4, 8, 10, 12, or even 20 sides. These games also have a specific notation for indicating which dice to roll. For example, 3d6 means rolling three six-sided dice, while 1d10+2 means rolling one ten-sided die and adding a two-point bonus to the roll. This program simulates this dice rolling, in case you forgot to bring your own. It can also simulate rolling dice that don't physically exist, such as a 38-sided die.

The Program in Action

When you run *diceroller.py*, the output will look like this:

```
Dice Roller, by Al Sweigart al@inventwithpython.com
--snip--
> 3d6
7 (3, 2, 2)
> 1d10+2
9 (7, +2)
> 2d38-1
32 (20, 13, -1)
> 100d6
364 (3, 3, 2, 4, 2, 1, 4, 2, 4, 6, 4, 5, 4, 3, 3, 3, 2, 5, 1, 5, 6, 6, 6, 4,
5, 5, 1, 5, 2, 2, 2, 5, 1, 1, 2, 1, 4, 5, 6, 2, 4, 3, 4, 3, 5, 2, 2, 1, 1, 5,
1, 3, 6, 6, 6, 6, 5, 2, 6, 5, 4, 4, 5, 1, 6, 6, 6, 4, 2, 6, 2, 6, 2, 2, 4, 3,
6, 4, 6, 4, 2, 4, 3, 3, 1, 6, 3, 3, 4, 4, 5, 5, 5, 6, 2, 3, 6, 1, 1, 1)
--snip--
```

How It Works

Most of the code in this program is dedicated to ensuring that the input the user entered is properly formatted. The actual random dice rolls themselves are simple calls to random.randint(). This function has no bias: each integer in the range passed to it is equally likely to be returned. This makes random .randint() ideal for simulating dice rolls.

```
 1. """Dice Roller, by Al Sweigart al@inventwithpython.com
 2. Simulates dice rolls using the Dungeons & Dragons dice roll notation.
 3. View this code at https://nostarch.com/big-book-small-python-projects
 4. Tags: short, simulation"""
 5.
 6. import random, sys
 7.
 8. print('''Dice Roller, by Al Sweigart al@inventwithpython.com
 9.
10. Enter what kind and how many dice to roll. The format is the number of
11. dice, followed by "d", followed by the number of sides the dice have.
12. You can also add a plus or minus adjustment.
13.
14. Examples:
15.    3d6 rolls three 6-sided dice
16.    1d10+2 rolls one 10-sided die, and adds 2
17.    2d38-1 rolls two 38-sided die, and subtracts 1
18.    QUIT quits the program
19. ''')
20.
21. while True:  # Main program loop:
22.     try:
23.         diceStr = input('> ')  # The prompt to enter the dice string.
24.         if diceStr.upper() == 'QUIT':
25.             print('Thanks for playing!')
26.             sys.exit()
```

```
27.
28.         # Clean up the dice string:
29.         diceStr = diceStr.lower().replace(' ', '')
30.
31.         # Find the "d" in the dice string input:
32.         dIndex = diceStr.find('d')
33.         if dIndex == -1:
34.             raise Exception('Missing the "d" character.')
35.
36.         # Get the number of dice. (The "3" in "3d6+1"):
37.         numberOfDice = diceStr[:dIndex]
38.         if not numberOfDice.isdecimal():
39.             raise Exception('Missing the number of dice.')
40.         numberOfDice = int(numberOfDice)
41.
42.         # Find if there is a plus or minus sign for a modifier:
43.         modIndex = diceStr.find('+')
44.         if modIndex == -1:
45.             modIndex = diceStr.find('-')
46.
47.         # Find the number of sides. (The "6" in "3d6+1"):
48.         if modIndex == -1:
49.             numberOfSides = diceStr[dIndex + 1 :]
50.         else:
51.             numberOfSides = diceStr[dIndex + 1 : modIndex]
52.         if not numberOfSides.isdecimal():
53.             raise Exception('Missing the number of sides.')
54.         numberOfSides = int(numberOfSides)
55.
56.         # Find the modifier amount. (The "1" in "3d6+1"):
57.         if modIndex == -1:
58.             modAmount = 0
59.         else:
60.             modAmount = int(diceStr[modIndex + 1 :])
61.             if diceStr[modIndex] == '-':
62.                 # Change the modification amount to negative:
63.                 modAmount = -modAmount
64.
65.         # Simulate the dice rolls:
66.         rolls = []
67.         for i in range(numberOfDice):
68.             rollResult = random.randint(1, numberOfSides)
69.             rolls.append(rollResult)
70.
71.         # Display the total:
72.         print('Total:', sum(rolls) + modAmount, '(Each die:', end='')
73.
74.         # Display the individual rolls:
75.         for i, roll in enumerate(rolls):
76.             rolls[i] = str(roll)
77.         print(', '.join(rolls), end='')
78.
79.         # Display the modifier amount:
80.         if modAmount != 0:
81.             modSign = diceStr[modIndex]
```

```
82.                print(', {}{}'.format(modSign, abs(modAmount)), end='')
83.          print(')')
84.
85.      except Exception as exc:
86.          # Catch any exceptions and display the message to the user:
87.          print('Invalid input. Enter something like "3d6" or "1d10+2".')
88.          print('Input was invalid because: ' + str(exc))
89.          continue  # Go back to the dice string prompt.
```

After entering the source code and running it a few times, try making experimental changes to it. On your own, you can also try to figure out how to do the following:

- Add a multiplication modifier to complement the addition and subtraction modifier.
- Add the ability to automatically remove the lowest die roll.

Exploring the Program

Try to find the answers to the following questions. Experiment with some modifications to the code and rerun the program to see what effect the changes have.

1. What happens if you delete or comment out rolls.append(rollResult) on line 69?
2. What happens if you change rolls.append(rollResult) on line 69 to rolls.append(-rollResult)?
3. What happens if you delete or comment out print(', '.join(rolls), end='') on line 77?
4. What happens if instead of a dice roll you enter nothing?

19

DIGITAL CLOCK

This program displays a digital clock with the current time. Rather than render numeric characters directly, the *sevseg.py* module from Project 64, "Seven-Segment Display Module," generates the drawings for each digit. This program is similar to Project 14, "Countdown."

The Program in Action

When you run *digitalclock.py*, the output will look like this:

```
 _  _    *  _  _    *  _  _
| | _|   *  _| _|   *  _||_
|_| _|   *  _| _|   *  _||_|
```

Press Ctrl-C to quit.

How It Works

The digital clock program looks similar to Project 14, "Countdown." Not only do they both import the *sevseg.py* module, but they must split up the multiline strings returned by sevseg.getSevSegStr() with the splitlines() method. This allows us to put a colon made of asterisks in between the digits for the hour, minute, and second sections of the clock. Compare this code with the code in Countdown to see how it is similar and how it is different.

```
 1. """Digital Clock, by Al Sweigart al@inventwithpython.com
 2. Displays a digital clock of the current time with a seven-segment
 3. display. Press Ctrl-C to stop.
 4. More info at https://en.wikipedia.org/wiki/Seven-segment_display
 5. Requires sevseg.py to be in the same folder.
 6. View this code at https://nostarch.com/big-book-small-python-projects
 7. Tags: tiny, artistic"""
 8.
 9. import sys, time
10. import sevseg  # Imports our sevseg.py program.
11.
12. try:
13.     while True:  # Main program loop.
14.         # Clear the screen by printing several newlines:
15.         print('\n' * 60)
16.
17.         # Get the current time from the computer's clock:
18.         currentTime = time.localtime()
19.         # % 12 so we use a 12-hour clock, not 24:
20.         hours = str(currentTime.tm_hour % 12)
21.         if hours == '0':
22.             hours = '12'  # 12-hour clocks show 12:00, not 00:00.
23.         minutes = str(currentTime.tm_min)
24.         seconds = str(currentTime.tm_sec)
25.
26.         # Get the digit strings from the sevseg module:
27.         hDigits = sevseg.getSevSegStr(hours, 2)
28.         hTopRow, hMiddleRow, hBottomRow = hDigits.splitlines()
29.
30.         mDigits = sevseg.getSevSegStr(minutes, 2)
31.         mTopRow, mMiddleRow, mBottomRow = mDigits.splitlines()
32.
33.         sDigits = sevseg.getSevSegStr(seconds, 2)
```

```
34.        sTopRow, sMiddleRow, sBottomRow = sDigits.splitlines()
35.
36.        # Display the digits:
37.        print(hTopRow    + '     ' + mTopRow    + '     ' + sTopRow)
38.        print(hMiddleRow + '  *  ' + mMiddleRow + '  *  ' + sMiddleRow)
39.        print(hBottomRow + '  *  ' + mBottomRow + '  *  ' + sBottomRow)
40.        print()
41.        print('Press Ctrl-C to quit.')
42.
43.        # Keep looping until the second changes:
44.        while True:
45.            time.sleep(0.01)
46.            if time.localtime().tm_sec != currentTime.tm_sec:
47.                break
48. except KeyboardInterrupt:
49.     print('Digital Clock, by Al Sweigart al@inventwithpython.com')
50.     sys.exit()  # When Ctrl-C is pressed, end the program.
```

Exploring the Program

Try to find the answers to the following questions. Experiment with some modifications to the code and rerun the program to see what effect the changes have.

1. What happens if you change time.sleep(0.01) on line 45 to time.sleep(2)?
2. What happens if you change the 2 on lines 27, 30, and 33 to 1?
3. What happens if you delete or comment out print('\n' * 60) on line 15?
4. What error message do you get if you delete or comment out import sevseg on line 10?

#20

DIGITAL STREAM

This program mimics the "digital stream" visualization from the science fiction movie *The Matrix*. Random beads of binary "rain" stream up from the bottom of the screen, creating a cool, hacker-like visualization. (Unfortunately, due to the way text moves as the screen scrolls down, it's not possible to make the streams fall downward without using a module such as bext.)

The Program in Action

When you run *digitalstream.py*, the output will look like this:

```
Digital Stream Screensaver, by Al Sweigart al@inventwithpython.com
Press Ctrl-C to quit.
                    0                       0
                    0                       0
    1           0   0   1               1 0                             1
    0           0   0   1           0   0 0           0                 0
    0           1   0   0           0   1 0 0         1           0     1
    0           1   0   0           1   011 1         1           0       1 0
    0           1   0   0           0   000 11        0           0     1 1 0
    1       1   0 1 0   1           1   110 10  1  0              1   0 1 0
            1   101 0       0           1   000 11  1  1              11 1 1 1
            0   100 1       0               11  00  0  1             01        0
        1 1   001 1       1               0   1  10  0             10        0
        0 0   010 0       1                   1  11  11            0         0
--snip--
```

How It Works

Like Project 15, "Deep Cave," this program uses the scrolling caused by print() calls to create an animation. Each column is represented by an integer in the columns list: columns[0] is an integer for the leftmost column, columns[1] is an integer for the column to the right of that one, and so on. The program initially sets these integers to 0, meaning it prints ' ' (an empty space string) instead of a stream in that column. Randomly, it changes each integer to a value between MIN_STREAM_LENGTH and MAX_STREAM _LENGTH. That integer decreases by 1 each time a line is printed. As long as a column's integer is greater than 0, the program prints a random 1 or 0 in that column. This produces the "digital stream" effect you see on the screen.

```
1. """Digital Stream, by Al Sweigart al@inventwithpython.com
2. A screensaver in the style of The Matrix movie's visuals.
3. View this code at https://nostarch.com/big-book-small-python-projects
4. Tags: tiny, artistic, beginner, scrolling"""
5.
6. import random, shutil, sys, time
7.
8. # Set up the constants:
9. MIN_STREAM_LENGTH = 6  # (!) Try changing this to 1 or 50.
10. MAX_STREAM_LENGTH = 14  # (!) Try changing this to 100.
11. PAUSE = 0.1  # (!) Try changing this to 0.0 or 2.0.
12. STREAM_CHARS = ['0', '1']  # (!) Try changing this to other characters.
13.
14. # Density can range from 0.0 to 1.0:
15. DENSITY = 0.02  # (!) Try changing this to 0.10 or 0.30.
16.
17. # Get the size of the terminal window:
18. WIDTH = shutil.get_terminal_size()[0]
```

```
19. # We can't print to the last column on Windows without it adding a
20. # newline automatically, so reduce the width by one:
21. WIDTH -= 1
22.
23. print('Digital Stream, by Al Sweigart al@inventwithpython.com')
24. print('Press Ctrl-C to quit.')
25. time.sleep(2)
26.
27. try:
28.     # For each column, when the counter is 0, no stream is shown.
29.     # Otherwise, it acts as a counter for how many times a 1 or 0
30.     # should be displayed in that column.
31.     columns = [0] * WIDTH
32.     while True:
33.         # Set up the counter for each column:
34.         for i in range(WIDTH):
35.             if columns[i] == 0:
36.                 if random.random() <= DENSITY:
37.                     # Restart a stream on this column.
38.                     columns[i] = random.randint(MIN_STREAM_LENGTH,
39.                                                 MAX_STREAM_LENGTH)
40.
41.             # Display an empty space or a 1/0 character.
42.             if columns[i] > 0:
43.                 print(random.choice(STREAM_CHARS), end='')
44.                 columns[i] -= 1
45.             else:
46.                 print(' ', end='')
47.         print()  # Print a newline at the end of the row of columns.
48.         sys.stdout.flush()  # Make sure text appears on the screen.
49.         time.sleep(PAUSE)
50. except KeyboardInterrupt:
51.     sys.exit()  # When Ctrl-C is pressed, end the program.
```

After entering the source code and running it a few times, try making experimental changes to it. The comments marked with (!) have suggestions for small changes you can make. On your own, you can also try to figure out how to do the following:

- Include characters besides just 1s and 0s.
- Include shapes besides lines, including rectangles, triangles, and diamonds.

Exploring the Program

Try to find the answers to the following questions. Experiment with some modifications to the code and rerun the program to see what effect the changes have.

1. What happens if you change print(' ', end='') on line 46 to print('.', end='')?

2. What error message do your get if you change PAUSE = 0.1 on line 11 to PAUSE = -0.1?

3. What happens if you change columns[i] > 0 on line 42 to columns[i] < 0?

4. What happens if you change columns[i] > 0 on line 42 to columns[i] <= 0?

5. What happens if you change columns[i] -= 1 on line 44 to columns[i] += 1?

#21

DNA VISUALIZATION

 Deoxyribonucleic acid is a tiny molecule that exists in every cell of our bodies and contains the blueprint for how our bodies grow. It looks like a *double helix* (a sort of twisted ladder) of pairs of nucleotide molecules: guanine, cytosine, adenine, and thymine. These are represented by the letters G, C, A, and T. DNA is a long molecule; it's microscopic, but if it were stretched out, its 3 billion base pairs would be 2 meters long! This program is a simple animation of DNA.

The Program in Action

When you run *dna.py*, the output will look like this:

```
DNA Animation, by Al Sweigart al@inventwithpython.com
Press Ctrl-C to quit...
       #G-C#
       #C---G#
      #T-----A#
      #T------A#
     #A------T#
     #G-----C#
      #G---C#
      #C-G#
       ##
      #T-A#
      #C---G#
     #G-----C#
     #G------C#
      #T------A#
       #A-----T#
        #C---G#
        #G-C#
         ##
        #T-A#
        #T---A#
       #A-----T#
--snip--
```

How It Works

Similar to Project 15, "Deep Cave," and Project 20, "Digital Stream," this program creates a scrolling animation by printing strings from the ROWS list. The AT and CG pairs are inserted into each string with the format() string method.

```
1. """DNA, by Al Sweigart al@inventwithpython.com
2. A simple animation of a DNA double-helix. Press Ctrl-C to stop.
3. Inspired by matoken https://asciinema.org/a/155441
4. View this code at https://nostarch.com/big-book-small-python-projects
5. Tags: short, artistic, scrolling, science"""
6.
7. import random, sys, time
8.
9. PAUSE = 0.15  # (!) Try changing this to 0.5 or 0.0.
10.
11. # These are the individual rows of the DNA animation:
12. ROWS = [
13.     #123456789 <- Use this to measure the number of spaces:
14.     '          ##',  # Index 0 has no {}.
15.     '         #{}-{}#',
16.     '         #{}---{}#',
```

```
17.    '      #{}-----{}#',
18.    '     #{}------{}#',
19.    '    #{}------{}#',
20.    '    #{}-----{}#',
21.    '     #{}---{}#',
22.    '      #{}-{}#',
23.    '       ##',   # Index 9 has no {}.
24.    '      #{}-{}#',
25.    '     #{}---{}#',
26.    '    #{}-----{}#',
27.    '    #{}------{}#',
28.    '     #{}------{}#',
29.    '      #{}-----{}#',
30.    '       #{}---{}#',
31.    '        #{}-{}#']
32.    #123456789 <- Use this to measure the number of spaces:
33.
34. try:
35.     print('DNA Animation, by Al Sweigart al@inventwithpython.com')
36.     print('Press Ctrl-C to quit...')
37.     time.sleep(2)
38.     rowIndex = 0
39.
40.     while True:  # Main program loop.
41.         # Increment rowIndex to draw next row:
42.         rowIndex = rowIndex + 1
43.         if rowIndex == len(ROWS):
44.             rowIndex = 0
45.
46.         # Row indexes 0 and 9 don't have nucleotides:
47.         if rowIndex == 0 or rowIndex == 9:
48.             print(ROWS[rowIndex])
49.             continue
50.
51.         # Select random nucleotide pairs, guanine-cytosine and
52.         # adenine-thymine:
53.         randomSelection = random.randint(1, 4)
54.         if randomSelection == 1:
55.             leftNucleotide, rightNucleotide = 'A', 'T'
56.         elif randomSelection == 2:
57.             leftNucleotide, rightNucleotide = 'T', 'A'
58.         elif randomSelection == 3:
59.             leftNucleotide, rightNucleotide = 'C', 'G'
60.         elif randomSelection == 4:
61.             leftNucleotide, rightNucleotide = 'G', 'C'
62.
63.         # Print the row.
64.         print(ROWS[rowIndex].format(leftNucleotide, rightNucleotide))
65.         time.sleep(PAUSE)  # Add a slight pause.
66. except KeyboardInterrupt:
67.     sys.exit()  # When Ctrl-C is pressed, end the program.
```

Exploring the Program

Try to find the answers to the following questions. Experiment with some modifications to the code and rerun the program to see what effect the changes have.

1. What happens if you change `rowIndex = rowIndex + 1` on line 42 to `rowIndex = rowIndex + 2`?

2. What happens if you change `random.randint(1, 4)` on line 53 to `random.randint(1, 2)`?

3. What error message do you get if you set `PAUSE = 0.15` on line 9 to `PAUSE = -0.15`?

#22

DUCKLINGS

This program creates a scrolling field of ducklings. Each duckling has slight variations: they can face left or right and have two different body sizes, four types of eyes, two types of mouths, and three positions for their wings. This gives us 96 different possible variations, which the Ducklings program produces endlessly.

The Program in Action

When you run *ducklings.py*, the output will look like this:

```
Duckling Screensaver, by Al Sweigart al@inventwithpython.com
Press Ctrl-C to quit...
                                              =" )
=")                                          (  v)=")
( ^)                                          ^ ^ ( v) >'')
  ^^                                              ^^  (  ^)
                          >")                            ^ ^
                          ( v)      =^^)
("< ("<                   >")    ^^   ( >)
(^ ) (< )                 ( ^)        ^ ^
  ^^    ^^           ("<   ^^                  (``<>^^)
(^^=                 (^ )                      (<  )(  ^)
(v  ) ( "<             ^^                        ^ ^  ^ ^
--snip--
```

How It Works

This program represents ducklings with a Duckling class. The random features of each ducking are chosen in the __init__() method of this class, while the various body parts of each duckling are returned by the getHeadStr(), getBodyStr(), and getFeetStr() methods.

```
1. """Duckling Screensaver, by Al Sweigart al@inventwithpython.com
2. A screensaver of many many ducklings.
3.
4. >" )   =^^)    (``=   ("= >")    ("=
5. ( >)  (  ^)   (v  )  (^ ) ( >)  (v )
6.  ^ ^    ^ ^    ^ ^    ^^   ^^    ^^
7.
8. View this code at https://nostarch.com/big-book-small-python-projects
9. Tags: large, artistic, object-oriented, scrolling"""
10.
11. import random, shutil, sys, time
12.
13. # Set up the constants:
14. PAUSE = 0.2  # (!) Try changing this to 1.0 or 0.0.
15. DENSITY = 0.10  # (!) Try changing this to anything from 0.0 to 1.0.
16.
17. DUCKLING_WIDTH = 5
18. LEFT = 'left'
19. RIGHT = 'right'
20. BEADY = 'beady'
21. WIDE = 'wide'
22. HAPPY = 'happy'
23. ALOOF = 'aloof'
24. CHUBBY = 'chubby'
25. VERY_CHUBBY = 'very chubby'
26. OPEN = 'open'
27. CLOSED = 'closed'
```

```
28. OUT = 'out'
29. DOWN = 'down'
30. UP = 'up'
31. HEAD = 'head'
32. BODY = 'body'
33. FEET = 'feet'
34.
35. # Get the size of the terminal window:
36. WIDTH = shutil.get_terminal_size()[0]
37. # We can't print to the last column on Windows without it adding a
38. # newline automatically, so reduce the width by one:
39. WIDTH -= 1
40.
41.
42. def main():
43.     print('Duckling Screensaver, by Al Sweigart')
44.     print('Press Ctrl-C to quit...')
45.     time.sleep(2)
46.
47.     ducklingLanes = [None] * (WIDTH // DUCKLING_WIDTH)
48.
49.     while True:  # Main program loop.
50.         for laneNum, ducklingObj in enumerate(ducklingLanes):
51.             # See if we should create a duckling in this lane:
52.             if (ducklingObj == None and random.random() <= DENSITY):
53.                     # Place a duckling in this lane:
54.                     ducklingObj = Duckling()
55.                     ducklingLanes[laneNum] = ducklingObj
56.
57.             if ducklingObj != None:
58.                 # Draw a duckling if there is one in this lane:
59.                 print(ducklingObj.getNextBodyPart(), end='')
60.                 # Delete the duckling if we've finished drawing it:
61.                 if ducklingObj.partToDisplayNext == None:
62.                     ducklingLanes[laneNum] = None
63.             else:
64.                 # Draw five spaces since there is no duckling here.
65.                 print(' ' * DUCKLING_WIDTH, end='')
66.
67.         print()  # Print a newline.
68.         sys.stdout.flush()  # Make sure text appears on the screen.
69.         time.sleep(PAUSE)
70.
71.
72. class Duckling:
73.     def __init__(self):
74.         """Create a new duckling with random body features."""
75.         self.direction = random.choice([LEFT, RIGHT])
76.         self.body = random.choice([CHUBBY, VERY_CHUBBY])
77.         self.mouth = random.choice([OPEN, CLOSED])
78.         self.wing = random.choice([OUT, UP, DOWN])
79.
80.         if self.body == CHUBBY:
81.             # Chubby ducklings can only have beady eyes.
82.             self.eyes = BEADY
```

```
 83.          else:
 84.              self.eyes = random.choice([BEADY, WIDE, HAPPY, ALOOF])
 85.
 86.          self.partToDisplayNext = HEAD
 87.
 88.      def getHeadStr(self):
 89.          """Returns the string of the duckling's head."""
 90.          headStr = ''
 91.          if self.direction == LEFT:
 92.              # Get the mouth:
 93.              if self.mouth == OPEN:
 94.                  headStr += '>'
 95.              elif self.mouth == CLOSED:
 96.                  headStr += '='
 97.
 98.              # Get the eyes:
 99.              if self.eyes == BEADY and self.body == CHUBBY:
100.                  headStr += '"'
101.              elif self.eyes == BEADY and self.body == VERY_CHUBBY:
102.                  headStr += '" '
103.              elif self.eyes == WIDE:
104.                  headStr += "'''"
105.              elif self.eyes == HAPPY:
106.                  headStr += '^^'
107.              elif self.eyes == ALOOF:
108.                  headStr += '``'
109.
110.              headStr += ') '   # Get the back of the head.
111.
112.          if self.direction == RIGHT:
113.              headStr += ' ('   # Get the back of the head.
114.
115.              # Get the eyes:
116.              if self.eyes == BEADY and self.body == CHUBBY:
117.                  headStr += '"'
118.              elif self.eyes == BEADY and self.body == VERY_CHUBBY:
119.                  headStr += ' "'
120.              elif self.eyes == WIDE:
121.                  headStr += "'''"
122.              elif self.eyes == HAPPY:
123.                  headStr += '^^'
124.              elif self.eyes == ALOOF:
125.                  headStr += '``'
126.
127.              # Get the mouth:
128.              if self.mouth == OPEN:
129.                  headStr += '<'
130.              elif self.mouth == CLOSED:
131.                  headStr += '='
132.
133.          if self.body == CHUBBY:
134.              # Get an extra space so chubby ducklings are the same
135.              # width as very chubby ducklings.
136.              headStr += ' '
137.
```

```
138.        return headStr
139.
140.    def getBodyStr(self):
141.        """Returns the string of the duckling's body."""
142.        bodyStr = '('  # Get the left side of the body.
143.        if self.direction == LEFT:
144.            # Get the interior body space:
145.            if self.body == CHUBBY:
146.                bodyStr += ' '
147.            elif self.body == VERY_CHUBBY:
148.                bodyStr += '  '
149.
150.            # Get the wing:
151.            if self.wing == OUT:
152.                bodyStr += '>'
153.            elif self.wing == UP:
154.                bodyStr += '^'
155.            elif self.wing == DOWN:
156.                bodyStr += 'v'
157.
158.        if self.direction == RIGHT:
159.            # Get the wing:
160.            if self.wing == OUT:
161.                bodyStr += '<'
162.            elif self.wing == UP:
163.                bodyStr += '^'
164.            elif self.wing == DOWN:
165.                bodyStr += 'v'
166.
167.            # Get the interior body space:
168.            if self.body == CHUBBY:
169.                bodyStr += ' '
170.            elif self.body == VERY_CHUBBY:
171.                bodyStr += '  '
172.
173.        bodyStr += ')'  # Get the right side of the body.
174.
175.        if self.body == CHUBBY:
176.            # Get an extra space so chubby ducklings are the same
177.            # width as very chubby ducklings.
178.            bodyStr += ' '
179.
180.        return bodyStr
181.
182.    def getFeetStr(self):
183.        """Returns the string of the duckling's feet."""
184.        if self.body == CHUBBY:
185.            return ' ^^ '
186.        elif self.body == VERY_CHUBBY:
187.            return ' ^ ^ '
188.
189.    def getNextBodyPart(self):
190.        """Calls the appropriate display method for the next body
191.        part that needs to be displayed. Sets partToDisplayNext to
192.        None when finished."""
```

```
193.          if self.partToDisplayNext == HEAD:
194.              self.partToDisplayNext = BODY
195.              return self.getHeadStr()
196.          elif self.partToDisplayNext == BODY:
197.              self.partToDisplayNext = FEET
198.              return self.getBodyStr()
199.          elif self.partToDisplayNext == FEET:
200.              self.partToDisplayNext = None
201.              return self.getFeetStr()
202.
203.
204.
205. # If this program was run (instead of imported), run the game:
206. if __name__ == '__main__':
207.     try:
208.         main()
209.     except KeyboardInterrupt:
210.         sys.exit()  # When Ctrl-C is pressed, end the program.
```

After entering the source code and running it a few times, try making experimental changes to it. The comments marked with (!) have suggestions for small changes you can make.

Exploring the Program

Try to find the answers to the following questions. Experiment with some modifications to the code and rerun the program to see what effect the changes have.

1. What happens if you change random.choice([LEFT, RIGHT]) on line 75 to random.choice([LEFT])?

2. What happens if you change self.partToDisplayNext = BODY on line 194 to self.partToDisplayNext = None?

3. What happens if you change self.partToDisplayNext = FEET on line 197 to self.partToDisplayNext = BODY?

4. What happens if you change return self.getHeadStr() on line 195 to return self.getFeetStr()?

#23

ETCHING DRAWER

When you move a pen point around the
screen with the WASD keys, the etching
drawer forms a picture by tracing a continu-
ous line, like the Etch A Sketch toy. Let your
artistic side break out and see what images you can
create! This program also lets you save your drawings to a text file so you can print them out later.
Plus, you can copy and paste the WASD movements
of other drawings into this program, like the WASD
commands for the Hilbert Curve fractal presented on
lines 6 to 14 of the source code.

The Program in Action

When you run *etchingdrawer.py*, the output will look like Figure 23-1.

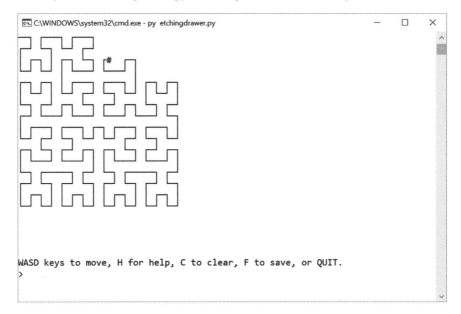

Figure 23-1: A drawing made in the etching drawer program

How It Works

Like Project 17, "Dice Math," this program uses a dictionary stored in a variable named canvas to record the lines of the drawing. The keys are (x, y) tuples and the values are strings representing the line shape to draw at those x, y coordinates on the screen. A full list of Unicode characters you can use in your Python programs is given in Appendix B.

Line 126 has a function call to open() that passes an encoding='utf-8' argument. The reasons are beyond the scope of this book, but this is necessary for Windows to write the line characters to a text file.

```
 1. """Etching Drawer, by Al Sweigart al@inventwithpython.com
 2. An art program that draws a continuous line around the screen using the
 3. WASD keys. Inspired by Etch A Sketch toys.
 4.
 5. For example, you can draw Hilbert Curve fractal with:
 6. SDWDDSASDSAAWASSDSASSDWDSDWWAWDDDSASSDWDSDWWAWDWWASAAWDWAWDDSDW
 7.
 8. Or an even larger Hilbert Curve fractal with:
 9. DDSAASSDDWDDSDDWWAAWDDDDSDDWDDDDSAASDDSAAAAWAASSSDDWDDDDSAASDDSAAAAWA
10. ASAAAAWDDWWAASAAWAASSDDSAASSDDWDDDDSAASDDSAAAAWAASSDDSAASSDDWDDSDDWWA
11. AWDDDDDDSAASSDDWDDSDDWWAAWDDWWAASAAAAWDDWAAWDDDDSDDWDDSDDWDDDDSAASDDS
12. AAAAWAASSDDSAASSDDWDDSDDWWAAWDDDDDDSAASSDDWDDSDDWWAAWDDWWAASAAAAWDDWA
13. AWDDDDDSDDWWAAWDDWWAASAAWAASSDDSAAAAWAASAAAAWDDWAAWDDDDSDDWWWAASAAAAWD
14. DWAAWDDDDSDDWDDDDSAASSDDWDDSDDWWAAWDD
```

```
15.
16. View this code at https://nostarch.com/big-book-small-python-projects
17. Tags: large, artistic"""
18.
19. import shutil, sys
20.
21. # Set up the constants for line characters:
22. UP_DOWN_CHAR          = chr(9474)  # Character 9474 is '│'
23. LEFT_RIGHT_CHAR       = chr(9472)  # Character 9472 is '─'
24. DOWN_RIGHT_CHAR       = chr(9484)  # Character 9484 is '┌'
25. DOWN_LEFT_CHAR        = chr(9488)  # Character 9488 is '┐'
26. UP_RIGHT_CHAR         = chr(9492)  # Character 9492 is '└'
27. UP_LEFT_CHAR          = chr(9496)  # Character 9496 is '┘'
28. UP_DOWN_RIGHT_CHAR    = chr(9500)  # Character 9500 is '├'
29. UP_DOWN_LEFT_CHAR     = chr(9508)  # Character 9508 is '┤'
30. DOWN_LEFT_RIGHT_CHAR  = chr(9516)  # Character 9516 is '┬'
31. UP_LEFT_RIGHT_CHAR    = chr(9524)  # Character 9524 is '┴'
32. CROSS_CHAR            = chr(9532)  # Character 9532 is '┼'
33. # A list of chr() codes is at https://inventwithpython.com/chr
34.
35. # Get the size of the terminal window:
36. CANVAS_WIDTH, CANVAS_HEIGHT = shutil.get_terminal_size()
37. # We can't print to the last column on Windows without it adding a
38. # newline automatically, so reduce the width by one:
39. CANVAS_WIDTH -= 1
40. # Leave room at the bottom few rows for the command info lines.
41. CANVAS_HEIGHT -= 5
42.
43. """The keys for canvas will be (x, y) integer tuples for the coordinate,
44. and the value is a set of letters W, A, S, D that tell what kind of line
45. should be drawn."""
46. canvas = {}
47. cursorX = 0
48. cursorY = 0
49.
50.
51. def getCanvasString(canvasData, cx, cy):
52.     """Returns a multiline string of the line drawn in canvasData."""
53.     canvasStr = ''
54.
55.     """canvasData is a dictionary with (x, y) tuple keys and values that
56.     are sets of 'W', 'A', 'S', and/or 'D' strings to show which
57.     directions the lines are drawn at each xy point."""
58.     for rowNum in range(CANVAS_HEIGHT):
59.         for columnNum in range(CANVAS_WIDTH):
60.             if columnNum == cx and rowNum == cy:
61.                 canvasStr += '#'
62.                 continue
63.
64.             # Add the line character for this point to canvasStr.
65.             cell = canvasData.get((columnNum, rowNum))
66.             if cell in (set(['W', 'S']), set(['W']), set(['S'])):
67.                 canvasStr += UP_DOWN_CHAR
68.             elif cell in (set(['A', 'D']), set(['A']), set(['D'])):
69.                 canvasStr += LEFT_RIGHT_CHAR
```

```
70.              elif cell == set(['S', 'D']):
71.                  canvasStr += DOWN_RIGHT_CHAR
72.              elif cell == set(['A', 'S']):
73.                  canvasStr += DOWN_LEFT_CHAR
74.              elif cell == set(['W', 'D']):
75.                  canvasStr += UP_RIGHT_CHAR
76.              elif cell == set(['W', 'A']):
77.                  canvasStr += UP_LEFT_CHAR
78.              elif cell == set(['W', 'S', 'D']):
79.                  canvasStr += UP_DOWN_RIGHT_CHAR
80.              elif cell == set(['W', 'S', 'A']):
81.                  canvasStr += UP_DOWN_LEFT_CHAR
82.              elif cell == set(['A', 'S', 'D']):
83.                  canvasStr += DOWN_LEFT_RIGHT_CHAR
84.              elif cell == set(['W', 'A', 'D']):
85.                  canvasStr += UP_LEFT_RIGHT_CHAR
86.              elif cell == set(['W', 'A', 'S', 'D']):
87.                  canvasStr += CROSS_CHAR
88.              elif cell == None:
89.                  canvasStr += ' '
90.          canvasStr += '\n'  # Add a newline at the end of each row.
91.      return canvasStr
92.
93.
94. moves = []
95. while True:  # Main program loop.
96.      # Draw the lines based on the data in canvas:
97.      print(getCanvasString(canvas, cursorX, cursorY))
98.
99.      print('WASD keys to move, H for help, C to clear, '
100.         + 'F to save, or QUIT.')
101.     response = input('> ').upper()
102.
103.     if response == 'QUIT':
104.         print('Thanks for playing!')
105.         sys.exit()  # Quit the program.
106.     elif response == 'H':
107.         print('Enter W, A, S, and D characters to move the cursor and')
108.         print('draw a line behind it as it moves. For example, ddd')
109.         print('draws a line going right and sssdddwwwaaa draws a box.')
110.         print()
111.         print('You can save your drawing to a text file by entering F.')
112.         input('Press Enter to return to the program...')
113.         continue
114.     elif response == 'C':
115.         canvas = {}  # Erase the canvas data.
116.         moves.append('C')  # Record this move.
117.     elif response == 'F':
118.         # Save the canvas string to a text file:
119.         try:
120.             print('Enter filename to save to:')
121.             filename = input('> ')
122.
123.             # Make sure the filename ends with .txt:
124.             if not filename.endswith('.txt'):
```

```
125.              filename += '.txt'
126.          with open(filename, 'w', encoding='utf-8') as file:
127.              file.write(''.join(moves) + '\n')
128.              file.write(getCanvasString(canvas, None, None))
129.      except:
130.          print('ERROR: Could not save file.')
131.
132.  for command in response:
133.      if command not in ('W', 'A', 'S', 'D'):
134.          continue  # Ignore this letter and continue to the next one.
135.      moves.append(command)  # Record this move.
136.
137.      # The first line we add needs to form a full line:
138.      if canvas == {}:
139.          if command in ('W', 'S'):
140.              # Make the first line a horizontal one:
141.              canvas[(cursorX, cursorY)] = set(['W', 'S'])
142.          elif command in ('A', 'D'):
143.              # Make the first line a vertical one:
144.              canvas[(cursorX, cursorY)] = set(['A', 'D'])
145.
146.      # Update x and y:
147.      if command == 'W' and cursorY > 0:
148.          canvas[(cursorX, cursorY)].add(command)
149.          cursorY = cursorY - 1
150.      elif command == 'S' and cursorY < CANVAS_HEIGHT - 1:
151.          canvas[(cursorX, cursorY)].add(command)
152.          cursorY = cursorY + 1
153.      elif command == 'A' and cursorX > 0:
154.          canvas[(cursorX, cursorY)].add(command)
155.          cursorX = cursorX - 1
156.      elif command == 'D' and cursorX < CANVAS_WIDTH - 1:
157.          canvas[(cursorX, cursorY)].add(command)
158.          cursorX = cursorX + 1
159.      else:
160.          # If the cursor doesn't move because it would have moved off
161.          # the edge of the canvas, then don't change the set at
162.          # canvas[(cursorX, cursorY)].
163.          continue
164.
165.      # If there's no set for (cursorX, cursorY), add an empty set:
166.      if (cursorX, cursorY) not in canvas:
167.          canvas[(cursorX, cursorY)] = set()
168.
169.      # Add the direction string to this xy point's set:
170.      if command == 'W':
171.          canvas[(cursorX, cursorY)].add('S')
172.      elif command == 'S':
173.          canvas[(cursorX, cursorY)].add('W')
174.      elif command == 'A':
175.          canvas[(cursorX, cursorY)].add('D')
176.      elif command == 'D':
177.          canvas[(cursorX, cursorY)].add('A')
```

Exploring the Program

Try to find the answers to the following questions. Experiment with some modifications to the code and rerun the program to see what effect the changes have.

1. What happens if you change `response = input('> ').upper()` on line 101 to `response = input('> ')`?

2. What happens if you change `canvasStr += '#'` on line 61 to `canvasStr += '@'`?

3. What happens if you change `canvasStr += ' '` on line 89 to `canvasStr += '.'`?

4. What happens if you change `moves = []` on line 94 to `moves = list('SDWDDSASDSAAWASSDSAS')`?

#24

FACTOR FINDER

A number's factors are any two other numbers that, when multiplied with each other, produce the number. For example, 2 × 13 = 26, so 2 and 13 are factors of 26. Also, 1 × 26 = 26, so 1 and 26 are also factors of 26. Therefore, we say that 26 has four factors: 1, 2, 13, and 26.

If a number only has two factors (1 and itself), we call that a prime number. Otherwise, we call it a composite number. Use the factor finder to discover some new prime numbers! (Hint: Prime numbers always end with an odd number that isn't 5.) You can also have the computer calculate them with Project 56, "Prime Numbers."

The math for this program isn't too heavy, making it an ideal project for beginners.

The Program in Action

When you run *factorfinder.py*, the output will look like this:

```
Factor Finder, by Al Sweigart al@inventwithpython.com
--snip--
Enter a number to factor (or "QUIT" to quit):
> 26
1, 2, 13, 26
Enter a number to factor (or "QUIT" to quit):
> 4352784
1, 2, 3, 4, 6, 8, 12, 16, 24, 29, 48, 53, 58, 59, 87, 106, 116, 118, 159,
174, 177, 212, 232, 236, 318, 348, 354, 424, 464, 472, 636, 696, 708, 848,
944, 1272, 1392, 1416, 1537, 1711, 2544, 2832, 3074, 3127, 3422, 4611, 5133,
6148, 6254, 6844, 9222, 9381, 10266, 12296, 12508, 13688, 18444, 18762, 20532,
24592, 25016, 27376, 36888, 37524, 41064, 50032, 73776, 75048, 82128, 90683,
150096, 181366, 272049, 362732, 544098, 725464, 1088196, 1450928, 2176392,
4352784
Enter a number to factor (or "QUIT" to quit):
> 9787
1, 9787
Enter a number to factor (or "QUIT" to quit):
> quit
```

How It Works

We can tell if a number is a factor of another number by checking if the second number evenly divides the first number. For example, 7 is a factor of 21 because $21 \div 7$ is 3. This also gives us another of 21's factors: 3. However, 8 is not a factor of 21 because $21 \div 8 = 2.625$. The fractional remainder component tells us this equation did not divide evenly.

The % mod operator will perform division and tell us if there's a remainder: 21 % 7 evaluates to 0, meaning there is no remainder and 7 is a factor of 21, whereas 21 % 8 evaluates to 1, a nonzero value, meaning that it isn't a factor. The factor finder program uses this technique on line 35 to determine which numbers are factors.

The math.sqrt() function returns the square root of the number passed to it. For example, math.sqrt(25) returns 5.0 because 5 times itself is 25, making it the square root of 25.

```
 1. """Factor Finder, by Al Sweigart al@inventwithpython.com
 2. Finds all the factors of a number.
 3. View this code at https://nostarch.com/big-book-small-python-projects
 4. Tags: tiny, beginner, math"""
 5.
 6. import math, sys
 7.
 8. print('''Factor Finder, by Al Sweigart al@inventwithpython.com
 9.
10. A number's factors are two numbers that, when multiplied with each
```

```
11. other, produce the number. For example, 2 x 13 = 26, so 2 and 13 are
12. factors of 26. 1 x 26 = 26, so 1 and 26 are also factors of 26. We
13. say that 26 has four factors: 1, 2, 13, and 26.
14.
15. If a number only has two factors (1 and itself), we call that a prime
16. number. Otherwise, we call it a composite number.
17.
18. Can you discover some prime numbers?
19. ''')
20.
21. while True:  # Main program loop.
22.     print('Enter a positive whole number to factor (or QUIT):')
23.     response = input('> ')
24.     if response.upper() == 'QUIT':
25.         sys.exit()
26.
27.     if not (response.isdecimal() and int(response) > 0):
28.         continue
29.     number = int(response)
30.
31.     factors = []
32.
33.     # Find the factors of number:
34.     for i in range(1, int(math.sqrt(number)) + 1):
35.         if number % i == 0:  # If there's no remainder, it is a factor.
36.             factors.append(i)
37.             factors.append(number // i)
38.
39.     # Convert to a set to get rid of duplicate factors:
40.     factors = list(set(factors))
41.     factors.sort()
42.
43.     # Display the results:
44.     for i, factor in enumerate(factors):
45.         factors[i] = str(factor)
46.     print(', '.join(factors))
```

Exploring the Program

Try to find the answers to the following questions. Experiment with some modifications to the code and rerun the program to see what effect the changes have.

1. What happens if you delete or comment out factors.append(i) on line 36?

2. What happens if you delete or comment out factors = list(set(factors)) on line 40? (Hint: Enter a square number such as 25 or 36 or 49.)

3. What happens if you delete or comment out factors.sort() on line 41?

4. What error message do you get if you change factors = [] on line 31 to factors = ''?

5. What happens if you change factors = [] on line 31 to factors = [-42]?

6. What error message do you get if you change factors = [] on line 31 to factors = ['hello']?

#25

FAST DRAW

 This program tests your reaction speed: press ENTER as soon as you see the word DRAW. But careful, though. Press it before DRAW appears, and you lose. Are you the fastest keyboard in the west?

The Program in Action

When you run *fastdraw.py*, the output will look like this:

```
Fast Draw, by Al Sweigart al@inventwithpython.com

Time to test your reflexes and see if you are the fastest
draw in the west!
When you see "DRAW", you have 0.3 seconds to press Enter.
But you lose if you press Enter before "DRAW" appears.

Press Enter to begin...

It is high noon...
DRAW!

You took 0.3485 seconds to draw. Too slow!
Enter QUIT to stop, or press Enter to play again.
> quit
Thanks for playing!
```

How It Works

The input() function pauses the program while waiting for the user to enter a string. This simple behavior means that we can't create real-time games with just input(). However, your programs will *buffer* keyboard input, meaning that if you pressed the C, A, and T keys before input() is called, those characters will be saved, and they'll appear immediately once input() executes.

By recording the time just before the input() call on line 22 and the time just after the input() call on line 24, we can determine how long the player took to press ENTER. However, if they pressed ENTER before input() was called, the buffered ENTER press causes input() to return immediately (usually in about 3 milliseconds). This is why line 26 checks if the time was less than 0.01 seconds, or 10 milliseconds, to determine that the player pressed ENTER too soon.

```
1. """Fast Draw, by Al Sweigart al@inventwithpython.com
2. Test your reflexes to see if you're the fastest draw in the west.
3. View this code at https://nostarch.com/big-book-small-python-projects
4. Tags: tiny, beginner, game"""
5.
6. import random, sys, time
7.
8. print('Fast Draw, by Al Sweigart al@inventwithpython.com')
9. print()
10. print('Time to test your reflexes and see if you are the fastest')
11. print('draw in the west!')
12. print('When you see "DRAW", you have 0.3 seconds to press Enter.')
13. print('But you lose if you press Enter before "DRAW" appears.')
14. print()
15. input('Press Enter to begin...')
```

```
16.
17. while True:
18.     print()
19.     print('It is high noon...')
20.     time.sleep(random.randint(20, 50) / 10.0)
21.     print('DRAW!')
22.     drawTime = time.time()
23.     input()  # This function call doesn't return until Enter is pressed.
24.     timeElapsed = time.time() - drawTime
25.
26.     if timeElapsed < 0.01:
27.         # If the player pressed Enter before DRAW! appeared, the input()
28.         # call returns almost instantly.
29.         print('You drew before "DRAW" appeared! You lose.')
30.     elif timeElapsed > 0.3:
31.         timeElapsed = round(timeElapsed, 4)
32.         print('You took', timeElapsed, 'seconds to draw. Too slow!')
33.     else:
34.         timeElapsed = round(timeElapsed, 4)
35.         print('You took', timeElapsed, 'seconds to draw.')
36.         print('You are the fastest draw in the west! You win!')
37.
38.     print('Enter QUIT to stop, or press Enter to play again.')
39.     response = input('> ').upper()
40.     if response == 'QUIT':
41.         print('Thanks for playing!')
42.         sys.exit()
```

Exploring the Program

Try to find the answers to the following questions. Experiment with some modifications to the code and rerun the program to see what effect the changes have.

1. What happens if you change drawTime = time.time() on line 22 to drawTime = 0?

2. What happens if you change timeElapsed > 0.3 on line 30 to timeElapsed < 0.3?

3. What happens if you change time.time() - drawTime on line 24 to time.time() + drawTime?

4. What happens if you delete or comment out input('Press Enter to begin...') on line 15?

#26

FIBONACCI

 The Fibonacci sequence is a famous mathematical pattern credited to Italian mathematician Fibonacci in the 13th century (though others had discovered it even earlier). The sequence begins with 0 and 1, and the next number is always the sum of the previous two numbers. The sequence continues forever:

0, 1, 1, 2, 3, 5, 8, 13, 21, 34, 55, 89, 144, 233, 377, 610, 987 . . .

The Fibonacci sequence has applications in music composition, stock market prediction, the pattern of florets in the head of sunflowers, and many other areas. This program lets you calculate the sequence as high as you are willing to go. More information about the Fibonacci sequence can be found at *https://en.wikipedia.org/wiki/Fibonacci_number.*

The Program in Action

When you run *fibonacci.py*, the output will look like this:

```
Fibonacci Sequence, by Al Sweigart al@inventwithpython.com
--snip--
Enter the Nth Fibonacci number you wish to
calculate (such as 5, 50, 1000, 9999), or QUIT to quit:
> 50

0, 1, 1, 2, 3, 5, 8, 13, 21, 34, 55, 89, 144, 233, 377, 610, 987, 1597, 2584,
4181, 6765, 10946, 17711, 28657, 46368, 75025, 121393, 196418, 317811, 514229,
832040, 1346269, 2178309, 3524578, 5702887, 9227465, 14930352, 24157817,
39088169, 63245986, 102334155, 165580141, 267914296, 433494437, 701408733,
1134903170, 1836311903, 2971215073, 4807526976, 7778742049
```

How It Works

Because Fibonacci numbers quickly become very large, lines 46 to 50 check if the user has entered a number that's 10,000 or larger and displays a warning that it may take some time for the output to finish displaying on the screen. While your programs can quickly do millions of calculations almost instantly, printing text to the screen is relatively slow and could take several seconds. The warning in our program reminds the user they can always terminate the program by pressing CTRL-C.

```python
 1. """Fibonacci Sequence, by Al Sweigart al@inventwithpython.com
 2. Calculates numbers of the Fibonacci sequence: 0, 1, 1, 2, 3, 5, 8, 13...
 3. View this code at https://nostarch.com/big-book-small-python-projects
 4. Tags: short, math"""
 5.
 6. import sys
 7.
 8. print('''Fibonacci Sequence, by Al Sweigart al@inventwithpython.com
 9.
10. The Fibonacci sequence begins with 0 and 1, and the next number is the
11. sum of the previous two numbers. The sequence continues forever:
12.
13. 0, 1, 1, 2, 3, 5, 8, 13, 21, 34, 55, 89, 144, 233, 377, 610, 987...
14. ''')
15.
16. while True:  # Main program loop.
17.     while True:  # Keep asking until the user enters valid input.
18.         print('Enter the Nth Fibonacci number you wish to')
19.         print('calculate (such as 5, 50, 1000, 9999), or QUIT to quit:')
20.         response = input('> ').upper()
21.
22.         if response == 'QUIT':
23.             print('Thanks for playing!')
24.             sys.exit()
25.
26.         if response.isdecimal() and int(response) != 0:
27.             nth = int(response)
```

```
28.                    break  # Exit the loop when the user enters a valid number.
29.
30.            print('Please enter a number greater than 0, or QUIT.')
31.    print()
32.
33.        # Handle the special cases if the user entered 1 or 2:
34.        if nth == 1:
35.            print('0')
36.            print()
37.            print('The #1 Fibonacci number is 0.')
38.            continue
39.        elif nth == 2:
40.            print('0, 1')
41.            print()
42.            print('The #2 Fibonacci number is 1.')
43.            continue
44.
45.        # Display warning if the user entered a large number:
46.        if nth >= 10000:
47.            print('WARNING: This will take a while to display on the')
48.            print('screen. If you want to quit this program before it is')
49.            print('done, press Ctrl-C.')
50.            input('Press Enter to begin...')
51.
52.        # Calculate the Nth Fibonacci number:
53.        secondToLastNumber = 0
54.        lastNumber = 1
55.        fibNumbersCalculated = 2
56.        print('0, 1, ', end='')  # Display the first two Fibonacci numbers.
57.
58.        # Display all the later numbers of the Fibonacci sequence:
59.        while True:
60.            nextNumber = secondToLastNumber + lastNumber
61.            fibNumbersCalculated += 1
62.
63.            # Display the next number in the sequence:
64.            print(nextNumber, end='')
65.
66.            # Check if we've found the Nth number the user wants:
67.            if fibNumbersCalculated == nth:
68.                print()
69.                print()
70.                print('The #', fibNumbersCalculated, ' Fibonacci ',
71.                      'number is ', nextNumber, sep='')
72.                break
73.
74.            # Print a comma in between the sequence numbers:
75.            print(', ', end='')
76.
77.            # Shift the last two numbers:
78.            secondToLastNumber = lastNumber
79.            lastNumber = nextNumber
```

After entering the source code and running it a few times, try making experimental changes to it. On your own, you can also try to figure out how to do the following:

- Use different starting numbers than 0 and 1.
- Create the next number by adding the previous three numbers instead of the previous two.

Exploring the Program

This is a base program, so there aren't many options to customize it. Instead, consider: how could you use this program? What other useful sequences could be programmed?

#27

FISH TANK

Watch your own virtual fish in a virtual
fish tank, complete with air bubblers and
kelp plants. Each time you run the program,
it randomly generates the fish using different
fish types and colors. Take a break and enjoy the calm
serenity of this software aquarium, or try programming
in some virtual sharks to terrorize its inhabitants! You
can't run this program from your IDE or editor. This
program uses the bext module and must be run from
the Command Prompt or Terminal in order to display
correctly. More information about the bext module can
be found at *https://pypi.org/project/bext/*.

The Program in Action

Figure 27-1 show what the output will look like when you run *fishtank.py*.

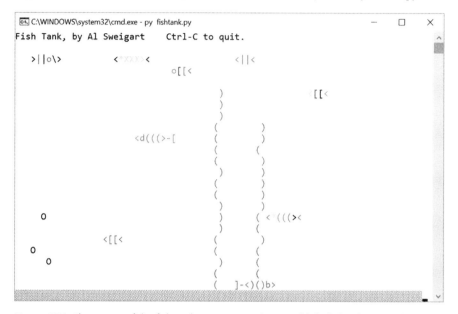

Figure 27-1: The output of the fish tank program, with several fish, kelp plants, and bubbles

How It Works

Modern graphical programs often generate animations by erasing their entire window and redrawing it 30 or 60 times a second. This gives them a *frame rate* of 30 or 60 frames per second (FPS). The higher the FPS, the more fluid the animated movement appears.

Drawing to terminal windows is much slower. If we erased the entire terminal window to redraw its contents with the bext module, we typically would only get about 3 or 4 FPS. This would cause a noticeable flicker in the window.

We can speed this up by only drawing characters to the parts of the terminal window that have changed. Most of the fish tank program's output is empty space, so to make the elements move, the clearAquarium() only has to draw ' ' space characters to the places where the fish, kelp, and bubbles currently are. This increases our frame rate, reduces flickering, and makes for a much more pleasant fish tank animation.

---

1. """Fish Tank, by Al Sweigart al@inventwithpython.com
2. A peaceful animation of a fish tank. Press Ctrl-C to stop.
3. Similar to ASCIIQuarium or @EmojiAquarium, but mine is based on an
4. older ASCII fish tank program for DOS.
5. https://robobunny.com/projects/asciiquarium/html/
6. https://twitter.com/EmojiAquarium

```
 7. View this code at https://nostarch.com/big-book-small-python-projects
 8. Tags: extra-large, artistic, bext"""
 9.
10. import random, sys, time
11.
12. try:
13.     import bext
14. except ImportError:
15.     print('This program requires the bext module, which you')
16.     print('can install by following the instructions at')
17.     print('https://pypi.org/project/Bext/')
18.     sys.exit()
19.
20. # Set up the constants:
21. WIDTH, HEIGHT = bext.size()
22. # We can't print to the last column on Windows without it adding a
23. # newline automatically, so reduce the width by one:
24. WIDTH -= 1
25.
26. NUM_KELP = 2  # (!) Try changing this to 10.
27. NUM_FISH = 10  # (!) Try changing this to 2 or 100.
28. NUM_BUBBLERS = 1  # (!) Try changing this to 0 or 10.
29. FRAMES_PER_SECOND = 4  # (!) Try changing this number to 1 or 60.
30. # (!) Try changing the constants to create a fish tank with only kelp,
31. # or only bubblers.
32.
33. # NOTE: Every string in a fish dictionary should be the same length.
34. FISH_TYPES = [
35.     {'right': ['><>'],          'left': ['<><']},
36.     {'right': ['>||>'],         'left': ['<||<']},
37.     {'right': ['>))>'],         'left': ['<[[<']},
38.     {'right': ['>||o', '>||.'], 'left': ['o||<', '.||<']},
39.     {'right': ['>))o', '>)).'], 'left': ['o[[<', '.[[<']},
40.     {'right': ['>-==>'],        'left': ['<==-<']},
41.     {'right': [r'>\\>'],        'left': ['<//<']},
42.     {'right': ['><)))*>'],      'left': ['<*(((><']},
43.     {'right': ['}-[[[*>'],      'left': ['<*]]]-{']},
44.     {'right': [']-<)))b>'],     'left': ['<d(((>-[']},
45.     {'right': ['><XXX*>'],      'left': ['<*XXX><']},
46.     {'right': ['_.-._.-^=>', '.-._.-.-^=>',
47.                '-._.-._^=>', '._.-._.^=>'],
48.      'left':  ['<=^-._.-._', '<=^.-._.-.',
49.                '<=^_.-._.-', '<=^._.-._.']},
50.     ]  # (!) Try adding your own fish to FISH_TYPES.
51. LONGEST_FISH_LENGTH = 10  # Longest single string in FISH_TYPES.
52.
53. # The x and y positions where a fish runs into the edge of the screen:
54. LEFT_EDGE = 0
55. RIGHT_EDGE = WIDTH - 1 - LONGEST_FISH_LENGTH
56. TOP_EDGE = 0
57. BOTTOM_EDGE = HEIGHT - 2
58.
59.
60. def main():
61.     global FISHES, BUBBLERS, BUBBLES, KELPS, STEP
```

```
62.      bext.bg('black')
63.      bext.clear()
64.
65.      # Generate the global variables:
66.      FISHES = []
67.      for i in range(NUM_FISH):
68.          FISHES.append(generateFish())
69.
70.      # NOTE: Bubbles are drawn, but not the bubblers themselves.
71.      BUBBLERS = []
72.      for i in range(NUM_BUBBLERS):
73.          # Each bubbler starts at a random position.
74.          BUBBLERS.append(random.randint(LEFT_EDGE, RIGHT_EDGE))
75.      BUBBLES = []
76.
77.      KELPS = []
78.      for i in range(NUM_KELP):
79.          kelpx = random.randint(LEFT_EDGE, RIGHT_EDGE)
80.          kelp = {'x': kelpx, 'segments': []}
81.          # Generate each segment of the kelp:
82.          for i in range(random.randint(6, HEIGHT - 1)):
83.              kelp['segments'].append(random.choice(['(', ')']))
84.          KELPS.append(kelp)
85.
86.      # Run the simulation:
87.      STEP = 1
88.      while True:
89.          simulateAquarium()
90.          drawAquarium()
91.          time.sleep(1 / FRAMES_PER_SECOND)
92.          clearAquarium()
93.          STEP += 1
94.
95.
96.  def getRandomColor():
97.      """Return a string of a random color."""
98.      return random.choice(('black', 'red', 'green', 'yellow', 'blue',
99.                            'purple', 'cyan', 'white'))
100.
101.
102. def generateFish():
103.      """Return a dictionary that represents a fish."""
104.      fishType = random.choice(FISH_TYPES)
105.
106.      # Set up colors for each character in the fish text:
107.      colorPattern = random.choice(('random', 'head-tail', 'single'))
108.      fishLength = len(fishType['right'][0])
109.      if colorPattern == 'random':  # All parts are randomly colored.
110.          colors = []
111.          for i in range(fishLength):
112.              colors.append(getRandomColor())
113.      if colorPattern == 'single' or colorPattern == 'head-tail':
114.          colors = [getRandomColor()] * fishLength  # All the same color.
115.      if colorPattern == 'head-tail':  # Head/tail different from body.
116.          headTailColor = getRandomColor()
```

```
117.          colors[0] = headTailColor  # Set head color.
118.          colors[-1] = headTailColor  # Set tail color.
119.
120.      # Set up the rest of fish data structure:
121.      fish = {'right':            fishType['right'],
122.              'left':             fishType['left'],
123.              'colors':           colors,
124.              'hSpeed':           random.randint(1, 6),
125.              'vSpeed':           random.randint(5, 15),
126.              'timeToHDirChange': random.randint(10, 60),
127.              'timeToVDirChange': random.randint(2, 20),
128.              'goingRight':       random.choice([True, False]),
129.              'goingDown':        random.choice([True, False])}
130.
131.      # 'x' is always the leftmost side of the fish body:
132.      fish['x'] = random.randint(0, WIDTH - 1 - LONGEST_FISH_LENGTH)
133.      fish['y'] = random.randint(0, HEIGHT - 2)
134.      return fish
135.
136.
137. def simulateAquarium():
138.      """Simulate the movements in the aquarium for one step."""
139.      global FISHES, BUBBLERS, BUBBLES, KELP, STEP
140.
141.      # Simulate the fish for one step:
142.      for fish in FISHES:
143.          # Move the fish horizontally:
144.          if STEP % fish['hSpeed'] == 0:
145.              if fish['goingRight']:
146.                  if fish['x'] != RIGHT_EDGE:
147.                      fish['x'] += 1  # Move the fish right.
148.                  else:
149.                      fish['goingRight'] = False  # Turn the fish around.
150.                      fish['colors'].reverse()  # Turn the colors around.
151.              else:
152.                  if fish['x'] != LEFT_EDGE:
153.                      fish['x'] -= 1  # Move the fish left.
154.                  else:
155.                      fish['goingRight'] = True  # Turn the fish around.
156.                      fish['colors'].reverse()  # Turn the colors around.
157.
158.          # Fish can randomly change their horizontal direction:
159.          fish['timeToHDirChange'] -= 1
160.          if fish['timeToHDirChange'] == 0:
161.              fish['timeToHDirChange'] = random.randint(10, 60)
162.              # Turn the fish around:
163.              fish['goingRight'] = not fish['goingRight']
164.
165.          # Move the fish vertically:
166.          if STEP % fish['vSpeed'] == 0:
167.              if fish['goingDown']:
168.                  if fish['y'] != BOTTOM_EDGE:
169.                      fish['y'] += 1  # Move the fish down.
170.                  else:
171.                      fish['goingDown'] = False  # Turn the fish around.
```

```
172.                else:
173.                    if fish['y'] != TOP_EDGE:
174.                        fish['y'] -= 1  # Move the fish up.
175.                    else:
176.                        fish['goingDown'] = True  # Turn the fish around.
177.
178.            # Fish can randomly change their vertical direction:
179.            fish['timeToVDirChange'] -= 1
180.            if fish['timeToVDirChange'] == 0:
181.                fish['timeToVDirChange'] = random.randint(2, 20)
182.                # Turn the fish around:
183.                fish['goingDown'] = not fish['goingDown']
184.
185.        # Generate bubbles from bubblers:
186.        for bubbler in BUBBLERS:
187.            # There is a 1 in 5 chance of making a bubble:
188.            if random.randint(1, 5) == 1:
189.                BUBBLES.append({'x': bubbler, 'y': HEIGHT - 2})
190.
191.        # Move the bubbles:
192.        for bubble in BUBBLES:
193.            diceRoll = random.randint(1, 6)
194.            if (diceRoll == 1) and (bubble['x'] != LEFT_EDGE):
195.                bubble['x'] -= 1  # Bubble goes left.
196.            elif (diceRoll == 2) and (bubble['x'] != RIGHT_EDGE):
197.                bubble['x'] += 1  # Bubble goes right.
198.
199.            bubble['y'] -= 1  # The bubble always goes up.
200.
201.        # Iterate over BUBBLES in reverse because I'm deleting from BUBBLES
202.        # while iterating over it.
203.        for i in range(len(BUBBLES) - 1, -1, -1):
204.            if BUBBLES[i]['y'] == TOP_EDGE:  # Delete bubbles that reach the top.
205.                del BUBBLES[i]
206.
207.        # Simulate the kelp waving for one step:
208.        for kelp in KELPS:
209.            for i, kelpSegment in enumerate(kelp['segments']):
210.                # 1 in 20 chance to change waving:
211.                if random.randint(1, 20) == 1:
212.                    if kelpSegment == '(':
213.                        kelp['segments'][i] = ')'
214.                    elif kelpSegment == ')':
215.                        kelp['segments'][i] = '('
216.
217.
218. def drawAquarium():
219.     """Draw the aquarium on the screen."""
220.     global FISHES, BUBBLERS, BUBBLES, KELP, STEP
221.
222.     # Draw quit message.
223.     bext.fg('white')
224.     bext.goto(0, 0)
225.     print('Fish Tank, by Al Sweigart    Ctrl-C to quit.', end='')
226.
```

```
227.        # Draw the bubbles:
228.        bext.fg('white')
229.        for bubble in BUBBLES:
230.            bext.goto(bubble['x'], bubble['y'])
231.            print(random.choice(('o', 'O')), end='')
232.
233.        # Draw the fish:
234.        for fish in FISHES:
235.            bext.goto(fish['x'], fish['y'])
236.
237.            # Get the correct right- or left-facing fish text.
238.            if fish['goingRight']:
239.                fishText = fish['right'][STEP % len(fish['right'])]
240.            else:
241.                fishText = fish['left'][STEP % len(fish['left'])]
242.
243.            # Draw each character of the fish text in the right color.
244.            for i, fishPart in enumerate(fishText):
245.                bext.fg(fish['colors'][i])
246.                print(fishPart, end='')
247.
248.        # Draw the kelp:
249.        bext.fg('green')
250.        for kelp in KELPS:
251.            for i, kelpSegment in enumerate(kelp['segments']):
252.                if kelpSegment == '(':
253.                    bext.goto(kelp['x'], BOTTOM_EDGE - i)
254.                elif kelpSegment == ')':
255.                    bext.goto(kelp['x'] + 1, BOTTOM_EDGE - i)
256.                print(kelpSegment, end='')
257.
258.        # Draw the sand on the bottom:
259.        bext.fg('yellow')
260.        bext.goto(0, HEIGHT - 1)
261.        print(chr(9617) * (WIDTH - 1), end='')  # Draws sand.
262.
263.        sys.stdout.flush()  # (Required for bext-using programs.)
264.
265.
266. def clearAquarium():
267.     """Draw empty spaces over everything on the screen."""
268.     global FISHES, BUBBLERS, BUBBLES, KELP
269.
270.     # Draw the bubbles:
271.     for bubble in BUBBLES:
272.         bext.goto(bubble['x'], bubble['y'])
273.         print(' ', end='')
274.
275.     # Draw the fish:
276.     for fish in FISHES:
277.         bext.goto(fish['x'], fish['y'])
278.
279.         # Draw each character of the fish text in the right color.
280.         print(' ' * len(fish['left'][0]), end='')
281.
```

```
282.     # Draw the kelp:
283.     for kelp in KELPS:
284.         for i, kelpSegment in enumerate(kelp['segments']):
285.             bext.goto(kelp['x'], HEIGHT - 2 - i)
286.             print(' ', end='')
287.
288.     sys.stdout.flush()  # (Required for bext-using programs.)
289.
290.
291. # If this program was run (instead of imported), run the game:
292. if __name__ == '__main__':
293.     try:
294.         main()
295.     except KeyboardInterrupt:
296.         sys.exit()  # When Ctrl-C is pressed, end the program.
```

After entering the source code and running it a few times, try making experimental changes to it. The comments marked with (!) have suggestions for small changes you can make. On your own, you can also try to figure out how to do the following:

- Add crabs that move along on the sandy bottom.
- Add an ASCII-art castle that appears randomly on the sandy bottom.
- Make the fish randomly increase their speed for a short burst.

Exploring the Program

Try to find the answers to the following questions. Experiment with some modifications to the code and rerun the program to see what effect the changes have.

1. What happens if you change LONGEST_FISH_LENGTH = 10 on line 51 to LONGEST_FISH_LENGTH = 50?

2. What happens if you change 'right': fishType['right'] on line 121 to 'right': fishType['left']?

3. What happens if you change bext.fg('green') on line 249 to bext.fg('red')?

4. What happens if you delete or comment out clearAquarium() on line 92?

5. What happens if you change bext.fg(fish['colors'][i]) on line 245 to bext.fg('random')?

6. What happens if you change random.randint(10, 60) on line 161 to 1?

#28

FLOODER

 Flooder is a colorful game where a player
tries to fill the board with a single color
by changing the color of the tile in the
upper-left corner. This new color spreads to
all neighboring tiles that matched the original color.
It's similar to the Flood It mobile game. This program
also has a colorblind mode, which uses shapes instead
of flat colored tiles. It relies on the recursive flood
fill algorithm to paint the board and works similarly
to the "paint bucket" or "fill" tool in many painting
applications.

The Program in Action

Figure 28-1 shows what the output will look like when you run *flooder.py*.

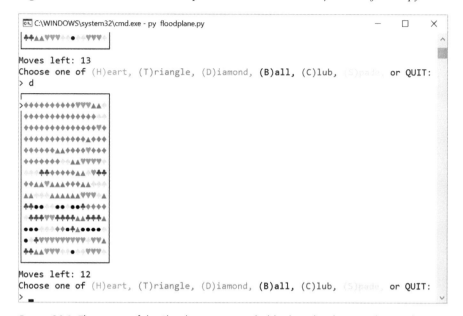

Figure 28-1: The output of the Flooder game in colorblind mode, showing distinct shapes instead of rectangles

How It Works

Accessibility is a large issue in video games, and addressing it can take many forms. For example, deuteranopia, or red-green colorblindness, causes shades of red and green to appear the same, making it hard to distinguish between red objects and green objects on the screen. We can make Flooder more accessible with a mode that uses distinct shapes instead of distinct colors. Note that even the colorblind mode still uses color. This means you can eliminate the "standard" mode, if you wish, and have even color-sighted users play in the colorblind mode. The best accessibility designs are those that incorporate accessibility considerations from the start rather than add them as a separate mode. This reduces the amount of code we have to write and makes any future bug fixes easier.

Other accessibility issues include making sure that text is large enough to be read without perfect vision, that sound effects have visual cues and spoken language has subtitles for those hard of hearing, and that controls can be remapped to other keyboard keys so people can play the game with one hand. The YouTube channel Game Maker's Toolkit has a video series called "Designing for Disability" that covers many aspects of designing your games with accessibility in mind.

```
 1. """Flooder, by Al Sweigart al@inventwithpython.com
 2. A colorful game where you try to fill the board with a single color. Has
 3. a mode for colorblind players.
 4. Inspired by the "Flood It!" game.
 5. View this code at https://nostarch.com/big-book-small-python-projects
 6. Tags: large, bext, game"""
 7.
 8. import random, sys
 9.
10. try:
11.     import bext
12. except ImportError:
13.     print('This program requires the bext module, which you')
14.     print('can install by following the instructions at')
15.     print('https://pypi.org/project/Bext/')
16.     sys.exit()
17.
18. # Set up the constants:
19. BOARD_WIDTH = 16  # (!) Try changing this to 4 or 40.
20. BOARD_HEIGHT = 14  # (!) Try changing this to 4 or 20.
21. MOVES_PER_GAME = 20  # (!) Try changing this to 3 or 300.
22.
23. # Constants for the different shapes used in colorblind mode:
24. HEART    = chr(9829)  # Character 9829 is '♥'.
25. DIAMOND  = chr(9830)  # Character 9830 is '♦'.
26. SPADE    = chr(9824)  # Character 9824 is '♠'.
27. CLUB     = chr(9827)  # Character 9827 is '♣'.
28. BALL     = chr(9679)  # Character 9679 is '●'.
29. TRIANGLE = chr(9650)  # Character 9650 is '▲'.
30.
31. BLOCK     = chr(9608)  # Character 9608 is '█'
32. LEFTRIGHT = chr(9472)  # Character 9472 is '─'
33. UPDOWN    = chr(9474)  # Character 9474 is '│'
34. DOWNRIGHT = chr(9484)  # Character 9484 is '┌'
35. DOWNLEFT  = chr(9488)  # Character 9488 is '┐'
36. UPRIGHT   = chr(9492)  # Character 9492 is '└'
37. UPLEFT    = chr(9496)  # Character 9496 is '┘'
38. # A list of chr() codes is at https://inventwithpython.com/chr
39.
40. # All the color/shape tiles used on the board:
41. TILE_TYPES = (0, 1, 2, 3, 4, 5)
42. COLORS_MAP = {0: 'red', 1: 'green', 2:'blue',
43.               3:'yellow', 4:'cyan', 5:'purple'}
44. COLOR_MODE = 'color mode'
45. SHAPES_MAP = {0: HEART, 1: TRIANGLE, 2: DIAMOND,
46.               3: BALL, 4: CLUB, 5: SPADE}
47. SHAPE_MODE = 'shape mode'
48.
49.
50. def main():
51.     bext.bg('black')
52.     bext.fg('white')
```

```
53.     bext.clear()
54.     print('''Flooder, by Al Sweigart al@inventwithpython.com
55.
56. Set the upper left color/shape, which fills in all the
57. adjacent squares of that color/shape. Try to make the
58. entire board the same color/shape.''')
59.
60.     print('Do you want to play in colorblind mode? Y/N')
61.     response = input('> ')
62.     if response.upper().startswith('Y'):
63.         displayMode = SHAPE_MODE
64.     else:
65.         displayMode = COLOR_MODE
66.
67.     gameBoard = getNewBoard()
68.     movesLeft = MOVES_PER_GAME
69.
70.     while True:  # Main game loop.
71.         displayBoard(gameBoard, displayMode)
72.
73.         print('Moves left:', movesLeft)
74.         playerMove = askForPlayerMove(displayMode)
75.         changeTile(playerMove, gameBoard, 0, 0)
76.         movesLeft -= 1
77.
78.         if hasWon(gameBoard):
79.             displayBoard(gameBoard, displayMode)
80.             print('You have won!')
81.             break
82.         elif movesLeft == 0:
83.             displayBoard(gameBoard, displayMode)
84.             print('You have run out of moves!')
85.             break
86.
87.
88. def getNewBoard():
89.     """Return a dictionary of a new Flood It board."""
90.
91.     # Keys are (x, y) tuples, values are the tile at that position.
92.     board = {}
93.
94.     # Create random colors for the board.
95.     for x in range(BOARD_WIDTH):
96.         for y in range(BOARD_HEIGHT):
97.             board[(x, y)] = random.choice(TILE_TYPES)
98.
99.     # Make several tiles the same as their neighbor. This creates groups
100.    # of the same color/shape.
101.    for i in range(BOARD_WIDTH * BOARD_HEIGHT):
102.        x = random.randint(0, BOARD_WIDTH - 2)
103.        y = random.randint(0, BOARD_HEIGHT - 1)
104.        board[(x + 1, y)] = board[(x, y)]
105.    return board
106.
107.
```

```
108. def displayBoard(board, displayMode):
109.     """Display the board on the screen."""
110.     bext.fg('white')
111.     # Display the top edge of the board:
112.     print(DOWNRIGHT + (LEFTRIGHT * BOARD_WIDTH) + DOWNLEFT)
113.
114.     # Display each row:
115.     for y in range(BOARD_HEIGHT):
116.         bext.fg('white')
117.         if y == 0:  # The first row begins with '>'.
118.             print('>', end='')
119.         else:  # Later rows begin with a white vertical line.
120.             print(UPDOWN, end='')
121.
122.         # Display each tile in this row:
123.         for x in range(BOARD_WIDTH):
124.             bext.fg(COLORS_MAP[board[(x, y)]])
125.             if displayMode == COLOR_MODE:
126.                 print(BLOCK, end='')
127.             elif displayMode == SHAPE_MODE:
128.                 print(SHAPES_MAP[board[(x, y)]], end='')
129.
130.         bext.fg('white')
131.         print(UPDOWN)  # Rows end with a white vertical line.
132.     # Display the bottom edge of the board:
133.     print(UPRIGHT + (LEFTRIGHT * BOARD_WIDTH) + UPLEFT)
134.
135.
136. def askForPlayerMove(displayMode):
137.     """Let the player select a color to paint the upper left tile."""
138.     while True:
139.         bext.fg('white')
140.         print('Choose one of ', end='')
141.
142.         if displayMode == COLOR_MODE:
143.             bext.fg('red')
144.             print('(R)ed ', end='')
145.             bext.fg('green')
146.             print('(G)reen ', end='')
147.             bext.fg('blue')
148.             print('(B)lue ', end='')
149.             bext.fg('yellow')
150.             print('(Y)ellow ', end='')
151.             bext.fg('cyan')
152.             print('(C)yan ', end='')
153.             bext.fg('purple')
154.             print('(P)urple ', end='')
155.         elif displayMode == SHAPE_MODE:
156.             bext.fg('red')
157.             print('(H)eart, ', end='')
158.             bext.fg('green')
159.             print('(T)riangle, ', end='')
160.             bext.fg('blue')
161.             print('(D)iamond, ', end='')
162.             bext.fg('yellow')
```

```
163.            print('(B)all, ', end='')
164.            bext.fg('cyan')
165.            print('(C)lub, ', end='')
166.            bext.fg('purple')
167.            print('(S)pade, ', end='')
168.        bext.fg('white')
169.        print('or QUIT:')
170.        response = input('> ').upper()
171.        if response == 'QUIT':
172.            print('Thanks for playing!')
173.            sys.exit()
174.        if displayMode == COLOR_MODE and response in tuple('RGBYCP'):
175.            # Return a tile type number based on the response:
176.            return {'R': 0, 'G': 1, 'B': 2,
177.                    'Y': 3, 'C': 4, 'P': 5}[response]
178.        if displayMode == SHAPE_MODE and response in tuple('HTDBCS'):
179.            # Return a tile type number based on the response:
180.            return {'H': 0, 'T': 1, 'D':2,
181.                    'B': 3, 'C': 4, 'S': 5}[response]
182.
183.
184. def changeTile(tileType, board, x, y, charToChange=None):
185.     """Change the color/shape of a tile using the recursive flood fill
186.     algorithm."""
187.     if x == 0 and y == 0:
188.         charToChange = board[(x, y)]
189.         if tileType == charToChange:
190.             return  # Base Case: Already is the same tile.
191.
192.     board[(x, y)] = tileType
193.
194.     if x > 0 and board[(x - 1, y)] == charToChange:
195.         # Recursive Case: Change the left neighbor's tile:
196.         changeTile(tileType, board, x - 1, y, charToChange)
197.     if y > 0 and board[(x, y - 1)] == charToChange:
198.         # Recursive Case: Change the top neighbor's tile:
199.         changeTile(tileType, board, x, y - 1, charToChange)
200.     if x < BOARD_WIDTH - 1 and board[(x + 1, y)] == charToChange:
201.         # Recursive Case: Change the right neighbor's tile:
202.         changeTile(tileType, board, x + 1, y, charToChange)
203.     if y < BOARD_HEIGHT - 1 and board[(x, y + 1)] == charToChange:
204.         # Recursive Case: Change the bottom neighbor's tile:
205.         changeTile(tileType, board, x, y + 1, charToChange)
206.
207.
208. def hasWon(board):
209.     """Return True if the entire board is one color/shape."""
210.     tile = board[(0, 0)]
211.
212.     for x in range(BOARD_WIDTH):
213.         for y in range(BOARD_HEIGHT):
214.             if board[(x, y)] != tile:
215.                 return False
216.     return True
217.
```

```
218.
219. # If this program was run (instead of imported), run the game:
220. if __name__ == '__main__':
221.     main()
```

After entering the source code and running it a few times, try making experimental changes to it. The comments marked with (!) have suggestions for small changes you can make. On your own, you can also try to figure out how to do the following:

- Add additional shapes and colors.
- Create other board shapes besides a rectangle.

Exploring the Program

Try to find the answers to the following questions. Experiment with some modifications to the code and rerun the program to see what effect the changes have.

1. What error message do you get if you change board = {} on line 92 to board = []?

2. What error message do you get if you change return board on line 105 to return None?

3. What happens if you change movesLeft -= 1 on line 76 to movesLeft -= 0?

#29

FOREST FIRE SIM

This simulation shows a forest whose trees are constantly growing and then being burned down. On each step of the simulation, there is a 1 percent chance that a blank space grows into a tree and a 1 percent chance that a tree is struck by lightning and burns. Fires will spread to adjacent trees, so a densely packed forest is more likely to suffer a larger fire than a sparsely packed one. This simulation was inspired by Nicky Case's Emoji Sim at *http://ncase.me/simulating/model/*.

The Program in Action

When you run *forestfiresim.py*, the output will look like this:

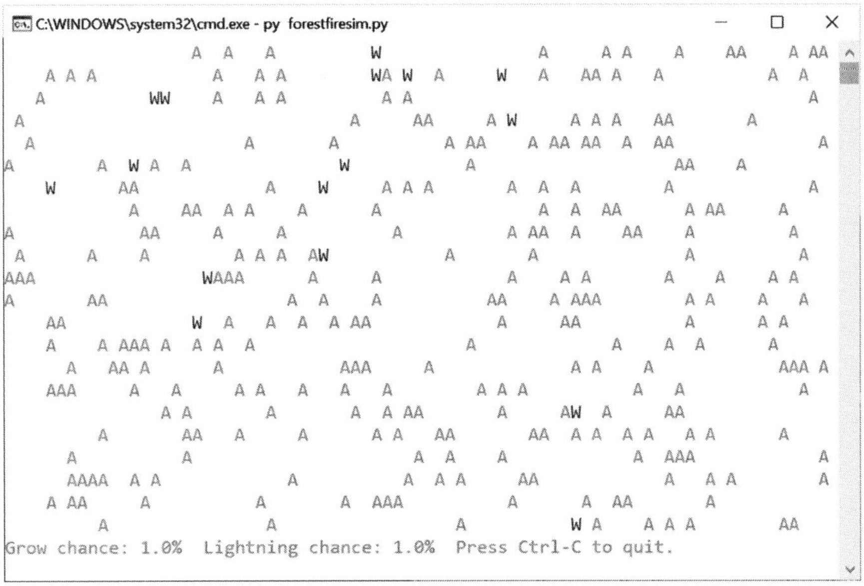

Figure 29-1: The forest fire simulation, with green As for trees and red Ws for flames

How It Works

This simulation is an example of *emergent behavior*—the interaction between simple parts in a system creating complicated patterns. Empty spaces grow into trees, lightning turns trees into fire, and fire turns trees back into empty spaces while spreading to neighboring trees. By adjusting the tree growth and lightning strike rate, you can cause the forest to display different phenomena. For example, a low lightning chance but high growth rate causes large, constant forest fires, since the trees tend to be near each other and quickly replenish. A low growth rate but high lightning strike chance creates several small fires that quickly extinguish due to a lack of nearby trees. We don't explicitly program any of this behavior; rather, it naturally emerges from the system that we created.

```
1. """Forest Fire Sim, by Al Sweigart al@inventwithpython.com
2. A simulation of wildfires spreading in a forest. Press Ctrl-C to stop.
3. Inspired by Nicky Case's Emoji Sim http://ncase.me/simulating/model/
4. View this code at https://nostarch.com/big-book-small-python-projects
5. Tags: short, bext, simulation"""
6.
7. import random, sys, time
8.
9. try:
10.     import bext
```

```python
11. except ImportError:
12.     print('This program requires the bext module, which you')
13.     print('can install by following the instructions at')
14.     print('https://pypi.org/project/Bext/')
15.     sys.exit()
16.
17. # Set up the constants:
18. WIDTH = 79
19. HEIGHT = 22
20.
21. TREE = 'A'
22. FIRE = 'W'
23. EMPTY = ' '
24.
25. # (!) Try changing these settings to anything between 0.0 and 1.0:
26. INITIAL_TREE_DENSITY = 0.20  # Amount of forest that starts with trees.
27. GROW_CHANCE = 0.01  # Chance a blank space turns into a tree.
28. FIRE_CHANCE = 0.01  # Chance a tree is hit by lightning & burns.
29.
30. # (!) Try setting the pause length to 1.0 or 0.0:
31. PAUSE_LENGTH = 0.5
32.
33.
34. def main():
35.     forest = createNewForest()
36.     bext.clear()
37.
38.     while True:  # Main program loop.
39.         displayForest(forest)
40.
41.         # Run a single simulation step:
42.         nextForest = {'width': forest['width'],
43.                       'height': forest['height']}
44.
45.         for x in range(forest['width']):
46.             for y in range(forest['height']):
47.                 if (x, y) in nextForest:
48.                     # If we've already set nextForest[(x, y)] on a
49.                     # previous iteration, just do nothing here:
50.                     continue
51.
52.                 if ((forest[(x, y)] == EMPTY
53.                     and (random.random() <= GROW_CHANCE)):
54.                     # Grow a tree in this empty space.
55.                     nextForest[(x, y)] = TREE
56.                 elif ((forest[(x, y)] == TREE)
57.                     and (random.random() <= FIRE_CHANCE)):
58.                     # Lightning sets this tree on fire.
59.                     nextForest[(x, y)] = FIRE
60.                 elif forest[(x, y)] == FIRE:
61.                     # This tree is currently burning.
62.                     # Loop through all the neighboring spaces:
63.                     for ix in range(-1, 2):
64.                         for iy in range(-1, 2):
```

```
65.                                          # Fire spreads to neighboring trees:
66.                                          if forest.get((x + ix, y + iy)) == TREE:
67.                                              nextForest[(x + ix, y + iy)] = FIRE
68.                                      # The tree has burned down now, so erase it:
69.                                      nextForest[(x, y)] = EMPTY
70.                              else:
71.                                  # Just copy the existing object:
72.                                  nextForest[(x, y)] = forest[(x, y)]
73.              forest = nextForest
74.
75.          time.sleep(PAUSE_LENGTH)
76.
77.
78. def createNewForest():
79.     """Returns a dictionary for a new forest data structure."""
80.     forest = {'width': WIDTH, 'height': HEIGHT}
81.     for x in range(WIDTH):
82.         for y in range(HEIGHT):
83.             if (random.random() * 100) <= INITIAL_TREE_DENSITY:
84.                 forest[(x, y)] = TREE  # Start as a tree.
85.             else:
86.                 forest[(x, y)] = EMPTY  # Start as an empty space.
87.     return forest
88.
89.
90. def displayForest(forest):
91.     """Display the forest data structure on the screen."""
92.     bext.goto(0, 0)
93.     for y in range(forest['height']):
94.         for x in range(forest['width']):
95.             if forest[(x, y)] == TREE:
96.                 bext.fg('green')
97.                 print(TREE, end='')
98.             elif forest[(x, y)] == FIRE:
99.                 bext.fg('red')
100.                print(FIRE, end='')
101.            elif forest[(x, y)] == EMPTY:
102.                print(EMPTY, end='')
103.        print()
104.    bext.fg('reset')  # Use the default font color.
105.    print('Grow chance: {}% '.format(GROW_CHANCE * 100), end='')
106.    print('Lightning chance: {}% '.format(FIRE_CHANCE * 100), end='')
107.    print('Press Ctrl-C to quit.')
108.
109.
110. # If this program was run (instead of imported), run the game:
111. if __name__ == '__main__':
112.     try:
113.         main()
114.     except KeyboardInterrupt:
115.         sys.exit()  # When Ctrl-C is pressed, end the program.
```

After entering the source code and running it a few times, try making experimental changes to it. The comments marked with (!) have suggestions for small changes you can make. On your own, you can also try to figure out how to do the following:

- Add randomly created lakes and rivers, which act as fire breaks that flames cannot cross.
- Add a percentage chance that a tree will catch fire from its neighbor.
- Add different types of trees with different chances of catching fire.
- Add different states of burning trees so that it takes multiple simulation steps for a tree to burn down.

Exploring the Program

Try to find the answers to the following questions. Experiment with some modifications to the code and rerun the program to see what effect the changes have.

1. What happens if you change `bext.fg('green')` on line 96 to `bext.fg('random')`?
2. What happens if you change `EMPTY = ' '` on line 23 to `EMPTY = '.'`?
3. What happens if you change `forest.get((x + ix, y + iy)) == TREE` on line 66 to `forest.get((x + ix, y + iy)) == EMPTY`?
4. What happens if you change `nextForest[(x, y)] = EMPTY` on line 69 to `nextForest[(x, y)] = FIRE`?
5. What happens if you change `forest[(x, y)] = EMPTY` on line 86 to `forest[(x, y)] = TREE`?

#30

FOUR IN A ROW

In this classic tile-dropping board game for two players, you must try to get four of your tiles in a row horizontally, vertically, or diagonally, while preventing your opponent from doing the same. This program is similar to Connect Four.

The Program in Action

When you run *fourinarow.py*, the output will look like this:

```
Four in a Row, by Al Sweigart al@inventwithpython.com
--snip--
     1234567
    +-------+
    |.......|
    |.......|
    |.......|
    |.......|
    |.......|
    |.......|
    +-------+
Player X, enter a column or QUIT:
> 3

     1234567
    +-------+
    |.......|
    |.......|
    |.......|
    |.......|
    |.......|
    |..X....|
    +-------+
Player O, enter a column or QUIT:
> 5
--snip--
Player O, enter a column or QUIT:
> 4

     1234567
    +-------+
    |.......|
    |.......|
    |XXX.XO.|
    |OOOOXO.|
    |OOOXOX.|
    |OXXXOXX|
    +-------+
Player O has won!
```

How It Works

The board game projects in this book follow a similar program structure. There's often a dictionary or list for representing the state of the board, a getNewBoard() function that returns a data structure for a board, a display Board() function for rendering a board data structure on the screen, and so on. You can check out the other projects in this book with the *board game* tag and compare them with each other, especially when you want to create your own original board game programs.

```
1.  """Four in a Row, by Al Sweigart al@inventwithpython.com
2.  A tile-dropping game to get four in a row, similar to Connect Four.
3.  View this code at https://nostarch.com/big-book-small-python-projects
4.  Tags: large, game, board game, two-player"""
5.
6.  import sys
7.
8.  # Constants used for displaying the board:
9.  EMPTY_SPACE = '.'  # A period is easier to count than a space.
10. PLAYER_X = 'X'
11. PLAYER_O = 'O'
12.
13. # Note: Update displayBoard() & COLUMN_LABELS if BOARD_WIDTH is changed.
14. BOARD_WIDTH = 7
15. BOARD_HEIGHT = 6
16. COLUMN_LABELS = ('1', '2', '3', '4', '5', '6', '7')
17. assert len(COLUMN_LABELS) == BOARD_WIDTH
18.
19.
20. def main():
21.     print("""Four in a Row, by Al Sweigart al@inventwithpython.com
22.
23. Two players take turns dropping tiles into one of seven columns, trying
24. to make four in a row horizontally, vertically, or diagonally.
25. """)
26.
27.     # Set up a new game:
28.     gameBoard = getNewBoard()
29.     playerTurn = PLAYER_X
30.
31.     while True:  # Run a player's turn.
32.         # Display the board and get player's move:
33.         displayBoard(gameBoard)
34.         playerMove = askForPlayerMove(playerTurn, gameBoard)
35.         gameBoard[playerMove] = playerTurn
36.
37.         # Check for a win or tie:
38.         if isWinner(playerTurn, gameBoard):
39.             displayBoard(gameBoard)  # Display the board one last time.
40.             print('Player ' + playerTurn + ' has won!')
41.             sys.exit()
42.         elif isFull(gameBoard):
43.             displayBoard(gameBoard)  # Display the board one last time.
44.             print('There is a tie!')
45.             sys.exit()
46.
47.         # Switch turns to other player:
48.         if playerTurn == PLAYER_X:
49.             playerTurn = PLAYER_O
50.         elif playerTurn == PLAYER_O:
51.             playerTurn = PLAYER_X
52.
53.
54. def getNewBoard():
```

```
55.      """Returns a dictionary that represents a Four in a Row board.
56.
57.      The keys are (columnIndex, rowIndex) tuples of two integers, and the
58.      values are one of the 'X', 'O' or '.' (empty space) strings."""
59.      board = {}
60.      for columnIndex in range(BOARD_WIDTH):
61.          for rowIndex in range(BOARD_HEIGHT):
62.              board[(columnIndex, rowIndex)] = EMPTY_SPACE
63.      return board
64.
65.
66. def displayBoard(board):
67.      """Display the board and its tiles on the screen."""
68.
69.      '''Prepare a list to pass to the format() string method for the
70.      board template. The list holds all of the board's tiles (and empty
71.      spaces) going left to right, top to bottom:'''
72.      tileChars = []
73.      for rowIndex in range(BOARD_HEIGHT):
74.          for columnIndex in range(BOARD_WIDTH):
75.              tileChars.append(board[(columnIndex, rowIndex)])
76.
77.      # Display the board:
78.      print("""
79.       1234567
80.      +-------+
81.      |{}{}{}{}{}{}{}|
82.      |{}{}{}{}{}{}{}|
83.      |{}{}{}{}{}{}{}|
84.      |{}{}{}{}{}{}{}|
85.      |{}{}{}{}{}{}{}|
86.      |{}{}{}{}{}{}{}|
87.      +-------+""".format(*tileChars))
88.
89.
90. def askForPlayerMove(playerTile, board):
91.      """Let a player select a column on the board to drop a tile into.
92.
93.      Returns a tuple of the (column, row) that the tile falls into."""
94.      while True:  # Keep asking player until they enter a valid move.
95.          print('Player {}, enter a column or QUIT:'.format(playerTile))
96.          response = input('> ').upper().strip()
97.
98.          if response == 'QUIT':
99.              print('Thanks for playing!')
100.             sys.exit()
101.
102.         if response not in COLUMN_LABELS:
103.             print('Enter a number from 1 to {}.'.format(BOARD_WIDTH))
104.             continue  # Ask player again for their move.
105.
106.         columnIndex = int(response) - 1  # -1 for 0-based the index.
107.
108.         # If the column is full, ask for a move again:
109.         if board[(columnIndex, 0)] != EMPTY_SPACE:
```

```
110.                    print('That column is full, select another one.')
111.                    continue  # Ask player again for their move.
112.
113.              # Starting from the bottom, find the first empty space.
114.              for rowIndex in range(BOARD_HEIGHT - 1, -1, -1):
115.                  if board[(columnIndex, rowIndex)] == EMPTY_SPACE:
116.                      return (columnIndex, rowIndex)
117.
118.
119. def isFull(board):
120.     """Returns True if the `board` has no empty spaces, otherwise
121.     returns False."""
122.     for rowIndex in range(BOARD_HEIGHT):
123.         for columnIndex in range(BOARD_WIDTH):
124.             if board[(columnIndex, rowIndex)] == EMPTY_SPACE:
125.                 return False  # Found an empty space, so return False.
126.     return True  # All spaces are full.
127.
128.
129. def isWinner(playerTile, board):
130.     """Returns True if `playerTile` has four tiles in a row on `board`,
131.     otherwise returns False."""
132.
133.     # Go through the entire board, checking for four-in-a-row:
134.     for columnIndex in range(BOARD_WIDTH - 3):
135.         for rowIndex in range(BOARD_HEIGHT):
136.             # Check for horizontal four-in-a-row going right:
137.             tile1 = board[(columnIndex, rowIndex)]
138.             tile2 = board[(columnIndex + 1, rowIndex)]
139.             tile3 = board[(columnIndex + 2, rowIndex)]
140.             tile4 = board[(columnIndex + 3, rowIndex)]
141.             if tile1 == tile2 == tile3 == tile4 == playerTile:
142.                 return True
143.
144.     for columnIndex in range(BOARD_WIDTH):
145.         for rowIndex in range(BOARD_HEIGHT - 3):
146.             # Check for vertical four-in-a-row going down:
147.             tile1 = board[(columnIndex, rowIndex)]
148.             tile2 = board[(columnIndex, rowIndex + 1)]
149.             tile3 = board[(columnIndex, rowIndex + 2)]
150.             tile4 = board[(columnIndex, rowIndex + 3)]
151.             if tile1 == tile2 == tile3 == tile4 == playerTile:
152.                 return True
153.
154.     for columnIndex in range(BOARD_WIDTH - 3):
155.         for rowIndex in range(BOARD_HEIGHT - 3):
156.             # Check for four-in-a-row going right-down diagonal:
157.             tile1 = board[(columnIndex, rowIndex)]
158.             tile2 = board[(columnIndex + 1, rowIndex + 1)]
159.             tile3 = board[(columnIndex + 2, rowIndex + 2)]
160.             tile4 = board[(columnIndex + 3, rowIndex + 3)]
161.             if tile1 == tile2 == tile3 == tile4 == playerTile:
162.                 return True
163.
164.             # Check for four-in-a-row going left-down diagonal:
```

```
165.                    tile1 = board[(columnIndex + 3, rowIndex)]
166.                    tile2 = board[(columnIndex + 2, rowIndex + 1)]
167.                    tile3 = board[(columnIndex + 1, rowIndex + 2)]
168.                    tile4 = board[(columnIndex, rowIndex + 3)]
169.                    if tile1 == tile2 == tile3 == tile4 == playerTile:
170.                        return True
171.        return False
172.
173.
174. # If the program is run (instead of imported), run the game:
175. if __name__ == '__main__':
176.     main()
```

After entering the source code and running it a few times, try making experimental changes to it. The comments marked with (!) have suggestions for small changes you can make. On your own, you can also try to figure out how to do the following:

- Create a three-in-a-row or five-in-a-row variant.
- Make a three-player variant of this game.
- Add a "wildcard" tile that randomly drops after the players' turns and can be used by either player.
- Add "block" tiles that cannot be used by either player.

Exploring the Program

Try to find the answers to the following questions. Experiment with some modifications to the code and rerun the program to see what effect the changes have.

1. What happens if you change PLAYER_O = 'O' on line 11 to PLAYER_O = 'X'?
2. What happens if you change return (columnIndex, rowIndex) on line 116 to return (columnIndex, 0)?
3. What happens if you change response == 'QUIT' on line 98 to response != 'QUIT'?
4. What error message do you get if you change tileChars = [] on line 72 to tileChars = {}?

#31

GUESS THE NUMBER

Guess the Number is a classic game for beginners to practice basic programming techniques. In this game, the computer thinks of a random number between 1 and 100. The player has 10 chances to guess the number. After each guess, the computer tells the player if it was too high or too low.

The Program in Action

When you run *guess.py*, the output will look like this:

```
Guess the Number, by Al Sweigart al@inventwithpython.com

I am thinking of a number between 1 and 100.
You have 10 guesses left. Take a guess.
> 50
Your guess is too high.
You have 9 guesses left. Take a guess.
> 25
Your guess is too low.
--snip--
You have 5 guesses left. Take a guess.
> 42
Yay! You guessed my number!
```

How It Works

Guess the Number uses several basic programming concepts: loops, if-else statements, functions, method calls, and random numbers. Python's random module generates pseudorandom numbers—numbers that look random but are technically predictable. Pseudorandom numbers are easier for computers to generate than truly random numbers, and they're considered "random enough" for applications such as video games and some scientific simulations.

Python's random module produces pseudorandom numbers from a seed value, and each stream of pseudorandom numbers generated from the same seed will be the same. For example, enter the following into the interactive shell:

```
>>> import random
>>> random.seed(42)
>>> random.randint(1, 10); random.randint(1, 10); random.randint(1, 10)
2
1
5
```

If you restart the interactive shell and run this code again, it produces the same pseudorandom numbers: 2, 1, 5. The video game *Minecraft* generates its pseudorandom virtual worlds from a starting seed value, which is why different players can re-create the same world by using the same seed.

```
1. """Guess the Number, by Al Sweigart al@inventwithpython.com
2. Try to guess the secret number based on hints.
3. View this code at https://nostarch.com/big-book-small-python-projects
4. Tags: tiny, beginner, game"""
5.
6. import random
7.
```

```
 8.
 9. def askForGuess():
10.     while True:
11.         guess = input('> ')  # Enter the guess.
12.
13.         if guess.isdecimal():
14.             return int(guess)  # Convert string guess to an integer.
15.         print('Please enter a number between 1 and 100.')
16.
17.
18. print('Guess the Number, by Al Sweigart al@inventwithpython.com')
19. print()
20. secretNumber = random.randint(1, 100)  # Select a random number.
21. print('I am thinking of a number between 1 and 100.')
22.
23. for i in range(10):  # Give the player 10 guesses.
24.     print('You have {} guesses left. Take a guess.'.format(10 - i))
25.
26.     guess = askForGuess()
27.     if guess == secretNumber:
28.         break  # Break out of the for loop if the guess is correct.
29.
30.     # Offer a hint:
31.     if guess < secretNumber:
32.         print('Your guess is too low.')
33.     if guess > secretNumber:
34.         print('Your guess is too high.')
35.
36. # Reveal the results:
37. if guess == secretNumber:
38.     print('Yay! You guessed my number!')
39. else:
40.     print('Game over. The number I was thinking of was', secretNumber)
```

After entering the source code and running it a few times, try making experimental changes to it. On your own, you can also try to figure out how to do the following:

- Create a "Guess the Letter" variant that gives hints based on the alphabetical order of the player's guess.
- Make the hints after each guess say "warmer" or "colder" based on the player's previous guess.

Exploring the Program

Try to find the answers to the following questions. Experiment with some modifications to the code and rerun the program to see what effect the changes have.

1. What happens if you change input('> ') on line 11 to input(secretNumber)?
2. What error message do you get if you change return int(guess) on line 14 to return guess?

3. What happens if you change `random.randint(1, 100)` on line 20 to `random.randint(1, 1)`?

4. What happens if you change `format(10 - i)` on line 24 to `format(i)`?

5. What error message do you get if you change `guess == secretNumber` on line 37 to `guess = secretNumber`?

#32

GULLIBLE

In this short and simple program, you can learn the secret and subtle art of keeping a gullible person busy for hours. I won't spoil the punch line here. Copy the code and run it for yourself. This project is great for beginners, whether you're smart or . . . not so smart.

The Program in Action

When you run *gullible.py*, the output will look like this:

```
Gullible, by Al Sweigart al@inventwithpython.com
Do you want to know how to keep a gullible person busy for hours? Y/N
> y
Do you want to know how to keep a gullible person busy for hours? Y/N
> y
Do you want to know how to keep a gullible person busy for hours? Y/N
> yes
Do you want to know how to keep a gullible person busy for hours? Y/N
> YES
Do you want to know how to keep a gullible person busy for hours? Y/N
> TELL ME HOW TO KEEP A GULLIBLE PERSON BUSY FOR HOURS
"TELL ME HOW TO KEEP A GULLIBLE PERSON BUSY FOR HOURS" is not a valid yes/no
response.
Do you want to know how to keep a gullible person busy for hours? Y/N
> y
Do you want to know how to keep a gullible person busy for hours? Y/N
> y
Do you want to know how to keep a gullible person busy for hours? Y/N
> n
Thank you. Have a nice day!
```

How It Works

To be more user friendly, your programs should attempt to interpret a range of possible inputs from the user. For example, this program asks the user a yes/no question, but it would be simpler for the player to simply enter "y" or "n" instead of enter the full word. The program can also understand the player's intent if their CAPS LOCK key is activated, because it calls the lower() string method on the string the player entered. This way, 'y', 'yes', 'Y', 'Yes', and 'YES', are all interpreted the same by the program. The same goes for a negative response from the player.

```
1. """Gullible, by Al Sweigart al@inventwithpython.com
2. How to keep a gullible person busy for hours. (This is a joke program.)
3. View this code at https://nostarch.com/big-book-small-python-projects
4. Tags: tiny, beginner, humor"""
5.
6. print('Gullible, by Al Sweigart al@inventwithpython.com')
7.
8. while True:  # Main program loop.
9.     print('Do you want to know how to keep a gullible person busy for
       hours? Y/N')
10.    response = input('> ')  # Get the user's response.
11.    if response.lower() == 'no' or response.lower() == 'n':
12.        break  # If "no", break out of this loop.
13.    if response.lower() == 'yes' or response.lower() == 'y':
14.        continue  # If "yes", continue to the start of this loop.
```

```
15.        print('"{}" is not a valid yes/no response.'.format(response))
16.
17. print('Thank you. Have a nice day!')
```

Exploring the Program

Try to find the answers to the following questions. Experiment with some modifications to the code and rerun the program to see what effect the changes have.

1. What happens if you change `response.lower() == 'no'` on line 11 to `response.lower() != 'no'`?

2. What happens if you change `while True:` on line 8 to `while False:`?

#33

HACKING MINIGAME

In this game, the player must hack a computer by guessing a seven-letter word used as the secret password. The computer's memory banks display the possible words, and the player is given hints as to how close each guess was. For example, if the secret password is MONITOR but the player guessed CONTAIN, they are given the hint that two out of seven letters were correct, because both MONITOR and CONTAIN have the letter *O* and *N* as their second and third letter. This game is similar to Project 1, "Bagels," and the hacking minigame in the *Fallout* series of video games.

The Program in Action

When you run *hacking.py*, the output will look like this:

```
Hacking Minigame, by Al Sweigart al@inventwithpython.com
Find the password in the computer's memory:
0x1150  $],>@|~~RESOLVE^      0x1250  {>+)<!?CHICKEN,%
0x1160  }@%_-:;/$^(|<|!(      0x1260  .][}}?#@#ADDRESS
0x1170  _;)][#?<&~$~+&}}      0x1270  ,#=)>{-;/DESPITE
0x1180  %[!]{REFUGEE@?~,      0x1280  }/.}!-DISPLAY%%/
0x1190  _[^%[@}^<_+{_@$~      0x1290  =>>,:*%?_?@+{%#.
0x11a0  )?~/)+PENALTY?-=      0x12a0  >[,?*#IMPROVE@$/
--snip--
Enter password: (4 tries remaining)
> resolve
Access Denied (2/7 correct)
Enter password: (3 tries remaining)
> improve
A C C E S S   G R A N T E D
```

How It Works

This game has a hacking theme, but it doesn't involve any actual computer hacking. If we'd just listed the possible words on the screen, the gameplay would have been identical. However, the cosmetic additions that mimic a computer's memory banks convey an exciting feeling of computer hacking. The attention to detail and user experience turn a plain, boring game into an exciting one.

```
 1. """Hacking Minigame, by Al Sweigart al@inventwithpython.com
 2. The hacking mini-game from "Fallout 3". Find out which seven-letter
 3. word is the password by using clues each guess gives you.
 4. View this code at https://nostarch.com/big-book-small-python-projects
 5. Tags: large, artistic, game, puzzle"""
 6.
 7. # NOTE: This program requires the sevenletterwords.txt file. You can
 8. # download it from https://inventwithpython.com/sevenletterwords.txt
 9.
10. import random, sys
11.
12. # Set up the constants:
13. # The garbage filler characters for the "computer memory" display.
14. GARBAGE_CHARS = '~!@#$%^&*()_+-={}[]|;:,.<>?/'
15.
16. # Load the WORDS list from a text file that has 7-letter words.
17. with open('sevenletterwords.txt') as wordListFile:
18.     WORDS = wordListFile.readlines()
19. for i in range(len(WORDS)):
20.     # Convert each word to uppercase and remove the trailing newline:
21.     WORDS[i] = WORDS[i].strip().upper()
22.
23.
```

```
24. def main():
25.     """Run a single game of Hacking."""
26.     print('''Hacking Minigame, by Al Sweigart al@inventwithpython.com
27. Find the password in the computer's memory. You are given clues after
28. each guess. For example, if the secret password is MONITOR but the
29. player guessed CONTAIN, they are given the hint that 2 out of 7 letters
30. were correct, because both MONITOR and CONTAIN have the letter O and N
31. as their 2nd and 3rd letter. You get four guesses.\n''')
32.     input('Press Enter to begin...')
33.
34.     gameWords = getWords()
35.     # The "computer memory" is just cosmetic, but it looks cool:
36.     computerMemory = getComputerMemoryString(gameWords)
37.     secretPassword = random.choice(gameWords)
38.
39.     print(computerMemory)
40.     # Start at 4 tries remaining, going down:
41.     for triesRemaining in range(4, 0, -1):
42.         playerMove = askForPlayerGuess(gameWords, triesRemaining)
43.         if playerMove == secretPassword:
44.             print('A C C E S S   G R A N T E D')
45.             return
46.         else:
47.             numMatches = numMatchingLetters(secretPassword, playerMove)
48.             print('Access Denied ({}/7 correct)'.format(numMatches))
49.     print('Out of tries. Secret password was {}.'.format(secretPassword))
50.
51.
52. def getWords():
53.     """Return a list of 12 words that could possibly be the password.
54.
55.     The secret password will be the first word in the list.
56.     To make the game fair, we try to ensure that there are words with
57.     a range of matching numbers of letters as the secret word."""
58.     secretPassword = random.choice(WORDS)
59.     words = [secretPassword]
60.
61.     # Find two more words; these have zero matching letters.
62.     # We use "< 3" because the secret password is already in words.
63.     while len(words) < 3:
64.         randomWord = getOneWordExcept(words)
65.         if numMatchingLetters(secretPassword, randomWord) == 0:
66.             words.append(randomWord)
67.
68.     # Find two words that have 3 matching letters (but give up at 500
69.     # tries if not enough can be found).
70.     for i in range(500):
71.         if len(words) == 5:
72.             break  # Found 5 words, so break out of the loop.
73.
74.         randomWord = getOneWordExcept(words)
75.         if numMatchingLetters(secretPassword, randomWord) == 3:
76.             words.append(randomWord)
77.
```

```
78.      # Find at least seven words that have at least one matching letter
79.      # (but give up at 500 tries if not enough can be found).
80.      for i in range(500):
81.          if len(words) == 12:
82.              break  # Found 7 or more words, so break out of the loop.
83.
84.          randomWord = getOneWordExcept(words)
85.          if numMatchingLetters(secretPassword, randomWord) != 0:
86.              words.append(randomWord)
87.
88.      # Add any random words needed to get 12 words total.
89.      while len(words) < 12:
90.          randomWord = getOneWordExcept(words)
91.          words.append(randomWord)
92.
93.      assert len(words) == 12
94.      return words
95.
96.
97. def getOneWordExcept(blocklist=None):
98.      """Returns a random word from WORDS that isn't in blocklist."""
99.      if blocklist == None:
100.         blocklist = []
101.
102.     while True:
103.         randomWord = random.choice(WORDS)
104.         if randomWord not in blocklist:
105.             return randomWord
106.
107.
108. def numMatchingLetters(word1, word2):
109.      """Returns the number of matching letters in these two words."""
110.      matches = 0
111.      for i in range(len(word1)):
112.          if word1[i] == word2[i]:
113.              matches += 1
114.      return matches
115.
116.
117. def getComputerMemoryString(words):
118.      """Return a string representing the "computer memory"."""
119.
120.      # Pick one line per word to contain a word. There are 16 lines, but
121.      # they are split into two halves.
122.      linesWithWords = random.sample(range(16 * 2), len(words))
123.      # The starting memory address (this is also cosmetic).
124.      memoryAddress = 16 * random.randint(0, 4000)
125.
126.      # Create the "computer memory" string.
127.      computerMemory = []  # Will contain 16 strings, one for each line.
128.      nextWord = 0  # The index in words of the word to put into a line.
129.      for lineNum in range(16):  # The "computer memory" has 16 lines.
130.          # Create a half line of garbage characters:
```

```
131.          leftHalf = ''
132.          rightHalf = ''
133.          for j in range(16):  # Each half line has 16 characters.
134.              leftHalf += random.choice(GARBAGE_CHARS)
135.              rightHalf += random.choice(GARBAGE_CHARS)
136.
137.          # Fill in the password from words:
138.          if lineNum in linesWithWords:
139.              # Find a random place in the half line to insert the word:
140.              insertionIndex = random.randint(0, 9)
141.              # Insert the word:
142.              leftHalf = (leftHalf[:insertionIndex] + words[nextWord]
143.                  + leftHalf[insertionIndex + 7:])
144.              nextWord += 1  # Update the word to put in the half line.
145.          if lineNum + 16 in linesWithWords:
146.              # Find a random place in the half line to insert the word:
147.              insertionIndex = random.randint(0, 9)
148.              # Insert the word:
149.              rightHalf = (rightHalf[:insertionIndex] + words[nextWord]
150.                  + rightHalf[insertionIndex + 7:])
151.              nextWord += 1  # Update the word to put in the half line.
152.
153.          computerMemory.append('0x' + hex(memoryAddress)[2:].zfill(4)
154.                          + ' ' + leftHalf + '    '
155.                          + '0x' + hex(memoryAddress + (16*16))[2:].zfill(4)
156.                          + ' ' + rightHalf)
157.
158.          memoryAddress += 16  # Jump from, say, 0xe680 to 0xe690.
159.
160.      # Each string in the computerMemory list is joined into one large
161.      # string to return:
162.      return '\n'.join(computerMemory)
163.
164.
165. def askForPlayerGuess(words, tries):
166.      """Let the player enter a password guess."""
167.      while True:
168.          print('Enter password: ({} tries remaining)'.format(tries))
169.          guess = input('> ').upper()
170.          if guess in words:
171.              return guess
172.          print('That is not one of the possible passwords listed above.')
173.          print('Try entering "{}" or "{}".'.format(words[0], words[1]))
174.
175.
176. # If this program was run (instead of imported), run the game:
177. if __name__ == '__main__':
178.      try:
179.          main()
180.      except KeyboardInterrupt:
181.          sys.exit()  # When Ctrl-C is pressed, end the program.
```

After entering the source code and running it a few times, try making experimental changes to it. On your own, you can also try to figure out how to do the following:

- Find a word list on the internet and create your own *sevenletterwords.txt* file, maybe one with six- or eight-letter words.
- Create a different visualization of the "computer memory."

Exploring the Program

Try to find the answers to the following questions. Experiment with some modifications to the code and rerun the program to see what effect the changes have.

1. What happens if you change `for j in range(16):` on line 133 to `for j in range(0):`?

2. What happens if you change `GARBAGE_CHARS = '~!@#$%^&*()_+-={}[]|;:,.<>?/'` on line 14 to `GARBAGE_CHARS = '.'`?

3. What happens if you change `gameWords = getWords()` on line 34 to `gameWords = ['MALKOVICH'] * 20`?

4. What error message do you get if you change `return words` on line 94 to `return`?

5. What happens if you change `randomWord = random.choice(WORDS)` on line 103 to `secretPassword = 'PASSWORD'`?

#34

HANGMAN AND GUILLOTINE

This classic word game has the player guess the letters to a secret word. For each incorrect letter, another part of the hangman is drawn. Try to guess the complete word before the hangman completes. The secret words in this version are all animals like RABBIT and PIGEON, but you can replace these with your own set of words.

The HANGMAN_PICS variable contains ASCII-art strings of each step of the hangman's noose:

```
+--+     +--+     +--+     +--+     +--+     +--+     +--+
|  |     |  |     |  |     |  |     |  |     |  |     |  |
|        0  |     0  |     0  |     0  |     0  |     0  |
|        |        |  |     /|  |    /|\ |    /|\ |    /|\ |
|        |        |        |        |        /   |    / \ |
|        |        |        |        |        |        |
=====    =====    =====    =====    =====    =====    =====
```

For a French twist on the game, you can replace the strings in the HANGMAN_PICS variable with the following strings depicting a guillotine:

```
|       |   |   |===|   |===|   |===|   |===|   |===|
|       |   |   |   |   |   |   |   |   || /|   || /|
|       |   |   |   |   |   |   |   |   ||/ |   ||/ |
|       |   |   |   |   |   |   |   |   |   |   |   |
|       |   |   |   |   |   |   |   |   |   |   |   |
|       |   |   |   |   |   |   |/-\|   |/-\|   |/-\|
|       |   |   |   |   |\ /|   |\ /|   |\ /|   |\0/|
|===   |===|   |===|   |===|   |===|   |===|   |===|
```

The Program in Action

When you run *hangman.py*, the output will look like this:

```
Hangman, by Al Sweigart al@inventwithpython.com

  +--+
  |  |
     |
     |
     |
     |
=====
The category is: Animals

Missed letters: No missed letters yet.


_ _ _ _ _
Guess a letter.
> e
--snip--
  +--+
  |  |
  0  |
 /|  |
     |
     |
=====
The category is: Animals

Missed letters: A I S
O T T E _
Guess a letter.
> r
Yes! The secret word is: OTTER
You have won!
```

How It Works

Hangman and Guillotine share the same game mechanics but have different presentations. This makes it easy to swap out the ASCII-art noose graphics with the ASCII-art guillotine graphics without having to change the main logic that the program follows. This separation of the presentation and logic parts of the program makes it easier to update with new features or different designs. In professional software development, this strategy is an example of a *software design pattern* or *software architecture*, which concerns itself with how to structure your programs for easy understanding and modification. This is mainly useful in large software applications, but you can also apply these principles to smaller projects.

```
1. """Hangman, by Al Sweigart al@inventwithpython.com
2. Guess the letters to a secret word before the hangman is drawn.
3. View this code at https://nostarch.com/big-book-small-python-projects
4. Tags: large, game, word, puzzle"""
5.
6. # A version of this game is featured in the book "Invent Your Own
7. # Computer Games with Python" https://nostarch.com/inventwithpython
8.
9. import random, sys
10.
11. # Set up the constants:
12. # (!) Try adding or changing the strings in HANGMAN_PICS to make a
13. # guillotine instead of a gallows.
14. HANGMAN_PICS = [r"""
15.  +--+
16.  |  |
17.     |
18.     |
19.     |
20.     |
21. ====="""",
22. r"""
23.  +--+
24.  |  |
25.  O  |
26.     |
27.     |
28.     |
29. ====="""",
30. r"""
31.  +--+
32.  |  |
33.  O  |
34.  |  |
35.     |
36.     |
37. ====="""",
38. r"""
39.  +--+
40.  |  |
41.  O  |
```

```
42. /|   |
43.    |
44.    |
45. ====="""",
46. r"""
47.  +--+
48.  |  |
49.  O  |
50. /|\ |
51.    |
52.    |
53. ====="""",
54. r"""
55.  +--+
56.  |  |
57.  O  |
58. /|\ |
59. /   |
60.    |
61. ====="""",
62. r"""
63.  +--+
64.  |  |
65.  O  |
66. /|\ |
67. / \ |
68.    |
69. =====""""]
70.
71. # (!) Try replacing CATEGORY and WORDS with new strings.
72. CATEGORY = 'Animals'
73. WORDS = 'ANT BABOON BADGER BAT BEAR BEAVER CAMEL CAT CLAM COBRA COUGAR
    COYOTE CROW DEER DOG DONKEY DUCK EAGLE FERRET FOX FROG GOAT GOOSE HAWK
    LION LIZARD LLAMA MOLE MONKEY MOOSE MOUSE MULE NEWT OTTER OWL PANDA PARROT
    PIGEON PYTHON RABBIT RAM RAT RAVEN RHINO SALMON SEAL SHARK SHEEP SKUNK
    SLOTH SNAKE SPIDER STORK SWAN TIGER TOAD TROUT TURKEY TURTLE WEASEL WHALE
    WOLF WOMBAT ZEBRA'.split()
74.
75.
76. def main():
77.     print('Hangman, by Al Sweigart al@inventwithpython.com')
78.
79.     # Setup variables for a new game:
80.     missedLetters = []  # List of incorrect letter guesses.
81.     correctLetters = [] # List of correct letter guesses.
82.     secretWord = random.choice(WORDS)  # The word the player must guess.
83.
84.     while True:  # Main game loop.
85.         drawHangman(missedLetters, correctLetters, secretWord)
86.
87.         # Let the player enter their letter guess:
88.         guess = getPlayerGuess(missedLetters + correctLetters)
89.
90.         if guess in secretWord:
91.             # Add the correct guess to correctLetters:
```

```
92.                 correctLetters.append(guess)
93.
94.             # Check if the player has won:
95.             foundAllLetters = True  # Start off assuming they've won.
96.             for secretWordLetter in secretWord:
97.                 if secretWordLetter not in correctLetters:
98.                     # There's a letter in the secret word that isn't
99.                     # yet in correctLetters, so the player hasn't won:
100.                    foundAllLetters = False
101.                    break
102.            if foundAllLetters:
103.                print('Yes! The secret word is:', secretWord)
104.                print('You have won!')
105.                break  # Break out of the main game loop.
106.        else:
107.            # The player has guessed incorrectly:
108.            missedLetters.append(guess)
109.
110.            # Check if player has guessed too many times and lost. (The
111.            # "- 1" is because we don't count the empty gallows in
112.            # HANGMAN_PICS.)
113.            if len(missedLetters) == len(HANGMAN_PICS) - 1:
114.                drawHangman(missedLetters, correctLetters, secretWord)
115.                print('You have run out of guesses!')
116.                print('The word was "{}"'.format(secretWord))
117.                break
118.
119.
120. def drawHangman(missedLetters, correctLetters, secretWord):
121.     """Draw the current state of the hangman, along with the missed and
122.     correctly-guessed letters of the secret word."""
123.     print(HANGMAN_PICS[len(missedLetters)])
124.     print('The category is:', CATEGORY)
125.     print()
126.
127.     # Show the incorrectly guessed letters:
128.     print('Missed letters: ', end='')
129.     for letter in missedLetters:
130.         print(letter, end=' ')
131.     if len(missedLetters) == 0:
132.         print('No missed letters yet.')
133.     print()
134.
135.     # Display the blanks for the secret word (one blank per letter):
136.     blanks = ['_'] * len(secretWord)
137.
138.     # Replace blanks with correctly guessed letters:
139.     for i in range(len(secretWord)):
140.         if secretWord[i] in correctLetters:
141.             blanks[i] = secretWord[i]
142.
143.     # Show the secret word with spaces in between each letter:
144.     print(' '.join(blanks))
145.
146.
```

```
147. def getPlayerGuess(alreadyGuessed):
148.     """Returns the letter the player entered. This function makes sure
149.     the player entered a single letter they haven't guessed before."""
150.     while True:  # Keep asking until the player enters a valid letter.
151.         print('Guess a letter.')
152.         guess = input('> ').upper()
153.         if len(guess) != 1:
154.             print('Please enter a single letter.')
155.         elif guess in alreadyGuessed:
156.             print('You have already guessed that letter. Choose again.')
157.         elif not guess.isalpha():
158.             print('Please enter a LETTER.')
159.         else:
160.             return guess
161.
162.
163. # If this program was run (instead of imported), run the game:
164. if __name__ == '__main__':
165.     try:
166.         main()
167.     except KeyboardInterrupt:
168.         sys.exit()  # When Ctrl-C is pressed, end the program.
```

After entering the source code and running it a few times, try making experimental changes to it. The comments marked with (!) have suggestions for small changes you can make. On your own, you can also try to figure out how to do the following:

- Add a "category select" feature and let the player choose what category of words they want to play.

- Add a selection feature so the player can choose between the hangman and guillotine versions of the game.

Exploring the Program

Try to find the answers to the following questions. Experiment with some modifications to the code and rerun the program to see what effect the changes have.

1. What happens if you delete or comment out missedLetters.append(guess) on line 108?

2. What happens if you change drawHangman(missedLetters, correctLetters, secretWord) on line 85 to drawHangman(correctLetters, missedLetters, secretWord)?

3. What happens if you change ['_'] on line 136 to ['*']?

4. What happens if you change print(' '.join(blanks)) on line 144 to print(secretWord)?

#35

HEX GRID

This short program produces a tessellated image of a hexagonal grid, similar to chicken wire. It shows that you don't need a lot of code to make something interesting. A slightly more complicated variation of this program is Project 65, "Shining Carpet."

Note that this program uses raw strings, which prefix the opening quote with a lowercase r so that the backslashes in the string aren't interpreted as escape characters.

The Program in Action

Figure 35-1 shows what the output will look like when you run *hexgrid.py*.

Figure 35-1: Output showing a tessellated image of a hexagonal grid

How It Works

The power behind programming is that it can make a computer carry out repetitive instructions quickly and without mistakes. This is how a dozen lines of code can create hundreds, thousands, or millions of hexagons on the screen.

In the Command Prompt or Terminal window, you can redirect a program's output from the screen to a text file. On Windows, run `py hexgrid.py > hextiles.txt` to create a text file that contains the hexagons. On Linux and macOS, run `python3 hexgrid.py > hextiles.txt`. Without the size of the screen as a limit, you can increase the X_REPEAT and Y_REPEAT constants and save the contents to a file. From there, it's easy to print the file on paper, send it in an email, or post it to social media. This applies to any computer-generated artwork you create.

```
1. """Hex Grid, by Al Sweigart al@inventwithpython.com
2. Displays a simple tessellation of a hexagon grid.
3. View this code at https://nostarch.com/big-book-small-python-projects
4. Tags: tiny, beginner, artistic"""
5.
6. # Set up the constants:
7. # (!) Try changing these values to other numbers:
8. X_REPEAT = 19  # How many times to tessellate horizontally.
9. Y_REPEAT = 12  # How many times to tessellate vertically.
10.
```

```
11. for y in range(Y_REPEAT):
12.     # Display the top half of the hexagon:
13.     for x in range(X_REPEAT):
14.         print(r'/ \_', end='')
15.     print()
16.
17.     # Display the bottom half of the hexagon:
18.     for x in range(X_REPEAT):
19.         print(r'\_/ ', end='')
20.     print()
```

After entering the source code and running it a few times, try making experimental changes to it. The comments marked with (!) have suggestions for small changes you can make. On your own, you can also try to figure out how to do the following:

- Create tiled hexagons of a larger size.
- Create tiled rectangular bricks instead of hexagons.

For practice, try re-creating this program with larger hexagon grids, such as the following patterns:

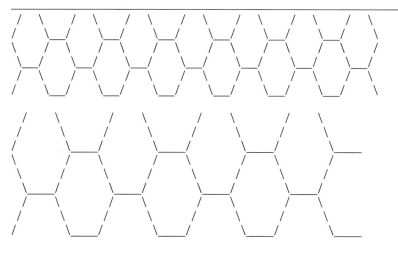

Exploring the Program

This is a base program, so there aren't many options to customize it. Instead, consider how you could similarly program patterns of other shapes.

#36

HOURGLASS

 This visualization program has a rough physics engine that simulates sand falling through the small aperture of an hourglass. The sand piles up in the bottom half of the hourglass; then the hourglass is turned over so the process repeats.

The Program in Action

Figure 36-1 shows what the output will look like when you run *hourglass.py.*

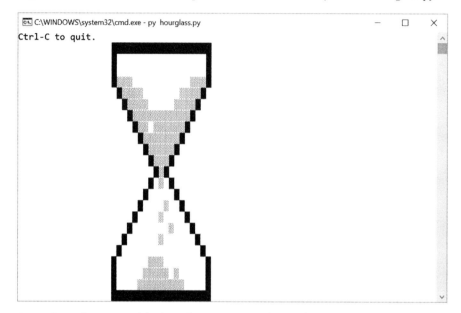

Figure 36-1: The output of the hourglass program with sand falling

How It Works

The hourglass program implements a rudimentary physics engine. A *physics engine* is software that simulates physical objects falling under gravity, colliding with each other, and moving according to the laws of physics. You'll find physics engines used in video games, computer animation, and scientific simulations. On lines 91 to 102, each "grain" of sand checks if the space beneath it is empty and moves down if it is. Otherwise, it checks if it can move down and to the left (lines 104 to 112) or down and to the right (lines 114 to 122). Of course, there is much more to *kinematics*, the branch of classical physics that deals with the motion of macroscopic objects, than this. However, you don't need a degree in physics to make a primitive simulation of sand in an hourglass that is enjoyable to look at.

```
 1. """Hourglass, by Al Sweigart al@inventwithpython.com
 2. An animation of an hourglass with falling sand. Press Ctrl-C to stop.
 3. View this code at https://nostarch.com/big-book-small-python-projects
 4. Tags: large, artistic, bext, simulation"""
 5.
 6. import random, sys, time
 7.
 8. try:
 9.     import bext
10. except ImportError:
11.     print('This program requires the bext module, which you')
```

```
12.        print('can install by following the instructions at')
13.        print('https://pypi.org/project/Bext/')
14.        sys.exit()
15.
16. # Set up the constants:
17. PAUSE_LENGTH = 0.2  # (!) Try changing this to 0.0 or 1.0.
18. # (!) Try changing this to any number between 0 and 100:
19. WIDE_FALL_CHANCE = 50
20.
21. SCREEN_WIDTH = 79
22. SCREEN_HEIGHT = 25
23. X = 0  # The index of X values in an (x, y) tuple is 0.
24. Y = 1  # The index of Y values in an (x, y) tuple is 1.
25. SAND = chr(9617)
26. WALL = chr(9608)
27.
28. # Set up the walls of the hourglass:
29. HOURGLASS = set()  # Has (x, y) tuples for where hourglass walls are.
30. # (!) Try commenting out some HOURGLASS.add() lines to erase walls:
31. for i in range(18, 37):
32.        HOURGLASS.add((i, 1))  # Add walls for the top cap of the hourglass.
33.        HOURGLASS.add((i, 23))  # Add walls for the bottom cap.
34. for i in range(1, 5):
35.        HOURGLASS.add((18, i))  # Add walls for the top left straight wall.
36.        HOURGLASS.add((36, i))  # Add walls for the top right straight wall.
37.        HOURGLASS.add((18, i + 19))  # Add walls for the bottom left.
38.        HOURGLASS.add((36, i + 19))  # Add walls for the bottom right.
39. for i in range(8):
40.        HOURGLASS.add((19 + i, 5 + i))  # Add the top left slanted wall.
41.        HOURGLASS.add((35 - i, 5 + i))  # Add the top right slanted wall.
42.        HOURGLASS.add((25 - i, 13 + i))  # Add the bottom left slanted wall.
43.        HOURGLASS.add((29 + i, 13 + i))  # Add the bottom right slanted wall.
44.
45. # Set up the initial sand at the top of the hourglass:
46. INITIAL_SAND = set()
47. for y in range(8):
48.        for x in range(19 + y, 36 - y):
49.            INITIAL_SAND.add((x, y + 4))
50.
51.
52. def main():
53.        bext.fg('yellow')
54.        bext.clear()
55.
56.        # Draw the quit message:
57.        bext.goto(0, 0)
58.        print('Ctrl-C to quit.', end='')
59.
60.        # Display the walls of the hourglass:
61.        for wall in HOURGLASS:
62.            bext.goto(wall[X], wall[Y])
63.            print(WALL, end='')
64.
65.        while True:  # Main program loop.
66.            allSand = list(INITIAL_SAND)
```

```
67.
68.            # Draw the initial sand:
69.            for sand in allSand:
70.                bext.goto(sand[X], sand[Y])
71.                print(SAND, end='')
72.
73.            runHourglassSimulation(allSand)
74.
75.
76.  def runHourglassSimulation(allSand):
77.      """Keep running the sand falling simulation until the sand stops
78.      moving."""
79.      while True:  # Keep looping until sand has run out.
80.          random.shuffle(allSand)  # Random order of grain simulation.
81.
82.          sandMovedOnThisStep = False
83.          for i, sand in enumerate(allSand):
84.              if sand[Y] == SCREEN_HEIGHT - 1:
85.                  # Sand is on the very bottom, so it won't move:
86.                  continue
87.
88.              # If nothing is under this sand, move it down:
89.              noSandBelow = (sand[X], sand[Y] + 1) not in allSand
90.              noWallBelow = (sand[X], sand[Y] + 1) not in HOURGLASS
91.              canFallDown = noSandBelow and noWallBelow
92.
93.              if canFallDown:
94.                  # Draw the sand in its new position down one space:
95.                  bext.goto(sand[X], sand[Y])
96.                  print(' ', end='')  # Clear the old position.
97.                  bext.goto(sand[X], sand[Y] + 1)
98.                  print(SAND, end='')
99.
100.                 # Set the sand in its new position down one space:
101.                 allSand[i] = (sand[X], sand[Y] + 1)
102.                 sandMovedOnThisStep = True
103.             else:
104.                 # Check if the sand can fall to the left:
105.                 belowLeft = (sand[X] - 1, sand[Y] + 1)
106.                 noSandBelowLeft = belowLeft not in allSand
107.                 noWallBelowLeft = belowLeft not in HOURGLASS
108.                 left = (sand[X] - 1, sand[Y])
109.                 noWallLeft = left not in HOURGLASS
110.                 notOnLeftEdge = sand[X] > 0
111.                 canFallLeft = (noSandBelowLeft and noWallBelowLeft
112.                     and noWallLeft and notOnLeftEdge)
113.
114.                 # Check if the sand can fall to the right:
115.                 belowRight = (sand[X] + 1, sand[Y] + 1)
116.                 noSandBelowRight = belowRight not in allSand
117.                 noWallBelowRight = belowRight not in HOURGLASS
118.                 right = (sand[X] + 1, sand[Y])
119.                 noWallRight = right not in HOURGLASS
120.                 notOnRightEdge = sand[X] < SCREEN_WIDTH - 1
121.                 canFallRight = (noSandBelowRight and noWallBelowRight
```

```
122.                         and noWallRight and notOnRightEdge)
123.
124.                 # Set the falling direction:
125.                 fallingDirection = None
126.                 if canFallLeft and not canFallRight:
127.                     fallingDirection = -1  # Set the sand to fall left.
128.                 elif not canFallLeft and canFallRight:
129.                     fallingDirection = 1  # Set the sand to fall right.
130.                 elif canFallLeft and canFallRight:
131.                     # Both are possible, so randomly set it:
132.                     fallingDirection = random.choice((-1, 1))
133.
134.                 # Check if the sand can "far" fall two spaces to
135.                 # the left or right instead of just one space:
136.                 if random.random() * 100 <= WIDE_FALL_CHANCE:
137.                     belowTwoLeft = (sand[X] - 2, sand[Y] + 1)
138.                     noSandBelowTwoLeft = belowTwoLeft not in allSand
139.                     noWallBelowTwoLeft = belowTwoLeft not in HOURGLASS
140.                     notOnSecondToLeftEdge = sand[X] > 1
141.                     canFallTwoLeft = (canFallLeft and noSandBelowTwoLeft
142.                         and noWallBelowTwoLeft and notOnSecondToLeftEdge)
143.
144.                     belowTwoRight = (sand[X] + 2, sand[Y] + 1)
145.                     noSandBelowTwoRight = belowTwoRight not in allSand
146.                     noWallBelowTwoRight = belowTwoRight not in HOURGLASS
147.                     notOnSecondToRightEdge = sand[X] < SCREEN_WIDTH - 2
148.                     canFallTwoRight = (canFallRight
149.                         and noSandBelowTwoRight and noWallBelowTwoRight
150.                         and notOnSecondToRightEdge)
151.
152.                     if canFallTwoLeft and not canFallTwoRight:
153.                         fallingDirection = -2
154.                     elif not canFallTwoLeft and canFallTwoRight:
155.                         fallingDirection = 2
156.                     elif canFallTwoLeft and canFallTwoRight:
157.                         fallingDirection = random.choice((-2, 2))
158.
159.                 if fallingDirection == None:
160.                     # This sand can't fall, so move on.
161.                     continue
162.
163.                 # Draw the sand in its new position:
164.                 bext.goto(sand[X], sand[Y])
165.                 print(' ', end='')  # Erase old sand.
166.                 bext.goto(sand[X] + fallingDirection, sand[Y] + 1)
167.                 print(SAND, end='')  # Draw new sand.
168.
169.                 # Move the grain of sand to its new position:
170.                 allSand[i] = (sand[X] + fallingDirection, sand[Y] + 1)
171.                 sandMovedOnThisStep = True
172.
173.         sys.stdout.flush()  # (Required for bext-using programs.)
174.         time.sleep(PAUSE_LENGTH)  # Pause after this
175.
176.         # If no sand has moved on this step, reset the hourglass:
```

```
177.        if not sandMovedOnThisStep:
178.            time.sleep(2)
179.            # Erase all of the sand:
180.            for sand in allSand:
181.                bext.goto(sand[X], sand[Y])
182.                print(' ', end='')
183.            break  # Break out of main simulation loop.
184.
185.
186. # If this program was run (instead of imported), run the game:
187. if __name__ == '__main__':
188.     try:
189.         main()
190.     except KeyboardInterrupt:
191.         sys.exit()  # When Ctrl-C is pressed, end the program.
```

After entering the source code and running it a few times, try making experimental changes to it. The comments marked with (!) have suggestions for small changes you can make. On your own, you can also try to figure out how to do the following:

- Create wall shapes other than an hourglass.
- Create points on the screen that continuously pour out new grains of sand.

Exploring the Program

Try to find the answers to the following questions. Experiment with some modifications to the code and rerun the program to see what effect the changes have.

1. What happens if you change range(18, 37) on line 31 to range(18, 30)?
2. What happens if you change range(8) on line 39 to range(0)?
3. What happens if you change sandMovedOnThisStep = False on line 82 to sandMovedOnThisStep = True?
4. What happens if you change fallingDirection = None on line 125 to fallingDirection = 1?
5. What happens if you change random.random() * 100 <= WIDE_FALL_CHANCE on line 136 to random.random() * 0 <= WIDE_FALL_CHANCE?

#37

HUNGRY ROBOTS

You are trapped in a maze with hungry robots! You don't know why robots need to eat, but you don't want to find out. The robots are badly programmed and will move directly toward you, even if blocked by walls. You must trick the robots into crashing into each other (or dead robots) without being caught.

You have a personal teleporter device that can send you to a random new place, but it only has enough battery for two trips. Also, you and the robots can slip through corners!

The Program in Action

When you run *hungryrobots.py*, the output will look like this:

```
Hungry Robots, by Al Sweigart al@inventwithpython.com
--snip--
```

```
(T)eleports remaining: 2
                    (Q) (W) ( )
                    (A) (S) (D)
Enter move or QUIT: (Z) (X) ( )
--snip--
```

How It Works

The x- and y- Cartesian coordinates that represent positions in this game allow us to use math to determine the direction in which the robots should move. In programming, x-coordinates increase going right, and y-coordinates increase going down. This means that if the robot's x-coordinate is larger than the player's coordinate, it should move left (that is, the code should subtract from its current x-coordinate) to move closer to the player. If the robot's x-coordinate is smaller, it should move right (that is, the code should add to its current x-coordinate) instead. The same applies to moving up and down based on their relative y-coordinates.

```
1. """Hungry Robots, by Al Sweigart al@inventwithpython.com
2. Escape the hungry robots by making them crash into each other.
3. View this code at https://nostarch.com/big-book-small-python-projects
4. Tags: large, game"""
5.
6. import random, sys
7.
8. # Set up the constants:
```

```
 9. WIDTH = 40            # (!) Try changing this to 70 or 10.
10. HEIGHT = 20           # (!) Try changing this to 10.
11. NUM_ROBOTS = 10       # (!) Try changing this to 1 or 30.
12. NUM_TELEPORTS = 2     # (!) Try changing this to 0 or 9999.
13. NUM_DEAD_ROBOTS = 2   # (!) Try changing this to 0 or 20.
14. NUM_WALLS = 100       # (!) Try changing this to 0 or 1000.
15.
16. EMPTY_SPACE = ' '     # (!) Try changing this to '.'.
17. PLAYER = '@'          # (!) Try changing this to 'R'.
18. ROBOT = 'R'           # (!) Try changing this to '@'.
19. DEAD_ROBOT = 'X'      # (!) Try changing this to 'R'.
20.
21. # (!) Try changing this to '#' or 'O' or ' ':
22. WALL = chr(9617)  # Character 9617 is '░'
23.
24.
25. def main():
26.     print('''Hungry Robots, by Al Sweigart al@inventwithpython.com
27.
28. You are trapped in a maze with hungry robots! You don't know why robots
29. need to eat, but you don't want to find out. The robots are badly
30. programmed and will move directly toward you, even if blocked by walls.
31. You must trick the robots into crashing into each other (or dead robots)
32. without being caught. You have a personal teleporter device, but it only
33. has enough battery for {} trips. Keep in mind, you and robots can slip
34. through the corners of two diagonal walls!
35. '''.format(NUM_TELEPORTS))
36.
37.     input('Press Enter to begin...')
38.
39.     # Set up a new game:
40.     board = getNewBoard()
41.     robots = addRobots(board)
42.     playerPosition = getRandomEmptySpace(board, robots)
43.     while True:  # Main game loop.
44.         displayBoard(board, robots, playerPosition)
45.
46.         if len(robots) == 0:  # Check if the player has won.
47.             print('All the robots have crashed into each other and you')
48.             print('lived to tell the tale! Good job!')
49.             sys.exit()
50.
51.         # Move the player and robots:
52.         playerPosition = askForPlayerMove(board, robots, playerPosition)
53.         robots = moveRobots(board, robots, playerPosition)
54.
55.         for x, y in robots:  # Check if the player has lost.
56.             if (x, y) == playerPosition:
57.                 displayBoard(board, robots, playerPosition)
58.                 print('You have been caught by a robot!')
59.                 sys.exit()
60.
61.
62. def getNewBoard():
63.     """Returns a dictionary that represents the board. The keys are
```

```
64.     (x, y) tuples of integer indexes for board positions, the values are
65.     WALL, EMPTY_SPACE, or DEAD_ROBOT. The dictionary also has the key
66.     'teleports' for the number of teleports the player has left.
67.     The living robots are stored separately from the board dictionary."""
68.     board = {'teleports': NUM_TELEPORTS}
69.
70.     # Create an empty board:
71.     for x in range(WIDTH):
72.         for y in range(HEIGHT):
73.             board[(x, y)] = EMPTY_SPACE
74.
75.     # Add walls on the edges of the board:
76.     for x in range(WIDTH):
77.         board[(x, 0)] = WALL  # Make top wall.
78.         board[(x, HEIGHT - 1)] = WALL  # Make bottom wall.
79.     for y in range(HEIGHT):
80.         board[(0, y)] = WALL  # Make left wall.
81.         board[(WIDTH - 1, y)] = WALL  # Make right wall.
82.
83.     # Add the random walls:
84.     for i in range(NUM_WALLS):
85.         x, y = getRandomEmptySpace(board, [])
86.         board[(x, y)] = WALL
87.
88.     # Add the starting dead robots:
89.     for i in range(NUM_DEAD_ROBOTS):
90.         x, y = getRandomEmptySpace(board, [])
91.         board[(x, y)] = DEAD_ROBOT
92.     return board
93.
94.
95. def getRandomEmptySpace(board, robots):
96.     """Return a (x, y) integer tuple of an empty space on the board."""
97.     while True:
98.         randomX = random.randint(1, WIDTH - 2)
99.         randomY = random.randint(1, HEIGHT - 2)
100.        if isEmpty(randomX, randomY, board, robots):
101.            break
102.    return (randomX, randomY)
103.
104.
105. def isEmpty(x, y, board, robots):
106.     """Return True if the (x, y) is empty on the board and there's also
107.     no robot there."""
108.     return board[(x, y)] == EMPTY_SPACE and (x, y) not in robots
109.
110.
111. def addRobots(board):
112.     """Add NUM_ROBOTS number of robots to empty spaces on the board and
113.     return a list of these (x, y) spaces where robots are now located."""
114.     robots = []
115.     for i in range(NUM_ROBOTS):
116.         x, y = getRandomEmptySpace(board, robots)
117.         robots.append((x, y))
118.     return robots
```

```
119.
120.
121. def displayBoard(board, robots, playerPosition):
122.     """Display the board, robots, and player on the screen."""
123.     # Loop over every space on the board:
124.     for y in range(HEIGHT):
125.         for x in range(WIDTH):
126.             # Draw the appropriate character:
127.             if board[(x, y)] == WALL:
128.                 print(WALL, end='')
129.             elif board[(x, y)] == DEAD_ROBOT:
130.                 print(DEAD_ROBOT, end='')
131.             elif (x, y) == playerPosition:
132.                 print(PLAYER, end='')
133.             elif (x, y) in robots:
134.                 print(ROBOT, end='')
135.             else:
136.                 print(EMPTY_SPACE, end='')
137.         print()  # Print a newline.
138.
139.
140. def askForPlayerMove(board, robots, playerPosition):
141.     """Returns the (x, y) integer tuple of the place the player moves
142.     next, given their current location and the walls of the board."""
143.     playerX, playerY = playerPosition
144.
145.     # Find which directions aren't blocked by a wall:
146.     q = 'Q' if isEmpty(playerX - 1, playerY - 1, board, robots) else ' '
147.     w = 'W' if isEmpty(playerX + 0, playerY - 1, board, robots) else ' '
148.     e = 'E' if isEmpty(playerX + 1, playerY - 1, board, robots) else ' '
149.     d = 'D' if isEmpty(playerX + 1, playerY + 0, board, robots) else ' '
150.     c = 'C' if isEmpty(playerX + 1, playerY + 1, board, robots) else ' '
151.     x = 'X' if isEmpty(playerX + 0, playerY + 1, board, robots) else ' '
152.     z = 'Z' if isEmpty(playerX - 1, playerY + 1, board, robots) else ' '
153.     a = 'A' if isEmpty(playerX - 1, playerY + 0, board, robots) else ' '
154.     allMoves = (q + w + e + d + c + x + a + z + 'S')
155.
156.     while True:
157.         # Get player's move:
158.         print('(T)eleports remaining: {}'.format(board["teleports"]))
159.         print('                       ({}) ({}) ({})'.format(q, w, e))
160.         print('                       ({}) (S) ({})'.format(a, d))
161.         print('Enter move or QUIT: ({}) ({}) ({})'.format(z, x, c))
162.
163.         move = input('> ').upper()
164.         if move == 'QUIT':
165.             print('Thanks for playing!')
166.             sys.exit()
167.         elif move == 'T' and board['teleports'] > 0:
168.             # Teleport the player to a random empty space:
169.             board['teleports'] -= 1
170.             return getRandomEmptySpace(board, robots)
171.         elif move != '' and move in allMoves:
172.             # Return the new player position based on their move:
173.             return {'Q': (playerX - 1, playerY - 1),
```

```
174.                           'W': (playerX + 0, playerY - 1),
175.                           'E': (playerX + 1, playerY - 1),
176.                           'D': (playerX + 1, playerY + 0),
177.                           'C': (playerX + 1, playerY + 1),
178.                           'X': (playerX + 0, playerY + 1),
179.                           'Z': (playerX - 1, playerY + 1),
180.                           'A': (playerX - 1, playerY + 0),
181.                           'S': (playerX, playerY)}[move]
182.
183.
184. def moveRobots(board, robotPositions, playerPosition):
185.     """Return a list of (x, y) tuples of new robot positions after they
186.     have tried to move toward the player."""
187.     playerx, playery = playerPosition
188.     nextRobotPositions = []
189.
190.     while len(robotPositions) > 0:
191.         robotx, roboty = robotPositions[0]
192.
193.         # Determine the direction the robot moves.
194.         if robotx < playerx:
195.             movex = 1  # Move right.
196.         elif robotx > playerx:
197.             movex = -1  # Move left.
198.         elif robotx == playerx:
199.             movex = 0  # Don't move horizontally.
200.
201.         if roboty < playery:
202.             movey = 1  # Move up.
203.         elif roboty > playery:
204.             movey = -1  # Move down.
205.         elif roboty == playery:
206.             movey = 0  # Don't move vertically.
207.
208.         # Check if the robot would run into a wall, and adjust course:
209.         if board[(robotx + movex, roboty + movey)] == WALL:
210.             # Robot would run into a wall, so come up with a new move:
211.             if board[(robotx + movex, roboty)] == EMPTY_SPACE:
212.                 movey = 0  # Robot can't move horizontally.
213.             elif board[(robotx, roboty + movey)] == EMPTY_SPACE:
214.                 movex = 0  # Robot can't move vertically.
215.             else:
216.                 # Robot can't move.
217.                 movex = 0
218.                 movey = 0
219.         newRobotx = robotx + movex
220.         newRoboty = roboty + movey
221.
222.         if (board[(robotx, roboty)] == DEAD_ROBOT
223.             or board[(newRobotx, newRoboty)] == DEAD_ROBOT):
224.             # Robot is at a crash site, remove it.
225.             del robotPositions[0]
226.             continue
227.
228.         # Check if it moves into a robot, then destroy both robots:
```

```
229.         if (newRobotx, newRoboty) in nextRobotPositions:
230.             board[(newRobotx, newRoboty)] = DEAD_ROBOT
231.             nextRobotPositions.remove((newRobotx, newRoboty))
232.         else:
233.             nextRobotPositions.append((newRobotx, newRoboty))
234.
235.         # Remove robots from robotPositions as they move.
236.         del robotPositions[0]
237.     return nextRobotPositions
238.
239.
240. # If this program was run (instead of imported), run the game:
241. if __name__ == '__main__':
242.     main()
```

After entering the source code and running it a few times, try making experimental changes to it. The comments marked with (!) have suggestions for small changes you can make. On your own, you can also try to figure out how to do the following:

- Create two different kinds of robots: those that can only move diagonally and those that can only move in cardinal directions.
- Give the player a limited number of traps they can leave behind to stop any robot that steps on one.
- Give the player a limited number of "instant walls" that they can put up for their own defense.

Exploring the Program

Try to find the answers to the following questions. Experiment with some modifications to the code and rerun the program to see what effect the changes have.

1. What happens if you change WALL = chr(9617) on line 22 to WALL = 'R'?
2. What happens if you change return nextRobotPositions on line 237 to return robotPositions?
3. What happens if you delete or comment out displayBoard(board, robots, playerPosition) on line 44?
4. What happens if you delete or comment out robots = moveRobots(board, robots, playerPosition) on line 53?

#38

J'ACCUSE!

You are the world-famous detective Mathilde Camus. Zophie the cat has gone missing, and you must sift through the clues. Suspects either always tell lies or always tell the truth. Will you find Zophie the cat in time and accuse the guilty party?

In this game, you take a taxi to different locations around the city. At each location is a suspect and an item. You can ask suspects about other suspects and items, compare their answers with your own exploration notes, and determine if they are lying or telling the truth. Some will know who has catnapped Zophie (or where she is, or what item is found at the location of the kidnapper), but you must determine if you can believe them. You have five minutes to find the criminal but will lose if you make three wrong accusations. This game is inspired by Homestar Runner's "Where's an Egg?" game.

The Program in Action

When you run *jaccuse.py*, the output will look like this:

```
J'ACCUSE! (a mystery game)
--snip--
Time left: 5 min, 0 sec
  You are in your TAXI. Where do you want to go?
(A)LBINO ALLIGATOR PIT
(B)OWLING ALLEY
(C)ITY HALL
(D)UCK POND
(H)IPSTER CAFE
(O)LD BARN
(U)NIVERSITY LIBRARY
(V)IDEO GAME MUSEUM
(Z)OO
> a

Time left: 4 min, 48 sec
  You are at the ALBINO ALLIGATOR PIT.
  ESPRESSA TOFFEEPOT with the ONE COWBOY BOOT is here.

(J) "J'ACCUSE!" (3 accusations left)
(Z) Ask if they know where ZOPHIE THE CAT is.
(T) Go back to the TAXI.
(1) Ask about ESPRESSA TOFFEEPOT
(2) Ask about ONE COWBOY BOOT
> z
  They give you this clue: "DUKE HAUTDOG"
Press Enter to continue...
--snip--
```

How It Works

To fully understand this program, you should pay close attention to the clues dictionary, which is set up on lines 51 to 109. You can uncomment lines 151 to 154 to display it on the screen. This dictionary has strings from the SUSPECTS list for the keys and "clue dictionaries" for the values. Each of these clue dictionaries contains strings from SUSPECTS and ITEMS. The original suspect will answer with these strings when asked about another suspect or item. For example, if clues['DUKE HAUTDOG']['CANDLESTICK'] is set to 'DUCK POND', then when the player asks Duke Hautdog about the Candlestick, they'll say it is at the Duck Pond. The suspects, items, locations, and culprit get shuffled each time the game is played.

The code for this program revolves around this data structure, so understanding it is necessary to unlocking your understanding of the rest of the program.

1. """J'ACCUSE!, by Al Sweigart al@inventwithpython.com
2. A mystery game of intrigue and a missing cat.
3. View this code at https://nostarch.com/big-book-small-python-projects

```
 4.    Tags: extra-large, game, humor, puzzle"""
 5.
 6. # Play the original Flash game at:
 7. # https://homestarrunner.com/videlectrix/wheresanegg.html
 8. # More info at: http://www.hrwiki.org/wiki/Where's_an_Egg%3F
 9.
10. import time, random, sys
11.
12. # Set up the constants:
13. SUSPECTS = ['DUKE HAUTDOG', 'MAXIMUM POWERS', 'BILL MONOPOLIS', 'SENATOR SCHMEAR',
    'MRS. FEATHERTOSS', 'DR. JEAN SPLICER', 'RAFFLES THE CLOWN', 'ESPRESSA TOFFEEPOT',
    'CECIL EDGAR VANDERTON']
14. ITEMS = ['FLASHLIGHT', 'CANDLESTICK', 'RAINBOW FLAG', 'HAMSTER WHEEL', 'ANIME VHS TAPE',
    'JAR OF PICKLES', 'ONE COWBOY BOOT', 'CLEAN UNDERPANTS', '5 DOLLAR GIFT CARD']
15. PLACES = ['ZOO', 'OLD BARN', 'DUCK POND', 'CITY HALL', 'HIPSTER CAFE', 'BOWLING ALLEY',
    'VIDEO GAME MUSEUM', 'UNIVERSITY LIBRARY', 'ALBINO ALLIGATOR PIT']
16. TIME_TO_SOLVE = 300  # 300 seconds (5 minutes) to solve the game.
17.
18. # First letters and longest length of places are needed for menu display:
19. PLACE_FIRST_LETTERS = {}
20. LONGEST_PLACE_NAME_LENGTH = 0
21. for place in PLACES:
22.     PLACE_FIRST_LETTERS[place[0]] = place
23.     if len(place) > LONGEST_PLACE_NAME_LENGTH:
24.         LONGEST_PLACE_NAME_LENGTH = len(place)
25.
26. # Basic sanity checks of the constants:
27. assert len(SUSPECTS) == 9
28. assert len(ITEMS) == 9
29. assert len(PLACES) == 9
30. # First letters must be unique:
31. assert len(PLACE_FIRST_LETTERS.keys()) == len(PLACES)
32.
33.
34. knownSuspectsAndItems = []
35. # visitedPlaces: Keys=places, values=strings of the suspect & item there.
36. visitedPlaces = {}
37. currentLocation = 'TAXI'  # Start the game at the taxi.
38. accusedSuspects = []  # Accused suspects won't offer clues.
39. liars = random.sample(SUSPECTS, random.randint(3, 4))
40. accusationsLeft = 3  # You can accuse up to 3 people.
41. culprit = random.choice(SUSPECTS)
42.
43. # Common indexes link these; e.g. SUSPECTS[0] and ITEMS[0] are at PLACES[0].
44. random.shuffle(SUSPECTS)
45. random.shuffle(ITEMS)
46. random.shuffle(PLACES)
47.
48. # Create data structures for clues the truth-tellers give about each
49. # item and suspect.
50. # clues: Keys=suspects being asked for a clue, value="clue dictionary".
51. clues = {}
52. for i, interviewee in enumerate(SUSPECTS):
53.     if interviewee in liars:
54.         continue  # Skip the liars for now.
```

```
55.
56.    # This "clue dictionary" has keys=items & suspects,
57.    # value=the clue given.
58.    clues[interviewee] = {}
59.    clues[interviewee]['debug_liar'] = False  # Useful for debugging.
60.    for item in ITEMS:  # Select clue about each item.
61.        if random.randint(0, 1) == 0:  # Tells where the item is:
62.            clues[interviewee][item] = PLACES[ITEMS.index(item)]
63.        else:  # Tells who has the item:
64.            clues[interviewee][item] = SUSPECTS[ITEMS.index(item)]
65.    for suspect in SUSPECTS:  # Select clue about each suspect.
66.        if random.randint(0, 1) == 0:  # Tells where the suspect is:
67.            clues[interviewee][suspect] = PLACES[SUSPECTS.index(suspect)]
68.        else:  # Tells what item the suspect has:
69.            clues[interviewee][suspect] = ITEMS[SUSPECTS.index(suspect)]
70.
71. # Create data structures for clues the liars give about each item
72. # and suspect:
73. for i, interviewee in enumerate(SUSPECTS):
74.    if interviewee not in liars:
75.        continue  # We've already handled the truth-tellers.
76.
77.    # This "clue dictionary" has keys=items & suspects,
78.    # value=the clue given:
79.    clues[interviewee] = {}
80.    clues[interviewee]['debug_liar'] = True  # Useful for debugging.
81.
82.    # This interviewee is a liar and gives wrong clues:
83.    for item in ITEMS:
84.        if random.randint(0, 1) == 0:
85.            while True:  # Select a random (wrong) place clue.
86.                # Lies about where the item is.
87.                clues[interviewee][item] = random.choice(PLACES)
88.                if clues[interviewee][item] != PLACES[ITEMS.index(item)]:
89.                    # Break out of the loop when wrong clue is selected.
90.                    break
91.        else:
92.            while True:  # Select a random (wrong) suspect clue.
93.                clues[interviewee][item] = random.choice(SUSPECTS)
94.                if clues[interviewee][item] != SUSPECTS[ITEMS.index(item)]:
95.                    # Break out of the loop when wrong clue is selected.
96.                    break
97.    for suspect in SUSPECTS:
98.        if random.randint(0, 1) == 0:
99.            while True:  # Select a random (wrong) place clue.
100.                clues[interviewee][suspect] = random.choice(PLACES)
101.                if clues[interviewee][suspect] != PLACES[ITEMS.index(item)]:
102.                    # Break out of the loop when wrong clue is selected.
103.                    break
104.        else:
105.            while True:  # Select a random (wrong) item clue.
106.                clues[interviewee][suspect] = random.choice(ITEMS)
107.                if clues[interviewee][suspect] != ITEMS[SUSPECTS.index(suspect)]:
108.                    # Break out of the loop when wrong clue is selected.
109.                    break
```

```
110.
111. # Create the data structures for clues given when asked about Zophie:
112. zophieClues = {}
113. for interviewee in random.sample(SUSPECTS, random.randint(3, 4)):
114.     kindOfClue = random.randint(1, 3)
115.     if kindOfClue == 1:
116.         if interviewee not in liars:
117.             # They tell you who has Zophie.
118.             zophieClues[interviewee] = culprit
119.         elif interviewee in liars:
120.             while True:
121.                 # Select a (wrong) suspect clue.
122.                 zophieClues[interviewee] = random.choice(SUSPECTS)
123.                 if zophieClues[interviewee] != culprit:
124.                     # Break out of the loop when wrong clue is selected.
125.                     break
126.
127.     elif kindOfClue == 2:
128.         if interviewee not in liars:
129.             # They tell you where Zophie is.
130.             zophieClues[interviewee] = PLACES[SUSPECTS.index(culprit)]
131.         elif interviewee in liars:
132.             while True:
133.                 # Select a (wrong) place clue.
134.                 zophieClues[interviewee] = random.choice(PLACES)
135.                 if zophieClues[interviewee] != PLACES[SUSPECTS.index(culprit)]:
136.                     # Break out of the loop when wrong clue is selected.
137.                     break
138.     elif kindOfClue == 3:
139.         if interviewee not in liars:
140.             # They tell you what item Zophie is near.
141.             zophieClues[interviewee] = ITEMS[SUSPECTS.index(culprit)]
142.         elif interviewee in liars:
143.             while True:
144.                 # Select a (wrong) item clue.
145.                 zophieClues[interviewee] = random.choice(ITEMS)
146.                 if zophieClues[interviewee] != ITEMS[SUSPECTS.index(culprit)]:
147.                     # Break out of the loop when wrong clue is selected.
148.                     break
149.
150. # EXPERIMENT: Uncomment this code to view the clue data structures:
151. #import pprint
152. #pprint.pprint(clues)
153. #pprint.pprint(zophieClues)
154. #print('culprit =', culprit)
155.
156. # START OF THE GAME
157. print("""J'ACCUSE! (a mystery game)")
158. By Al Sweigart al@inventwithpython.com
159. Inspired by Homestar Runner\'s "Where\'s an Egg?" game
160.
161. You are the world-famous detective Mathilde Camus.
162. ZOPHIE THE CAT has gone missing, and you must sift through the clues.
163. Suspects either always tell lies, or always tell the truth. Ask them
164. about other people, places, and items to see if the details they give are
```

```
165. truthful and consistent with your observations. Then you will know if
166. their clue about ZOPHIE THE CAT is true or not. Will you find ZOPHIE THE
167. CAT in time and accuse the guilty party?
168. """)
169. input('Press Enter to begin...')
170.
171.
172. startTime = time.time()
173. endTime = startTime + TIME_TO_SOLVE
174.
175. while True:  # Main game loop.
176.     if time.time() > endTime or accusationsLeft == 0:
177.         # Handle "game over" condition:
178.         if time.time() > endTime:
179.             print('You have run out of time!')
180.         elif accusationsLeft == 0:
181.             print('You have accused too many innocent people!')
182.         culpritIndex = SUSPECTS.index(culprit)
183.         print('It was {} at the {} with the {} who catnapped her!'.format(culprit,
              PLACES[culpritIndex], ITEMS[culpritIndex]))
184.         print('Better luck next time, Detective.')
185.         sys.exit()
186.
187.     print()
188.     minutesLeft = int(endTime - time.time()) // 60
189.     secondsLeft = int(endTime - time.time()) % 60
190.     print('Time left: {} min, {} sec'.format(minutesLeft, secondsLeft))
191.
192.     if currentLocation == 'TAXI':
193.         print('  You are in your TAXI. Where do you want to go?')
194.         for place in sorted(PLACES):
195.             placeInfo = ''
196.             if place in visitedPlaces:
197.                 placeInfo = visitedPlaces[place]
198.             nameLabel = '(' + place[0] + ')' + place[1:]
199.             spacing = " " * (LONGEST_PLACE_NAME_LENGTH - len(place))
200.             print('{} {}{}'.format(nameLabel, spacing, placeInfo))
201.         print('(Q)UIT GAME')
202.         while True:  # Keep asking until a valid response is given.
203.             response = input('> ').upper()
204.             if response == '':
205.                 continue  # Ask again.
206.             if response == 'Q':
207.                 print('Thanks for playing!')
208.                 sys.exit()
209.             if response in PLACE_FIRST_LETTERS.keys():
210.                 break
211.         currentLocation = PLACE_FIRST_LETTERS[response]
212.         continue  # Go back to the start of the main game loop.
213.
214.     # At a place; player can ask for clues.
215.     print('  You are at the {}.'.format(currentLocation))
216.     currentLocationIndex = PLACES.index(currentLocation)
217.     thePersonHere = SUSPECTS[currentLocationIndex]
218.     theItemHere = ITEMS[currentLocationIndex]
```

```
219.        print('  {} with the {} is here.'.format(thePersonHere, theItemHere))
220.
221.        # Add the suspect and item at this place to our list of known
222.        # suspects and items:
223.        if thePersonHere not in knownSuspectsAndItems:
224.            knownSuspectsAndItems.append(thePersonHere)
225.        if ITEMS[currentLocationIndex] not in knownSuspectsAndItems:
226.            knownSuspectsAndItems.append(ITEMS[currentLocationIndex])
227.        if currentLocation not in visitedPlaces.keys():
228.            visitedPlaces[currentLocation] = '({}, {})'.format(thePersonHere.lower(),
                 theItemHere.lower())
229.
230.        # If the player has accused this person wrongly before, they
231.        # won't give clues:
232.        if thePersonHere in accusedSuspects:
233.            print('They are offended that you accused them,')
234.            print('and will not help with your investigation.')
235.            print('You go back to your TAXI.')
236.            print()
237.            input('Press Enter to continue...')
238.            currentLocation = 'TAXI'
239.            continue  # Go back to the start of the main game loop.
240.
241.        # Display menu of known suspects & items to ask about:
242.        print()
243.        print('(J) "J\'ACCUSE!" ({} accusations left)'.format(accusationsLeft))
244.        print('(Z) Ask if they know where ZOPHIE THE CAT is.')
245.        print('(T) Go back to the TAXI.')
246.        for i, suspectOrItem in enumerate(knownSuspectsAndItems):
247.            print('({}) Ask about {}'.format(i + 1, suspectOrItem))
248.
249.        while True:  # Keep asking until a valid response is given.
250.            response = input('> ').upper()
251.            if response in 'JZT' or (response.isdecimal() and 0 < int(response) <=
                 len(knownSuspectsAndItems)):
252.                break
253.
254.        if response == 'J':  # Player accuses this suspect.
255.            accusationsLeft -= 1  # Use up an accusation.
256.            if thePersonHere == culprit:
257.                # You've accused the correct suspect.
258.                print('You\'ve cracked the case, Detective!')
259.                print('It was {} who had catnapped ZOPHIE THE CAT.'.format(culprit))
260.                minutesTaken = int(time.time() - startTime) // 60
261.                secondsTaken = int(time.time() - startTime) % 60
262.                print('Good job! You solved it in {} min, {} sec.'.format(minutesTaken,
                     secondsTaken))
263.                sys.exit()
264.            else:
265.                # You've accused the wrong suspect.
266.                accusedSuspects.append(thePersonHere)
267.                print('You have accused the wrong person, Detective!')
268.                print('They will not help you with anymore clues.')
269.                print('You go back to your TAXI.')
270.                currentLocation = 'TAXI'
```

```
271.
272.    elif response == 'Z':  # Player asks about Zophie.
273.        if thePersonHere not in zophieClues:
274.            print('"I don\'t know anything about ZOPHIE THE CAT."')
275.        elif thePersonHere in zophieClues:
276.            print('  They give you this clue: "{}"'.format(zophieClues[thePersonHere]))
277.            # Add non-place clues to the list of known things:
278.            if zophieClues[thePersonHere] not in knownSuspectsAndItems and
                zophieClues[thePersonHere] not in PLACES:
279.                knownSuspectsAndItems.append(zophieClues[thePersonHere])
280.
281.    elif response == 'T':  # Player goes back to the taxi.
282.        currentLocation = 'TAXI'
283.        continue   # Go back to the start of the main game loop.
284.
285.    else:  # Player asks about a suspect or item.
286.        thingBeingAskedAbout = knownSuspectsAndItems[int(response) - 1]
287.        if thingBeingAskedAbout in (thePersonHere, theItemHere):
288.            print('  They give you this clue: "No comment."')
289.        else:
290.            print('  They give you this clue:
                "{}"'.format(clues[thePersonHere][thingBeingAskedAbout]))
291.            # Add non-place clues to the list of known things:
292.            if clues[thePersonHere][thingBeingAskedAbout] not in knownSuspectsAndItems
                and clues[thePersonHere][thingBeingAskedAbout] not in PLACES:
293.                knownSuspectsAndItems.append(clues[thePersonHere][thingBeingAskedAbout])
294.
295.    input('Press Enter to continue...')
```

Exploring the Program

Try to find the answers to the following questions. Experiment with some modifications to the code and rerun the program to see what effect the changes have.

1. What happens if you change TIME_TO_SOLVE = 300 on line 16 to TIME_TO_SOLVE = 0?

2. What happens if you change time.time() > endTime or accusationsLeft == 0 on line 176 to time.time() > endTime and accusationsLeft == 0?

3. What happens if you change place[1:] on line 198 to place?

4. What happens if you change startTime + TIME_TO_SOLVE on line 173 to startTime * TIME_TO_SOLVE?

#39

LANGTON'S ANT

 Langton's Ant is a cellular automata simulation on a two-dimensional grid, similar to Project 13, "Conway's Game of Life." In the simulation, an "ant" begins on a square that is one of two colors. If the space is the first color, the ant switches it to the second color, turns 90 degrees to the right, and moves forward one space. If the space is the second color, the ant switches it to the first color, turns 90 degrees to the left, and moves forward one space.

Despite the very simple set of rules, the simulation displays complex emergent behavior. Simulations can feature multiple ants in the same space, causing interesting interactions when they cross paths with each other. Langton's Ant was invented by computer scientist Chris Langton in 1986. More information about Langton's Ant can be found at *https://en.wikipedia.org/wiki/Langton%27s_ant*.

The Program in Action

Figure 39-1 shows what the output will look like when you run *langtonsant.py*.

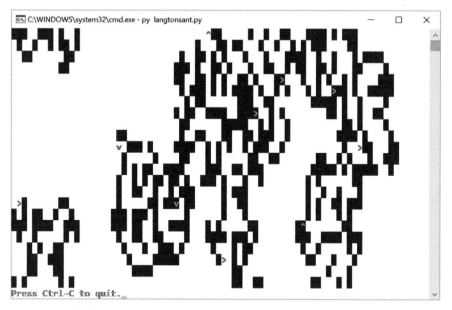

Figure 39-1: The hypnotic output of the Langton's Ant cellular automata

How It Works

This program uses two senses of "direction." On the one hand, the dictionaries that represent each ant store *cardinal directions*: north, south, east, and west. However, turning left or right (or counterclockwise and clockwise, since we are viewing the ants from above) is a *rotational direction*. Ants are supposed to turn left or right in response to the tile they're standing on, so lines 78 to 100 set a new cardinal direction based on the ant's current cardinal direction and the direction they are turning.

```
1. """Langton's Ant, by Al Sweigart al@inventwithpython.com
2. A cellular automata animation. Press Ctrl-C to stop.
3. More info: https://en.wikipedia.org/wiki/Langton%27s_ant
4. View this code at https://nostarch.com/big-book-small-python-projects
5. Tags: large, artistic, bext, simulation"""
6.
7. import copy, random, sys, time
8.
9. try:
10.     import bext
11. except ImportError:
12.     print('This program requires the bext module, which you')
13.     print('can install by following the instructions at')
14.     print('https://pypi.org/project/Bext/')
15.     sys.exit()
16.
```

```
17. # Set up the constants:
18. WIDTH, HEIGHT = bext.size()
19. # We can't print to the last column on Windows without it adding a
20. # newline automatically, so reduce the width by one:
21. WIDTH -= 1
22. HEIGHT -= 1  # Adjustment for the quit message at the bottom.
23.
24. NUMBER_OF_ANTS = 10  # (!) Try changing this to 1 or 50.
25. PAUSE_AMOUNT = 0.1  # (!) Try changing this to 1.0 or 0.0.
26.
27. # (!) Try changing these to make the ants look different:
28. ANT_UP = '^'
29. ANT_DOWN = 'v'
30. ANT_LEFT = '<'
31. ANT_RIGHT = '>'
32.
33. # (!) Try changing these colors to one of 'black', 'red', 'green',
34. # 'yellow', 'blue', 'purple', 'cyan', or 'white'. (These are the only
35. # colors that the bext module supports.)
36. ANT_COLOR = 'red'
37. BLACK_TILE = 'black'
38. WHITE_TILE = 'white'
39.
40. NORTH = 'north'
41. SOUTH = 'south'
42. EAST = 'east'
43. WEST = 'west'
44.
45.
46. def main():
47.     bext.fg(ANT_COLOR)  # The ants' color is the foreground color.
48.     bext.bg(WHITE_TILE)  # Set the background to white to start.
49.     bext.clear()
50.
51.     # Create a new board data structure:
52.     board = {'width': WIDTH, 'height': HEIGHT}
53.
54.     # Create ant data structures:
55.     ants = []
56.     for i in range(NUMBER_OF_ANTS):
57.         ant = {
58.             'x': random.randint(0, WIDTH - 1),
59.             'y': random.randint(0, HEIGHT - 1),
60.             'direction': random.choice([NORTH, SOUTH, EAST, WEST]),
61.         }
62.         ants.append(ant)
63.
64.     # Keep track of which tiles have changed and need to be redrawn on
65.     # the screen:
66.     changedTiles = []
67.
68.     while True:  # Main program loop.
69.         displayBoard(board, ants, changedTiles)
70.         changedTiles = []
71.
```

```
72.        # nextBoard is what the board will look like on the next step in
73.        # the simulation. Start with a copy of the current step's board:
74.        nextBoard = copy.copy(board)
75.
76.        # Run a single simulation step for each ant:
77.        for ant in ants:
78.            if board.get((ant['x'], ant['y']), False) == True:
79.                nextBoard[(ant['x'], ant['y'])] = False
80.                # Turn clockwise:
81.                if ant['direction'] == NORTH:
82.                    ant['direction'] = EAST
83.                elif ant['direction'] == EAST:
84.                    ant['direction'] = SOUTH
85.                elif ant['direction'] == SOUTH:
86.                    ant['direction'] = WEST
87.                elif ant['direction'] == WEST:
88.                    ant['direction'] = NORTH
89.            else:
90.                nextBoard[(ant['x'], ant['y'])] = True
91.                # Turn counter clockwise:
92.                if ant['direction'] == NORTH:
93.                    ant['direction'] = WEST
94.                elif ant['direction'] == WEST:
95.                    ant['direction'] = SOUTH
96.                elif ant['direction'] == SOUTH:
97.                    ant['direction'] = EAST
98.                elif ant['direction'] == EAST:
99.                    ant['direction'] = NORTH
100.            changedTiles.append((ant['x'], ant['y']))
101.
102.            # Move the ant forward in whatever direction it's facing:
103.            if ant['direction'] == NORTH:
104.                ant['y'] -= 1
105.            if ant['direction'] == SOUTH:
106.                ant['y'] += 1
107.            if ant['direction'] == WEST:
108.                ant['x'] -= 1
109.            if ant['direction'] == EAST:
110.                ant['x'] += 1
111.
112.            # If the ant goes past the edge of the screen,
113.            # it should wrap around to other side.
114.            ant['x'] = ant['x'] % WIDTH
115.            ant['y'] = ant['y'] % HEIGHT
116.
117.            changedTiles.append((ant['x'], ant['y']))
118.
119.        board = nextBoard
120.
121.
122. def displayBoard(board, ants, changedTiles):
123.     """Displays the board and ants on the screen. The changedTiles
124.     argument is a list of (x, y) tuples for tiles on the screen that
125.     have changed and need to be redrawn."""
126.
```

```
127.     # Draw the board data structure:
128.     for x, y in changedTiles:
129.         bext.goto(x, y)
130.         if board.get((x, y), False):
131.             bext.bg(BLACK_TILE)
132.         else:
133.             bext.bg(WHITE_TILE)
134.
135.         antIsHere = False
136.         for ant in ants:
137.             if (x, y) == (ant['x'], ant['y']):
138.                 antIsHere = True
139.                 if ant['direction'] == NORTH:
140.                     print(ANT_UP, end='')
141.                 elif ant['direction'] == SOUTH:
142.                     print(ANT_DOWN, end='')
143.                 elif ant['direction'] == EAST:
144.                     print(ANT_LEFT, end='')
145.                 elif ant['direction'] == WEST:
146.                     print(ANT_RIGHT, end='')
147.                 break
148.         if not antIsHere:
149.             print(' ', end='')
150.
151.     # Display the quit message at the bottom of the screen:
152.     bext.goto(0, HEIGHT)
153.     bext.bg(WHITE_TILE)
154.     print('Press Ctrl-C to quit.', end='')
155.
156.     sys.stdout.flush()  # (Required for bext-using programs.)
157.     time.sleep(PAUSE_AMOUNT)
158.
159.
160. # If this program was run (instead of imported), run the game:
161. if __name__ == '__main__':
162.     try:
163.         main()
164.     except KeyboardInterrupt:
165.         print("Langton's Ant, by Al Sweigart al@inventwithpython.com")
166.         sys.exit()  # When Ctrl-C is pressed, end the program.
```

After entering the source code and running it a few times, try making experimental changes to it. The comments marked with (!) have suggestions for small changes you can make. On your own, you can also try to figure out how to do the following:

- Let the player load and save the state of the board's tiles from and to a text file.
- Create additional tile states with new rules of movement and see what behavior emerges.
- Implement some of the ideas suggested in the Wikipedia article for Langton's Ant.

Exploring the Program

Try to find the answers to the following questions. Experiment with some modifications to the code and rerun the program to see what effect the changes have.

1. What happens if you change `print(' ', end='')` on line 149 to `print('.', end='')`?

2. What happens if you change `ant['y'] += 1` on line 106 to `ant['y'] -= 1`?

3. What happens if you change `nextBoard[(ant['x'], ant['y'])] = False` on line 79 to `nextBoard[(ant['x'], ant['y'])] = True`?

4. What happens if you change `WIDTH -= 1` on line 21 to `WIDTH -= 40`?

5. What happens if you change `board = nextBoard` on line 119 to `board = board`?

#40

LEETSPEAK

 There's no better way to demonstrate your mad hacker skills than by replacing letters in your text with numbers: m4d h4x0r 5k1llz!!! This word program automatically converts plain English into leetspeak, the coolest way to talk online. Or at least it was in 1993.

It takes a while to get used to, but with some practice, you'll eventually be able to read leetspeak fluently. For example, 1t +@]<3s 4 w|-|1le +o g37 |_|s3|) 70, b|_|+ y0u (an 3\/3nt|_|/-\11y r3a|) 133t$peak ph1|_|3n+ly. Leetspeak may be hard to read at first, but the program itself is simple and good for beginners. More information about leetspeak can be found at *https://en.wikipedia.org/wiki/Leet*.

The Program in Action

When you run *leetspeak.py*, the output will look like this:

```
L3375P34]< (leetspeek)
By Al Sweigart al@inventwithpython.com

Enter your leet message:
> I am a leet hacker. Fear my mad skills. The 90s were over two decades ago.

! @m a l33t h@(]<er. ph3@r my m4|) $k|ll$. +h3 90s w3r3 Over twO d3(ad3$ 4gO.
(Copied leetspeak to clipboard.)
```

How It Works

The dictionary in the charMapping variable on line 36 maps plain English characters to leetspeak characters. However, since there can be multiple possible leetspeak characters (such as '7' or '+' for the letter 't'), each value in the charMapping dictionary is a list of strings. When creating the new leetspeak string, the program has a 30 percent chance of simply using the character in the original English message and a 70 percent chance of using one of the leetspeak characters. This means the same English message has multiple possible leetspeak translations.

```
 1. """Leetspeak, by Al Sweigart al@inventwithpython.com
 2. Translates English messages into l33t5p34]<.
 3. View this code at https://nostarch.com/big-book-small-python-projects
 4. Tags: tiny, beginner, word"""
 5.
 6. import random
 7.
 8. try:
 9.     import pyperclip  # pyperclip copies text to the clipboard.
10. except ImportError:
11.     pass  # If pyperclip is not installed, do nothing. It's no big deal.
12.
13.
14. def main():
15.     print('''L3375P34]< (leetspeek)
16. By Al Sweigart al@inventwithpython.com
17.
18. Enter your leet message:''')
19.     english = input('> ')
20.     print()
21.     leetspeak = englishToLeetspeak(english)
22.     print(leetspeak)
23.
24.     try:
25.         # Trying to use pyperclip will raise a NameError exception if
26.         # it wasn't imported:
27.         pyperclip.copy(leetspeak)
28.         print('(Copied leetspeak to clipboard.)')
```

```
29.        except NameError:
30.            pass  # Do nothing if pyperclip wasn't installed.
31.
32.
33.  def englishToLeetspeak(message):
34.        """Convert the English string in message and return leetspeak."""
35.        # Make sure all the keys in `charMapping` are lowercase.
36.        charMapping = {
37.        'a': ['4', '@', '/-\\'], 'c': ['('], 'd': ['|)'], 'e': ['3'],
38.        'f': ['ph'], 'h': [']-[', '|-|'], 'i': ['1', '!', '|'], 'k': [']<'],
39.        'o': ['0'], 's': ['$', '5'], 't': ['7', '+'], 'u': ['|_|'],
40.        'v': ['\\/']}
41.        leetspeak = ''
42.        for char in message:  # Check each character:
43.            # There is a 70% chance we change the character to leetspeak.
44.            if char.lower() in charMapping and random.random() <= 0.70:
45.                possibleLeetReplacements = charMapping[char.lower()]
46.                leetReplacement = random.choice(possibleLeetReplacements)
47.                leetspeak = leetspeak + leetReplacement
48.            else:
49.                # Don't translate this character:
50.                leetspeak = leetspeak + char
51.        return leetspeak
52.
53.
54.  # If this program was run (instead of imported), run the game:
55.  if __name__ == '__main__':
56.        main()
```

After entering the source code and running it a few times, try making experimental changes to it. On your own, you can also try to figure out how to do the following:

- Modify the charMapping dictionary so that it supports new leetspeak characters.
- Add a feature that can convert leetspeak back into plain English.

Exploring the Program

Try to find the answers to the following questions. Experiment with some modifications to the code and rerun the program to see what effect the changes have.

1. What happens if you change return leetspeak on line 51 to return message?

2. What happens if you change char.lower() on line 44 to char?

3. What happens if you change char.lower() on line 44 to char.upper()?

4. What happens if you change leetspeak = leetspeak + leetReplacement on line 47 to leetspeak = leetReplacement?

#41

LUCKY STARS

In this push-your-luck game, you roll dice to collect stars. The more you roll, the more stars you can get, but if you get three skulls you lose everything! This quick multiplayer game can support as many players as you want, making it ideal for parties.

On your turn, you pull three random dice from the dice cup and roll them. You can roll Stars, Skulls, and Question Marks. If you end your turn, you get one point per Star. If you choose to roll again, you keep the Question Marks and pull new dice to replace the Stars and Skulls. If you collect three Skulls, you lose all your Stars and end your turn.

When a player gets 13 points, everyone else gets one more turn before the game ends. Whoever has the most points wins.

There are six gold dice, four silver dice, and three bronze dice in the cup. Gold dice have more Stars, bronze dice have more Skulls, and silver is even.

The Program in Action

When you run *luckystars.py*, the output will look like this:

```
Lucky Stars, by Al Sweigart al@inventwithpython.com
--snip--
SCORES: Alice=0, Bob=0
It is Alice's turn.

+-----------+ +-----------+ +-----------+
|           | |     .     | |           |
|           | |    ,0,    | |           |
|     ?     | | 'oo000oo' | |     ?     |
|           | |   `000`   | |           |
|           | |   0' '0   | |           |
+-----------+ +-----------+ +-----------+
     GOLD          GOLD         BRONZE
Stars collected: 1    Skulls collected: 0
Do you want to roll again? Y/N
> y

+-----------+ +-----------+ +-----------+
|     .     | |    ___    | |           |
|    ,0,    | |   /   \   | |           |
| 'oo000oo' | |  |() ()|  | |     ?     |
|   `000`   | |   \ ^ /   | |           |
|   0' '0   | |    VVV    | |           |
+-----------+ +-----------+ +-----------+
     GOLD         BRONZE        BRONZE
Stars collected: 2    Skulls collected: 1
Do you want to roll again? Y/N
--snip--
```

How It Works

The text-based graphics in this program are stored as strings in a list in the STAR_FACE, SKULL_FACE, and QUESTION_FACE variables. This format makes them easy to write in a code editor, while the code in lines 154 to 157 display them on the screen. Note that because three dice are shown together, this code must print each horizontal row of text on a die face at a time. Simply running code like print(STAR_FACE) would result in each of the three dice appearing on top of each other, instead of side by side.

```
1. """Lucky Stars, by Al Sweigart al@inventwithpython.com
2. A "press your luck" game where you roll dice to gather as many stars
3. as possible. You can roll as many times as you want, but if you roll
4. three skulls you lose all your stars.
5.
6. Inspired by the Zombie Dice game from Steve Jackson Games.
7. View this code at https://nostarch.com/big-book-small-python-projects
8. Tags: large, game, multiplayer"""
9.
10. import random
```

```python
11.
12. # Set up the constants:
13. GOLD = 'GOLD'
14. SILVER = 'SILVER'
15. BRONZE = 'BRONZE'
16.
17. STAR_FACE = ["+-----------+",
18.              "|     .     |",
19.              "|    ,0,    |",
20.              "| 'oo00Ooo' |",
21.              "|  `000`    |",
22.              "|   0' 'O   |",
23.              "+-----------+"]
24. SKULL_FACE = ['+-----------+',
25.               '|    ___    |',
26.               '|   / _ \\   |',
27.               '|   |() ()|  |',
28.               '|   \\\\ ^ /   |',
29.               '|    VVV    |',
30.               '+-----------+']
31. QUESTION_FACE = ['+-----------+',
32.                  '|           |',
33.                  '|           |',
34.                  '|     ?     |',
35.                  '|           |',
36.                  '|           |',
37.                  '+-----------+']
38. FACE_WIDTH = 13
39. FACE_HEIGHT = 7
40.
41. print("""Lucky Stars, by Al Sweigart al@inventwithpython.com
42.
43. A "press your luck" game where you roll dice with Stars, Skulls, and
44. Question Marks.
45.
46. On your turn, you pull three random dice from the dice cup and roll
47. them. You can roll Stars, Skulls, and Question Marks. You can end your
48. turn and get one point per Star. If you choose to roll again, you keep
49. the Question Marks and pull new dice to replace the Stars and Skulls.
50. If you collect three Skulls, you lose all your Stars and end your turn.
51.
52. When a player gets 13 points, everyone else gets one more turn before
53. the game ends. Whoever has the most points wins.
54.
55. There are 6 Gold dice, 4 Silver dice, and 3 Bronze dice in the cup.
56. Gold dice have more Stars, Bronze dice have more Skulls, and Silver is
57. even.
58. """)
59.
60. print('How many players are there?')
61. while True:  # Loop until the user enters a number.
62.     response = input('> ')
63.     if response.isdecimal() and int(response) > 1:
64.         numPlayers = int(response)
65.         break
```

```
66.        print('Please enter a number larger than 1.')
67.
68. playerNames = []  # List of strings of player names.
69. playerScores = {}  # Keys are player names, values are integer scores.
70. for i in range(numPlayers):
71.     while True:  # Keep looping until a name is entered.
72.         print('What is player #' + str(i + 1) + '\'s name?')
73.         response = input('> ')
74.         if response != '' and response not in playerNames:
75.             playerNames.append(response)
76.             playerScores[response] = 0
77.             break
78.         print('Please enter a name.')
79. print()
80.
81. turn = 0  # The player at playerNames[0] will go first.
82. # (!) Uncomment to let a player named 'Al' start with three points:
83. #playerScores['Al'] = 3
84. endGameWith = None
85. while True:  # Main game loop.
86.     # Display everyone's score:
87.     print()
88.     print('SCORES: ', end='')
89.     for i, name in enumerate(playerNames):
90.         print(name + ' = ' + str(playerScores[name]), end='')
91.         if i != len(playerNames) - 1:
92.             # All but the last player have commas separating their names.
93.             print(', ', end='')
94.     print('\n')
95.
96.     # Start the number of collected stars and skulls at 0.
97.     stars = 0
98.     skulls = 0
99.     # A cup has 6 gold, 4 silver, and 3 bronze dice:
100.    cup = ([GOLD] * 6) + ([SILVER] * 4) + ([BRONZE] * 3)
101.    hand = []  # Your hand starts with no dice.
102.    print('It is ' + playerNames[turn] + '\'s turn.')
103.    while True:  # Each iteration of this loop is rolling the dice.
104.        print()
105.
106.        # Check that there's enough dice left in the cup:
107.        if (3 - len(hand)) > len(cup):
108.            # End this turn because there are not enough dice:
109.            print('There aren\'t enough dice left in the cup to '
110.                + 'continue ' + playerNames[turn] + '\'s turn.')
111.            break
112.
113.        # Pull dice from the cup until you have 3 in your hand:
114.        random.shuffle(cup)  # Shuffle the dice in the cup.
115.        while len(hand) < 3:
116.            hand.append(cup.pop())
117.
118.        # Roll the dice:
119.        rollResults = []
120.        for dice in hand:
```

```
121.                roll = random.randint(1, 6)
122.            if dice == GOLD:
123.                # Roll a gold die (3 stars, 2 questions, 1 skull):
124.                if 1 <= roll <= 3:
125.                    rollResults.append(STAR_FACE)
126.                    stars += 1
127.                elif 4 <= roll <= 5:
128.                    rollResults.append(QUESTION_FACE)
129.                else:
130.                    rollResults.append(SKULL_FACE)
131.                    skulls += 1
132.            if dice == SILVER:
133.                # Roll a silver die (2 stars, 2 questions, 2 skulls):
134.                if 1 <= roll <= 2:
135.                    rollResults.append(STAR_FACE)
136.                    stars += 1
137.                elif 3 <= roll <= 4:
138.                    rollResults.append(QUESTION_FACE)
139.                else:
140.                    rollResults.append(SKULL_FACE)
141.                    skulls += 1
142.            if dice == BRONZE:
143.                # Roll a bronze die (1 star, 2 questions, 3 skulls):
144.                if roll == 1:
145.                    rollResults.append(STAR_FACE)
146.                    stars += 1
147.                elif 2 <= roll <= 4:
148.                    rollResults.append(QUESTION_FACE)
149.                else:
150.                    rollResults.append(SKULL_FACE)
151.                    skulls += 1
152.
153.        # Display roll results:
154.        for lineNum in range(FACE_HEIGHT):
155.            for diceNum in range(3):
156.                print(rollResults[diceNum][lineNum] + ' ', end='')
157.            print()  # Print a newline.
158.
159.        # Display the type of dice each one is (gold, silver, bronze):
160.        for diceType in hand:
161.            print(diceType.center(FACE_WIDTH) + ' ', end='')
162.        print()  # Print a newline.
163.
164.        print('Stars collected:', stars, '  Skulls collected:', skulls)
165.
166.        # Check if they've collected 3 or more skulls:
167.        if skulls >= 3:
168.            print('3 or more skulls means you\'ve lost your stars!')
169.            input('Press Enter to continue...')
170.            break
171.
172.        print(playerNames[turn] + ', do you want to roll again? Y/N')
173.        while True:  # Keep asking the player until they enter Y or N:
174.            response = input('> ').upper()
175.            if response != '' and response[0] in ('Y', 'N'):
```

```
176.                    break
177.               print('Please enter Yes or No.')
178.
179.          if response.startswith('N'):
180.              print(playerNames[turn], 'got', stars, 'stars!')
181.              # Add stars to this player's point total:
182.              playerScores[playerNames[turn]] += stars
183.
184.              # Check if they've reached 13 or more points:
185.              # (!) Try changing this to 5 or 50 points.
186.              if (endGameWith == None
187.                  and playerScores[playerNames[turn]] >= 13):
188.                  # Since this player reached 13 points, play one more
189.                  # round for all other players:
190.                  print('\n\n' + ('!' * 60))
191.                  print(playerNames[turn] + ' has reached 13 points!!!')
192.                  print('Everyone else will get one more turn!')
193.                  print(('!' * 60) + '\n\n')
194.                  endGameWith = playerNames[turn]
195.              input('Press Enter to continue...')
196.              break
197.
198.          # Discard the stars and skulls, but keep the question marks:
199.          nextHand = []
200.          for i in range(3):
201.              if rollResults[i] == QUESTION_FACE:
202.                  nextHand.append(hand[i])  # Keep the question marks.
203.          hand = nextHand
204.
205.      # Move on to the next player's turn:
206.      turn = (turn + 1) % numPlayers
207.
208.      # If the game has ended, break out of this loop:
209.      if endGameWith == playerNames[turn]:
210.          break  # End the game.
211.
212. print('The game has ended...')
213.
214. # Display everyone's score:
215. print()
216. print('SCORES: ', end='')
217. for i, name in enumerate(playerNames):
218.     print(name + ' = ' + str(playerScores[name]), end='')
219.     if i != len(playerNames) - 1:
220.         # All but the last player have commas separating their names.
221.         print(', ', end='')
222. print('\n')
223.
224. # Find out who the winners are:
225. highestScore = 0
226. winners = []
227. for name, score in playerScores.items():
228.     if score > highestScore:
229.         # This player has the highest score:
230.         highestScore = score
```

```
231.         winners = [name]  # Overwrite any previous winners.
232.     elif score == highestScore:
233.         # This player is tied with the highest score.
234.         winners.append(name)
235.
236. if len(winners) == 1:
237.     # There is only one winner:
238.     print('The winner is ' + winners[0] + '!!!')
239. else:
240.     # There are multiple tied winners:
241.     print('The winners are: ' + ', '.join(winners))
242.
243. print('Thanks for playing!')
```

After entering the source code and running it a few times, try making experimental changes to it. The comments marked with (!) have suggestions for small changes you can make.

Exploring the Program

Try to find the answers to the following questions. Experiment with some modifications to the code and rerun the program to see what effect the changes have.

1. What happens if you delete or comment out random.shuffle(cup) on line 114?
2. What happens if you change skulls >= 3 on line 167 to skulls > 3?
3. What error message do you get if you change (turn + 1) % numPlayers on line 206 to (turn + 1)?
4. What happens if you change endGameWith = None on line 84 to endGameWith = playerNames[0]?
5. What happens if you delete or comment out break on line 170?
6. What happens if you change playerScores[response] = 0 on line 76 to playerScores[response] = 10?

#42

MAGIC FORTUNE BALL

The Magic Fortune Ball can predict the future and answer your yes/no questions with 100 percent accuracy using the power of Python's random number module. This program is similar to a Magic 8 Ball toy, except you don't have to shake it. It also features a function for slowly printing text strings with spaces in between each character, giving the messages a spooky, mysterious effect.

Most of the code is dedicated to setting the eerie atmosphere. The program itself simply selects a message to display in response to a random number.

The Program in Action

When you run *magicfortuneball.py*, the output will look like this:

```
M A G i C   F O R T U N E   B A L L ,   B Y   A L   S W E i G A R T

A S K   M E   Y O U R   Y E S / N O   Q U E S T i O N .

> Isn't fortune telling just a scam to trick money out of gullible people?
L E T   M E   T H i N K   O N   T H i S . . .


. . . . . . . .

i   H A V E   A N   A N S W E R . . .

A F F i R M A T i V E
```

How It Works

The only thing the Magic Fortune Ball actually does is display a randomly chosen string. It completely ignores the user's question. Sure, line 28 calls input('> '), but it doesn't store the return value in any variable because the program doesn't actually use this text. Letting users enter their questions gives them the sense that the program has an aura of clairvoyance.

The slowSpacePrint() function displays the uppercase text with any letter *I* in lowercase, making the message look unique. The function also inserts spaces between each character of the string and then displays them slowly, with pauses. A program doesn't need to be sophisticated enough to predict the future to be fun!

```
1. """Magic Fortune Ball, by Al Sweigart al@inventwithpython.com
2. Ask a yes/no question about your future. Inspired by the Magic 8 Ball.
3. View this code at https://nostarch.com/big-book-small-python-projects
4. Tags: tiny, beginner, humor"""
5.
6. import random, time
7.
8.
9. def slowSpacePrint(text, interval=0.1):
10.     """Slowly display text with spaces in between each letter and
11.     lowercase letter i's."""
12.     for character in text:
13.         if character == 'I':
14.             # I's are displayed in lowercase for style:
15.             print('i ', end='', flush=True)
16.         else:
17.             # All other characters are displayed normally:
18.             print(character + ' ', end='', flush=True)
19.         time.sleep(interval)
20.     print()  # Print two newlines at the end.
21.     print()
22.
```

```
23.
24. # Prompt for a question:
25. slowSpacePrint('MAGIC FORTUNE BALL, BY AL SWEiGART')
26. time.sleep(0.5)
27. slowSpacePrint('ASK ME YOUR YES/NO QUESTION.')
28. input('> ')
29.
30. # Display a brief reply:
31. replies = [
32.     'LET ME THINK ON THIS...',
33.     'AN INTERESTING QUESTION...',
34.     'HMMM... ARE YOU SURE YOU WANT TO KNOW..?',
35.     'DO YOU THINK SOME THINGS ARE BEST LEFT UNKNOWN..?',
36.     'I MIGHT TELL YOU, BUT YOU MIGHT NOT LIKE THE ANSWER...',
37.     'YES... NO... MAYBE... I WILL THINK ON IT...',
38.     'AND WHAT WILL YOU DO WHEN YOU KNOW THE ANSWER? WE SHALL SEE...',
39.     'I SHALL CONSULT MY VISIONS...',
40.     'YOU MAY WANT TO SIT DOWN FOR THIS...',
41. ]
42. slowSpacePrint(random.choice(replies))
43.
44. # Dramatic pause:
45. slowSpacePrint('.' * random.randint(4, 12), 0.7)
46.
47. # Give the answer:
48. slowSpacePrint('I HAVE AN ANSWER...', 0.2)
49. time.sleep(1)
50. answers = [
51.     'YES, FOR SURE',
52.     'MY ANSWER IS NO',
53.     'ASK ME LATER',
54.     'I AM PROGRAMMED TO SAY YES',
55.     'THE STARS SAY YES, BUT I SAY NO',
56.     'I DUNNO MAYBE',
57.     'FOCUS AND ASK ONCE MORE',
58.     'DOUBTFUL, VERY DOUBTFUL',
59.     'AFFIRMATIVE',
60.     'YES, THOUGH YOU MAY NOT LIKE IT',
61.     'NO, BUT YOU MAY WISH IT WAS SO',
62. ]
63. slowSpacePrint(random.choice(answers), 0.05)
```

After entering the source code and running it a few times, try making experimental changes to it. On your own, you can also try to figure out how to do the following:

- Check that the player's question ends in a question mark.
- Add other answers the program can give.

Exploring the Program

Try to find the answers to the following questions. Experiment with some modifications to the code and rerun the program to see what effect the changes have.

1. What happens if you change `random.randint(4, 12)` on line 45 to `random.randint(4, 9999)`?

2. What error do you get if you change `time.sleep(1)` on line 49 to `time.sleep(-1)`?

#43

MANCALA

The board game Mancala is at least 2,000 years old, making it almost as old as Project 63, "Royal Game of Ur." It is a "seed-sowing" game in which two players select pockets of seeds to spread across the other pockets on the board while trying to collect as many in their store as possible. There are several variants of this game across different cultures. The name comes from the Arab word *naqala*, meaning "to move."

To play, grab the seeds from a pit on your side of the board and place one in each subsequent pit, going counterclockwise and skipping your opponent's store. If your last seed lands in an empty pit of yours, move the opposite pit's seeds into that pit. If the last placed seed is in your store, you get a free turn.

The game ends when all of one player's pits are empty. The other player claims the remaining seeds for their store, and the winner is the one with the most seeds. More information about Mancala and its variants can be found at *https://en.wikipedia.org/wiki/Mancala*.

The Program in Action

When you run *mancala.py*, the output will look like this:

```
Mancala, by Al Sweigart al@inventwithpython.com
--snip--

+------+------+--<<<<<-Player 2----+------+------+------+
2     |G     |H     |I     |J     |K     |L     |        1
      |   4  |   4  |   4  |   4  |   4  |   4  |
S     |      |      |      |      |      |      |        S
T   0 +------+------+------+------+------+------+  0   T
O     |A     |B     |C     |D     |E     |F     |        O
R     |   4  |   4  |   4  |   4  |   4  |   4  |        R
E     |      |      |      |      |      |      |        E
+------+------+------+-Player 1->>>>>-----+------+------+


Player 1, choose move: A-F (or QUIT)
> f

+------+------+--<<<<<-Player 2----+------+------+------+
2     |G     |H     |I     |J     |K     |L     |        1
      |   4  |   4  |   4  |   5  |   5  |   5  |
S     |      |      |      |      |      |      |        S
T   0 +------+------+------+------+------+------+  1   T
O     |A     |B     |C     |D     |E     |F     |        O
R     |   4  |   4  |   4  |   4  |   4  |   0  |        R
E     |      |      |      |      |      |      |        E
+------+------+------+-Player 1->>>>>-----+------+------+
Player 2, choose move: G-L (or QUIT)
--snip--
```

How It Works

Mancala uses ASCII art to display the board. Notice that each pocket needs to have not only the number of seeds in it but a label as well. To avoid confusion, the labels use the letters *A* through *L* so they won't be mistaken for the number of seeds in each pocket. The dictionaries NEXT_PIT and OPPOSITE_PIT map the letter of one pocket to the letter of the pit next to or opposite it, respectively. This lets the expression NEXT_PIT['A'] evaluate to 'B' and the expression OPPOSITE_PIT['A'] evaluate to 'G'. Pay attention to how the code uses these dictionaries. Without them, our Mancala program would require long series of if and elif statements to carry out the same game steps.

```
 1. """Mancala, by Al Sweigart al@inventwithpython.com
 2. The ancient seed-sowing game.
 3. View this code at https://nostarch.com/big-book-small-python-projects
 4. Tags: large, board game, game, two-player"""
 5.
 6. import sys
 7.
 8. # A tuple of the player's pits:
 9. PLAYER_1_PITS = ('A', 'B', 'C', 'D', 'E', 'F')
10. PLAYER_2_PITS = ('G', 'H', 'I', 'J', 'K', 'L')
11.
12. # A dictionary whose keys are pits and values are opposite pit:
13. OPPOSITE_PIT = {'A': 'G', 'B': 'H', 'C': 'I', 'D': 'J', 'E': 'K',
14.                 'F': 'L', 'G': 'A', 'H': 'B', 'I': 'C', 'J': 'D',
15.                 'K': 'E', 'L': 'F'}
16.
17. # A dictionary whose keys are pits and values are the next pit in order:
18. NEXT_PIT = {'A': 'B', 'B': 'C', 'C': 'D', 'D': 'E', 'E': 'F', 'F': '1',
19.             '1': 'L', 'L': 'K', 'K': 'J', 'J': 'I', 'I': 'H', 'H': 'G',
20.             'G': '2', '2': 'A'}
21.
22. # Every pit label, in counterclockwise order starting with A:
23. PIT_LABELS = 'ABCDEF1LKJIHG2'
24.
25. # How many seeds are in each pit at the start of a new game:
26. STARTING_NUMBER_OF_SEEDS = 4  # (!) Try changing this to 1 or 10.
27.
28.
29. def main():
30.     print('''Mancala, by Al Sweigart al@inventwithpython.com
31.
32. The ancient two-player seed-sowing game. Grab the seeds from a pit on
33. your side and place one in each following pit, going counterclockwise
34. and skipping your opponent's store. If your last seed lands in an empty
35. pit of yours, move the opposite pit's seeds into that pit. The
36. goal is to get the most seeds in your store on the side of the board.
37. If the last placed seed is in your store, you get a free turn.
38.
39. The game ends when all of one player's pits are empty. The other player
40. claims the remaining seeds for their store, and the winner is the one
41. with the most seeds.
42.
43. More info at https://en.wikipedia.org/wiki/Mancala
44. ''')
45.     input('Press Enter to begin...')
46.
47.     gameBoard = getNewBoard()
48.     playerTurn = '1'  # Player 1 goes first.
49.
50.     while True:  # Run a player's turn.
51.         # "Clear" the screen by printing many newlines, so the old
52.         # board isn't visible anymore.
53.         print('\n' * 60)
54.         # Display board and get the player's move:
```

```
55.            displayBoard(gameBoard)
56.            playerMove = askForPlayerMove(playerTurn, gameBoard)
57.
58.            # Carry out the player's move:
59.            playerTurn = makeMove(gameBoard, playerTurn, playerMove)
60.
61.            # Check if the game ended and a player has won:
62.            winner = checkForWinner(gameBoard)
63.            if winner == '1' or winner == '2':
64.                displayBoard(gameBoard)  # Display the board one last time.
65.                print('Player ' + winner + ' has won!')
66.                sys.exit()
67.            elif winner == 'tie':
68.                displayBoard(gameBoard)  # Display the board one last time.
69.                print('There is a tie!')
70.                sys.exit()
71.
72.
73. def getNewBoard():
74.     """Return a dictionary representing a Mancala board in the starting
75.     state: 4 seeds in each pit and 0 in the stores."""
76.
77.     # Syntactic sugar - Use a shorter variable name:
78.     s = STARTING_NUMBER_OF_SEEDS
79.
80.     # Create the data structure for the board, with 0 seeds in the
81.     # stores and the starting number of seeds in the pits:
82.     return {'1': 0, '2': 0, 'A': s, 'B': s, 'C': s, 'D': s, 'E': s,
83.             'F': s, 'G': s, 'H': s, 'I': s, 'J': s, 'K': s, 'L': s}
84.
85.
86. def displayBoard(board):
87.     """Displays the game board as ASCII-art based on the board
88.     dictionary."""
89.
90.     seedAmounts = []
91.     # This 'GHIJKL21ABCDEF' string is the order of the pits left to
92.     # right and top to bottom:
93.     for pit in 'GHIJKL21ABCDEF':
94.         numSeedsInThisPit = str(board[pit]).rjust(2)
95.         seedAmounts.append(numSeedsInThisPit)
96.
97.     print("""
98. +------+------+--<<<<<-Player 2----+------+------+------+
99. 2      |G     |H     |I     |J     |K     |L     |       1
100.        |  {}  |  {}  |  {}  |  {}  |  {}  |  {}  |
101. S      |      |      |      |      |      |      |       S
102. T  {}  +------+------+------+------+------+------+  {}  T
103. 0      |A     |B     |C     |D     |E     |F     |       0
104. R      |  {}  |  {}  |  {}  |  {}  |  {}  |  {}  |       R
105. E      |      |      |      |      |      |      |       E
106. +------+------+------+-Player 1->>>>>-----+------+------+
107.
108. """.format(*seedAmounts))
109.
```

```
110.
111. def askForPlayerMove(playerTurn, board):
112.     """Asks the player which pit on their side of the board they
113.     select to sow seeds from. Returns the uppercase letter label of the
114.     selected pit as a string."""
115.
116.     while True:  # Keep asking the player until they enter a valid move.
117.         # Ask the player to select a pit on their side:
118.         if playerTurn == '1':
119.             print('Player 1, choose move: A-F (or QUIT)')
120.         elif playerTurn == '2':
121.             print('Player 2, choose move: G-L (or QUIT)')
122.         response = input('> ').upper().strip()
123.
124.         # Check if the player wants to quit:
125.         if response == 'QUIT':
126.             print('Thanks for playing!')
127.             sys.exit()
128.
129.         # Make sure it is a valid pit to select:
130.         if (playerTurn == '1' and response not in PLAYER_1_PITS) or (
131.             playerTurn == '2' and response not in PLAYER_2_PITS
132.         ):
133.             print('Please pick a letter on your side of the board.')
134.             continue  # Ask player again for their move.
135.         if board.get(response) == 0:
136.             print('Please pick a non-empty pit.')
137.             continue  # Ask player again for their move.
138.         return response
139.
140.
141. def makeMove(board, playerTurn, pit):
142.     """Modify the board data structure so that the player 1 or 2 in
143.     turn selected pit as their pit to sow seeds from. Returns either
144.     '1' or '2' for whose turn it is next."""
145.
146.     seedsToSow = board[pit]  # Get number of seeds from selected pit.
147.     board[pit] = 0  # Empty out the selected pit.
148.
149.     while seedsToSow > 0:  # Continue sowing until we have no more seeds.
150.         pit = NEXT_PIT[pit]  # Move on to the next pit.
151.         if (playerTurn == '1' and pit == '2') or (
152.             playerTurn == '2' and pit == '1'
153.         ):
154.             continue  # Skip opponent's store.
155.         board[pit] += 1
156.         seedsToSow -= 1
157.
158.     # If the last seed went into the player's store, they go again.
159.     if (pit == playerTurn == '1') or (pit == playerTurn == '2'):
160.         # The last seed landed in the player's store; take another turn.
161.         return playerTurn
162.
163.     # Check if last seed was in an empty pit; take opposite pit's seeds.
164.     if playerTurn == '1' and pit in PLAYER_1_PITS and board[pit] == 1:
```

```
165.            oppositePit = OPPOSITE_PIT[pit]
166.            board['1'] += board[oppositePit]
167.            board[oppositePit] = 0
168.        elif playerTurn == '2' and pit in PLAYER_2_PITS and board[pit] == 1:
169.            oppositePit = OPPOSITE_PIT[pit]
170.            board['2'] += board[oppositePit]
171.            board[oppositePit] = 0
172.
173.        # Return the other player as the next player:
174.        if playerTurn == '1':
175.            return '2'
176.        elif playerTurn == '2':
177.            return '1'
178.
179.
180. def checkForWinner(board):
181.        """Looks at board and returns either '1' or '2' if there is a
182.        winner or 'tie' or 'no winner' if there isn't. The game ends when a
183.        player's pits are all empty; the other player claims the remaining
184.        seeds for their store. The winner is whoever has the most seeds."""
185.
186.        player1Total = board['A'] + board['B'] + board['C']
187.        player1Total += board['D'] + board['E'] + board['F']
188.        player2Total = board['G'] + board['H'] + board['I']
189.        player2Total += board['J'] + board['K'] + board['L']
190.
191.        if player1Total == 0:
192.            # Player 2 gets all the remaining seeds on their side:
193.            board['2'] += player2Total
194.            for pit in PLAYER_2_PITS:
195.                board[pit] = 0  # Set all pits to 0.
196.        elif player2Total == 0:
197.            # Player 1 gets all the remaining seeds on their side:
198.            board['1'] += player1Total
199.            for pit in PLAYER_1_PITS:
200.                board[pit] = 0  # Set all pits to 0.
201.        else:
202.            return 'no winner'  # No one has won yet.
203.
204.        # Game is over, find player with largest score.
205.        if board['1'] > board['2']:
206.            return '1'
207.        elif board['2'] > board['1']:
208.            return '2'
209.        else:
210.            return 'tie'
211.
212.
213. # If the program is run (instead of imported), run the game:
214. if __name__ == '__main__':
215.     main()
```

After entering the source code and running it a few times, try making experimental changes to it. On your own, you can also try to figure out how to do the following:

- Change the board to have more pits.
- Randomly select a bonus pit that, when the last seed lands in it, lets the player take another turn.
- Create a square-shaped board for four players instead of two.

Exploring the Program

Try to find the answers to the following questions. Experiment with some modifications to the code and rerun the program to see what effect the changes have.

1. What happens if you change return '2' on line 175 to return '1'?
2. What happens if you change return '2' on line 208 to return '1'?
3. What happens if you change response == 'QUIT' on line 125 to response == 'quit'?
4. What happens if you change board[pit] = 0 on line 147 to board[pit] = 1?
5. What happens if you change print('\n' * 60) on line 53 to print('\n' * 0)?
6. What happens if you change playerTurn = '1' on line 48 to playerTurn = '2'?
7. What happens if you change board.get(response) == 0 on line 135 to board.get(response) == -1?

#44

MAZE RUNNER 2D

This two-dimensional maze runner shows the player a top-down, bird's-eye view of a maze file you create in a text editor, such as the IDE you use to write your *.py* files. Using the WASD keys, the player can move up, left, down, and right, respectively, to navigate the @ symbol toward the exit marked by the X character.

To make a maze file, open a text editor and create the following pattern. Don't type the numbers along the top and left side; they are only there for reference:

```
 123456789
1#########
2#S# # # #
3#########
4# # # # #
5#########
```

```
6# # # # #
7#########
8# # # #E#
9#########
```

The # characters represent walls, the S marks the start, and the E marks the exit. The # characters in bold represent walls that you can remove to form your maze. Don't remove the walls at odd-numbered columns and odd-numbered rows, and don't remove the borders of the maze. When you're done, save the maze as a *.txt* (text) file. It could look something like this:

```
#########
#S     # #
# ### # #
# #   # #
# ##### #
#   #   #
### # # #
#      #E#
#########
```

Of course, this is a simple maze. You can make maze files of any size as long as they have an odd number of rows and columns. Be sure it'll still fit on the screen, though! You can also download maze files from *https:// invpy.com/mazes/*.

The Program in Action

When you run *mazerunner2d.py*, the output will look like this:

```
Maze Runner 2D, by Al Sweigart al@inventwithpython.com

(Maze files are generated by mazemakerrec.py)
Enter the filename of the maze (or LIST or QUIT):
> maze65x11s1.txt
```

```
Enter direction, or QUIT: ASD
--snip--
```

How It Works

The program loads the data for the maze's walls from a text file and into a dictionary stored in the maze variable. This dictionary has (x, y) tuples for keys and the string in the WALL, EMPTY, START, or EXIT constants for values. Project 45, "Maze Runner 3D," uses a similar dictionary representation of the maze. The difference between the projects is in the code that renders that maze on the screen. Since Maze Runner 2D is simpler, I recommend becoming familiar with this program first before moving on to Maze Runner 3D.

```python
1. """Maze Runner 2D, by Al Sweigart al@inventwithpython.com
2. Move around a maze and try to escape. Maze files are generated by
3. mazemakerrec.py.
4. View this code at https://nostarch.com/big-book-small-python-projects
5. Tags: large, game, maze"""
6.
7. import sys, os
8.
9. # Maze file constants:
10. WALL = '#'
11. EMPTY = ' '
12. START = 'S'
13. EXIT = 'E'
14.
15. PLAYER = '@'  # (!) Try changing this to '+' or 'o'.
16. BLOCK = chr(9617)  # Character 9617 is '▒'
17.
18.
19. def displayMaze(maze):
20.     # Display the maze:
21.     for y in range(HEIGHT):
22.         for x in range(WIDTH):
23.             if (x, y) == (playerx, playery):
24.                 print(PLAYER, end='')
25.             elif (x, y) == (exitx, exity):
26.                 print('X', end='')
27.             elif maze[(x, y)] == WALL:
28.                 print(BLOCK, end='')
29.             else:
30.                 print(maze[(x, y)], end='')
31.         print()  # Print a newline after printing the row.
32.
33.
34. print('''Maze Runner 2D, by Al Sweigart al@inventwithpython.com
35.
36. (Maze files are generated by mazemakerrec.py)''')
37.
38. # Get the maze file's filename from the user:
39. while True:
40.     print('Enter the filename of the maze (or LIST or QUIT):')
41.     filename = input('> ')
42.
43.     # List all the maze files in the current folder:
```

```
44.     if filename.upper() == 'LIST':
45.         print('Maze files found in', os.getcwd())
46.         for fileInCurrentFolder in os.listdir():
47.             if (fileInCurrentFolder.startswith('maze') and
48.             fileInCurrentFolder.endswith('.txt')):
49.                 print('  ', fileInCurrentFolder)
50.         continue
51.
52.     if filename.upper() == 'QUIT':
53.         sys.exit()
54.
55.     if os.path.exists(filename):
56.         break
57.     print('There is no file named', filename)
58.
59. # Load the maze from a file:
60. mazeFile = open(filename)
61. maze = {}
62. lines = mazeFile.readlines()
63. playerx = None
64. playery = None
65. exitx = None
66. exity = None
67. y = 0
68. for line in lines:
69.     WIDTH = len(line.rstrip())
70.     for x, character in enumerate(line.rstrip()):
71.         assert character in (WALL, EMPTY, START, EXIT), 'Invalid character
            at column {}, line {}'.format(x + 1, y + 1)
72.         if character in (WALL, EMPTY):
73.             maze[(x, y)] = character
74.         elif character == START:
75.             playerx, playery = x, y
76.             maze[(x, y)] = EMPTY
77.         elif character == EXIT:
78.             exitx, exity = x, y
79.             maze[(x, y)] = EMPTY
80.     y += 1
81. HEIGHT = y
82.
83. assert playerx != None and playery != None, 'No start in maze file.'
84. assert exitx != None and exity != None, 'No exit in maze file.'
85.
86. while True:  # Main game loop.
87.     displayMaze(maze)
88.
89.     while True:  # Get user move.
90.         print('                        W')
91.         print('Enter direction, or QUIT: ASD')
92.         move = input('> ').upper()
93.
94.         if move == 'QUIT':
95.             print('Thanks for playing!')
96.             sys.exit()
97.
```

```
98.            if move not in ['W', 'A', 'S', 'D']:
99.                print('Invalid direction. Enter one of W, A, S, or D.')
100.               continue
101.
102.           # Check if the player can move in that direction:
103.           if move == 'W' and maze[(playerx, playery - 1)] == EMPTY:
104.               break
105.           elif move == 'S' and maze[(playerx, playery + 1)] == EMPTY:
106.               break
107.           elif move == 'A' and maze[(playerx - 1, playery)] == EMPTY:
108.               break
109.           elif move == 'D' and maze[(playerx + 1, playery)] == EMPTY:
110.               break
111.
112.           print('You cannot move in that direction.')
113.
114.       # Keep moving in this direction until you encounter a branch point.
115.       if move == 'W':
116.           while True:
117.               playery -= 1
118.               if (playerx, playery) == (exitx, exity):
119.                   break
120.               if maze[(playerx, playery - 1)] == WALL:
121.                   break  # Break if we've hit a wall.
122.               if (maze[(playerx - 1, playery)] == EMPTY
123.                   or maze[(playerx + 1, playery)] == EMPTY):
124.                   break  # Break if we've reached a branch point.
125.       elif move == 'S':
126.           while True:
127.               playery += 1
128.               if (playerx, playery) == (exitx, exity):
129.                   break
130.               if maze[(playerx, playery + 1)] == WALL:
131.                   break  # Break if we've hit a wall.
132.               if (maze[(playerx - 1, playery)] == EMPTY
133.                   or maze[(playerx + 1, playery)] == EMPTY):
134.                   break  # Break if we've reached a branch point.
135.       elif move == 'A':
136.           while True:
137.               playerx -= 1
138.               if (playerx, playery) == (exitx, exity):
139.                   break
140.               if maze[(playerx - 1, playery)] == WALL:
141.                   break  # Break if we've hit a wall.
142.               if (maze[(playerx, playery - 1)] == EMPTY
143.                   or maze[(playerx, playery + 1)] == EMPTY):
144.                   break  # Break if we've reached a branch point.
145.       elif move == 'D':
146.           while True:
147.               playerx += 1
148.               if (playerx, playery) == (exitx, exity):
149.                   break
150.               if maze[(playerx + 1, playery)] == WALL:
151.                   break  # Break if we've hit a wall.
152.               if (maze[(playerx, playery - 1)] == EMPTY
```

```
153.                    or maze[(playerx, playery + 1)] == EMPTY):
154.                break  # Break if we've reached a branch point.
155.
156.    if (playerx, playery) == (exitx, exity):
157.        displayMaze(maze)
158.        print('You have reached the exit! Good job!')
159.        print('Thanks for playing!')
160.        sys.exit()
```

Exploring the Program

Try to find the answers to the following questions. Experiment with some modifications to the code and rerun the program to see what effect the changes have.

1. What error message do you get if you change character == START on line 74 to character == EXIT?
2. What happens if you change playery + 1 on line 105 to playery - 1?
3. What happens if you change (exitx, exity) on line 156 to (None, None)?
4. What error message do you get if you change while True: on line 89 to while False:?
5. What happens if you change break on line 104 to continue?
6. What error message do you get if you change break on line 121 to continue?

#45

MAZE RUNNER 3D

This three-dimensional maze runner provides the player with a first-person view from inside a maze. Try to find your way out! You can generate maze files by following the instructions in Project 44, "Maze Runner 2D," or by downloading maze files from *https://invpy.com/mazes/*.

The Program in Action

When you run *mazerunner3d.py*, the output will look like this:

```
Maze Runner 3D, by Al Sweigart al@inventwithpython.com
(Maze files are generated by mazemakerrec.py)
Enter the filename of the maze (or LIST or QUIT):
> maze75x11s1.txt
::::::::::::::::::::::::::::::::::::
:: \              /    ::
:: \              /    ::
:: _____/     ::
::  |          |       ::
::  |          |       ::
::  |          |       ::
::  |          |       ::
::  |          |       ::
::  |          |       ::
::  |          |       ::
::  |          |       ::
::  |          |       ::
::  |_____|      ::
::  /          \       ::
::  /            \      ::
::::::::::::::::::::::::::::::::::::
Location (1, 1)  Direction: NORTH
                    (W)
Enter direction: (A) (D)  or QUIT.
> d
::::::::::::::::::::::::::::::::::::
:: \              ::
:: \              ::
:: _____  ::
::  |             ::
::  |             ::
::  |             ::
::  |             ::
::  |             ::
::  |             ::
::  |             ::
::  |             ::
::  |             ::
::  |_____ ::
::  /             ::
::  /             ::
::::::::::::::::::::::::::::::::::::
Location (1, 1)  Direction: EAST
--snip--
```

How It Works

This 3D-perspective ASCII art starts with the multiline string stored in ALL_OPEN. This string depicts a position in which no paths are closed off by walls. The program then draws the walls, stored in the CLOSED dictionary, on top of the ALL_OPEN string to generate the ASCII art for any possible combination of closed-off paths. For example, here's how the program generates the view in which the wall is to the left of the player:

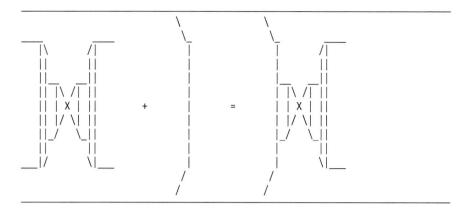

The periods in the ASCII art in the source code get removed before the strings are displayed; they only exist to make entering the code easier, so you don't insert or leave out blank spaces.

Here is the source code for the 3D maze:

```
1. """Maze 3D, by Al Sweigart al@inventwithpython.com
2. Move around a maze and try to escape... in 3D!
3. View this code at https://nostarch.com/big-book-small-python-projects
4. Tags: extra-large, artistic, game, maze"""
5.
6. import copy, sys, os
7.
8. # Set up the constants:
9. WALL = '#'
10. EMPTY = ' '
11. START = 'S'
12. EXIT = 'E'
13. BLOCK = chr(9617)  # Character 9617 is '░'
14. NORTH = 'NORTH'
15. SOUTH = 'SOUTH'
16. EAST = 'EAST'
17. WEST = 'WEST'
18.
19.
20. def wallStrToWallDict(wallStr):
21.     """Takes a string representation of a wall drawing (like those in
22.     ALL_OPEN or CLOSED) and returns a representation in a dictionary
23.     with (x, y) tuples as keys and single-character strings of the
24.     character to draw at that x, y location."""
25.     wallDict = {}
26.     height = 0
27.     width = 0
28.     for y, line in enumerate(wallStr.splitlines()):
29.         if y > height:
30.             height = y
31.         for x, character in enumerate(line):
32.             if x > width:
33.                 width = x
34.             wallDict[(x, y)] = character
35.     wallDict['height'] = height + 1
```

```
36.        wallDict['width'] = width + 1
37.        return wallDict
38.
39. EXIT_DICT = {(0, 0): 'E', (1, 0): 'X', (2, 0): 'I',
40.             (3, 0): 'T', 'height': 1, 'width': 4}
41.
42. # The way we create the strings to display is by converting the pictures
43. # in these multiline strings to dictionaries using wallStrToWallDict().
44. # Then we compose the wall for the player's location and direction by
45. # "pasting" the wall dictionaries in CLOSED on top of the wall dictionary
46. # in ALL_OPEN.
47.
48. ALL_OPEN = wallStrToWallDict(r'''
49. ................
50. ____.........____
51. ...|\......../|...
52. ...||........||...
53. ...||__...__||...
54. ...||.|\./|.||...
55. ...||.|.X.|.||...
56. ...||.|/.\|.||...
57. ...||_/...\_||...
58. ...||........||...
59. ___|/........\|___
60. ................
61. ................'''.strip())
62. # The strip() call is used to remove the newline
63. # at the start of this multiline string.
64.
65. CLOSED = {}
66. CLOSED['A'] = wallStrToWallDict(r'''
67. _____
68. .....
69. .....
70. .....
71. _____'''.strip()) # Paste to 6, 4.
72.
73. CLOSED['B'] = wallStrToWallDict(r'''
74. .\.
75. ..\
76. ...
77. ...
78. ...
79. ../
80. ./.'''.strip()) # Paste to 4, 3.
81.
82. CLOSED['C'] = wallStrToWallDict(r'''
83. _____
84. ..........
85. ..........
86. ..........
87. ..........
88. ..........
89. ..........
90. ..........
```

```
91.  ..........
92.  _____'''.strip()) # Paste to 3, 1.
93.
94. CLOSED['D'] = wallStrToWallDict(r'''
95.  ./.
96.  /..
97.  ...
98.  ...
99.  ...
100. \..
101. .\.'''.strip()) # Paste to 10, 3.
102.
103. CLOSED['E'] = wallStrToWallDict(r'''
104. ..\..
105. ...\_
106. ....|
107. ....|
108. ....|
109. ....|
110. ....|
111. ....|
112. ....|
113. ....|
114. ....|
115. .../.
116. ../..'''.strip()) # Paste to 0, 0.
117.
118. CLOSED['F'] = wallStrToWallDict(r'''
119. ../..
120. _/...
121. |....
122. |....
123. |....
124. |....
125. |....
126. |....
127. |....
128. |....
129. |....
130. .\...
131. ..\..'''.strip()) # Paste to 12, 0.
132.
133. def displayWallDict(wallDict):
134.     """Display a wall dictionary, as returned by wallStrToWallDict(), on
135.     the screen."""
136.     print(BLOCK * (wallDict['width'] + 2))
137.     for y in range(wallDict['height']):
138.         print(BLOCK, end='')
139.         for x in range(wallDict['width']):
140.             wall = wallDict[(x, y)]
141.             if wall == '.':
142.                 wall = ' '
143.             print(wall, end='')
144.         print(BLOCK)  # Print block with a newline.
145.     print(BLOCK * (wallDict['width'] + 2))
```

```
146.
147.
148. def pasteWallDict(srcWallDict, dstWallDict, left, top):
149.     """Copy the wall representation dictionary in srcWallDict on top of
150.     the one in dstWallDict, offset to the position given by left, top."""
151.     dstWallDict = copy.copy(dstWallDict)
152.     for x in range(srcWallDict['width']):
153.         for y in range(srcWallDict['height']):
154.             dstWallDict[(x + left, y + top)] = srcWallDict[(x, y)]
155.     return dstWallDict
156.
157.
158. def makeWallDict(maze, playerx, playery, playerDirection, exitx, exity):
159.     """From the player's position and direction in the maze (which has
160.     an exit at exitx, exity), create the wall representation dictionary
161.     by pasting wall dictionaries on top of ALL_OPEN, then return it."""
162.
163.     # The A-F "sections" (which are relative to the player's direction)
164.     # determine which walls in the maze we check to see if we need to
165.     # paste them over the wall representation dictionary we're creating.
166.
167.     if playerDirection == NORTH:
168.         # Map of the sections, relative  A
169.         # to the player @:               BCD (Player facing north)
170.         #                                E@F
171.         offsets = (('A', 0, -2), ('B', -1, -1), ('C', 0, -1),
172.                    ('D', 1, -1), ('E', -1, 0), ('F', 1, 0))
173.     if playerDirection == SOUTH:
174.         # Map of the sections, relative F@E
175.         # to the player @:              DCB (Player facing south)
176.         #                                A
177.         offsets = (('A', 0, 2), ('B', 1, 1), ('C', 0, 1),
178.                    ('D', -1, 1), ('E', 1, 0), ('F', -1, 0))
179.     if playerDirection == EAST:
180.         # Map of the sections, relative EB
181.         # to the player @:              @CA (Player facing east)
182.         #                                FD
183.         offsets = (('A', 2, 0), ('B', 1, -1), ('C', 1, 0),
184.                    ('D', 1, 1), ('E', 0, -1), ('F', 0, 1))
185.     if playerDirection == WEST:
186.         # Map of the sections, relative  DF
187.         # to the player @:              AC@ (Player facing west)
188.         #                                 BE
189.         offsets = (('A', -2, 0), ('B', -1, 1), ('C', -1, 0),
190.                    ('D', -1, -1), ('E', 0, 1), ('F', 0, -1))
191.
192.     section = {}
193.     for sec, xOff, yOff in offsets:
194.         section[sec] = maze.get((playerx + xOff, playery + yOff), WALL)
195.         if (playerx + xOff, playery + yOff) == (exitx, exity):
196.             section[sec] = EXIT
197.
198.     wallDict = copy.copy(ALL_OPEN)
199.     PASTE_CLOSED_TO = {'A': (6, 4), 'B': (4, 3), 'C': (3, 1),
200.                        'D': (10, 3), 'E': (0, 0), 'F': (12, 0)}
```

```
201.     for sec in 'ABDCEF':
202.         if section[sec] == WALL:
203.             wallDict = pasteWallDict(CLOSED[sec], wallDict,
204.                 PASTE_CLOSED_TO[sec][0], PASTE_CLOSED_TO[sec][1])
205.
206.     # Draw the EXIT sign if needed:
207.     if section['C'] == EXIT:
208.         wallDict = pasteWallDict(EXIT_DICT, wallDict, 7, 9)
209.     if section['E'] == EXIT:
210.         wallDict = pasteWallDict(EXIT_DICT, wallDict, 0, 11)
211.     if section['F'] == EXIT:
212.         wallDict = pasteWallDict(EXIT_DICT, wallDict, 13, 11)
213.
214.     return wallDict
215.
216.
217. print('Maze Runner 3D, by Al Sweigart al@inventwithpython.com')
218. print('(Maze files are generated by mazemakerrec.py)')
219.
220. # Get the maze file's filename from the user:
221. while True:
222.     print('Enter the filename of the maze (or LIST or QUIT):')
223.     filename = input('> ')
224.
225.     # List all the maze files in the current folder:
226.     if filename.upper() == 'LIST':
227.         print('Maze files found in', os.getcwd())
228.         for fileInCurrentFolder in os.listdir():
229.             if (fileInCurrentFolder.startswith('maze')
230.             and fileInCurrentFolder.endswith('.txt')):
231.                 print('  ', fileInCurrentFolder)
232.         continue
233.
234.     if filename.upper() == 'QUIT':
235.         sys.exit()
236.
237.     if os.path.exists(filename):
238.         break
239.     print('There is no file named', filename)
240.
241. # Load the maze from a file:
242. mazeFile = open(filename)
243. maze = {}
244. lines = mazeFile.readlines()
245. px = None
246. py = None
247. exitx = None
248. exity = None
249. y = 0
250. for line in lines:
251.     WIDTH = len(line.rstrip())
252.     for x, character in enumerate(line.rstrip()):
253.         assert character in (WALL, EMPTY, START, EXIT), 'Invalid character
             at column {}, line {}'.format(x + 1, y + 1)
254.         if character in (WALL, EMPTY):
```

```
255.              maze[(x, y)] = character
256.          elif character == START:
257.              px, py = x, y
258.              maze[(x, y)] = EMPTY
259.          elif character == EXIT:
260.              exitx, exity = x, y
261.              maze[(x, y)] = EMPTY
262.      y += 1
263. HEIGHT = y
264.
265. assert px != None and py != None, 'No start point in file.'
266. assert exitx != None and exity != None, 'No exit point in file.'
267. pDir = NORTH
268.
269.
270. while True:  # Main game loop.
271.     displayWallDict(makeWallDict(maze, px, py, pDir, exitx, exity))
272.
273.     while True: # Get user move.
274.         print('Location ({}, {})  Direction: {}'.format(px, py, pDir))
275.         print('                     (W)')
276.         print('Enter direction: (A) (D)  or QUIT.')
277.         move = input('> ').upper()
278.
279.         if move == 'QUIT':
280.             print('Thanks for playing!')
281.             sys.exit()
282.
283.         if (move not in ['F', 'L', 'R', 'W', 'A', 'D']
284.             and not move.startswith('T')):
285.             print('Please enter one of F, L, or R (or W, A, D).')
286.             continue
287.
288.         # Move the player according to their intended move:
289.         if move == 'F' or move == 'W':
290.             if pDir == NORTH and maze[(px, py - 1)] == EMPTY:
291.                 py -= 1
292.                 break
293.             if pDir == SOUTH and maze[(px, py + 1)] == EMPTY:
294.                 py += 1
295.                 break
296.             if pDir == EAST and maze[(px + 1, py)] == EMPTY:
297.                 px += 1
298.                 break
299.             if pDir == WEST and maze[(px - 1, py)] == EMPTY:
300.                 px -= 1
301.                 break
302.         elif move == 'L' or move == 'A':
303.             pDir = {NORTH: WEST, WEST: SOUTH,
304.                     SOUTH: EAST, EAST: NORTH}[pDir]
305.             break
306.         elif move == 'R' or move == 'D':
307.             pDir = {NORTH: EAST, EAST: SOUTH,
308.                     SOUTH: WEST, WEST: NORTH}[pDir]
309.             break
```

```
310.        elif move.startswith('T'):  # Cheat code: 'T x,y'
311.            px, py = move.split()[1].split(',')
312.            px = int(px)
313.            py = int(py)
314.            break
315.        else:
316.            print('You cannot move in that direction.')
317.
318.    if (px, py) == (exitx, exity):
319.        print('You have reached the exit! Good job!')
320.        print('Thanks for playing!')
321.        sys.exit()
```

Exploring the Program

Try to find the answers to the following questions. Experiment with some modifications to the code and rerun the program to see what effect the changes have.

1. What bug do you cause if you change move == 'QUIT' on line 279 to move == 'quit'?

2. How can you remove the teleportation cheat?

#46

MILLION DICE ROLL STATISTICS SIMULATOR

When you roll two six-sided dice, there's a 17 percent chance you'll roll a 7. That's much better than the odds of rolling a 2: just 3 percent. That's because there's only one combination of dice rolls that gives you 2 (the one that occurs when both dice roll a 1), but many combinations add up to seven: 1 and 6, 2 and 5, 3 and 4, and so on.

But what about when you roll three dice? Or four? Or 1,000? You could mathematically calculate the theoretical probabilities, or you can have the computer roll a number of dice one million times to empirically figure them out. This program takes that latter approach. In this program, you tell the computer to roll *N* dice one million times and remember the results. It then displays the percentage chance of each sum.

This program does a massive amount of computation, but the computation itself isn't hard to understand.

The Program in Action

When you run *milliondicestats.py*, the output will look like this:

```
Million Dice Roll Statistics Simulator
By Al Sweigart al@inventwithpython.com

Enter how many six-sided dice you want to roll:
> 2
Simulating 1,000,000 rolls of 2 dice...
36.2% done...
73.4% done...
TOTAL - ROLLS - PERCENTAGE
  2 - 27590 rolls - 2.8%
  3 - 55730 rolls - 5.6%
  4 - 83517 rolls - 8.4%
  5 - 111526 rolls - 11.2%
  6 - 139015 rolls - 13.9%
  7 - 166327 rolls - 16.6%
  8 - 139477 rolls - 13.9%
  9 - 110268 rolls - 11.0%
 10 - 83272 rolls - 8.3%
 11 - 55255 rolls - 5.5%
 12 - 28023 rolls - 2.8%
```

How It Works

We simulate the roll of a single six-sided die by calling random.randint(1, 6) on line 30. This returns a random number between 1 and 6, which gets added to the running total for however many dice are rolled together. The random.randint() function has a uniform distribution, meaning each number is just as likely as any other to be returned.

The program stores the results of this roll with the results dictionary. The keys to this dictionary are each possible dice roll total, and the values are how many times this total has been encountered. To get the frequency percentage, we divide the number of times a total has been encountered by 1,000,000 (the number of dice rolls in this simulation) and multiply it by 100 (to get a percentage between 0.0 and 100.0 instead of 0.0 and 1.0). By doing some algebra, we can figure out that this is the same as dividing the number of encounters by 10,000, which we do on line 37.

```
1. """Million Dice Roll Statistics Simulator
2. By Al Sweigart al@inventwithpython.com
3. A simulation of one million dice rolls.
4. View this code at https://nostarch.com/big-book-small-python-projects
5. Tags: tiny, beginner, math, simulation"""
6.
7. import random, time
8.
9. print('''Million Dice Roll Statistics Simulator
10. By Al Sweigart al@inventwithpython.com
11.
```

```
12. Enter how many six-sided dice you want to roll:''')
13. numberOfDice = int(input('> '))
14.
15. # Set up a dictionary to store the results of each dice roll:
16. results = {}
17. for i in range(numberOfDice, (numberOfDice * 6) + 1):
18.     results[i] = 0
19.
20. # Simulate dice rolls:
21. print('Simulating 1,000,000 rolls of {} dice...'.format(numberOfDice))
22. lastPrintTime = time.time()
23. for i in range(1000000):
24.     if time.time() > lastPrintTime + 1:
25.         print('{}% done...'.format(round(i / 10000, 1)))
26.         lastPrintTime = time.time()
27.
28.     total = 0
29.     for j in range(numberOfDice):
30.         total = total + random.randint(1, 6)
31.     results[total] = results[total] + 1
32.
33. # Display results:
34. print('TOTAL - ROLLS - PERCENTAGE')
35. for i in range(numberOfDice, (numberOfDice * 6) + 1):
36.     roll = results[i]
37.     percentage = round(results[i] / 10000, 1)
38.     print('  {} - {} rolls - {}%'.format(i, roll, percentage))
```

After entering the source code and running it a few times, try making experimental changes to it. On your own, you can also try to figure out how to do the following:

- Try rolling 8-, 10-, 12-, or 20-sided dice.
- Try simulating two-sided coin tosses.

Exploring the Program

Try to find the answers to the following questions. Experiment with some modifications to the code and rerun the program to see what effect the changes have.

1. What happens if you change lastPrintTime + 1 on line 24 to lastPrintTime + 2?

2. What bug do you cause if you delete or comment out results[total] = results[total] + 1 on line 31?

3. What error happens if the user types letters instead of a number for the number of six-sided dice to roll?

#47

MONDRIAN ART GENERATOR

Piet Mondrian was a 20th-century Dutch painter and one of the founders of neoplasticism, an abstract art movement. His most iconic paintings relied on blocks of primary colors (blue, yellow, red), black, and white. Using a minimalist approach, he separated these colors with horizontal and vertical elements.

This program generates random paintings that follow Mondrian's style. You can find out more about Piet Mondrian at *https://en.wikipedia.org/wiki/ Piet_Mondrian*.

The Program in Action

The bext module allows our Python program to display bright primary colors in the text output, even though this book only shows black-and-white images. Figure 47-1 shows what the output will look like when you run *mondrian.py*.

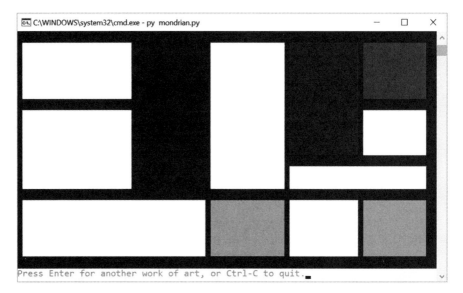

Figure 47-1: The Mondrian art program's computer-generated art. A different image is generated each time the program runs.

How It Works

The algorithm works by creating a data structure (the canvas dictionary) with randomly spaced vertical and horizontal lines, as in Figure 47-2.

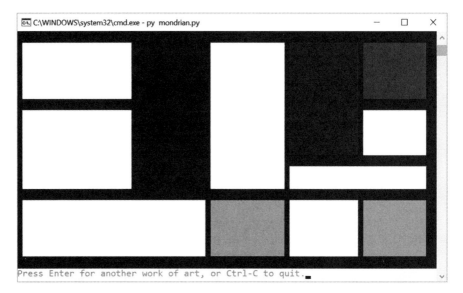

Figure 47-2: The first step of the Mondrian art algorithm creates a grid.

Next, it removes some of the line segments to create larger rectangles, as shown in Figure 47-3.

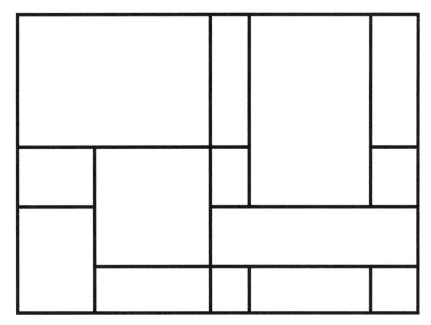

Figure 47-3: The second step of the Mondrian art algorithm removes some lines at random.

Finally, the algorithm randomly fills some rectangles with yellow, red, blue, or black, as in Figure 47-4.

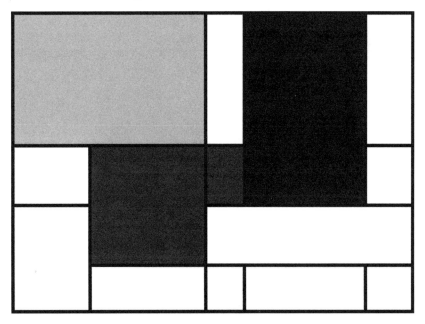

Figure 47-4: The third step of the Mondrian art algorithm randomly selects rectangles to fill with color.

You can find another version of this Mondrian art generator at *https://github.com/asweigart/mondrian_art_generator/* along with several sample images.

```
1. """Mondrian Art Generator, by Al Sweigart al@inventwithpython.com
2. Randomly generates art in the style of Piet Mondrian.
3. More info at: https://en.wikipedia.org/wiki/Piet_Mondrian
4. View this code at https://nostarch.com/big-book-small-python-projects
5. Tags: large, artistic, bext"""
6.
7. import sys, random
8.
9. try:
10.     import bext
11. except ImportError:
12.     print('This program requires the bext module, which you')
13.     print('can install by following the instructions at')
14.     print('https://pypi.org/project/Bext/')
15.     sys.exit()
16.
17. # Set up the constants:
18. MIN_X_INCREASE = 6
19. MAX_X_INCREASE = 16
20. MIN_Y_INCREASE = 3
21. MAX_Y_INCREASE = 6
22. WHITE = 'white'
23. BLACK = 'black'
24. RED = 'red'
25. YELLOW = 'yellow'
26. BLUE = 'blue'
27.
28. # Setup the screen:
29. width, height = bext.size()
30. # We can't print to the last column on Windows without it adding a
31. # newline automatically, so reduce the width by one:
32. width -= 1
33.
34. height -= 3
35.
36. while True:  # Main application loop.
37.     # Pre-populate the canvas with blank spaces:
38.     canvas = {}
39.     for x in range(width):
40.         for y in range(height):
41.             canvas[(x, y)] = WHITE
42.
43.     # Generate vertical lines:
44.     numberOfSegmentsToDelete = 0
45.     x = random.randint(MIN_X_INCREASE, MAX_X_INCREASE)
46.     while x < width - MIN_X_INCREASE:
47.         numberOfSegmentsToDelete += 1
48.         for y in range(height):
49.             canvas[(x, y)] = BLACK
50.         x += random.randint(MIN_X_INCREASE, MAX_X_INCREASE)
```

```
51.
52.    # Generate horizontal lines:
53.    y = random.randint(MIN_Y_INCREASE, MAX_Y_INCREASE)
54.    while y < height - MIN_Y_INCREASE:
55.        numberOfSegmentsToDelete += 1
56.        for x in range(width):
57.            canvas[(x, y)] = BLACK
58.        y += random.randint(MIN_Y_INCREASE, MAX_Y_INCREASE)
59.
60.    numberOfRectanglesToPaint = numberOfSegmentsToDelete - 3
61.    numberOfSegmentsToDelete = int(numberOfSegmentsToDelete * 1.5)
62.
63.    # Randomly select points and try to remove them.
64.    for i in range(numberOfSegmentsToDelete):
65.        while True:  # Keep selecting segments to try to delete.
66.            # Get a random start point on an existing segment:
67.            startx = random.randint(1, width - 2)
68.            starty = random.randint(1, height - 2)
69.            if canvas[(startx, starty)] == WHITE:
70.                continue
71.
72.            # Find out if we're on a vertical or horizontal segment:
73.            if (canvas[(startx - 1, starty)] == WHITE and
74.                canvas[(startx + 1, starty)] == WHITE):
75.                orientation = 'vertical'
76.            elif (canvas[(startx, starty - 1)] == WHITE and
77.                  canvas[(startx, starty + 1)] == WHITE):
78.                orientation = 'horizontal'
79.            else:
80.                # The start point is on an intersection,
81.                # so get a new random start point:
82.                continue
83.
84.            pointsToDelete = [(startx, starty)]
85.
86.            canDeleteSegment = True
87.            if orientation == 'vertical':
88.                # Go up one path from the start point, and
89.                # see if we can remove this segment:
90.                for changey in (-1, 1):
91.                    y = starty
92.                    while 0 < y < height - 1:
93.                        y += changey
94.                        if (canvas[(startx - 1, y)] == BLACK and
95.                            canvas[(startx + 1, y)] == BLACK):
96.                            # We've found a four-way intersection.
97.                            break
98.                        elif ((canvas[(startx - 1, y)] == WHITE and
99.                               canvas[(startx + 1, y)] == BLACK) or
100.                              (canvas[(startx - 1, y)] == BLACK and
101.                               canvas[(startx + 1, y)] == WHITE)):
102.                            # We've found a T-intersection; we can't
103.                            # delete this segment:
104.                            canDeleteSegment = False
105.                            break
```

```python
106.                             else:
107.                                 pointsToDelete.append((startx, y))
108.
109.                     elif orientation == 'horizontal':
110.                         # Go up one path from the start point, and
111.                         # see if we can remove this segment:
112.                         for changex in (-1, 1):
113.                             x = startx
114.                             while 0 < x < width - 1:
115.                                 x += changex
116.                                 if (canvas[(x, starty - 1)] == BLACK and
117.                                     canvas[(x, starty + 1)] == BLACK):
118.                                     # We've found a four-way intersection.
119.                                     break
120.                                 elif ((canvas[(x, starty - 1)] == WHITE and
121.                                         canvas[(x, starty + 1)] == BLACK) or
122.                                       (canvas[(x, starty - 1)] == BLACK and
123.                                         canvas[(x, starty + 1)] == WHITE)):
124.                                     # We've found a T-intersection; we can't
125.                                     # delete this segment:
126.                                     canDeleteSegment = False
127.                                     break
128.                                 else:
129.                                     pointsToDelete.append((x, starty))
130.                     if not canDeleteSegment:
131.                         continue  # Get a new random start point.
132.                     break  # Move on to delete the segment.
133.
134.             # If we can delete this segment, set all the points to white:
135.             for x, y in pointsToDelete:
136.                 canvas[(x, y)] = WHITE
137.
138.     # Add the border lines:
139.     for x in range(width):
140.         canvas[(x, 0)] = BLACK  # Top border.
141.         canvas[(x, height - 1)] = BLACK  # Bottom border.
142.     for y in range(height):
143.         canvas[(0, y)] = BLACK  # Left border.
144.         canvas[(width - 1, y)] = BLACK  # Right border.
145.
146.     # Paint the rectangles:
147.     for i in range(numberOfRectanglesToPaint):
148.         while True:
149.             startx = random.randint(1, width - 2)
150.             starty = random.randint(1, height - 2)
151.
152.             if canvas[(startx, starty)] != WHITE:
153.                 continue  # Get a new random start point.
154.             else:
155.                 break
156.
157.         # Flood fill algorithm:
158.         colorToPaint = random.choice([RED, YELLOW, BLUE, BLACK])
159.         pointsToPaint = set([(startx, starty)])
160.         while len(pointsToPaint) > 0:
```

```
161.            x, y = pointsToPaint.pop()
162.            canvas[(x, y)] = colorToPaint
163.            if canvas[(x - 1, y)] == WHITE:
164.                pointsToPaint.add((x - 1, y))
165.            if canvas[(x + 1, y)] == WHITE:
166.                pointsToPaint.add((x + 1, y))
167.            if canvas[(x, y - 1)] == WHITE:
168.                pointsToPaint.add((x, y - 1))
169.            if canvas[(x, y + 1)] == WHITE:
170.                pointsToPaint.add((x, y + 1))
171.
172.    # Draw the canvas data structure:
173.    for y in range(height):
174.        for x in range(width):
175.            bext.bg(canvas[(x, y)])
176.            print(' ', end='')
177.
178.        print()
179.
180.    # Prompt user to create a new one:
181.    try:
182.        input('Press Enter for another work of art, or Ctrl-C to quit.')
183.    except KeyboardInterrupt:
184.        sys.exit()
```

After entering the source code and running it a few times, try making experimental changes to it. On your own, you can also try to figure out how to do the following:

- Create programs with different color palettes.
- Use the Pillow module to produce image files of Mondrian art. You can learn about this module from Chapter 19 of *Automate the Boring Stuff with Python* at *https://automatetheboringstuff.com/2e/chapter19/*.

Exploring the Program

Try to find the answers to the following questions. Experiment with some modifications to the code and rerun the program to see what effect the changes have.

1. What error happens if you change canvas[(x, y)] = WHITE on line 41 to canvas[(x, y)] = RED?
2. What happens if you change print(' ', end='') on line 176 to print('A', end='')?

#48

MONTY HALL PROBLEM

The Monty Hall Problem illustrates a surprising fact of probability. The problem is loosely based on the old game show *Let's Make a Deal* and its host, Monty Hall. In the Monty Hall Problem, you can pick one of three doors. Behind one door is a prize: a new car. Each of the other two doors opens onto a worthless goat. Say you pick Door #1. Before the door you choose is opened, the host opens another door (either #2 or #3), which leads to a goat. You can choose to either open the door you originally picked or switch to the other unopened door.

It may seem like it doesn't matter if you switch or not, but your odds do improve if you switch doors! This program demonstrates the Monty Hall problem by letting you do repeated experiments.

To understand why your odds improve, consider a version of the Monty Hall Problem with one thousand doors instead of three. You pick one door, and then the host opens 998 doors, which all reveal goats. The only two doors that are unopened are the one you selected and one other door. If you correctly picked the car door to begin with (a 1 in 1,000 chance), then the host left a random goat door closed. If you picked a goat door (a 999 in a 1,000 chance), the host specifically chose the car door to leave closed. The choice of which doors to open isn't random; the host knows to leave the car door closed. It's almost certain that you didn't pick the car door to begin with, so you should switch to the other door.

Another way to think of it is that you have 1,000 boxes and one box contains a prize. You guess which box the prize is in and the host puts it in your hands. Do you think the prize is in your box or one of the 999 other boxes? You don't need the host to open 998 of the 999 boxes that don't contain a prize; the amount of choice is the same as with the 1,000 doors. The odds that you guessed correctly in the beginning are 1 in 1,000, while the odds that you did not (and that the prize is in one of the other boxes) is a near certain 999 in 1,000.

More information about the Monty Hall Problem can be found at *https://en.wikipedia.org/wiki/Monty_Hall_problem*.

The Program in Action

When you run *montyhall.py*, the output will look like this:

```
The Monty Hall Problem, by Al Sweigart al@inventwithpython.com
--snip--
+------+ +------+ +------+
|      | |      | |      |
|  1   | |  2   | |  3   |
|      | |      | |      |
|      | |      | |      |
|      | |      | |      |
+------+ +------+ +------+
Pick a door 1, 2, or 3 (or "quit" to stop):
> 1

+------+ +------+ +------+
|      | |      | | ((   |
|  1   |.|  2   | | oo   |
|      | |      | | /_/|_|
|      | |      | |    | |
|      | |      | |GOAT| |
+------+ +------+ +------+
Door 3 contains a goat!
Do you want to swap doors? Y/N
> y

+------+ +------+ +------+
| ((   | | CAR! | | ((   |
| oo   | |    _ | | oo   |
| /_/|_| |   _/ | | /_/|_|
|    | | | /_ _|| |    | |
|GOAT| | |  O   | |GOAT| |
+------+ +------+ +------+
```

```
Door 2 has the car!
You won!

Swapping:     1 wins, 0 losses, success rate 100.0%
Not swapping: 0 wins, 0 losses, success rate 0.0%

Press Enter to repeat the experiment...
--snip--
```

How It Works

The multiline strings for the ASCII-art doors are stored in several constant variables, such as ALL_CLOSED, FIRST_GOAT, and FIRST_CAR_OTHERS_GOAT. The code that uses these constants, like print(FIRST_GOAT) on line 125, stays the same even if we update the graphics. By placing the multiline strings together toward the top of the source code file, we'll have an easier time comparing them to make sure the graphics are consistent.

```
1. """The Monty Hall Problem, by Al Sweigart al@inventwithpython.com
2. A simulation of the Monty Hall game show problem.
3. More info at https://en.wikipedia.org/wiki/Monty_Hall_problem
4. View this code at https://nostarch.com/big-book-small-python-projects
5. Tags: large, game, math, simulation"""
6.
7. import random, sys
8.
9. ALL_CLOSED = """
10. +------+ +------+ +------+
11. |      | |      | |      |
12. |  1   | |  2   | |  3   |
13. |      | |      | |      |
14. |      | |      | |      |
15. |      | |      | |      |
16. +------+ +------+ +------+"""
17.
18. FIRST_GOAT = """
19. +------+ +------+ +------+
20. |  ((  | |      | |      |
21. |  oo  | |  2   | |  3   |
22. | /_/|_| |      | |      |
23. |   || | |      | |      |
24. |GOAT||| |      | |      |
25. +------+ +------+ +------+"""
26.
27. SECOND_GOAT = """
28. +------+ +------+ +------+
29. |      | |  ((  | |      |
30. |  1   | |  oo  | |  3   |
31. |      | | /_/|_| |      |
32. |      | |   || | |      |
33. |      | |GOAT||| |      |
34. +------+ +------+ +------+"""
35.
```

```
36. THIRD_GOAT = """
37. +------+  +------+  +------+
38. |      |  |      |  |  ((  |
39. |   1  |  |   2  |  |  oo  |
40. |      |  |      |  | /_/|_|
41. |      |  |      |  |    | |
42. |      |  |      |  |GOAT| |
43. +------+  +------+  +------+"""
44.
45. FIRST_CAR_OTHERS_GOAT = """
46. +------+  +------+  +------+
47. | CAR! |  |  ((  |  |  ((  |
48. |    _|  |  oo  |  |  oo  |
49. |   _/  |  | /_/|_|  | /_/|_|
50. | /__|  |  |    | |  |    | |
51. |   0  |  |GOAT| |  |GOAT| |
52. +------+  +------+  +------+"""
53.
54. SECOND_CAR_OTHERS_GOAT = """
55. +------+  +------+  +------+
56. |  ((  |  | CAR! |  |  ((  |
57. |  oo  |  |    _|  |  oo  |
58. | /_/|_|  |   _/  |  | /_/|_|
59. |    | |  | /__|  |  |    | |
60. |GOAT| |  |   0  |  |GOAT| |
61. +------+  +------+  +------+"""
62.
63. THIRD_CAR_OTHERS_GOAT = """
64. +------+  +------+  +------+
65. |  ((  |  |  ((  |  | CAR! |
66. |  oo  |  |  oo  |  |    _|
67. | /_/|_|  | /_/|_|  |   _/  |
68. |    | |  |    | |  | /__|  |
69. |GOAT| |  |GOAT| |  |   0  |
70. +------+  +------+  +------+"""
71.
72. print('''The Monty Hall Problem, by Al Sweigart al@inventwithpython.com
73.
74. In the Monty Hall game show, you can pick one of three doors. One door
75. has a new car for a prize. The other two doors have worthless goats:
76. {}
77. Say you pick Door #1.
78. Before the door you choose is opened, another door with a goat is opened:
79. {}
80. You can choose to either open the door you originally picked or swap
81. to the other unopened door.
82.
83. It may seem like it doesn't matter if you swap or not, but your odds
84. do improve if you swap doors! This program demonstrates the Monty Hall
85. problem by letting you do repeated experiments.
86.
87. You can read an explanation of why swapping is better at
88. https://en.wikipedia.org/wiki/Monty_Hall_problem
89. '''.format(ALL_CLOSED, THIRD_GOAT))
90.
```

```
91.  input('Press Enter to start...')
92.
93.
94.  swapWins = 0
95.  swapLosses = 0
96.  stayWins = 0
97.  stayLosses = 0
98.  while True:  # Main program loop.
99.      # The computer picks which door has the car:
100.     doorThatHasCar = random.randint(1, 3)
101.
102.     # Ask the player to pick a door:
103.     print(ALL_CLOSED)
104.     while True:  # Keep asking the player until they enter a valid door.
105.         print('Pick a door 1, 2, or 3 (or "quit" to stop):')
106.         response = input('> ').upper()
107.         if response == 'QUIT':
108.             # End the game.
109.             print('Thanks for playing!')
110.             sys.exit()
111.
112.         if response == '1' or response == '2' or response == '3':
113.             break
114.     doorPick = int(response)
115.
116.     # Figure out which goat door to show the player:
117.     while True:
118.         # Select a door that is a goat and not picked by the player:
119.         showGoatDoor = random.randint(1, 3)
120.         if showGoatDoor != doorPick and showGoatDoor != doorThatHasCar:
121.             break
122.
123.     # Show this goat door to the player:
124.     if showGoatDoor == 1:
125.         print(FIRST_GOAT)
126.     elif showGoatDoor == 2:
127.         print(SECOND_GOAT)
128.     elif showGoatDoor == 3:
129.         print(THIRD_GOAT)
130.
131.     print('Door {} contains a goat!'.format(showGoatDoor))
132.
133.     # Ask the player if they want to swap:
134.     while True:  # Keep asking until the player enters Y or N.
135.         print('Do you want to swap doors? Y/N')
136.         swap = input('> ').upper()
137.         if swap == 'Y' or swap == 'N':
138.             break
139.
140.     # Swap the player's door if they wanted to swap:
141.     if swap == 'Y':
142.         if doorPick == 1 and showGoatDoor == 2:
143.             doorPick = 3
144.         elif doorPick == 1 and showGoatDoor == 3:
145.             doorPick = 2
```

```
146.        elif doorPick == 2 and showGoatDoor == 1:
147.            doorPick = 3
148.        elif doorPick == 2 and showGoatDoor == 3:
149.            doorPick = 1
150.        elif doorPick == 3 and showGoatDoor == 1:
151.            doorPick = 2
152.        elif doorPick == 3 and showGoatDoor == 2:
153.            doorPick = 1
154.
155.    # Open all the doors:
156.    if doorThatHasCar == 1:
157.        print(FIRST_CAR_OTHERS_GOAT)
158.    elif doorThatHasCar == 2:
159.        print(SECOND_CAR_OTHERS_GOAT)
160.    elif doorThatHasCar == 3:
161.        print(THIRD_CAR_OTHERS_GOAT)
162.
163.    print('Door {} has the car!'.format(doorThatHasCar))
164.
165.    # Record wins and losses for swapping and not swapping:
166.    if doorPick == doorThatHasCar:
167.        print('You won!')
168.        if swap == 'Y':
169.            swapWins += 1
170.        elif swap == 'N':
171.            stayWins += 1
172.    else:
173.        print('Sorry, you lost.')
174.        if swap == 'Y':
175.            swapLosses += 1
176.        elif swap == 'N':
177.            stayLosses += 1
178.
179.    # Calculate success rate of swapping and not swapping:
180.    totalSwaps = swapWins + swapLosses
181.    if totalSwaps != 0:  # Prevent zero-divide error.
182.        swapSuccess = round(swapWins / totalSwaps * 100, 1)
183.    else:
184.        swapSuccess = 0.0
185.
186.    totalStays = stayWins + stayLosses
187.    if (stayWins + stayLosses) != 0:  # Prevent zero-divide.
188.        staySuccess = round(stayWins / totalStays * 100, 1)
189.    else:
190.        staySuccess = 0.0
191.
192.    print()
193.    print('Swapping:     ', end='')
194.    print('{} wins, {} losses, '.format(swapWins, swapLosses), end='')
195.    print('success rate {}%'.format(swapSuccess))
196.    print('Not swapping: ', end='')
197.    print('{} wins, {} losses, '.format(stayWins, stayLosses), end='')
198.    print('success rate {}%'.format(staySuccess))
199.    print()
200.    input('Press Enter to repeat the experiment...')
```

Exploring the Program

Try to find the answers to the following questions. Experiment with some modifications to the code and rerun the program to see what effect the changes have.

1. What happens if you change doorThatHasCar = random.randint(1, 3) on line 100 to doorThatHasCar = 1?

2. What happens if you replace lines 124 to 129 with print([FIRST_GOAT, SECOND_GOAT, THIRD_GOAT][showGoatDoor - 1])?

#49

MULTIPLICATION TABLE

This program generates a multiplication table from 0 × 0 to 12 × 12. While simple, it provides a useful demonstration of nested loops.

The Program in Action

When you run *multiplicationtable.py*, the output will look like this:

```
Multiplication Table, by Al Sweigart al@inventwithpython.com
  | 0  1  2  3  4  5  6  7  8  9 10 11 12
--+-------------------------------------------------------
 0| 0  0  0  0  0  0  0  0  0  0  0  0  0
 1| 0  1  2  3  4  5  6  7  8  9 10 11 12
 2| 0  2  4  6  8 10 12 14 16 18 20 22 24
 3| 0  3  6  9 12 15 18 21 24 27 30 33 36
 4| 0  4  8 12 16 20 24 28 32 36 40 44 48
 5| 0  5 10 15 20 25 30 35 40 45 50 55 60
 6| 0  6 12 18 24 30 36 42 48 54 60 66 72
 7| 0  7 14 21 28 35 42 49 56 63 70 77 84
 8| 0  8 16 24 32 40 48 56 64 72 80 88 96
 9| 0  9 18 27 36 45 54 63 72 81 90 99 108
10| 0 10 20 30 40 50 60 70 80 90 100 110 120
11| 0 11 22 33 44 55 66 77 88 99 110 121 132
12| 0 12 24 36 48 60 72 84 96 108 120 132 144
```

How It Works

Line 9 prints the top row of the table. Notice that it sets a large enough distance between the numbers to accommodate products that are a maximum of three digits long. Since this is a 12 × 12 multiplication table, this spacing can fit the largest product, 144. If you want to create a larger table, you may need to increase the spacing for the columns as well. Keep in mind that the standard terminal window is 80 columns wide and 24 rows tall, so you cannot create much larger multiplication tables without having the rows wrap around the right edge of the window.

```python
1. """Multiplication Table, by Al Sweigart al@inventwithpython.com
2. Print a multiplication table.
3. View this code at https://nostarch.com/big-book-small-python-projects
4. Tags: tiny, beginner, math"""
5.
6. print('Multiplication Table, by Al Sweigart al@inventwithpython.com')
7.
8. # Print the horizontal number labels:
9. print('  | 0  1  2  3  4  5  6  7  8  9 10 11 12')
10. print('--+-------------------------------------------------------')
11.
12. # Display each row of products:
13. for number1 in range(0, 13):
14.
15.     # Print the vertical numbers labels:
16.     print(str(number1).rjust(2), end='')
17.
18.     # Print a separating bar:
19.     print('|', end='')
20.
```

```
21.      for number2 in range(0, 13):
22.          # Print the product followed by a space:
23.          print(str(number1 * number2).rjust(3), end=' ')
24.
25.      print()  # Finish the row by printing a newline.
```

Exploring the Program

Try to find the answers to the following questions. Experiment with some modifications to the code and rerun the program to see what effect the changes have.

1. What happens if you change range(0, 13) on line 13 to range(0, 80)?
2. What happens if you change range(0, 13) on line 13 to range(0, 100)?

#50

NINETY-NINE BOTTLES

"Ninety-Nine Bottles" is a folk song of undetermined origin known for its length and repetitiveness. The lyrics go, "Ninety-nine bottles of milk on the wall, ninety-nine bottles of milk. Take one down, pass it around, ninety-eight bottles of milk on the wall." As the lyrics repeat, the number of bottles falls from ninety-eight to ninety-seven, then from ninety-seven to ninety-six, until it reaches zero: "One bottle of milk on the wall, one bottle of milk. Take it down, pass it around, no more bottles of milk on the wall!"

Luckily for us, computers are excellent at performing repetitive tasks, and this program reproduces all of the lyrics programmatically. An extended version of this program is in Project 51, "niNety-nniinE BoOttels."

The Program in Action

When you run *ninetyninebottles.py*, the output will look like this:

```
Ninety-Nine Bottles, by Al Sweigart al@inventwithpython.com

(Press Ctrl-C to quit.)
99 bottles of milk on the wall,
99 bottles of milk,
Take one down, pass it around,
98 bottles of milk on the wall!

98 bottles of milk on the wall,
98 bottles of milk,
Take one down, pass it around,
97 bottles of milk on the wall!
--snip--
```

How It Works

The repetition in this song makes it easy to use a for loop (from lines 20 to 30) to display the first 98 stanzas. However, the last stanza has some minor differences and requires separate code to display (lines 33 to 39). This is because the last line, 'No more bottles of milk on the wall!', deviates from the line repeated in the loop, and because the word "bottle" is singular rather than plural.

```python
1. """Ninety-Nine Bottles of Milk on the Wall
2. By Al Sweigart al@inventwithpython.com
3. Print the full lyrics to one of the longest songs ever! Press
4. Ctrl-C to stop.
5. View this code at https://nostarch.com/big-book-small-python-projects
6. Tags: tiny, beginner, scrolling"""
7.
8. import sys, time
9.
10. print('Ninety-Nine Bottles, by Al Sweigart al@inventwithpython.com')
11. print()
12. print('(Press Ctrl-C to quit.)')
13.
14. time.sleep(2)
15.
16. bottles = 99  # This is the starting number of bottles.
17. PAUSE = 2  # (!) Try changing this to 0 to see the full song at once.
18.
19. try:
20.     while bottles > 1:  # Keep looping and display the lyrics.
21.         print(bottles, 'bottles of milk on the wall,')
22.         time.sleep(PAUSE)  # Pause for PAUSE number of seconds.
23.         print(bottles, 'bottles of milk,')
24.         time.sleep(PAUSE)
25.         print('Take one down, pass it around,')
26.         time.sleep(PAUSE)
```

```
27.          bottles = bottles - 1  # Decrease the number of bottles by one.
28.          print(bottles, 'bottles of milk on the wall!')
29.          time.sleep(PAUSE)
30.          print()  # Print a newline.
31.
32.      # Display the last stanza:
33.      print('1 bottle of milk on the wall,')
34.      time.sleep(PAUSE)
35.      print('1 bottle of milk,')
36.      time.sleep(PAUSE)
37.      print('Take it down, pass it around,')
38.      time.sleep(PAUSE)
39.      print('No more bottles of milk on the wall!')
40. except KeyboardInterrupt:
41.      sys.exit()  # When Ctrl-C is pressed, end the program.
```

After entering the source code and running it a few times, try making experimental changes to it. On your own, you can also try to figure out how to do the following:

- Create a program for the repetitive song "The Twelve Days of Christmas."

- Create programs for other cumulative songs. You can find a list of them at *https://en.wikipedia.org/wiki/Cumulative_song*.

Exploring the Program

Try to find the answers to the following questions. Experiment with some modifications to the code and rerun the program to see what effect the changes have.

1. What happens if you change bottles = bottles - 1 on line 27 to bottles = bottles - 2?

2. What happens if you change while bottles > 1: on line 20 to while bottles < 1:?

#51

NINETY-NNIINE BOOTTELS

In this version of the song "Ninety-Nine Bottles," the program introduces small imperfections in each stanza by either removing a letter, swapping the casing of a letter, transposing two letters, or doubling a letter.

As the song continues to play, these mutations add up, resulting in a very silly song. It's a good idea to try Project 50, "Ninety-Nine Bottles," before attempting this one.

The Program in Action

When you run *ninetyninebottles2.py*, the output will look like this:

```
niNety-nniinE BoOttels, by Al Sweigart al@inventwithpython.com
--snip--
99 bottles of milk on the wall,
99 bottles of milk,
Take one down, pass it around,
98 bottles of milk on the wall!

98 bottles of milk on the wall,
98 bottles of milk,
Take one d wn, pass it around,
97 bottles of milk on the wall!

97 bottles of milk on the wall,
97 bottels of milk,
Take one d wn,  pass it around,
96 bottles of milk on the wall!
--snip--
75b otlte  of mIl  on teh wall,
75   ottels  f miLk,
Take one d wn,  pass it ar und,
74 bbOttles of milk on t e wall!
--snip--
1  otlE t of iml  oo nteh  lall,
1   o  Tle   FF FmMLIIkk,
Taake on  d wn,  pAasSs itt au nn d,
No more bottles of milk on the wall!
```

How It Works

String values in Python are *immutable*, meaning they cannot be changed. If the string 'Hello' is stored in a variable called greeting, the code greeting = greeting + ' world!' doesn't actually change the 'Hello' string. Rather, it creates a new string, 'Hello world!', to replace the 'Hello' string in greeting. The technical reasons for this are beyond the scope of this book, but it's important to understand the distinction, because it means code like greeting[0] = 'h' isn't allowed, since strings are immutable. However, since lists are mutable, we can create a list of single-character strings (as line 62 does), change the characters in the list, and then create a string from the list (line 85). This is how our program seemingly changes, or *mutates*, the strings containing the song lyrics.

```
1. """niNety-nniinE BoOttels of Mlik On teh waLl
2. By Al Sweigart al@inventwithpython.com
3. Print the full lyrics to one of the longest songs ever! The song
4. gets sillier and sillier with each verse. Press Ctrl-C to stop.
5. View this code at https://nostarch.com/big-book-small-python-projects
6. Tags: short, scrolling, word"""
7.
```

```
 8. import random, sys, time
 9.
10. # Set up the constants:
11. # (!) Try changing both of these to 0 to print all the lyrics at once.
12. SPEED = 0.01  # The pause in between printing letters.
13. LINE_PAUSE = 1.5  # The pause at the end of each line.
14.
15.
16. def slowPrint(text, pauseAmount=0.1):
17.     """Slowly print out the characters in text one at a time."""
18.     for character in text:
19.         # Set flush=True here so the text is immediately printed:
20.         print(character, flush=True, end='')  # end='' means no newline.
21.         time.sleep(pauseAmount)  # Pause in between each character.
22.     print()  # Print a newline.
23.
24.
25. print('niNety-nniinE BoOttels, by Al Sweigart al@inventwithpython.com')
26. print()
27. print('(Press Ctrl-C to quit.)')
28.
29. time.sleep(2)
30.
31. bottles = 99  # This is the starting number of bottles.
32.
33. # This list holds the string used for the lyrics:
34. lines = [' bottles of milk on the wall,',
35.          ' bottles of milk,',
36.          'Take one down, pass it around,',
37.          ' bottles of milk on the wall!']
38.
39. try:
40.     while bottles > 0:  # Keep looping and display the lyrics.
41.         slowPrint(str(bottles) + lines[0], SPEED)
42.         time.sleep(LINE_PAUSE)
43.         slowPrint(str(bottles) + lines[1], SPEED)
44.         time.sleep(LINE_PAUSE)
45.         slowPrint(lines[2], SPEED)
46.         time.sleep(LINE_PAUSE)
47.         bottles = bottles - 1  # Decrease the number of bottles by one.
48.
49.         if bottles > 0:  # Print the last line of the current stanza.
50.             slowPrint(str(bottles) + lines[3], SPEED)
51.         else:  # Print the last line of the entire song.
52.             slowPrint('No more bottles of milk on the wall!', SPEED)
53.
54.         time.sleep(LINE_PAUSE)
55.         print()  # Print a newline.
56.
57.         # Choose a random line to make "sillier":
58.         lineNum = random.randint(0, 3)
59.
60.         # Make a list from the line string so we can edit it. (Strings
61.         # in Python are immutable.)
62.         line = list(lines[lineNum])
```

```
63.
64.         effect = random.randint(0, 3)
65.         if effect == 0:  # Replace a character with a space.
66.             charIndex = random.randint(0, len(line) - 1)
67.             line[charIndex] = ' '
68.         elif effect == 1:  # Change the casing of a character.
69.             charIndex = random.randint(0, len(line) - 1)
70.             if line[charIndex].isupper():
71.                 line[charIndex] = line[charIndex].lower()
72.             elif line[charIndex].islower():
73.                 line[charIndex] = line[charIndex].upper()
74.         elif effect == 2:  # Transpose two characters.
75.             charIndex = random.randint(0, len(line) - 2)
76.             firstChar = line[charIndex]
77.             secondChar = line[charIndex + 1]
78.             line[charIndex] = secondChar
79.             line[charIndex + 1] = firstChar
80.         elif effect == 3:  # Double a character.
81.             charIndex = random.randint(0, len(line) - 2)
82.             line.insert(charIndex, line[charIndex])
83.
84.         # Convert the line list back to a string and put it in lines:
85.         lines[lineNum] = ''.join(line)
86. except KeyboardInterrupt:
87.     sys.exit()  # When Ctrl-C is pressed, end the program.
```

After entering the source code and running it a few times, try making experimental changes to it. The comments marked with (!) have suggestions for small changes you can make. On your own, you can also try to figure out how to do the following:

- Swap the order of two adjacent words, where a "word" is text separated by spaces.
- On rare occasions, have the song start counting upward for a few iterations.
- Change the case of an entire word.

Exploring the Program

Try to find the answers to the following questions. Experiment with some modifications to the code and rerun the program to see what effect the changes have.

1. What happens if you change bottles = bottles - 1 on line 47 to bottles = bottles - 2?

2. What happens if you change effect = random.randint(0, 3) on line 64 to effect = 0?

3. What error happens if you delete or comment out line = list(lines [lineNum]) on line 62?

#52

NUMERAL SYSTEM COUNTERS

We're used to counting in the decimal numeral system, which uses 10 digits: 0 through 9. This system likely developed because humans counted on their fingers, and most people have 10 fingers. But other number systems exist. Computers make use of *binary*, a numeral system with only two digits, 0 and 1. Programmers also sometimes use hexadecimal, which is a base-16 numeral system that uses the digits 0 to 9 but also extends into the letters *A* to *F*.

We can represent any number in any numeral system, and this program displays a range of numbers in decimal, binary, and hexadecimal.

The Program in Action

When you run *numeralsystems.py*, the output will look like this:

```
Numeral System Counters, by Al Sweigart al@inventwithpython.com

--snip--
Enter the starting number (e.g. 0) > 0
Enter how many numbers to display (e.g. 1000) > 20
DEC: 0    HEX: 0    BIN: 0
DEC: 1    HEX: 1    BIN: 1
DEC: 2    HEX: 2    BIN: 10
DEC: 3    HEX: 3    BIN: 11
DEC: 4    HEX: 4    BIN: 100
DEC: 5    HEX: 5    BIN: 101
DEC: 6    HEX: 6    BIN: 110
DEC: 7    HEX: 7    BIN: 111
DEC: 8    HEX: 8    BIN: 1000
DEC: 9    HEX: 9    BIN: 1001
DEC: 10   HEX: A    BIN: 1010
DEC: 11   HEX: B    BIN: 1011
DEC: 12   HEX: C    BIN: 1100
DEC: 13   HEX: D    BIN: 1101
DEC: 14   HEX: E    BIN: 1110
DEC: 15   HEX: F    BIN: 1111
DEC: 16   HEX: 10   BIN: 10000
DEC: 17   HEX: 11   BIN: 10001
DEC: 18   HEX: 12   BIN: 10010
DEC: 19   HEX: 13   BIN: 10011
```

How It Works

You can get the binary and hexadecimal representations of a number in Python by calling the bin() and hex() functions, respectively:

```
>>> bin(42)
'0b101010'
>>> hex(42)
'0x2a'
```

Convert these strings back into decimal integers by calling int() and supplying the base to convert from, like so:

```
>>> int('0b101010', 2)
42
>>> int('0x2a', 16)
42
```

Keep in mind that the binary and hexadecimal "numbers" returned by bin() and hex() are actually string values: bin(42) returns the string '0b101010' and hex(42) returns the string '0x2a'. In programming, it is convention to add a 0b prefix to binary numbers and 0x prefix to hexadecimal numbers.

That way, no one will confuse the binary number 10000 (the number 16 in decimal) with the decimal number "ten thousand." The numeral systems program removes these prefixes before displaying the number.

```
1. """Numeral System Counters, by Al Sweigart al@inventwithpython.com
2. Shows equivalent numbers in decimal, hexadecimal, and binary.
3. View this code at https://nostarch.com/big-book-small-python-projects
4. Tags: tiny, math"""
5.
6.
7. print('''Numeral System Counters, by Al Sweigart al@inventwithpython.com
8.
9. This program shows you equivalent numbers in decimal (base 10),
10. hexadecimal (base 16), and binary (base 2) numeral systems.
11.
12. (Ctrl-C to quit.)
13. ''')
14.
15. while True:
16.     response = input('Enter the starting number (e.g. 0) > ')
17.     if response == '':
18.         response = '0'  # Start at 0 by default.
19.         break
20.     if response.isdecimal():
21.         break
22.     print('Please enter a number greater than or equal to 0.')
23. start = int(response)
24.
25. while True:
26.     response = input('Enter how many numbers to display (e.g. 1000) > ')
27.     if response == '':
28.         response = '1000'  # Display 1000 numbers by default.
29.         break
30.     if response.isdecimal():
31.         break
32.     print('Please enter a number.')
33. amount = int(response)
34.
35. for number in range(start, start + amount):  # Main program loop.
36.     # Convert to hexadecimal/binary and remove the prefix:
37.     hexNumber = hex(number)[2:].upper()
38.     binNumber = bin(number)[2:]
39.
40.     print('DEC:', number, '   HEX:', hexNumber, '   BIN:', binNumber)
```

After entering the source code and running it a few times, try making experimental changes to it. On your own, you can also try to figure out how to do the following:

- Enter a new row for *octal*, the base-8 number system, using Python's oct() function.
- Search the internet for "number system conversion" to find out how to implement your own bin(), oct(), and hex() functions.

Exploring the Program

Try to find the answers to the following questions. Experiment with some modifications to the code and rerun the program to see what effect the changes have.

1. What happens if you change hex(number)[2:].upper() on line 37 to hex(number)[2:]?

2. What error do you cause if you change int(response) on line 33 to response?

#53

PERIODIC TABLE OF THE ELEMENTS

The periodic table of the elements organizes all known chemical elements into a single table. This program presents this table and lets the player access additional information about each element, such as its atomic number, symbol, melting point, and so on. I compiled this information from Wikipedia and stored it in a file called *periodictable.csv* that you can download from *https://inventwithpython.com/periodictable.csv*.

The Program in Action

When you run *periodictable.py*, the output will look like this:

```
Periodic Table of Elements
By Al Sweigart al@inventwithpython.com

            Periodic Table of Elements
    1  2  3  4  5  6  7  8  9  10 11 12 13 14 15 16 17 18
 1  H                                                  He
 2  Li Be                               B  C  N  O  F  Ne
 3  Na Mg                               Al Si P  S  Cl Ar
 4  K  Ca Sc Ti V  Cr Mn Fe Co Ni Cu Zn Ga Ge As Se Br Kr
 5  Rb Sr Y  Zr Nb Mo Tc Ru Rh Pd Ag Cd In Sn Sb Te I  Xe
 6  Cs Ba La Hf Ta W  Re Os Ir Pt Au Hg Tl Pb Bi Po At Rn
 7  Fr Ra Ac Rf Db Sg Bh Hs Mt Ds Rg Cn Nh Fl Mc Lv Ts Og

            Ce Pr Nd Pm Sm Eu Gd Tb Dy Ho Er Tm Yb Lu
            Th Pa U  Np Pu Am Cm Bk Cf Es Fm Md No Lr
Enter a symbol or atomic number to examine, or QUIT to quit.
> 42
            Atomic Number: 42
                   Symbol: Mo
                  Element: Molybdenum
           Origin of name: Greek molýbdaina, 'piece of lead', from mólybdos, 'lead'
                    Group: 6
                   Period: 5
            Atomic weight: 95.95(1) u
                  Density: 10.22 g/cm^3
            Melting point: 2896 K
            Boiling point: 4912 K
   Specific heat capacity: 0.251 J/(g*K)
        Electronegativity: 2.16
Abundance in earth's crust: 1.2 mg/kg
Press Enter to continue...
--snip--
```

How It Works

A *.csv*, or *comma-separated values*, file is a text file that represents a primitive spreadsheet. Each line in the *.csv* file is a row, and commas separate the columns. For example, the first three lines in *periodictable.csv* look like this:

```
1,H,Hydrogen,"Greek elements hydro- and -gen, meaning 'water-forming--snip--
2,He,Helium,"Greek hélios, 'sun'",18,1,4.002602(2)[III][V],0.0001785--snip--
3,Li,Lithium,"Greek líthos, 'stone'",1,2,6.94[III][IV][V][VIII][VI],--snip--
```

Python's csv module makes it easy to import data from a *.csv* file and into a list of lists of strings, as lines 15 to 18 do. Lines 32 to 58 turn this list of lists into a dictionary so that the rest of the program can easily summon the information by an element's name or atomic number.

```
 1.  """Periodic Table of Elements, by Al Sweigart al@inventwithpython.com
 2.  Displays atomic information for all the elements.
 3.  View this code at https://nostarch.com/big-book-small-python-projects
 4.  Tags: short, science"""
 5.
 6.  # Data from https://en.wikipedia.org/wiki/List_of_chemical_elements
 7.  # Highlight the table, copy it, then paste it into a spreadsheet program
 8.  # like Excel or Google Sheets like in https://invpy.com/elements
 9.  # Then save this file as periodictable.csv.
10.  # Or download this csv file from https://invpy.com/periodictable.csv
11.
12.  import csv, sys, re
13.
14.  # Read in all the data from periodictable.csv.
15.  elementsFile = open('periodictable.csv', encoding='utf-8')
16.  elementsCsvReader = csv.reader(elementsFile)
17.  elements = list(elementsCsvReader)
18.  elementsFile.close()
19.
20.  ALL_COLUMNS = ['Atomic Number', 'Symbol', 'Element', 'Origin of name',
21.                 'Group', 'Period', 'Atomic weight', 'Density',
22.                 'Melting point', 'Boiling point',
23.                 'Specific heat capacity', 'Electronegativity',
24.                 'Abundance in earth\'s crust']
25.
26.  # To justify the text, we need to find the longest string in ALL_COLUMNS.
27.  LONGEST_COLUMN = 0
28.  for key in ALL_COLUMNS:
29.      if len(key) > LONGEST_COLUMN:
30.          LONGEST_COLUMN = len(key)
31.
32.  # Put all the elements data into a data structure:
33.  ELEMENTS = {}  # The data structure that stores all the element data.
34.  for line in elements:
35.      element = {'Atomic Number':  line[0],
36.                 'Symbol':         line[1],
37.                 'Element':        line[2],
38.                 'Origin of name': line[3],
39.                 'Group':          line[4],
40.                 'Period':         line[5],
41.                 'Atomic weight':  line[6] + ' u', # atomic mass unit
42.                 'Density':        line[7] + ' g/cm^3', # grams/cubic cm
43.                 'Melting point':  line[8] + ' K', # kelvin
44.                 'Boiling point':  line[9] + ' K', # kelvin
45.                 'Specific heat capacity':    line[10] + ' J/(g*K)',
46.                 'Electronegativity':         line[11],
47.                 'Abundance in earth\'s crust': line[12] + ' mg/kg'}
48.
49.      # Some of the data has bracketed text from Wikipedia that we want to
50.      # remove, such as the atomic weight of Boron:
51.      # "10.81[III][IV][V][VI]" should be "10.81"
52.
53.      for key, value in element.items():
54.          # Remove the [roman numeral] text:
```

```
55.         element[key] = re.sub(r'\[(I|V|X)+\]', '', value)
56.
57.     ELEMENTS[line[0]] = element  # Map the atomic number to the element.
58.     ELEMENTS[line[1]] = element  # Map the symbol to the element.
59.
60. print('Periodic Table of Elements')
61. print('By Al Sweigart al@inventwithpython.com')
62. print()
63.
64. while True:  # Main program loop.
65.     # Show table and let the user select an element:
66.     print('''          Periodic Table of Elements
67.       1  2  3  4  5  6  7  8  9  10 11 12 13 14 15 16 17 18
68.     1 H                                                  He
69.     2 Li Be                          B  C  N  O  F  Ne
70.     3 Na Mg                          Al Si P  S  Cl Ar
71.     4 K  Ca Sc Ti V  Cr Mn Fe Co Ni Cu Zn Ga Ge As Se Br Kr
72.     5 Rb Sr Y  Zr Nb Mo Tc Ru Rh Pd Ag Cd In Sn Sb Te I  Xe
73.     6 Cs Ba La Hf Ta W  Re Os Ir Pt Au Hg Tl Pb Bi Po At Rn
74.     7 Fr Ra Ac Rf Db Sg Bh Hs Mt Ds Rg Cn Nh Fl Mc Lv Ts Og
75.
76.           Ce Pr Nd Pm Sm Eu Gd Tb Dy Ho Er Tm Yb Lu
77.           Th Pa U  Np Pu Am Cm Bk Cf Es Fm Md No Lr''')
78.     print('Enter a symbol or atomic number to examine, or QUIT to quit.')
79.     response = input('> ').title()
80.
81.     if response == 'Quit':
82.         sys.exit()
83.
84.     # Display the selected element's data:
85.     if response in ELEMENTS:
86.         for key in ALL_COLUMNS:
87.             keyJustified = key.rjust(LONGEST_COLUMN)
88.             print(keyJustified + ': ' + ELEMENTS[response][key])
89.         input('Press Enter to continue...')
```

Exploring the Program

Try to find the answers to the following questions. Experiment with some modifications to the code and rerun the program to see what effect the changes have.

1. What bug do you cause if you change response == 'Quit' on line 81 to response == 'quit'?

2. What happens if you delete or comment out lines 53 and 55?

#54

PIG LATIN

Pig Latin is a word game that transforms English words into a parody of Latin. In Pig Latin, if a word begins with a consonant, the speaker removes this letter and puts it at the end, followed by "ay." For example, "pig" becomes "igpay" and "latin" becomes "atinlay." Otherwise, if the word begins with a vowel, the speaker simply adds "yay" to the end of it. For example, "elephant" becomes "elephantyay" and "umbrella" becomes "umbrellayay."

The Program in Action

When you run *piglatin.py*, the output will look like this:

```
Igpay Atinlay (Pig Latin)
By Al Sweigart al@inventwithpython.com

Enter your message:
> This is a very serious message.
Isthay isyay ayay eryvay erioussay essagemay.
(Copied pig latin to clipboard.)
```

How It Works

The englishToPigLatin() function takes a string of English text and returns a string of its Pig Latin equivalent. The main() function only gets called if a user runs the program directly. You could also write your own Python programs, import *piglatin.py* with an import piglatin statement, then call piglatin.englishToPigLatin() to make use of the englishToPigLatin() function. This reuse technique can save you the time and effort required to reinvent this code yourself.

```
 1. """Pig Latin, by Al Sweigart al@inventwithpython.com
 2. Translates English messages into Igpay Atinlay.
 3. View this code at https://nostarch.com/big-book-small-python-projects
 4. Tags: short, word"""
 5.
 6. try:
 7.     import pyperclip  # pyperclip copies text to the clipboard.
 8. except ImportError:
 9.     pass  # If pyperclip is not installed, do nothing. It's no big deal.
10.
11. VOWELS = ('a', 'e', 'i', 'o', 'u', 'y')
12.
13.
14. def main():
15.     print('''Igpay Atinlay (Pig Latin)
16. By Al Sweigart al@inventwithpython.com
17.
18. Enter your message:''')
19.     pigLatin = englishToPigLatin(input('> '))
20.
21.     # Join all the words back together into a single string:
22.     print(pigLatin)
23.
24.     try:
25.         pyperclip.copy(pigLatin)
26.         print('(Copied pig latin to clipboard.)')
27.     except NameError:
28.         pass  # Do nothing if pyperclip wasn't installed.
29.
```

```
30.
31. def englishToPigLatin(message):
32.     pigLatin = ''  # A string of the pig latin translation.
33.     for word in message.split():
34.         # Separate the non-letters at the start of this word:
35.         prefixNonLetters = ''
36.         while len(word) > 0 and not word[0].isalpha():
37.             prefixNonLetters += word[0]
38.             word = word[1:]
39.         if len(word) == 0:
40.             pigLatin = pigLatin + prefixNonLetters + ' '
41.             continue
42.
43.         # Separate the non-letters at the end of this word:
44.         suffixNonLetters = ''
45.         while not word[-1].isalpha():
46.             suffixNonLetters = word[-1] + suffixNonLetters
47.             word = word[:-1]
48.
49.         # Remember if the word was in uppercase or titlecase.
50.         wasUpper = word.isupper()
51.         wasTitle = word.istitle()
52.
53.         word = word.lower()  # Make the word lowercase for translation.
54.
55.         # Separate the consonants at the start of this word:
56.         prefixConsonants = ''
57.         while len(word) > 0 and not word[0] in VOWELS:
58.             prefixConsonants += word[0]
59.             word = word[1:]
60.
61.         # Add the pig latin ending to the word:
62.         if prefixConsonants != '':
63.             word += prefixConsonants + 'ay'
64.         else:
65.             word += 'yay'
66.
67.         # Set the word back to uppercase or titlecase:
68.         if wasUpper:
69.             word = word.upper()
70.         if wasTitle:
71.             word = word.title()
72.
73.         # Add the non-letters back to the start or end of the word.
74.         pigLatin += prefixNonLetters + word + suffixNonLetters + ' '
75.     return pigLatin
76.
77.
78. if __name__ == '__main__':
79.     main()
```

Exploring the Program

Try to find the answers to the following questions. Experiment with some modifications to the code and rerun the program to see what effect the changes have.

1. What happens if you change `message.split()` on line 33 to `message`?
2. What happens if you change `('a', 'e', 'i', 'o', 'u', 'y')` on line 11 to `()`?
3. What happens if you change `('a', 'e', 'i', 'o', 'u', 'y')` on line 11 to `('A', 'E', 'I', 'O', 'U', 'Y')`?

#55

POWERBALL LOTTERY

The Powerball Lottery is an exciting way to lose small amounts of money. If you purchase a $2 ticket, you can pick six numbers: five drawn from 1 to 69, and a sixth "Powerball" number drawn from 1 to 26. The order of the numbers doesn't matter. If the lottery selects your six numbers, you win $1.586 billion dollars! Except you won't win, because your odds are 1 in 292,201,338. But if you spent $200 on 100 tickets, your odds would be . . . 1 in 2,922,013. You won't win that either, but at least you'll lose 100 times as much money. The more you like losing money, the more fun the lottery is!

To help you visualize how often you won't win the lottery, this program simulates up to one million Powerball drawings and then compares them with the numbers you picked. Now you can have all the excitement of losing the lottery without spending money.

Fun fact: every set of six numbers is just as likely to win as any other. So the next time you want to buy a lottery ticket, pick the numbers 1, 2, 3, 4, 5, and 6. Those numbers are just as likely to come up as a more complex set.

The Program in Action

When you run *powerballlottery.py*, the output will look like this:

```
Powerball Lottery, by Al Sweigart al@inventwithpython.com

Each powerball lottery ticket costs $2. The jackpot for this game
is $1.586 billion! It doesn't matter what the jackpot is, though,
because the odds are 1 in 292,201,338, so you won't win.

This simulation gives you the thrill of playing without wasting money.

Enter 5 different numbers from 1 to 69, with spaces between
each number. (For example: 5 17 23 42 50 51)
> 1 2 3 4 5
Enter the powerball number from 1 to 26.
> 6
How many times do you want to play? (Max: 1000000)
> 1000000
It costs $2000000 to play 1000000 times, but don't
worry. I'm sure you'll win it all back.
Press Enter to start...
The winning numbers are: 12 29 48 11 4 and 13  You lost.
The winning numbers are: 54 39 3 42 16 and 12  You lost.
The winning numbers are: 56 4 63 23 38 and 24  You lost.
--snip--
The winning numbers are: 46 29 10 62 17 and 21 You lost.
The winning numbers are: 5 20 18 65 30 and 10  You lost.
The winning numbers are: 54 30 58 10 1 and 18  You lost.
You have wasted $2000000
Thanks for playing!
```

How It Works

The output from this program looks fairly uniform because the allWinning Nums.ljust(21) code on line 109 pads the numbers with enough spaces to take up 21 columns, no matter how many digits the winning numbers have. This makes the "You lost." text always appear in the same place on the screen, so it remains readable even as the program quickly outputs several lines.

```
1. """Powerball Lottery, by Al Sweigart al@inventwithpython.com
2. A simulation of the lottery so you can experience the thrill of
3. losing the lottery without wasting your money.
4. View this code at https://nostarch.com/big-book-small-python-projects
5. Tags: short, humor, simulation"""
6.
```

```
 7. import random
 8.
 9. print('''Powerball Lottery, by Al Sweigart al@inventwithpython.com
10.
11. Each powerball lottery ticket costs $2. The jackpot for this game
12. is $1.586 billion! It doesn't matter what the jackpot is, though,
13. because the odds are 1 in 292,201,338, so you won't win.
14.
15. This simulation gives you the thrill of playing without wasting money.
16. ''')
17.
18. # Let the player enter the first five numbers, 1 to 69:
19. while True:
20.     print('Enter 5 different numbers from 1 to 69, with spaces between')
21.     print('each number. (For example: 5 17 23 42 50)')
22.     response = input('> ')
23.
24.     # Check that the player entered 5 things:
25.     numbers = response.split()
26.     if len(numbers) != 5:
27.         print('Please enter 5 numbers, separated by spaces.')
28.         continue
29.
30.     # Convert the strings into integers:
31.     try:
32.         for i in range(5):
33.             numbers[i] = int(numbers[i])
34.     except ValueError:
35.         print('Please enter numbers, like 27, 35, or 62.')
36.         continue
37.
38.     # Check that the numbers are between 1 and 69:
39.     for i in range(5):
40.         if not (1 <= numbers[i] <= 69):
41.             print('The numbers must all be between 1 and 69.')
42.             continue
43.
44.     # Check that the numbers are unique:
45.     # (Create a set from number to remove duplicates.)
46.     if len(set(numbers)) != 5:
47.         print('You must enter 5 different numbers.')
48.         continue
49.
50.     break
51.
52. # Let the player select the powerball, 1 to 26:
53. while True:
54.     print('Enter the powerball number from 1 to 26.')
55.     response = input('> ')
56.
57.     # Convert the strings into integers:
58.     try:
59.         powerball = int(response)
60.     except ValueError:
61.         print('Please enter a number, like 3, 15, or 22.')
```

```
62.            continue
63.
64.        # Check that the number is between 1 and 26:
65.        if not (1 <= powerball <= 26):
66.            print('The powerball number must be between 1 and 26.')
67.            continue
68.
69.        break
70.
71. # Enter the number of times you want to play:
72. while True:
73.        print('How many times do you want to play? (Max: 1000000)')
74.        response = input('> ')
75.
76.        # Convert the strings into integers:
77.        try:
78.            numPlays = int(response)
79.        except ValueError:
80.            print('Please enter a number, like 3, 15, or 22000.')
81.            continue
82.
83.        # Check that the number is between 1 and 1000000:
84.        if not (1 <= numPlays <= 1000000):
85.            print('You can play between 1 and 1000000 times.')
86.            continue
87.
88.        break
89.
90. # Run the simulation:
91. price = '$' + str(2 * numPlays)
92. print('It costs', price, 'to play', numPlays, 'times, but don\'t')
93. print('worry. I\'m sure you\'ll win it all back.')
94. input('Press Enter to start...')
95.
96. possibleNumbers = list(range(1, 70))
97. for i in range(numPlays):
98.        # Come up with lottery numbers:
99.        random.shuffle(possibleNumbers)
100.       winningNumbers = possibleNumbers[0:5]
101.       winningPowerball = random.randint(1, 26)
102.
103.       # Display winning numbers:
104.       print('The winning numbers are: ', end='')
105.       allWinningNums = ''
106.       for i in range(5):
107.           allWinningNums += str(winningNumbers[i]) + ' '
108.       allWinningNums += 'and ' + str(winningPowerball)
109.       print(allWinningNums.ljust(21), end='')
110.
111.       # NOTE: Sets are not ordered, so it doesn't matter what order the
112.       # integers in set(numbers) and set(winningNumbers) are.
113.       if (set(numbers) == set(winningNumbers)
114.           and powerball == winningPowerball):
115.               print()
116.               print('You have won the Powerball Lottery! Congratulations,')
```

```
117.            print('you would be a billionaire if this was real!')
118.            break
119.    else:
120.        print(' You lost.')  # The leading space is required here.
121.
122. print('You have wasted', price)
123. print('Thanks for playing!')
```

Exploring the Program

Try to find the answers to the following questions. Experiment with some modifications to the code and rerun the program to see what effect the changes have.

1. What happens if you change possibleNumbers[0:5] on line 100 to numbers and random.randint(1, 26) on line 101 to powerball?

2. What error do you get if you delete or comment out possibleNumbers = list(range(1, 70)) on line 96?

#56

PRIME NUMBERS

 A *prime number* is a number that is evenly divisible only by one and itself. Prime numbers have a variety of practical applications, but no algorithm can predict them; we must calculate them one at a time. However, we do know that there is an infinite number of prime numbers to be discovered.

This program finds prime numbers through brute-force calculation. Its code is similar to Project 24, "Factor Finder." (Another way to describe a prime number is that one and the number itself are its only factors.) You can find out more about prime numbers from *https://en.wikipedia.org/wiki/Prime_number*.

The Program in Action

When you run *primenumbers.py*, the output will look like this:

```
Prime Numbers, by Al Sweigart al@inventwithpython.com
--snip--
Enter a number to start searching for primes from:
(Try 0 or 1000000000000 (12 zeros) or another number.)
> 0
Press Ctrl-C at any time to quit. Press Enter to begin...
2, 3, 5, 7, 11, 13, 17, 19, 23, 29, 31, 37, 41, 43, 47, 53, 59, 61, 67, 71,
73, 79, 83, 89, 97, 101, 103, 107, 109, 113, 127, 131, 137, 139, 149, 151,
157, 163, 167, 173, 179, 181, 191, 193, 197, 199, 211, 223, 227, 229, 233,
239, 241, 251, 257, 263, 269, 271, 277, 281, 283, 293, 307, 311, 313, 317,
331, 337, 347, 349, 353, 359, 367, 373, 379, 383, 389, 397, 401, 409, 419,
421, 431, 433, 439, 443, 449, 457, 461, 463, 467, 479, 487, 491, 499, 503,
509, 521, 523, 541, 547, 557, 563, 569, 571, 577, 587, 593, 599, 601, 607,
613, 617, 619, 631, 641, 643, 647, --snip--
```

How It Works

The isPrime() function accepts an integer and returns True if it is a prime number. Otherwise, it returns False. Project 24 is worth studying if you're trying to understand this program. The isPrime() function essentially looks for any factors in the given number and returns False if it finds any.

The algorithm in this program can quickly find large prime numbers. The number one trillion has a mere 10 digits. But to find prime numbers that are as big as a googol (a one followed by 100 zeros), you need to use an advanced algorithm such as the Rabin-Miller primality test. Chapter 22 of my book *Cracking Codes with Python* (No Starch Press, 2018) has a Python implementation of this algorithm.

```
1. """Prime Numbers, by Al Sweigart al@inventwithpython.com
2. Calculates prime numbers, which are numbers that are only evenly
3. divisible by one and themselves. They are used in a variety of practical
4. applications.
5. More info at: https://en.wikipedia.org/wiki/Prime_number
6. View this code at https://nostarch.com/big-book-small-python-projects
7. Tags: tiny, math, scrolling"""
8.
9. import math, sys
10.
11. def main():
12.     print('Prime Numbers, by Al Sweigart al@inventwithpython.com')
13.     print('Prime numbers are numbers that are only evenly divisible by')
14.     print('one and themselves. They are used in a variety of practical')
15.     print('applications, but cannot be predicted. They must be')
16.     print('calculated one at a time.')
17.     print()
18.     while True:
19.         print('Enter a number to start searching for primes from:')
20.         print('(Try 0 or 1000000000000 (12 zeros) or another number.)')
```

```
21.            response = input('> ')
22.            if response.isdecimal():
23.                num = int(response)
24.                break
25.
26.        input('Press Ctrl-C at any time to quit. Press Enter to begin...')
27.
28.        while True:
29.            # Print out any prime numbers:
30.            if isPrime(num):
31.                print(str(num) + ', ', end='', flush=True)
32.            num = num + 1  # Go to the next number.
33.
34.
35. def isPrime(number):
36.        """Returns True if number is prime, otherwise returns False."""
37.        # Handle special cases:
38.        if number < 2:
39.            return False
40.        elif number == 2:
41.            return True
42.
43.        # Try to evenly divide number by all numbers from 2 up to number's
44.        # square root.
45.        for i in range(2, int(math.sqrt(number)) + 1):
46.            if number % i == 0:
47.                return False
48.        return True
49.
50.
51. # If this program was run (instead of imported), run the game:
52. if __name__ == '__main__':
53.        try:
54.            main()
55.        except KeyboardInterrupt:
56.            sys.exit()  # When Ctrl-C is pressed, end the program.
```

Exploring the Program

Try to find the answers to the following questions. Experiment with some modifications to the code and rerun the program to see what effect the changes have.

1. What error do you get if you change `response.isdecimal()` on line 22 to `response` and enter a non-number for the number from which to start searching for primes?

2. What happens if you change `number < 2` on line 38 to `number > 2`?

3. What happens if you change `number % 1 == 0` on line 46 to `number % i != 0`?

#57

PROGRESS BAR

A *progress bar* is a visual element that shows how much of a task has been completed. Progress bars are often used alongside downloading files or software installations. This project creates a getProgressBar() function that returns a progress bar string based on the arguments passed to it. It simulates a downloading file, but you can reuse the progress bar code in your own projects.

The Program in Action

When you run *progressbar.py*, the output will look like this:

```
Progress Bar Simulation, by Al Sweigart
[████████████                              ] 24.6% 1007/4098
```

How It Works

The progress bar relies on a certain trick that programs running in terminal windows can perform. Just as '\n' and '\t' are escape characters for newline and tab characters, respectively, '\b' is an escape character for backspace characters. If you "print" a backspace character, the text cursor will move to the left and erase the previously printed character. This only works for the current line the text cursor is on. If you run the code print('Hello\b\b\b\b\bHowdy'), Python will print the text "Hello," move the text cursor back five spaces, and then print the text "Howdy." The "Howdy" text will overwrite "Hello," making it look as though you called "Howdy."

We can use this technique to create an animated progress bar on a single line by printing one version of the bar, moving the text cursor back to the start, then printing an updated progress bar. This effect can generate any text animation without requiring a module such as bext, though it will be limited to taking up a single line in the terminal window.

Once you've created this program, you can display progress bars in your other Python programs by running import progressbar and printing the string returned from progressbar.getProgressBar().

```python
1. """Progress Bar Simulation, by Al Sweigart al@inventwithpython.com
2. A sample progress bar animation that can be used in other programs.
3. View this code at https://nostarch.com/big-book-small-python-projects
4. Tags: tiny, module"""
5.
6. import random, time
7.
8. BAR = chr(9608) # Character 9608 is '█'
9.
10. def main():
11.     # Simulate a download:
12.     print('Progress Bar Simulation, by Al Sweigart')
13.     bytesDownloaded = 0
14.     downloadSize = 4096
15.     while bytesDownloaded < downloadSize:
16.         # "Download" a random amount of "bytes":
17.         bytesDownloaded += random.randint(0, 100)
18.
19.         # Get the progress bar string for this amount of progress:
20.         barStr = getProgressBar(bytesDownloaded, downloadSize)
21.
22.         # Don't print a newline at the end, and immediately flush the
23.         # printed string to the screen:
24.         print(barStr, end='', flush=True)
25.
```

```
26.           time.sleep(0.2)  # Pause for a little bit:
27.
28.           # Print backspaces to move the text cursor to the line's start:
29.           print('\b' * len(barStr), end='', flush=True)
30.
31.
32. def getProgressBar(progress, total, barWidth=40):
33.     """Returns a string that represents a progress bar that has barWidth
34.     bars and has progressed progress amount out of a total amount."""
35.
36.     progressBar = ''   # The progress bar will be a string value.
37.     progressBar += '['  # Create the left end of the progress bar.
38.
39.     # Make sure that the amount of progress is between 0 and total:
40.     if progress > total:
41.         progress = total
42.     if progress < 0:
43.         progress = 0
44.
45.     # Calculate the number of "bars" to display:
46.     numberOfBars = int((progress / total) * barWidth)
47.
48.     progressBar += BAR * numberOfBars  # Add the progress bar.
49.     progressBar += ' ' * (barWidth - numberOfBars)  # Add empty space.
50.     progressBar += ']'   # Add the right end of the progress bar.
51.
52.     # Calculate the percentage complete:
53.     percentComplete = round(progress / total * 100, 1)
54.     progressBar += ' ' + str(percentComplete) + '%'  # Add percentage.
55.
56.     # Add the numbers:
57.     progressBar += ' ' + str(progress) + '/' + str(total)
58.
59.     return progressBar  # Return the progress bar string.
60.
61.
62. # If the program is run (instead of imported), run the game:
63. if __name__ == '__main__':
64.     main()
```

After entering the source code and running it a few times, try making experimental changes to it. On your own, you can also try to figure out how to do the following:

- Create a one-line animation of a spinner that alternates between the characters |, /, -, and \ to produce a rotating effect.

- Create a program that can display a scrolling marquee of text moving from left to right.

- Create a one-line animation that displays a set of four equal signs moving back and forth as a single unit, similar to the red scanning light on the robot car from the TV show *Knight Rider* or the Cylon robot face from the TV show *Battlestar Galactica*.

Exploring the Program

Try to find the answers to the following questions. Experiment with some modifications to the code and rerun the program to see what effect the changes have.

1. What happens if you delete or comment out print('\b' * len(barStr), end='', flush=True) on line 29?

2. What happens if you switch the order of lines 48 and 49?

3. What happens if you change round(progress / total * 100, 1) on line 53 to round(progress / total * 100)?

#58

RAINBOW

Rainbow is a simple program that shows a colorful rainbow traveling back and forth across the screen. The program makes use of the fact that when new lines of text appear, the existing text scrolls up, causing it to look like it's moving. This program is good for beginners, and it's similar to Project 15, "Deep Cave."

The Program in Action

Figure 58-1 shows what the output will look like when you run *rainbow.py*.

Figure 58-1: The zigzag output of the rainbow, which is in color on the screen

How It Works

This program continuously prints the same rainbow pattern. What changes is the number of space characters printed to the left of it. Increasing this number moves the rainbow to the right, and decreasing it moves the rainbow to the left. The indent variable keeps track of the number of spaces. The indentIncreasing variable is set to True to note that indent should increase until it reaches 60, at which point it changes to False. The rest of the code decreases the number of spaces. Once it reaches 0, it changes back to True again to repeat the zigzag of the rainbow.

```
1. """Rainbow, by Al Sweigart al@inventwithpython.com
2. Shows a simple rainbow animation. Press Ctrl-C to stop.
3. View this code at https://nostarch.com/big-book-small-python-projects
4. Tags: tiny, artistic, bext, beginner, scrolling"""
5.
6. import time, sys
7.
8. try:
9.     import bext
10. except ImportError:
11.     print('This program requires the bext module, which you')
12.     print('can install by following the instructions at')
13.     print('https://pypi.org/project/Bext/')
14.     sys.exit()
```

```
15.
16. print('Rainbow, by Al Sweigart al@inventwithpython.com')
17. print('Press Ctrl-C to stop.')
18. time.sleep(3)
19.
20. indent = 0  # How many spaces to indent.
21. indentIncreasing = True  # Whether the indentation is increasing or not.
22.
23. try:
24.     while True:  # Main program loop.
25.         print(' ' * indent, end='')
26.         bext.fg('red')
27.         print('##', end='')
28.         bext.fg('yellow')
29.         print('##', end='')
30.         bext.fg('green')
31.         print('##', end='')
32.         bext.fg('blue')
33.         print('##', end='')
34.         bext.fg('cyan')
35.         print('##', end='')
36.         bext.fg('purple')
37.         print('##')
38.
39.         if indentIncreasing:
40.             # Increase the number of spaces:
41.             indent = indent + 1
42.             if indent == 60:  # (!) Change this to 10 or 30.
43.                 # Change direction:
44.                 indentIncreasing = False
45.         else:
46.             # Decrease the number of spaces:
47.             indent = indent - 1
48.             if indent == 0:
49.                 # Change direction:
50.                 indentIncreasing = True
51.
52.         time.sleep(0.02)  # Add a slight pause.
53. except KeyboardInterrupt:
54.     sys.exit()  # When Ctrl-C is pressed, end the program.
```

Exploring the Program

Try to find the answers to the following questions. Experiment with some modifications to the code and rerun the program to see what effect the changes have.

1. What happens if you change False on line 44 to True?

2. What happens if you change the argument to all bext.fg() calls to 'random'?

#59

ROCK PAPER SCISSORS

In this version of the two-player hand game also known as Rochambeau or jan-ken-pon, the player faces off against the computer. You can pick either rock, paper, or scissors. Rock beats scissors, scissors beats paper, and paper beats rock. This program adds some brief pauses for suspense.

For a variation of this game, see Project 60, "Rock Paper Scissors (Always-Win Version)."

The Program in Action

When you run *rockpaperscissors.py*, the output will look like this:

```
Rock, Paper, Scissors, by Al Sweigart al@inventwithpython.com
- Rock beats scissors.
- Paper beats rocks.
- Scissors beats paper.

0 Wins, 0 Losses, 0 Ties
Enter your move: (R)ock (P)aper (S)cissors or (Q)uit
> r
ROCK versus...
1...
2...
3...
SCISSORS
You win!
1 Wins, 0 Losses, 0 Ties
Enter your move: (R)ock (P)aper (S)cissors or (Q)uit
--snip--
```

How It Works

The game logic for Rock Paper Scissors is fairly straightforward, and we implement it here with if-elif statements. To add a bit of suspense, lines 45 to 51 count down before revealing the opponent's move, with brief pauses between counts. This gives the player a period in which their excitement builds about the results of the game. Without this pause, the results would appear as soon as the player entered their move—a bit anticlimactic. It doesn't take a lot of code to improve the user experience for the player.

```python
 1. """Rock, Paper, Scissors, by Al Sweigart al@inventwithpython.com
 2. The classic hand game of luck.
 3. View this code at https://nostarch.com/big-book-small-python-projects
 4. Tags: short, game"""
 5.
 6. import random, time, sys
 7.
 8. print('''Rock, Paper, Scissors, by Al Sweigart al@inventwithpython.com
 9. - Rock beats scissors.
10. - Paper beats rocks.
11. - Scissors beats paper.
12. ''')
13.
14. # These variables keep track of the number of wins, losses, and ties.
15. wins = 0
16. losses = 0
17. ties = 0
18.
19. while True:  # Main game loop.
20.     while True:  # Keep asking until player enters R, P, S, or Q.
21.         print('{} Wins, {} Losses, {} Ties'.format(wins, losses, ties))
```

```
22.         print('Enter your move: (R)ock (P)aper (S)cissors or (Q)uit')
23.         playerMove = input('> ').upper()
24.         if playerMove == 'Q':
25.             print('Thanks for playing!')
26.             sys.exit()
27.
28.         if playerMove == 'R' or playerMove == 'P' or playerMove == 'S':
29.             break
30.         else:
31.             print('Type one of R, P, S, or Q.')
32.
33.     # Display what the player chose:
34.     if playerMove == 'R':
35.         print('ROCK versus...')
36.         playerMove = 'ROCK'
37.     elif playerMove == 'P':
38.         print('PAPER versus...')
39.         playerMove = 'PAPER'
40.     elif playerMove == 'S':
41.         print('SCISSORS versus...')
42.         playerMove = 'SCISSORS'
43.
44.     # Count to three with dramatic pauses:
45.     time.sleep(0.5)
46.     print('1...')
47.     time.sleep(0.25)
48.     print('2...')
49.     time.sleep(0.25)
50.     print('3...')
51.     time.sleep(0.25)
52.
53.     # Display what the computer chose:
54.     randomNumber = random.randint(1, 3)
55.     if randomNumber == 1:
56.         computerMove = 'ROCK'
57.     elif randomNumber == 2:
58.         computerMove = 'PAPER'
59.     elif randomNumber == 3:
60.         computerMove = 'SCISSORS'
61.     print(computerMove)
62.     time.sleep(0.5)
63.
64.     # Display and record the win/loss/tie:
65.     if playerMove == computerMove:
66.         print('It\'s a tie!')
67.         ties = ties + 1
68.     elif playerMove == 'ROCK' and computerMove == 'SCISSORS':
69.         print('You win!')
70.         wins = wins + 1
71.     elif playerMove == 'PAPER' and computerMove == 'ROCK':
72.         print('You win!')
73.         wins = wins + 1
74.     elif playerMove == 'SCISSORS' and computerMove == 'PAPER':
75.         print('You win!')
76.         wins = wins + 1
```

```
77.    elif playerMove == 'ROCK' and computerMove == 'PAPER':
78.        print('You lose!')
79.        losses = losses + 1
80.    elif playerMove == 'PAPER' and computerMove == 'SCISSORS':
81.        print('You lose!')
82.        losses = losses + 1
83.    elif playerMove == 'SCISSORS' and computerMove == 'ROCK':
84.        print('You lose!')
85.        losses = losses + 1
```

After entering the source code and running it a few times, try making experimental changes to it. On your own, you can also try to figure out how to do the following:

- Add "Lizard" and "Spock" moves to the game. Lizard poisons Spock and eats paper, but is crushed by rock and decapitated by scissors. Spock breaks scissors and vaporizes rock, but is poisoned by lizard and disproved by paper.

- Allow the player to win a point for each victory and lose a point for each defeat. Upon winning, the player can also take "double or nothing" risks to possibly win 2, 4, 8, 16, and an increasing number of points in subsequent rounds.

Exploring the Program

Try to find the answers to the following questions. Experiment with some modifications to the code and rerun the program to see what effect the changes have.

1. What error do you get if you change random.randint(1, 3) on line 54 to random.randint(1, 300)?

2. What happens if you change playerMove == computerMove on line 65 to True?

#60

ROCK PAPER SCISSORS
(ALWAYS-WIN VERSION)

This variant of Rock Paper Scissors is identical to Project 59, "Rock Paper Scissors," except the player will always win. The code selecting the computer's move is set so that it always chooses the losing move. You can offer this game to your friends, who may be excited when they win . . . at first. See how long it takes before they catch on to the fact that the game is rigged in their favor.

The Program in Action

When you run *rockpaperscissorsalwayswin.py*, the output will look like this:

```
Rock, Paper, Scissors, by Al Sweigart al@inventwithpython.com
- Rock beats scissors.
- Paper beats rocks.
- Scissors beats paper.

0 Wins, 0 Losses, 0 Ties
Enter your move: (R)ock (P)aper (S)cissors or (Q)uit
> p
PAPER versus...
1...
2...
3...
ROCK
You win!
1 Wins, 0 Losses, 0 Ties
Enter your move: (R)ock (P)aper (S)cissors or (Q)uit
> s
SCISSORS versus...
1...
2...
3...
PAPER
You win!
2 Wins, 0 Losses, 0 Ties
--snip--
SCISSORS versus...
1...
2...
3...
PAPER
You win!
413 Wins, 0 Losses, 0 Ties
Enter your move: (R)ock (P)aper (S)cissors or (Q)uit
--snip--
```

How It Works

You may notice that this version of the program is shorter than Project 59. This makes sense: when you don't have to randomly generate a move for the computer and compute the results of the game, you can remove quite a bit of code from the original. There are also no variables to track the number of losses and ties, since these would be zero all the time anyway.

```
1. """Rock, Paper, Scissors (Always Win version)
2. By Al Sweigart al@inventwithpython.com
3. The classic hand game of luck, except you always win.
4. View this code at https://nostarch.com/big-book-small-python-projects
5. Tags: tiny, game, humor"""
6.
```

```
 7. import time, sys
 8.
 9. print('''Rock, Paper, Scissors, by Al Sweigart al@inventwithpython.com
10. - Rock beats scissors.
11. - Paper beats rocks.
12. - Scissors beats paper.
13. ''')
14.
15. # These variables keep track of the number of wins.
16. wins = 0
17.
18. while True:  # Main game loop.
19.     while True:  # Keep asking until player enters R, P, S, or Q.
20.         print('{} Wins, 0 Losses, 0 Ties'.format(wins))
21.         print('Enter your move: (R)ock (P)aper (S)cissors or (Q)uit')
22.         playerMove = input('> ').upper()
23.         if playerMove == 'Q':
24.             print('Thanks for playing!')
25.             sys.exit()
26.
27.         if playerMove == 'R' or playerMove == 'P' or playerMove == 'S':
28.             break
29.         else:
30.             print('Type one of R, P, S, or Q.')
31.
32.     # Display what the player chose:
33.     if playerMove == 'R':
34.         print('ROCK versus...')
35.     elif playerMove == 'P':
36.         print('PAPER versus...')
37.     elif playerMove == 'S':
38.         print('SCISSORS versus...')
39.
40.     # Count to three with dramatic pauses:
41.     time.sleep(0.5)
42.     print('1...')
43.     time.sleep(0.25)
44.     print('2...')
45.     time.sleep(0.25)
46.     print('3...')
47.     time.sleep(0.25)
48.
49.     # Display what the computer chose:
50.     if playerMove == 'R':
51.         print('SCISSORS')
52.     elif playerMove == 'P':
53.         print('ROCK')
54.     elif playerMove == 'S':
55.         print('PAPER')
56.
57.     time.sleep(0.5)
58.
59.     print('You win!')
60.     wins = wins + 1
```

After entering the source code and running it a few times, try making experimental changes to it. On your own, you can also try to figure out how to do the following:

- Add "Lizard" and "Spock" moves to the game. Lizard poisons Spock and eats paper, but is crushed by rock and decapitated by scissors. Spock breaks scissors and vaporizes rock, but is poisoned by lizard and disproved by paper.
- Allow the player to win a point for each victory. Upon winning, the player can also take "double or nothing" risks to possibly win 2, 4, 8, 16, and an increasing number of points.

Exploring the Program

Try to find the answers to the following questions. Experiment with some modifications to the code and rerun the program to see what effect the changes have.

1. What happens if you delete or comment out lines 33 to 57?
2. What happens if you change input('> ').upper() on line 22 to input('> ')?

#61

ROT13 CIPHER

The ROT13 cipher, one of the simplest encryption algorithms, stands for "rotate 13 spaces." The cypher represents the letters *A* to *Z* as the numbers 0 to 25 in such a way that the encrypted letter is 13 spaces from the plaintext letter: *A* becomes *N*, *B* becomes *O*, and so on. The encryption process is identical to the decryption process, making it trivial to program. However, the encryption is also trivial to break. Because of this, you'll most often find ROT13 used to conceal non-sensitive information, such as spoilers or trivia answers, so it's not read unintentionally. More information about the ROT13 cipher can be found at *https://en.wikipedia.org/ wiki/ROT13*. If you'd like to learn about ciphers and code breaking more generally, you can read my book *Cracking Codes with Python* (No Starch Press, 2018; *https://nostarch.com/crackingcodes/*).

The Program in Action

When you run *rot13cipher.py*, the output will look like this:

```
ROT13 Cipher, by Al Sweigart al@inventwithpython.com

Enter a message to encrypt/decrypt (or QUIT):
> Meet me by the rose bushes tonight.
The translated message is:
Zrrg zr ol gur ebfr ohfurf gbavtug.

(Copied to clipboard.)
Enter a message to encrypt/decrypt (or QUIT):
--snip--
```

How It Works

ROT13 shares a lot of code with Project 6, "Caesar Cipher," although it's much simpler because it always uses the key 13. Since the same code performs both the encryption and decryption (lines 27 to 39), there's no need to ask the player which mode they want to use.

One difference is that this program maintains the casing of the original message instead of automatically converting the message to uppercase. For example, "Hello" encrypts to "Uryyb," whereas "HELLO" encrypts to "URYYB."

```
 1. """ROT13 Cipher, by Al Sweigart al@inventwithpython.com
 2. The simplest shift cipher for encrypting and decrypting text.
 3. More info at https://en.wikipedia.org/wiki/ROT13
 4. View this code at https://nostarch.com/big-book-small-python-projects
 5. Tags: tiny, cryptography"""
 6.
 7. try:
 8.     import pyperclip  # pyperclip copies text to the clipboard.
 9. except ImportError:
10.     pass  # If pyperclip is not installed, do nothing. It's no big deal.
11.
12. # Set up the constants:
13. UPPER_LETTERS = 'ABCDEFGHIJKLMNOPQRSTUVWXYZ'
14. LOWER_LETTERS = 'abcdefghijklmnopqrstuvwxyz'
15.
16. print('ROT13 Cipher, by Al Sweigart al@inventwithpython.com')
17. print()
18.
19. while True:  # Main program loop.
20.     print('Enter a message to encrypt/decrypt (or QUIT):')
21.     message = input('> ')
22.
23.     if message.upper() == 'QUIT':
24.         break  # Break out of the main program loop.
25.
26.     # Rotate the letters in message by 13 characters.
```

```
27.      translated = ''
28.      for character in message:
29.          if character.isupper():
30.              # Concatenate uppercase translated character.
31.              transCharIndex = (UPPER_LETTERS.find(character) + 13) % 26
32.              translated += UPPER_LETTERS[transCharIndex]
33.          elif character.islower():
34.              # Concatenate lowercase translated character.
35.              transCharIndex = (LOWER_LETTERS.find(character) + 13) % 26
36.              translated += LOWER_LETTERS[transCharIndex]
37.          else:
38.              # Concatenate the character untranslated.
39.              translated += character
40.
41.      # Display the translation:
42.      print('The translated message is:')
43.      print(translated)
44.      print()
45.
46.      try:
47.          # Copy the translation to the clipboard:
48.          pyperclip.copy(translated)
49.          print('(Copied to clipboard.)')
50.      except:
51.          pass
```

Exploring the Program

Try to find the answers to the following questions. Experiment with some modifications to the code and rerun the program to see what effect the changes have.

1. What happens if you change character.isupper() on line 29 to character.islower()?

2. What happens if you change print(translated) on line 43 to print(message)?

#62

ROTATING CUBE

This project features an animation of a 3D cube rotating using trigonometric functions. You can adapt the 3D point rotation math and the line() function in your own animation programs.

Although the block text characters we'll use to draw the cube don't look like thin, straight lines, this kind of drawing is called a *wireframe model* because it renders only the edges of an object's surfaces. Figure 62-1 shows the wireframe model for a cube and an icosphere, a rough sphere made of triangles.

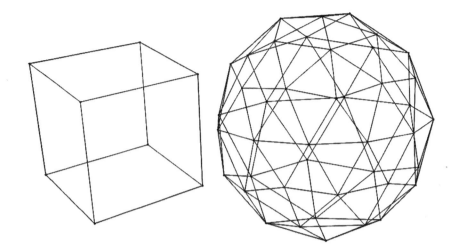

Figure 62-1: The wireframe models for a cube (left) and an icosphere (right)

The Program in Action

Figure 62-2 shows what the output will look like when you run *rotatingcube.py*.

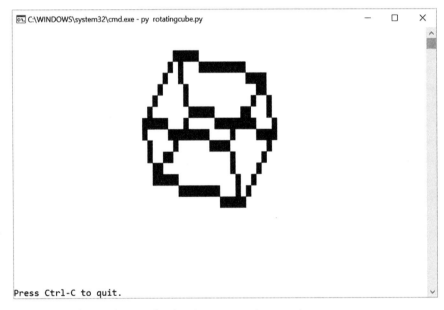

Figure 62-2: The wireframe cube that the program draws to the screen

How It Works

This algorithm has two main parts: the line() function and the rotatePoint() function. The cube has eight points, one for each corner. The program stores these corners as (*x*, *y*, *z*) tuples in the CUBE_CORNERS list. These points also define the connections for the cube's edge lines. When all the points rotate in the same direction by the same amount, they give the illusion of a cube rotating.

```
1.  """Rotating Cube, by Al Sweigart al@inventwithpython.com
2.  A rotating cube animation. Press Ctrl-C to stop.
3.  View this code at https://nostarch.com/big-book-small-python-projects
4.  Tags: large, artistic, math"""
5.
6.  # This program MUST be run in a Terminal/Command Prompt window.
7.
8.  import math, time, sys, os
9.
10. # Set up the constants:
11. PAUSE_AMOUNT = 0.1  # Pause length of one-tenth of a second.
12. WIDTH, HEIGHT = 80, 24
13. SCALEX = (WIDTH - 4) // 8
14. SCALEY = (HEIGHT - 4) // 8
15. # Text cells are twice as tall as they are wide, so set scaley:
16. SCALEY *= 2
17. TRANSLATEX = (WIDTH - 4) // 2
18. TRANSLATEY = (HEIGHT - 4) // 2
19.
20. # (!) Try changing this to '#' or '*' or some other character:
21. LINE_CHAR = chr(9608)  # Character 9608 is '█'
22.
23. # (!) Try setting two of these values to zero to rotate the cube only
24. # along a single axis:
25. X_ROTATE_SPEED = 0.03
26. Y_ROTATE_SPEED = 0.08
27. Z_ROTATE_SPEED = 0.13
28.
29. # This program stores XYZ coordinates in lists, with the X coordinate
30. # at index 0, Y at 1, and Z at 2. These constants make our code more
31. # readable when accessing the coordinates in these lists.
32. X = 0
33. Y = 1
34. Z = 2
35.
36.
37. def line(x1, y1, x2, y2):
38.     """Returns a list of points in a line between the given points.
39.
40.     Uses the Bresenham line algorithm. More info at:
41.     https://en.wikipedia.org/wiki/Bresenham%27s_line_algorithm"""
42.     points = []  # Contains the points of the line.
43.     # "Steep" means the slope of the line is greater than 45 degrees or
44.     # less than -45 degrees:
45.
```

```
46.     # Check for the special case where the start and end points are
47.     # certain neighbors, which this function doesn't handle correctly,
48.     # and return a hard coded list instead:
49.     if (x1 == x2 and y1 == y2 + 1) or (y1 == y2 and x1 == x2 + 1):
50.         return [(x1, y1), (x2, y2)]
51.
52.     isSteep = abs(y2 - y1) > abs(x2 - x1)
53.     if isSteep:
54.         # This algorithm only handles non-steep lines, so let's change
55.         # the slope to non-steep and change it back later.
56.         x1, y1 = y1, x1  # Swap x1 and y1
57.         x2, y2 = y2, x2  # Swap x2 and y2
58.     isReversed = x1 > x2  # True if the line goes right-to-left.
59.
60.     if isReversed:  # Get the points on the line going right-to-left.
61.         x1, x2 = x2, x1  # Swap x1 and x2
62.         y1, y2 = y2, y1  # Swap y1 and y2
63.
64.         deltax = x2 - x1
65.         deltay = abs(y2 - y1)
66.         extray = int(deltax / 2)
67.         currenty = y2
68.         if y1 < y2:
69.             ydirection = 1
70.         else:
71.             ydirection = -1
72.         # Calculate the y for every x in this line:
73.         for currentx in range(x2, x1 - 1, -1):
74.             if isSteep:
75.                 points.append((currenty, currentx))
76.             else:
77.                 points.append((currentx, currenty))
78.             extray -= deltay
79.             if extray <= 0:  # Only change y once extray <= 0.
80.                 currenty -= ydirection
81.                 extray += deltax
82.     else:  # Get the points on the line going left to right.
83.         deltax = x2 - x1
84.         deltay = abs(y2 - y1)
85.         extray = int(deltax / 2)
86.         currenty = y1
87.         if y1 < y2:
88.             ydirection = 1
89.         else:
90.             ydirection = -1
91.         # Calculate the y for every x in this line:
92.         for currentx in range(x1, x2 + 1):
93.             if isSteep:
94.                 points.append((currenty, currentx))
95.             else:
96.                 points.append((currentx, currenty))
97.             extray -= deltay
98.             if extray < 0:  # Only change y once extray < 0.
99.                 currenty += ydirection
100.                extray += deltax
```

```
101.    return points
102.
103.
104. def rotatePoint(x, y, z, ax, ay, az):
105.     """Returns an (x, y, z) tuple of the x, y, z arguments rotated.
106.
107.     The rotation happens around the 0, 0, 0 origin by angles
108.     ax, ay, az (in radians).
109.        Directions of each axis:
110.          -y
111.          |
112.          +-- +x
113.         /
114.        +z
115.     """
116.
117.     # Rotate around x axis:
118.     rotatedX = x
119.     rotatedY = (y * math.cos(ax)) - (z * math.sin(ax))
120.     rotatedZ = (y * math.sin(ax)) + (z * math.cos(ax))
121.     x, y, z = rotatedX, rotatedY, rotatedZ
122.
123.     # Rotate around y axis:
124.     rotatedX = (z * math.sin(ay)) + (x * math.cos(ay))
125.     rotatedY = y
126.     rotatedZ = (z * math.cos(ay)) - (x * math.sin(ay))
127.     x, y, z = rotatedX, rotatedY, rotatedZ
128.
129.     # Rotate around z axis:
130.     rotatedX = (x * math.cos(az)) - (y * math.sin(az))
131.     rotatedY = (x * math.sin(az)) + (y * math.cos(az))
132.     rotatedZ = z
133.
134.     return (rotatedX, rotatedY, rotatedZ)
135.
136.
137. def adjustPoint(point):
138.     """Adjusts the 3D XYZ point to a 2D XY point fit for displaying on
139.     the screen. This resizes this 2D point by a scale of SCALEX and
140.     SCALEY, then moves the point by TRANSLATEX and TRANSLATEY."""
141.     return (int(point[X] * SCALEX + TRANSLATEX),
142.             int(point[Y] * SCALEY + TRANSLATEY))
143.
144.
145. """CUBE_CORNERS stores the XYZ coordinates of the corners of a cube.
146. The indexes for each corner in CUBE_CORNERS are marked in this diagram:
147.      0---1
148.     /|  /|
149.    2---3 |
150.    | 4-|-5
151.    |/  |/
152.    6---7"""
153. CUBE_CORNERS = [[-1, -1, -1], # Point 0
154.                 [ 1, -1, -1], # Point 1
155.                 [-1, -1,  1], # Point 2
```

```
156.                        [ 1, -1,  1], # Point 3
157.                        [-1,  1, -1], # Point 4
158.                        [ 1,  1, -1], # Point 5
159.                        [-1,  1,  1], # Point 6
160.                        [ 1,  1,  1]] # Point 7
161. # rotatedCorners stores the XYZ coordinates from CUBE_CORNERS after
162. # they've been rotated by rx, ry, and rz amounts:
163. rotatedCorners = [None, None, None, None, None, None, None, None]
164. # Rotation amounts for each axis:
165. xRotation = 0.0
166. yRotation = 0.0
167. zRotation = 0.0
168.
169. try:
170.     while True:  # Main program loop.
171.         # Rotate the cube along different axes by different amounts:
172.         xRotation += X_ROTATE_SPEED
173.         yRotation += Y_ROTATE_SPEED
174.         zRotation += Z_ROTATE_SPEED
175.         for i in range(len(CUBE_CORNERS)):
176.             x = CUBE_CORNERS[i][X]
177.             y = CUBE_CORNERS[i][Y]
178.             z = CUBE_CORNERS[i][Z]
179.             rotatedCorners[i] = rotatePoint(x, y, z, xRotation,
180.                 yRotation, zRotation)
181.
182.         # Get the points of the cube lines:
183.         cubePoints = []
184.         for fromCornerIndex, toCornerIndex in ((0, 1), (1, 3), (3, 2),
             (2, 0), (0, 4), (1, 5), (2, 6), (3, 7), (4, 5), (5, 7), (7, 6),
             (6, 4)):
185.             fromX, fromY = adjustPoint(rotatedCorners[fromCornerIndex])
186.             toX, toY = adjustPoint(rotatedCorners[toCornerIndex])
187.             pointsOnLine = line(fromX, fromY, toX, toY)
188.             cubePoints.extend(pointsOnLine)
189.
190.         # Get rid of duplicate points:
191.         cubePoints = tuple(frozenset(cubePoints))
192.
193.         # Display the cube on the screen:
194.         for y in range(HEIGHT):
195.             for x in range(WIDTH):
196.                 if (x, y) in cubePoints:
197.                     # Display full block:
198.                     print(LINE_CHAR, end='', flush=False)
199.                 else:
200.                     # Display empty space:
201.                     print(' ', end='', flush=False)
202.             print(flush=False)
203.         print('Press Ctrl-C to quit.', end='', flush=True)
204.
205.         time.sleep(PAUSE_AMOUNT)  # Pause for a bit.
206.
207.         # Clear the screen:
208.         if sys.platform == 'win32':
```

```
209.            os.system('cls')  # Windows uses the cls command.
210.        else:
211.            os.system('clear')  # macOS and Linux use the clear command.
212.
213. except KeyboardInterrupt:
214.     print('Rotating Cube, by Al Sweigart al@inventwithpython.com')
215.     sys.exit()  # When Ctrl-C is pressed, end the program.
```

After entering the source code and running it a few times, try making experimental changes to it. The comments marked with (!) have suggestions for small changes you can make. On your own, you can also try to figure out how to do the following:

- Modify CUBE_CORNERS and the tuple on line 184 to create different wireframe models such as a pyramid and a flat hexagon.
- Increase the coordinates of CUBE_CORNERS by 1.5 so that the cube revolves around the center of the screen, rather than rotating around its own center.

Exploring the Program

Try to find the answers to the following questions. Experiment with some modifications to the code and rerun the program to see what effect the changes have.

1. What happens if you delete or comment out lines 208 to 211?
2. What happens if you change the tuples on line 184 to <((0, 1), (1, 3), (3, 2), (2, 0), (0,4), (4, 5), (5, 1))>?

#63

ROYAL GAME OF UR

The Royal Game of Ur is a 5,000-year-old game from Mesopotamia. Archeologists rediscovered the game in the Royal Cemetery at Ur, in modern-day southern Iraq, during excavations between 1922 and 1934. The rules were reconstructed from the game board (shown in Figure 63-1) and a Babylonian clay tablet, and they're similar to Parcheesi. You'll need both luck and skill to win.

Figure 63-1: One of the five game boards found in the Royal Cemetery at Ur

Two players each begin with seven tokens in their home, and the first player to move all seven to the goal is the winner. Players take turns throwing four dice. These dice are four-pointed pyramid shapes called tetrahedrons. Each die has two marked points, giving an even chance that the dice come up marked or unmarked. Instead of dice, our game uses coins whose heads act as the marked point. The player can move a token one space for each marked point that comes up. This means they can move a single token between zero and four spaces, though they're most likely to roll two spaces.

The tokens travel along the path indicated in Figure 63-2. Only one token may exist on a space at a time. If a token lands on an opponent's token while in the shared middle path, the opponent's token is sent back home. If a token lands on the middle flower square, it is safe from being landed on. If a token lands on any of the other four flower tiles, the player gets to roll again. Our game will represent the tokens with the letters *X* and *O*.

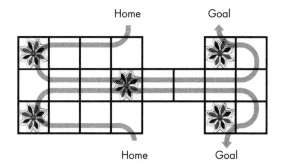

Figure 63-2: The path each player's token takes from their home to their goal

A video featuring YouTuber Tom Scott and British Museum curator Irving Finkel discussing the Royal Game of Ur can be found at *https://www.youtube.com/watch?v=WZskjLq04OI*.

The Program in Action

When you run *royalgameofur.py*, the output will look like this:

```
The Royal Game of Ur, by Al Sweigart
--snip--
                    XXXXXXX              .......
                    Home                 Goal
                     v                    ^
+-----+-----+-----+--v--+       +--^--+-----+
|*****|     |     |     |       |*****|     |
|*   *|<    <     <     |       |*   *|<    |
|****h|  g|  f|   e|            |****t|   s|
+--v--+-----+-----+-----+-----+-----+-----+--^--+
|     |     |     |*****|     |     |     |     |
|  >    >    >|*    *|>   >     >     >     |
|   i|   j|   k|****l|   m|   n|   o|   p|
+--^--+-----+-----+-----+-----+-----+-----+--v--+
|*****|     |     |     |       |*****|     |
|*   *|<    <     <     |       |*   *|<    |
|****d|  c|  b|   a|            |****r|   q|
+-----+-----+-----+--^--+       +--v--+-----+
                     ^                    v
                    Home                 Goal
                    OOOOOOO              .......
```

```
It is O's turn. Press Enter to flip...
Flips: H-H-H-H   Select token to move 4 spaces: home quit
> home
O landed on a flower space and gets to go again.
Press Enter to continue...
--snip--
```

How It Works

Like in Project 43, "Mancala," the spaces on the ASCII-art game board are labeled with the letters *a* through *t*. After rolling, the player can select a space that contains their token to move that token, or they can select home to begin moving a token from their home to the board. The program represents the board as a dictionary with the keys 'a' to 't' and the values of 'X' and 'O' for the tokens (or ' ' for a blank space).

Additionally, this dictionary has keys 'x_home', 'o_home', 'x_goal', and 'o_goal', and the values for these keys are seven-character strings that represent how full the homes and goals are. The 'X' or 'O' characters in these strings represent tokens at the home or goal, and '.' represents an empty slot. The displayBoard() function displays these seven-character strings on the screen.

1. """The Royal Game of Ur, by Al Sweigart al@inventwithpython.com
2. A 5,000 year old board game from Mesopotamia. Two players knock each
3. other back as they race for the goal.
4. More info https://en.wikipedia.org/wiki/Royal_Game_of_Ur
5. View this code at https://nostarch.com/big-book-small-python-projects

```
 6.    Tags: large, board game, game, two-player
 7.    """
 8.
 9.    import random, sys
10.
11.    X_PLAYER = 'X'
12.    O_PLAYER = 'O'
13.    EMPTY = ' '
14.
15.    # Set up constants for the space labels:
16.    X_HOME = 'x_home'
17.    O_HOME = 'o_home'
18.    X_GOAL = 'x_goal'
19.    O_GOAL = 'o_goal'
20.
21.    # The spaces in left to right, top to bottom order:
22.    ALL_SPACES = 'hgfetsijklmnopdcbarq'
23.    X_TRACK = 'HefghijklmnopstG'  # (H stands for Home, G stands for Goal.)
24.    O_TRACK = 'HabcdijklmnopqrG'
25.
26.    FLOWER_SPACES = ('h', 't', 'l', 'd', 'r')
27.
28.    BOARD_TEMPLATE = """
29.                    {}              {}
30.                   Home            Goal
31.                    v               ^
32.    +-----+-----+-----+--v--+       +--^--+-----+
33.    |*****|     |     |     |       |*****|     |
34.    |* {} *< {} < {} < {} |         |* {} *< {} |
35.    |****h|   g|   f|   e|         |****t|   s|
36.    +--v--+-----+-----+-----+-----+-----+-----+--^--+
37.    |     |     |     |*****|     |     |     |     |
38.    | {} > {} > {} >* {} *> {} > {} > {} > {} |
39.    |   i|   j|   k|****l|   m|   n|   o|   p|
40.    +--^--+-----+-----+-----+-----+-----+-----+--v--+
41.    |*****|     |     |     |       |*****|     |
42.    |* {} *< {} < {} < {} |         |* {} *< {} |
43.    |****d|   c|   b|   a|         |****r|   q|
44.    +-----+-----+-----+--^--+       +--v--+-----+
45.                    ^               v
46.                   Home            Goal
47.                    {}              {}
48.    """
49.
50.
51.    def main():
52.        print('''The Royal Game of Ur, by Al Sweigart
53.
54.    This is a 5,000 year old game. Two players must move their tokens
55.    from their home to their goal. On your turn you flip four coins and can
56.    move one token a number of spaces equal to the heads you got.
57.
58.    Ur is a racing game; the first player to move all seven of their tokens
59.    to their goal wins. To do this, tokens must travel from their home to
60.    their goal:
```

```
61.
62.                X Home        X Goal
63.                   v             ^
64. +---+---+---+---+-v-+      +-^-+---+
65. |v<<<<<<<<<<<<<<  |        |  ^<|<< |
66. |v  |   |   |   |        |   | ^  |
67. +v--+---+---+---+---+---+---+---+-^-+
68. |>>>>>>>>>>>>>>>>>>>>>>>>>>>>^  |
69. |>>>>>>>>>>>>>>>>>>>>>>>>>>>>>v  |
70. +^--+---+---+---+---+---+---+-v-+
71. |^  |   |   |   |        |   | v |
72. |^<<<<<<<<<<<<<<  |        | v<<<< |
73. +---+---+---+-^-+      +-v-+---+
74.                   ^             v
75.                O Home        O Goal
76.
77. If you land on an opponent's token in the middle track, it gets sent
78. back home. The **flower** spaces let you take another turn. Tokens in
79. the middle flower space are safe and cannot be landed on.''')
80.     input('Press Enter to begin...')
81.
82.     gameBoard = getNewBoard()
83.     turn = O_PLAYER
84.     while True:  # Main game loop.
85.         # Set up some variables for this turn:
86.         if turn == X_PLAYER:
87.             opponent = O_PLAYER
88.             home = X_HOME
89.             track = X_TRACK
90.             goal = X_GOAL
91.             opponentHome = O_HOME
92.         elif turn == O_PLAYER:
93.             opponent = X_PLAYER
94.             home = O_HOME
95.             track = O_TRACK
96.             goal = O_GOAL
97.             opponentHome = X_HOME
98.
99.         displayBoard(gameBoard)
100.
101.         input('It is ' + turn + '\'s turn. Press Enter to flip...')
102.
103.         flipTally = 0
104.         print('Flips: ', end='')
105.         for i in range(4):  # Flip 4 coins.
106.             result = random.randint(0, 1)
107.             if result == 0:
108.                 print('T', end='')  # Tails.
109.             else:
110.                 print('H', end='')  # Heads.
111.             if i != 3:
112.                 print('-', end='')  # Print separator.
113.             flipTally += result
114.         print('  ', end='')
115.
```

```
116.          if flipTally == 0:
117.              input('You lose a turn. Press Enter to continue...')
118.              turn = opponent  # Swap turns to the other player.
119.              continue
120.
121.          # Ask the player for their move:
122.          validMoves = getValidMoves(gameBoard, turn, flipTally)
123.
124.          if validMoves == []:
125.              print('There are no possible moves, so you lose a turn.')
126.              input('Press Enter to continue...')
127.              turn = opponent  # Swap turns to the other player.
128.              continue
129.
130.          while True:
131.              print('Select move', flipTally, 'spaces: ', end='')
132.              print(' '.join(validMoves) + ' quit')
133.              move = input('> ').lower()
134.
135.              if move == 'quit':
136.                  print('Thanks for playing!')
137.                  sys.exit()
138.              if move in validMoves:
139.                  break  # Exit the loop when a valid move is selected.
140.
141.              print('That is not a valid move.')
142.
143.          # Perform the selected move on the board:
144.          if move == 'home':
145.              # Subtract tokens at home if moving from home:
146.              gameBoard[home] -= 1
147.              nextTrackSpaceIndex = flipTally
148.          else:
149.              gameBoard[move] = EMPTY  # Set the "from" space to empty.
150.              nextTrackSpaceIndex = track.index(move) + flipTally
151.
152.          movingOntoGoal = nextTrackSpaceIndex == len(track) - 1
153.          if movingOntoGoal:
154.              gameBoard[goal] += 1
155.              # Check if the player has won:
156.              if gameBoard[goal] == 7:
157.                  displayBoard(gameBoard)
158.                  print(turn, 'has won the game!')
159.                  print('Thanks for playing!')
160.                  sys.exit()
161.          else:
162.              nextBoardSpace = track[nextTrackSpaceIndex]
163.              # Check if the opponent has a tile there:
164.              if gameBoard[nextBoardSpace] == opponent:
165.                  gameBoard[opponentHome] += 1
166.
167.              # Set the "to" space to the player's token:
168.              gameBoard[nextBoardSpace] = turn
169.
170.          # Check if the player landed on a flower space and can go again:
```

```
171.          if nextBoardSpace in FLOWER_SPACES:
172.              print(turn, 'landed on a flower space and goes again.')
173.              input('Press Enter to continue...')
174.          else:
175.              turn = opponent  # Swap turns to the other player.
176.
177. def getNewBoard():
178.     """
179.     Returns a dictionary that represents the state of the board. The
180.     keys are strings of the space labels, the values are X_PLAYER,
181.     O_PLAYER, or EMPTY. There are also counters for how many tokens are
182.     at the home and goal of both players.
183.     """
184.     board = {X_HOME: 7, X_GOAL: 0, O_HOME: 7, O_GOAL: 0}
185.     # Set each space as empty to start:
186.     for spaceLabel in ALL_SPACES:
187.         board[spaceLabel] = EMPTY
188.     return board
189.
190.
191. def displayBoard(board):
192.     """Display the board on the screen."""
193.     # "Clear" the screen by printing many newlines, so the old
194.     # board isn't visible anymore.
195.     print('\n' * 60)
196.
197.     xHomeTokens = ('X' * board[X_HOME]).ljust(7, '.')
198.     xGoalTokens = ('X' * board[X_GOAL]).ljust(7, '.')
199.     oHomeTokens = ('O' * board[O_HOME]).ljust(7, '.')
200.     oGoalTokens = ('O' * board[O_GOAL]).ljust(7, '.')
201.
202.     # Add the strings that should populate BOARD_TEMPLATE in order,
203.     # going from left to right, top to bottom.
204.     spaces = []
205.     spaces.append(xHomeTokens)
206.     spaces.append(xGoalTokens)
207.     for spaceLabel in ALL_SPACES:
208.         spaces.append(board[spaceLabel])
209.     spaces.append(oHomeTokens)
210.     spaces.append(oGoalTokens)
211.
212.     print(BOARD_TEMPLATE.format(*spaces))
213.
214.
215. def getValidMoves(board, player, flipTally):
216.     validMoves = []  # Contains the spaces with tokens that can move.
217.     if player == X_PLAYER:
218.         opponent = O_PLAYER
219.         track = X_TRACK
220.         home = X_HOME
221.     elif player == O_PLAYER:
222.         opponent = X_PLAYER
223.         track = O_TRACK
224.         home = O_HOME
225.
```

```
226.        # Check if the player can move a token from home:
227.        if board[home] > 0 and board[track[flipTally]] == EMPTY:
228.            validMoves.append('home')
229.
230.        # Check which spaces have a token the player can move:
231.        for trackSpaceIndex, space in enumerate(track):
232.            if space == 'H' or space == 'G' or board[space] != player:
233.                continue
234.            nextTrackSpaceIndex = trackSpaceIndex + flipTally
235.            if nextTrackSpaceIndex >= len(track):
236.                # You must flip an exact number of moves onto the goal,
237.                # otherwise you can't move on the goal.
238.                continue
239.            else:
240.                nextBoardSpaceKey = track[nextTrackSpaceIndex]
241.                if nextBoardSpaceKey == 'G':
242.                    # This token can move off the board:
243.                    validMoves.append(space)
244.                    continue
245.            if board[nextBoardSpaceKey] in (EMPTY, opponent):
246.                # If the next space is the protected middle space, you
247.                # can only move there if it is empty:
248.                if nextBoardSpaceKey == 'l' and board['l'] == opponent:
249.                    continue  # Skip this move, the space is protected.
250.                validMoves.append(space)
251.
252.    return validMoves
253.
254.
255. if __name__ == '__main__':
256.    main()
```

Exploring the Program

Try to find the answers to the following questions. Experiment with some modifications to the code and rerun the program to see what effect the changes have.

1. What happens if you change nextTrackSpaceIndex == len(track) - 1 on line 152 to nextTrackSpaceIndex == 1?

2. What happens if you change result = random.randint(0, 1) on line 106 to result = 1?

3. What error do you cause if you change board = {X_HOME: 7, X_GOAL: 0, O_HOME: 7, O_GOAL: 0} on line 184 to board = {}?

#**64**

SEVEN-SEGMENT DISPLAY MODULE

 A seven-segment display is a type of LCD component used to display numbers in pocket calculators, microwave ovens, and other small electronic devices. Through different combinations of seven line-shaped segments in an LCD, a seven-segment display can represent the digits 0 through 9. They look like this:

```
 _     _  _     _  _  _  _  _
| |  | _| _| |_||_ |_   ||_||_|
|_|  ||_  _|  | _||_|  ||_| _|
```

The benefit of this program is that other programs can import it as a module. Project 14, "Countdown," and Project 19, "Digital Clock," import the *sevseg.py* file so they can use its getSevSegStr() function. You can find more information about seven-segment displays and other variations at *https://en.wikipedia.org/wiki/Seven-segment_display*.

The Program in Action

Even though it's a module, *sevseg.py* outputs a sample demo of the digits it produces when you run the program directly. The output will look like this:

```
This module is meant to be imported rather than run.
For example, this code:
    import sevseg
    myNumber = sevseg.getSevSegStr(42, 3)
    print(myNumber)

Will print 42, zero-padded to three digits:

 __   |  |__|   __|
|__|     |  |  |__
```

How It Works

The getSevSegStr() function first creates a list of three strings. The strings represent the top, middle, and bottom row of the numeric digits. Lines 27 to 75 have a long list of if-elif statements for each digit (and the decimal point and minus sign) that concatenates the rows of each digit to these strings. These three strings are joined together with newlines on line 84 so that the function returns a single multiline string suitable to pass to print().

```
 1. """Sevseg, by Al Sweigart al@inventwithpython.com
 2. A seven-segment number display module, used by the Countdown and Digital
 3. Clock programs.
 4. More info at https://en.wikipedia.org/wiki/Seven-segment_display
 5. View this code at https://nostarch.com/big-book-small-python-projects
 6. Tags: short, module"""
 7.
 8. """A labeled seven-segment display, with each segment labeled A to G:
 9.  __A__
10. |     |      Each digit in a seven-segment display:
11. F     B
12. |__G__|    __     __  __       __   __  __   __   __
13. |     |   |  |   | __| __| |__| |__  |__  | |__| |__|
14. E     C   |__|   | |__  __|   |  __| |__| | |__|  __|
15. |__D__|"""
16.
17.
18. def getSevSegStr(number, minWidth=0):
19.     """Return a seven-segment display string of number. The returned
20.     string will be padded with zeros if it is smaller than minWidth."""
21.
22.     # Convert number to string in case it's an int or float:
23.     number = str(number).zfill(minWidth)
24.
25.     rows = ['', '', '']
26.     for i, numeral in enumerate(number):
27.         if numeral == '.':  # Render the decimal point.
28.             rows[0] += ' '
```

```
29.                    rows[1] += ' '
30.                    rows[2] += '.'
31.                    continue  # Skip the space in between digits.
32.                elif numeral == '-':  # Render the negative sign:
33.                    rows[0] += '     '
34.                    rows[1] += ' __  '
35.                    rows[2] += '     '
36.                elif numeral == '0':  # Render the 0.
37.                    rows[0] += ' __  '
38.                    rows[1] += '|  |'
39.                    rows[2] += '|__|'
40.                elif numeral == '1':  # Render the 1.
41.                    rows[0] += '     '
42.                    rows[1] += '   |'
43.                    rows[2] += '   |'
44.                elif numeral == '2':  # Render the 2.
45.                    rows[0] += ' __  '
46.                    rows[1] += ' __|'
47.                    rows[2] += '|__ '
48.                elif numeral == '3':  # Render the 3.
49.                    rows[0] += ' __  '
50.                    rows[1] += ' __|'
51.                    rows[2] += ' __|'
52.                elif numeral == '4':  # Render the 4.
53.                    rows[0] += '     '
54.                    rows[1] += '|__|'
55.                    rows[2] += '   |'
56.                elif numeral == '5':  # Render the 5.
57.                    rows[0] += ' __  '
58.                    rows[1] += '|__ '
59.                    rows[2] += ' __|'
60.                elif numeral == '6':  # Render the 6.
61.                    rows[0] += ' __  '
62.                    rows[1] += '|__ '
63.                    rows[2] += '|__|'
64.                elif numeral == '7':  # Render the 7.
65.                    rows[0] += ' __  '
66.                    rows[1] += '   |'
67.                    rows[2] += '   |'
68.                elif numeral == '8':  # Render the 8.
69.                    rows[0] += ' __  '
70.                    rows[1] += '|__|'
71.                    rows[2] += '|__|'
72.                elif numeral == '9':  # Render the 9.
73.                    rows[0] += ' __  '
74.                    rows[1] += '|__|'
75.                    rows[2] += ' __|'
76.
77.                # Add a space (for the space in between numerals) if this
78.                # isn't the last numeral:
79.                if i != len(number) - 1:
80.                    rows[0] += ' '
81.                    rows[1] += ' '
82.                    rows[2] += ' '
83.
```

```
84.    return '\n'.join(rows)
85.
86.
87. # If this program isn't being imported, display the numbers 00 to 99.
88. if __name__ == '__main__':
89.    print('This module is meant to be imported rather than run.')
90.    print('For example, this code:')
91.    print('    import sevseg')
92.    print('    myNumber = sevseg.getSevSegStr(42, 3)')
93.    print('    print(myNumber)')
94.    print()
95.    print('...will print 42, zero-padded to three digits:')
96.    print('  __      __ ')
97.    print('|  | | |_| _|')
98.    print('|__|   | |_ ')
```

After entering the source code and running it a few times, try making experimental changes to it. On your own, you can also try to figure out how to do the following:

- Create new fonts for numbers, such as using five rows and the block character string returned by chr(9608).

- Look at the Wikipedia article for seven-segment displays to find out how to display letters and then add those to *sevseg.py*.

- Learn about sixteen-segment displays from *https://en.wikipedia.org/wiki/Sixteen-segment_display* and create a *sixteenseg.py* module to generate numbers in that style.

Exploring the Program

Try to find the answers to the following questions. Experiment with some modifications to the code and rerun the program to see what effect the changes have.

1. What happens if you change the single-space strings on lines 80, 81, and 82 to empty strings?

2. What happens if you change the minWidth=0 default argument on line 18 to minWidth=8?

#65

SHINING CARPET

The Shining, a 1980 psychological horror film directed by Stanley Kubrick, takes place at the haunted Overlook Hotel. The hotel carpet's hexagonal design became an iconic part of this famous movie. The carpet features alternating and interlocking hexagons whose mesmerizing effect is well-suited for such an unnerving film. The short program in this project, similar to Project 35, "Hex Grid," prints this repetitive pattern on the screen.

Note that this program uses raw strings, which prefix the opening quote with a lowercase r, so that the backslashes in the string aren't interpreted as escape characters.

The Program in Action

When you run *shiningcarpet.py*, the output will look like this:

How It Works

The creation of a program like this (or the similar Project 35) doesn't begin with coding but rather just drawing tessellating shapes in a text editor. Once you've written out the pattern, you can cut it down to the smallest unit to be tiled:

After you've copied and pasted this text into the source code, you can write the rest of the program around it. Software is not just a matter of sitting down and writing code from beginning to end. Every professional software developer goes through several iterations of tinkering, experimentation, and debugging. The end result may be just nine lines of code, but a small program doesn't necessarily imply that a small amount of effort went into making it.

```
1. """Shining Carpet, by Al Sweigart al@inventwithpython.com
2. Displays a tessellation of the carpet pattern from The Shining.
3. View this code at https://nostarch.com/big-book-small-python-projects
4. Tags: tiny, beginner, artistic"""
5.
6. # Set up the constants:
```

```
 7. X_REPEAT = 6  # How many times to tessellate horizontally.
 8. Y_REPEAT = 4  # How many times to tessellate vertically.
 9.
10. for i in range(Y_REPEAT):
11.     print(r'_ \ \ \_/ _' * X_REPEAT)
12.     print(r' \ \ \__/ _' * X_REPEAT)
13.     print(r'\ \ \____/ ' * X_REPEAT)
14.     print(r'/ / / ___ \' * X_REPEAT)
15.     print(r'_/ / / _\_' * X_REPEAT)
16.     print(r'__/ / / \___' * X_REPEAT)
```

Exploring the Program

For practice, try creating patterns such as the following:

#66

SIMPLE SUBSTITUTION CIPHER

The Simple Substitution Cipher substitutes one letter for another. Since there are 26 possible substitutions for the letter *A*, 25 possible substitutions for *B*, 24 for *C*, and so on, the total number of possible keys is 26 × 25 × 24 × 23 × ... × 1, or 403,291,461,126,605,635,584,000,000 keys! That's far too many keys for even a supercomputer to brute force, so the code-breaking method used in Project 7, "Caesar Hacker," can't be used against the simple cipher. Unfortunately, devious attackers can take advantage of known weakness to break the code. If you'd like to learn more about ciphers and code breaking, you can read my book *Cracking Codes with Python* (No Starch Press, 2018; *https://nostarch.com/crackingcodes/*).

The Program in Action

When you run *simplesubcipher.py*, the output will look like this:

```
Simple Substitution Cipher, by Al Sweigart
A simple substitution cipher has a one-to-one translation for each
symbol in the plaintext and each symbol in the ciphertext.
Do you want to (e)ncrypt or (d)ecrypt?
> e
Please specify the key to use.
Or enter RANDOM to have one generated for you.
> random
The key is WNOMTRCEHDXBFVSLKAGZIPYJQU. KEEP THIS SECRET!
Enter the message to encrypt.
> Meet me by the rose bushes tonight.
The encrypted message is:
Fttz ft nq zet asgt nigetg zsvhcez.
Full encrypted text copied to clipboard.

Simple Substitution Cipher, by Al Sweigart
A simple substitution cipher has a one-to-one translation for each
symbol in the plaintext and each symbol in the ciphertext.
Do you want to (e)ncrypt or (d)ecrypt?
> d
Please specify the key to use.
> WNOMTRCEHDXBFVSLKAGZIPYJQU
Enter the message to decrypt.
> Fttz ft nq zet asgt nigetg zsvhcez.
The decrypted message is:
Meet me by the rose bushes tonight.
Full decrypted text copied to clipboard.
```

How It Works

The position of each of the key's 26 letters corresponds to the letter of the alphabet at that same position:

```
A B C D E F G H I J K L M N O P Q R S T U V W X Y Z
↕ ↕ ↕ ↕ ↕ ↕ ↕ ↕ ↕ ↕ ↕ ↕ ↕ ↕ ↕ ↕ ↕ ↕ ↕ ↕ ↕ ↕ ↕ ↕ ↕ ↕
W N O M T R C E H D X B F V S L K A G Z I P Y J Q U
```

Figure 66-1: How the letters of the alphabet encrypt with a key that begins with WNOM. To decrypt, replace letters at the bottom with the corresponding letters above them.

With this key, the letter *A* encrypts to *W* (and *W* decrypts to *A*), the letter *B* encrypts to *N*, and so on. The LETTERS and key variables are assigned to charsA and charsB (or the other way around if decrypting). Any message characters in charsA are substituted with the corresponding character in charsB to produce the final translated message.

```
1. """Simple Substitution Cipher, by Al Sweigart al@inventwithpython.com
2. A simple substitution cipher has a one-to-one translation for each
3. symbol in the plaintext and each symbol in the ciphertext.
```

```
 4. More info at: https://en.wikipedia.org/wiki/Substitution_cipher
 5. View this code at https://nostarch.com/big-book-small-python-projects
 6. Tags: short, cryptography, math"""
 7.
 8. import random
 9.
10. try:
11.     import pyperclip  # pyperclip copies text to the clipboard.
12. except ImportError:
13.     pass  # If pyperclip is not installed, do nothing. It's no big deal.
14.
15. # Every possible symbol that can be encrypted/decrypted:
16. LETTERS = 'ABCDEFGHIJKLMNOPQRSTUVWXYZ'
17.
18. def main():
19.     print('''Simple Substitution Cipher, by Al Sweigart
20. A simple substitution cipher has a one-to-one translation for each
21. symbol in the plaintext and each symbol in the ciphertext.''')
22.
23.     # Let the user specify if they are encrypting or decrypting:
24.     while True:  # Keep asking until the user enters e or d.
25.         print('Do you want to (e)ncrypt or (d)ecrypt?')
26.         response = input('> ').lower()
27.         if response.startswith('e'):
28.             myMode = 'encrypt'
29.             break
30.         elif response.startswith('d'):
31.             myMode = 'decrypt'
32.             break
33.         print('Please enter the letter e or d.')
34.
35.     # Let the user specify the key to use:
36.     while True:  # Keep asking until the user enters a valid key.
37.         print('Please specify the key to use.')
38.         if myMode == 'encrypt':
39.             print('Or enter RANDOM to have one generated for you.')
40.         response = input('> ').upper()
41.         if response == 'RANDOM':
42.             myKey = generateRandomKey()
43.             print('The key is {}. KEEP THIS SECRET!'.format(myKey))
44.             break
45.         else:
46.             if checkKey(response):
47.                 myKey = response
48.                 break
49.
50.     # Let the user specify the message to encrypt/decrypt:
51.     print('Enter the message to {}.'.format(myMode))
52.     myMessage = input('> ')
53.
54.     # Perform the encryption/decryption:
55.     if myMode == 'encrypt':
56.         translated = encryptMessage(myMessage, myKey)
57.     elif myMode == 'decrypt':
58.         translated = decryptMessage(myMessage, myKey)
```

```
59.
60.     # Display the results:
61.     print('The %sed message is:' % (myMode))
62.     print(translated)
63.
64.     try:
65.         pyperclip.copy(translated)
66.         print('Full %sed text copied to clipboard.' % (myMode))
67.     except:
68.         pass  # Do nothing if pyperclip wasn't installed.
69.
70.
71. def checkKey(key):
72.     """Return True if key is valid. Otherwise return False."""
73.     keyList = list(key)
74.     lettersList = list(LETTERS)
75.     keyList.sort()
76.     lettersList.sort()
77.     if keyList != lettersList:
78.         print('There is an error in the key or symbol set.')
79.         return False
80.     return True
81.
82.
83. def encryptMessage(message, key):
84.     """Encrypt the message using the key."""
85.     return translateMessage(message, key, 'encrypt')
86.
87.
88. def decryptMessage(message, key):
89.     """Decrypt the message using the key."""
90.     return translateMessage(message, key, 'decrypt')
91.
92.
93. def translateMessage(message, key, mode):
94.     """Encrypt or decrypt the message using the key."""
95.     translated = ''
96.     charsA = LETTERS
97.     charsB = key
98.     if mode == 'decrypt':
99.         # For decrypting, we can use the same code as encrypting. We
100.        # just need to swap where the key and LETTERS strings are used.
101.        charsA, charsB = charsB, charsA
102.
103.    # Loop through each symbol in the message:
104.    for symbol in message:
105.        if symbol.upper() in charsA:
106.            # Encrypt/decrypt the symbol:
107.            symIndex = charsA.find(symbol.upper())
108.            if symbol.isupper():
109.                translated += charsB[symIndex].upper()
110.            else:
111.                translated += charsB[symIndex].lower()
112.        else:
113.            # The symbol is not in LETTERS, just add it unchanged.
```

```
114.              translated += symbol
115.
116.     return translated
117.
118.
119. def generateRandomKey():
120.     """Generate and return a random encryption key."""
121.     key = list(LETTERS)  # Get a list from the LETTERS string.
122.     random.shuffle(key)  # Randomly shuffle the list.
123.     return ''.join(key)  # Get a string from the list.
124.
125.
126. # If this program was run (instead of imported), run the program:
127. if __name__ == '__main__':
128.     main()
```

Exploring the Program

Try to find the answers to the following questions. Experiment with some modifications to the code and rerun the program to see what effect the changes have.

1. What happens if you delete or comment out random.shuffle(key) on line 122 and enter RANDOM for the key?

2. What happens if you extend the LETTERS string on line 16 to become 'ABCDEFGHIJKLMNOPQRSTUVWXYZ1234567890'?

#67

SINE MESSAGE

This program displays a message of the user's choice in a wavy pattern as the text scrolls up. It accomplishes this effect with math.sin(), which implements the trigonometric sine wave function. But even if you don't understand the math, this program is rather short and easy to copy.

The Program in Action

When you run *sinemessage.py*, the output will look like this:

```
Sine Message, by Al Sweigart al@inventwithpython.com
(Press Ctrl-C to quit.)

What message do you want to display? (Max 39 chars.)
> I <3 Programming!
                              I <3 Programming!
                          I <3 Programming!
                            I <3 Programming!
                             I <3 Programming!
                              I <3 Programming!
                               I <3 Programming!
                                I <3 Programming!
                                I <3 Programming!
                               I <3 Programming!
                             I <3 Programming!
                           I <3 Programming!
                         I <3 Programming!
                      I <3 Programming!
                  I <3 Programming!
              I <3 Programming!
          I <3 Programming!
      I <3 Programming!
   I <3 Programming!
I <3 Programming!
I <3 Programming!
 I <3 Programming!
    I <3 Programming!
        I <3 Programming!
--snip--
```

How It Works

The math.sin() function in Python's math module takes an argument, which we'll call *x*, and returns another number called the *sine of x*. Several mathematical applications use the sine function; in our program, its purpose is merely to create a neat wave effect. We pass a variable named step to math .sin(). This variable starts at 0 and increases by 0.25 on each iteration of the main program loop.

We'll use the return value of math.sin() to figure out how many spaces of padding we should print on either side of the user's message. Since math .sin() returns a floating point number between -1.0 and 1.0, but the minimum amount of padding we want is zero, not a negative value, line 31 adds 1 to the return value of math.sin(), making the effective range 0.0 to 2.0. We'll certainly need more than zero to two spaces, so line 31 multiplies this number by a variable named multiplier to increase the amount of padding. The product of this multiplication is the number of spaces of padding to add to the left side before printing the user's message.

The result is the waving message animation you see when you run the program.

```
1. """Sine Message, by Al Sweigart al@inventwithpython.com
2. Create a sine-wavy message.
3. View this code at https://nostarch.com/big-book-small-python-projects
4. Tags: tiny, artistic"""
5.
6. import math, shutil, sys, time
7.
8. # Get the size of the terminal window:
9. WIDTH, HEIGHT = shutil.get_terminal_size()
10. # We can't print to the last column on Windows without it adding a
11. # newline automatically, so reduce the width by one:
12. WIDTH -= 1
13.
14. print('Sine Message, by Al Sweigart al@inventwithpython.com')
15. print('(Press Ctrl-C to quit.)')
16. print()
17. print('What message do you want to display? (Max', WIDTH // 2, 'chars.)')
18. while True:
19.     message = input('> ')
20.     if 1 <= len(message) <= (WIDTH // 2):
21.         break
22.     print('Message must be 1 to', WIDTH // 2, 'characters long.')
23.
24.
25. step = 0.0  # The "step" determines how far into the sine wave we are.
26. # Sine goes from -1.0 to 1.0, so we need to change it by a multiplier:
27. multiplier = (WIDTH - len(message)) / 2
28. try:
29.     while True:  # Main program loop.
30.         sinOfStep = math.sin(step)
31.         padding = ' ' * int((sinOfStep + 1) * multiplier)
32.         print(padding + message)
33.         time.sleep(0.1)
34.         step += 0.25  # (!) Try changing this to 0.1 or 0.5.
35. except KeyboardInterrupt:
36.     sys.exit()  # When Ctrl-C is pressed, end the program.
```

After entering the source code and running it a few times, try making experimental changes to it. The comments marked with (!) have suggestions for small changes you can make.

Exploring the Program

Try to find the answers to the following questions. Experiment with some modifications to the code and rerun the program to see what effect the changes have.

1. What happens if you change math.sin(step) on line 30 to math.cos(step)?

2. What happens if you change math.sin(step) on line 30 to math.sin(0)?

#68

SLIDING TILE PUZZLE

This classic puzzle relies on a 4 × 4 board with 15 numbered tiles and one free space. The objective is to slide the tiles until the numbers are in the correct order, going left to right and top to bottom. Tiles can only slide; you're not allowed to directly pick them up and rearrange them. Some versions of this puzzle toy feature scrambled images that form a complete picture once solved.

More information about sliding tile puzzles can be found at *https://en.wikipedia.org/wiki/Sliding_puzzle.*

The Program in Action

When you run *slidingtilepuzzle.py*, the output will look like this:

```
Sliding Tile Puzzle, by Al Sweigart al@inventwithpython.com

    Use the WASD keys to move the tiles
    back into their original order:
         1  2  3  4
         5  6  7  8
         9 10 11 12
        13 14 15
Press Enter to begin...


+------+------+------+------+
|      |      |      |      |
|  5   |  10  |      |  11  |
|      |      |      |      |
+------+------+------+------+
|      |      |      |      |
|  6   |  3   |  7   |  2   |
|      |      |      |      |
+------+------+------+------+
|      |      |      |      |
|  14  |  1   |  15  |  8   |
|      |      |      |      |
+------+------+------+------+
|      |      |      |      |
|  9   |  13  |  4   |  12  |
|      |      |      |      |
+------+------+------+------+

                          (W)
Enter WASD (or QUIT): (A) ( ) (D)
> w


+------+------+------+------+
|      |      |      |      |
|  5   |  10  |  7   |  11  |
|      |      |      |      |
+------+------+------+------+
|      |      |      |      |
|  6   |  3   |      |  2   |
|      |      |      |      |
+------+------+------+------+
|      |      |      |      |
|  14  |  1   |  15  |  8   |
|      |      |      |      |
+------+------+------+------+
|      |      |      |      |
|  9   |  13  |  4   |  12  |
|      |      |      |      |
+------+------+------+------+
```

```
                              (W)
Enter WASD (or QUIT): (A) (S) (D)
--snip--
```

How It Works

The data structure that represents the sliding tile game board is a list of lists. The inner lists each represent one column of the 4 × 4 board and contain strings for the numbered tiles (or the BLANK string to represent the blank space). The getNewBoard() function returns this list of lists with all tiles in their starting positions and the blank space in the lower-right corner.

Python can swap the values in two variables with a statement like a, b = b, a. The program uses this technique on lines 101 to 108 to swap the blank space and a neighboring tile and simulate sliding a numbered tile into the blank space. The getNewPuzzle() function generates new puzzles by performing 200 of these swaps randomly.

```python
1. """Sliding Tile Puzzle, by Al Sweigart al@inventwithpython.com
2. Slide the numbered tiles into the correct order.
3. View this code at https://nostarch.com/big-book-small-python-projects
4. Tags: large, game, puzzle"""
5.
6. import random, sys
7.
8. BLANK = '  '  # Note: This string is two spaces, not one.
9.
10.
11. def main():
12.     print('''Sliding Tile Puzzle, by Al Sweigart al@inventwithpython.com
13.
14.     Use the WASD keys to move the tiles
15.     back into their original order:
16.          1  2  3  4
17.          5  6  7  8
18.          9 10 11 12
19.         13 14 15    ''')
20.     input('Press Enter to begin...')
21.
22.     gameBoard = getNewPuzzle()
23.
24.     while True:
25.         displayBoard(gameBoard)
26.         playerMove = askForPlayerMove(gameBoard)
27.         makeMove(gameBoard, playerMove)
28.
29.         if gameBoard == getNewBoard():
30.             print('You won!')
31.             sys.exit()
32.
33.
34. def getNewBoard():
35.     """Return a list of lists that represents a new tile puzzle."""
```

```
36.     return [['1 ', '5 ', '9 ', '13'], ['2 ', '6 ', '10', '14'],
37.              ['3 ', '7 ', '11', '15'], ['4 ', '8 ', '12', BLANK]]
38.
39.
40. def displayBoard(board):
41.     """Display the given board on the screen."""
42.     labels = [board[0][0], board[1][0], board[2][0], board[3][0],
43.               board[0][1], board[1][1], board[2][1], board[3][1],
44.               board[0][2], board[1][2], board[2][2], board[3][2],
45.               board[0][3], board[1][3], board[2][3], board[3][3]]
46.     boardToDraw = """
47. +------+------+------+------+
48. |      |      |      |      |
49. |  {}  |  {}  |  {}  |  {}  |
50. |      |      |      |      |
51. +------+------+------+------+
52. |      |      |      |      |
53. |  {}  |  {}  |  {}  |  {}  |
54. |      |      |      |      |
55. +------+------+------+------+
56. |      |      |      |      |
57. |  {}  |  {}  |  {}  |  {}  |
58. |      |      |      |      |
59. +------+------+------+------+
60. |      |      |      |      |
61. |  {}  |  {}  |  {}  |  {}  |
62. |      |      |      |      |
63. +------+------+------+------+
64. """.format(*labels)
65.     print(boardToDraw)
66.
67.
68. def findBlankSpace(board):
69.     """Return an (x, y) tuple of the blank space's location."""
70.     for x in range(4):
71.         for y in range(4):
72.             if board[x][y] == '  ':
73.                 return (x, y)
74.
75.
76. def askForPlayerMove(board):
77.     """Let the player select a tile to slide."""
78.     blankx, blanky = findBlankSpace(board)
79.
80.     w = 'W' if blanky != 3 else ' '
81.     a = 'A' if blankx != 3 else ' '
82.     s = 'S' if blanky != 0 else ' '
83.     d = 'D' if blankx != 0 else ' '
84.
85.     while True:
86.         print('                         ({})'.format(w))
87.         print('Enter WASD (or QUIT): ({}) ({}) ({})'.format(a, s, d))
88.
89.         response = input('> ').upper()
90.         if response == 'QUIT':
```

```
91.            sys.exit()
92.          if response in (w + a + s + d).replace(' ', ''):
93.            return response
94.
95.
96. def makeMove(board, move):
97.      """Carry out the given move on the given board."""
98.      # Note: This function assumes that the move is valid.
99.      bx, by = findBlankSpace(board)
100.
101.      if move == 'W':
102.          board[bx][by], board[bx][by+1] = board[bx][by+1], board[bx][by]
103.      elif move == 'A':
104.          board[bx][by], board[bx+1][by] = board[bx+1][by], board[bx][by]
105.      elif move == 'S':
106.          board[bx][by], board[bx][by-1] = board[bx][by-1], board[bx][by]
107.      elif move == 'D':
108.          board[bx][by], board[bx-1][by] = board[bx-1][by], board[bx][by]
109.
110.
111. def makeRandomMove(board):
112.      """Perform a slide in a random direction."""
113.      blankx, blanky = findBlankSpace(board)
114.      validMoves = []
115.      if blanky != 3:
116.          validMoves.append('W')
117.      if blankx != 3:
118.          validMoves.append('A')
119.      if blanky != 0:
120.          validMoves.append('S')
121.      if blankx != 0:
122.          validMoves.append('D')
123.
124.      makeMove(board, random.choice(validMoves))
125.
126.
127. def getNewPuzzle(moves=200):
128.      """Get a new puzzle by making random slides from a solved state."""
129.      board = getNewBoard()
130.
131.      for i in range(moves):
132.          makeRandomMove(board)
133.      return board
134.
135.
136. # If this program was run (instead of imported), run the game:
137. if __name__ == '__main__':
138.      main()
```

After entering the source code and running it a few times, try making experimental changes to it. On your own, you can also try to figure out how to do the following:

- Create a more difficult 5 × 5 variant of the sliding tile puzzle.

- Create a "solve automatically" mode, which saves the current arrangement of the tiles and then attempts up to 40 random moves and stops if they have solved the puzzle. Otherwise, the puzzle loads the saved state and attempts another 40 random moves.

Exploring the Program

Try to find the answers to the following questions. Experiment with some modifications to the code and rerun the program to see what effect the changes have.

1. What happens if you change getNewPuzzle() on line 22 to getNewPuzzle(1)?
2. What happens if you change getNewPuzzle() on line 22 to getNewPuzzle(0)?
3. What happens if you delete or comment out sys.exit() on line 31?

#69

SNAIL RACE

You won't be able to handle the fast-paced excitement of these racing . . . snails. But what they lack in speed they make up for in ASCII-art cuteness. Each snail (represented by an @ character for the shell and v for the two eyestalks) moves slowly but surely toward the finish line. Up to eight snails, each with a custom name, can race each other, leaving a slime trail in their wake. This program is good for beginners.

The Program in Action

When you run *snailrace.py*, the output will look like this:

```
Snail Race, by Al Sweigart al@inventwithpython.com

    @v <-- snail

How many snails will race? Max: 8
> 3
Enter snail #1's name:
> Alice
Enter snail #2's name:
> Bob
Enter snail #3's name:
> Carol
START                           FINISH
|                               |
      Alice
......@v
      Bob
.....@v
       Carol
.......@v
--snip--
```

How It Works

This program makes use of two data structures, stored in two variables: snailNames is a list of strings of each snail's name, and snailProgress is a dictionary whose keys are the snails' names and whose values are integers representing how many spaces the snails have moved. Lines 79 to 82 read the data in these two variables to draw the snails at appropriate places on the screen.

```
1. """Snail Race, by Al Sweigart al@inventwithpython.com
2. Fast-paced snail racing action!
3. View this code at https://nostarch.com/big-book-small-python-projects
4. Tags: short, artistic, beginner, game, multiplayer"""
5.
6. import random, time, sys
7.
8. # Set up the constants:
9. MAX_NUM_SNAILS = 8
10. MAX_NAME_LENGTH = 20
11. FINISH_LINE = 40  # (!) Try modifying this number.
12.
13. print('''Snail Race, by Al Sweigart al@inventwithpython.com
14.
15.     @v <-- snail
16.
17. ''')
18.
```

```
19. # Ask how many snails to race:
20. while True:  # Keep asking until the player enters a number.
21.     print('How many snails will race? Max:', MAX_NUM_SNAILS)
22.     response = input('> ')
23.     if response.isdecimal():
24.         numSnailsRacing = int(response)
25.         if 1 < numSnailsRacing <= MAX_NUM_SNAILS:
26.             break
27.     print('Enter a number between 2 and', MAX_NUM_SNAILS)
28.
29. # Enter the names of each snail:
30. snailNames = []  # List of the string snail names.
31. for i in range(1, numSnailsRacing + 1):
32.     while True:  # Keep asking until the player enters a valid name.
33.         print('Enter snail #' + str(i) + "'s name:")
34.         name = input('> ')
35.         if len(name) == 0:
36.             print('Please enter a name.')
37.         elif name in snailNames:
38.             print('Choose a name that has not already been used.')
39.         else:
40.             break  # The entered name is acceptable.
41.     snailNames.append(name)
42.
43. # Display each snail at the start line.
44. print('\n' * 40)
45. print('START' + (' ' * (FINISH_LINE - len('START')) + 'FINISH'))
46. print('|' + (' ' * (FINISH_LINE - len('|')) + '|'))
47. snailProgress = {}
48. for snailName in snailNames:
49.     print(snailName[:MAX_NAME_LENGTH])
50.     print('@v')
51.     snailProgress[snailName] = 0
52.
53. time.sleep(1.5)  # The pause right before the race starts.
54.
55. while True:  # Main program loop.
56.     # Pick random snails to move forward:
57.     for i in range(random.randint(1, numSnailsRacing // 2)):
58.         randomSnailName = random.choice(snailNames)
59.         snailProgress[randomSnailName] += 1
60.
61.         # Check if a snail has reached the finish line:
62.         if snailProgress[randomSnailName] == FINISH_LINE:
63.             print(randomSnailName, 'has won!')
64.             sys.exit()
65.
66.     # (!) EXPERIMENT: Add a cheat here that increases a snail's progress
67.     # if it has your name.
68.
69.     time.sleep(0.5)  # (!) EXPERIMENT: Try changing this value.
70.
71.     # (!) EXPERIMENT: What happens if you comment this line out?
72.     print('\n' * 40)
73.
```

```
74.    # Display the start and finish lines:
75.    print('START' + (' ' * (FINISH_LINE - len('START')) + 'FINISH'))
76.    print('|' + (' ' * (FINISH_LINE - 1) + '|'))
77.
78.    # Display the snails (with name tags):
79.    for snailName in snailNames:
80.        spaces = snailProgress[snailName]
81.        print((' ' * spaces) + snailName[:MAX_NAME_LENGTH])
82.        print(('.' * snailProgress[snailName]) + '@v')
```

After entering the source code and running it a few times, try making experimental changes to it. The comments marked with (!) have suggestions for small changes you can make. On your own, you can also try to figure out how to do the following:

- Add a random "speed boost" that launches the snail four spaces ahead instead of one.
- Add a "sleep mode" that snails can randomly enter during the race. This mode causes them to stop for a few turns and zzz to appear next to them.
- Add support for ties, in case snails reach the finish line at the same time.

Exploring the Program

Try to find the answers to the following questions. Experiment with some modifications to the code and rerun the program to see what effect the changes have.

1. What happens if you change snailName[:MAX_NAME_LENGTH] on line 81 to snailNames[0]?
2. What happens if you change print('@v') on line 50 to print('v@')?

#70

SOROBAN JAPANESE ABACUS

An abacus, also called a counting frame, is a calculating tool used in many cultures long before electronic calculators were invented. Figure 70-1 shows the Japanese form of the abacus, called a soroban. Each wire represents a place in a positional numeral system, and the beads on the wire represent the digit at that place. For example, a soroban with two beads moved over on the rightmost wire and three beads moved over on the second-to-rightmost wire would represent the number 32. This program simulates a soroban. (The irony of using a computer to simulate a pre-computer computing tool is not lost on me.)

Figure 70-1: A soroban

Each column in the soroban represents a different digit. The rightmost column is the ones place, the column to its left is the tens place, the column to the left of that is the hundreds place, and so on. The Q, W, E, R, T, Y, U, I, O, and P keys along the top of your keyboard can increase the digit at their respective positions, while the A, S, D, F, G, H, J, K, L, and ; keys will decrease them. The beads on the virtual soroban will slide to reflect the current number. You can also enter numbers directly.

The four beads below the horizontal divider are "earth" beads, and lifting them up against the divider counts as 1 for that digit. The bead above the horizontal divider is a "heaven" bead, and pulling it down against the divider counts as 5 for that digit, so pulling down one heaven bead and pulling up three earth beads in the tens column represents the number 80. More information about abacuses and how to use them can be found at *https://en.wikipedia.org/wiki/Abacus*.

The Program in Action

When you run *soroban.py*, the output will look like this:

```
Soroban - The Japanese Abacus
By Al Sweigart al@inventwithpython.com


+================================+
I 0  0  0  0  0  0  0  0  0  0  I
I |  |  |  |  |  |  |  |  |  |  I
I |  |  |  |  |  |  |  |  |  |  I
+================================+
I |  |  |  |  |  |  |  |  |  |  I
I |  |  |  |  |  |  |  |  |  |  I
I 0  0  0  0  0  0  0  0  0  0  I
I 0  0  0  0  0  0  0  0  0  0  I
I 0  0  0  0  0  0  0  0  0  0  I
I 0  0  0  0  0  0  0  0  0  0  I
+==0==0==0==0==0==0==0==0==0==0==+
  +q  w  e  r  t  y  u  i  o  p
  -a  s  d  f  g  h  j  k  l  ;
(Enter a number, "quit", or a stream of up/down letters.)
> pppiiiii
```

```
+=================================+
I 0  0  0  0  0  0  0  |  0  0  I
I |  |  |  |  |  |  |  |  |  |  I
I |  |  |  |  |  |  |  0  |  |  I
+=================================+
I |  |  |  |  |  |  |  |  |  0  I
I |  |  |  |  |  |  |  |  |  0  I
I 0  0  0  0  0  0  0  0  0  0  I
I 0  0  0  0  0  0  0  0  0  |  I
I 0  0  0  0  0  0  0  0  0  |  I
I 0  0  0  0  0  0  0  0  0  0  I
+==0==0==0==0==0==0==5==0==3==+
 +q  w  e  r  t  y  u  i  o  p
 -a  s  d  f  g  h  j  k  l  ;
(Enter a number, "quit", or a stream of up/down letters.)
--snip--
```

How It Works

The displayAbacus() function accepts a number argument used to figure out where it should render beads on the abacus. The soroban always has exactly 80 possible locations for either '0' beads or '|' rod segments, as marked by the curly braces ({}) in the multiline string on lines 127 to 139. Another 10 curly braces represent the digits of the number argument.

We need to create a list of strings to fill in these curly braces, going from left to right, top to bottom. The code in displayAbacus() will populate a hasBead list with a True value to display a '0' bead and a False value to display a '|'. The first 10 values in this list are for the top "heaven" row. We'll put a bead in this row if the column's digit is 0, 1, 2, 3, or 4, since the heaven bead won't be in that row unless the digit for that column is 0 to 4. We add Boolean values to hasBead for the remaining rows.

Lines 118 to 123 use hasBead to create an abacusChar list that contains the actual '0' and '|' strings. When combined with numberList on line 126, the program forms a chars list that populates the curly braces ({}) for the multiline-string ASCII art of the soroban.

```
1. """Soroban Japanese Abacus, by Al Sweigart al@inventwithpython.com
2. A simulation of a Japanese abacus calculator tool.
3. More info at: https://en.wikipedia.org/wiki/Soroban
4. View this code at https://nostarch.com/big-book-small-python-projects
5. Tags: large, artistic, math, simulation"""
6.
7. NUMBER_OF_DIGITS = 10
8.
9.
10. def main():
11.     print('Soroban - The Japanese Abacus')
12.     print('By Al Sweigart al@inventwithpython.com')
13.     print()
14.
15.     abacusNumber = 0  # This is the number represented on the abacus.
```

```
16.
17.    while True:  # Main program loop.
18.        displayAbacus(abacusNumber)
19.        displayControls()
20.
21.        commands = input('> ')
22.        if commands == 'quit':
23.            # Quit the program:
24.            break
25.        elif commands.isdecimal():
26.            # Set the abacus number:
27.            abacusNumber = int(commands)
28.        else:
29.            # Handle increment/decrement commands:
30.            for letter in commands:
31.                if letter == 'q':
32.                    abacusNumber += 1000000000
33.                elif letter == 'a':
34.                    abacusNumber -= 1000000000
35.                elif letter == 'w':
36.                    abacusNumber += 100000000
37.                elif letter == 's':
38.                    abacusNumber -= 100000000
39.                elif letter == 'e':
40.                    abacusNumber += 10000000
41.                elif letter == 'd':
42.                    abacusNumber -= 10000000
43.                elif letter == 'r':
44.                    abacusNumber += 1000000
45.                elif letter == 'f':
46.                    abacusNumber -= 1000000
47.                elif letter == 't':
48.                    abacusNumber += 100000
49.                elif letter == 'g':
50.                    abacusNumber -= 100000
51.                elif letter == 'y':
52.                    abacusNumber += 10000
53.                elif letter == 'h':
54.                    abacusNumber -= 10000
55.                elif letter == 'u':
56.                    abacusNumber += 1000
57.                elif letter == 'j':
58.                    abacusNumber -= 1000
59.                elif letter == 'i':
60.                    abacusNumber += 100
61.                elif letter == 'k':
62.                    abacusNumber -= 100
63.                elif letter == 'o':
64.                    abacusNumber += 10
65.                elif letter == 'l':
66.                    abacusNumber -= 10
67.                elif letter == 'p':
68.                    abacusNumber += 1
69.                elif letter == ';':
70.                    abacusNumber -= 1
```

```
71.
72.         # The abacus can't show negative numbers:
73.         if abacusNumber < 0:
74.             abacusNumber = 0  # Change any negative numbers to 0.
75.         # The abacus can't show numbers larger than 9999999999:
76.         if abacusNumber > 9999999999:
77.             abacusNumber = 9999999999
78.
79.
80. def displayAbacus(number):
81.     numberList = list(str(number).zfill(NUMBER_OF_DIGITS))
82.
83.     hasBead = []  # Contains a True or False for each bead position.
84.
85.     # Top heaven row has a bead for digits 0, 1, 2, 3, and 4.
86.     for i in range(NUMBER_OF_DIGITS):
87.         hasBead.append(numberList[i] in '01234')
88.
89.     # Bottom heaven row has a bead for digits 5, 6, 7, 8, and 9.
90.     for i in range(NUMBER_OF_DIGITS):
91.         hasBead.append(numberList[i] in '56789')
92.
93.     # 1st (topmost) earth row has a bead for all digits except 0.
94.     for i in range(NUMBER_OF_DIGITS):
95.         hasBead.append(numberList[i] in '12346789')
96.
97.     # 2nd earth row has a bead for digits 2, 3, 4, 7, 8, and 9.
98.     for i in range(NUMBER_OF_DIGITS):
99.         hasBead.append(numberList[i] in '234789')
100.
101.     # 3rd earth row has a bead for digits 0, 3, 4, 5, 8, and 9.
102.     for i in range(NUMBER_OF_DIGITS):
103.         hasBead.append(numberList[i] in '034589')
104.
105.     # 4th earth row has a bead for digits 0, 1, 2, 4, 5, 6, and 9.
106.     for i in range(NUMBER_OF_DIGITS):
107.         hasBead.append(numberList[i] in '014569')
108.
109.     # 5th earth row has a bead for digits 0, 1, 2, 5, 6, and 7.
110.     for i in range(NUMBER_OF_DIGITS):
111.         hasBead.append(numberList[i] in '012567')
112.
113.     # 6th earth row has a bead for digits 0, 1, 2, 3, 5, 6, 7, and 8.
114.     for i in range(NUMBER_OF_DIGITS):
115.         hasBead.append(numberList[i] in '01235678')
116.
117.     # Convert these True or False values into O or | characters.
118.     abacusChar = []
119.     for i, beadPresent in enumerate(hasBead):
120.         if beadPresent:
121.             abacusChar.append('O')
122.         else:
123.             abacusChar.append('|')
124.
125.     # Draw the abacus with the O/| characters.
```

```
126.        chars = abacusChar + numberList
127.        print("""
128. +==================================+
129. I  {}  {}  {}  {}  {}  {}  {}  {}  {}  {}  I
130. I  |   |   |   |   |   |   |   |   |   |   I
131. I  {}  {}  {}  {}  {}  {}  {}  {}  {}  {}  I
132. +==================================+
133. I  {}  {}  {}  {}  {}  {}  {}  {}  {}  {}  I
134. I  {}  {}  {}  {}  {}  {}  {}  {}  {}  {}  I
135. I  {}  {}  {}  {}  {}  {}  {}  {}  {}  {}  I
136. I  {}  {}  {}  {}  {}  {}  {}  {}  {}  {}  I
137. I  {}  {}  {}  {}  {}  {}  {}  {}  {}  {}  I
138. I  {}  {}  {}  {}  {}  {}  {}  {}  {}  {}  I
139. +=={}=={}=={}=={}=={}=={}=={}=={}=={}=={}==+""".format(*chars))
140.
141.
142. def displayControls():
143.        print('  +q  w  e  r  t  y  u  i  o  p')
144.        print('  -a  s  d  f  g  h  j  k  l  ;')
145.        print('(Enter a number, "quit", or a stream of up/down letters.)')
146.
147.
148. if __name__ == '__main__':
149.        main()
```

Exploring the Program

Try to find the answers to the following questions. Experiment with some modifications to the code and rerun the program to see what effect the changes have.

1. What happens if you change abacusNumber = 0 on line 15 to abacusNumber = 9999?

2. What happens if you change abacusChar.append('0') on line 121 to abacusChar.append('@')?

#71

SOUND MIMIC

Similar to the Simon electronic toy, this memorization game uses the third-party playsound module to play four different sounds, which correspond to the A, S, D, and F keys on the keyboard. As you successfully repeat the pattern the game gives you, the patterns get longer and longer. How many sounds can you hold in your short-term memory?

If you look at the code, you'll see that the playsound.playsound() function is passed the filename of the sound to play. You can download the sound files from these URLs:

https://inventwithpython.com/soundA.wav
https://inventwithpython.com/soundS.wav
https://inventwithpython.com/soundD.wav
https://inventwithpython.com/soundF.wav

Place these files in the same folder as *soundmimic.py* before running the program. More information about the playsound module can be found at *https://pypi.org/project/playsound/*. Users on macOS must also install the pyobjc module from *https://pypi.org/project/pyobjc/* for playsound to work.

The Program in Action

When you run *soundmimic.py*, the output will look like this:

```
Sound Mimic, by Al Sweigart al@inventwithpython.com
Try to memorize a pattern of A S D F letters (each with its own sound)
as it gets longer and longer.
Press Enter to begin...
<screen clears>
Pattern: S
<screen clears>
Enter the pattern:
> s
Correct!
<screen clears>
Pattern: S F
<screen clears>
Enter the pattern:
> sf
Correct!
<screen clears>
Pattern: S F F
<screen clears>
Enter the pattern:
> sff
Correct!
<screen clears>
Pattern: S F F D
--snip--
```

How It Works

This program imports the playsound module, which can play sound files. The module has one function, playsound(), to which you can pass the filename of a *.wav* or *.mp3* file to play. On each round of the game, the program appends a randomly chosen letter (either A, S, D, or F) to the pattern list and plays the sounds in this list. As the pattern list grows longer, so does the pattern of sound files the player must memorize.

```
1. """Sound Mimic, by Al Sweigart al@inventwithpython.com
2. A pattern-matching game with sounds. Try to memorize an increasingly
3. longer and longer pattern of letters. Inspired by the electronic game
4. Simon.
5. View this code at https://nostarch.com/big-book-small-python-projects
6. Tags: short, beginner, game"""
7.
```

```
 8. import random, sys, time
 9.
10. # Download the sound files from these URLs (or use your own):
11. # https://inventwithpython.com/soundA.wav
12. # https://inventwithpython.com/soundS.wav
13. # https://inventwithpython.com/soundD.wav
14. # https://inventwithpython.com/soundF.wav
15.
16. try:
17.     import playsound
18. except ImportError:
19.     print('The playsound module needs to be installed to run this')
20.     print('program. On Windows, open a Command Prompt and run:')
21.     print('pip install playsound')
22.     print('On macOS and Linux, open a Terminal and run:')
23.     print('pip3 install playsound')
24.     sys.exit()
25.
26.
27. print('''Sound Mimic, by Al Sweigart al@inventwithpython.com
28. Try to memorize a pattern of A S D F letters (each with its own sound)
29. as it gets longer and longer.''')
30.
31. input('Press Enter to begin...')
32.
33. pattern = ''
34. while True:
35.     print('\n' * 60)  # Clear the screen by printing several newlines.
36.
37.     # Add a random letter to the pattern:
38.     pattern = pattern + random.choice('ASDF')
39.
40.     # Display the pattern (and play their sounds):
41.     print('Pattern: ', end='')
42.     for letter in pattern:
43.         print(letter, end=' ', flush=True)
44.         playsound.playsound('sound' + letter + '.wav')
45.
46.     time.sleep(1)  # Add a slight pause at the end.
47.     print('\n' * 60)  # Clear the screen by printing several newlines.
48.
49.     # Let the player enter the pattern:
50.     print('Enter the pattern:')
51.     response = input('> ').upper()
52.
53.     if response != pattern:
54.         print('Incorrect!')
55.         print('The pattern was', pattern)
56.     else:
57.         print('Correct!')
58.
59.     for letter in pattern:
60.         playsound.playsound('sound' + letter + '.wav')
61.
62.     if response != pattern:
```

```
63.        print('You scored', len(pattern) - 1, 'points.')
64.        print('Thanks for playing!')
65.        break
66.
67.    time.sleep(1)
```

Exploring the Program

Try to find the answers to the following questions. Experiment with some modifications to the code and rerun the program to see what effect the changes have.

1. What happens if you delete or comment out print('\n' * 60) on line 47?
2. What happens if you change response != pattern on line 62 to False?

#72

SPONGECASE

You've probably seen the "Mocking SpongeBob" meme: a picture of SpongeBob SquarePants, with a caption whose text alternates between upper- and lowercase letters to indicate sarcasm, like this: uSiNg SpOnGeBoB MeMeS dOeS NoT mAkE YoU wItTy. For some randomness, the text sometimes doesn't alternate capitalization.

This short program uses the upper() and lower() string methods to convert your message into "spongecase." The program is also set up so that other programs can import it as a module with import spongecase and then call the spongecase.englishToSpongecase() function.

tHe PrOgRaM iN AcTiOn

When you run *spongecase.py*, the output will look like this:

```
sPoNgEcAsE, bY aL sWeIGaRt Al@iNvEnTwItHpYtHoN.cOm

eNtEr YoUr MeSsAgE:
> Using SpongeBob memes does not make you witty.

uSiNg SpOnGeBoB MeMeS dOeS NoT mAkE YoU wItTy.
(cOpIed SpOnGeTexT to ClIpbOaRd.)
```

hOw It WoRkS

The code in this program uses a for loop on line 35 to iterate over every character in the message string. The useUpper variable contains a Boolean variable to indicate if the character should be made uppercase (if True) or lowercase (if False). Lines 46 and 47 *toggle* the Boolean value in useUpper (that is, set it to its opposite value) in 90 percent of the iterations. This means that the casing almost always switches between upper- and lowercase.

```
 1. """sPoNgEcAsE, by Al Sweigart al@inventwithpython.com
 2. Translates English messages into sPOnGEtExT.
 3. View this code at https://nostarch.com/big-book-small-python-projects
 4. Tags: tiny, beginner, word"""
 5.
 6. import random
 7.
 8. try:
 9.     import pyperclip  # pyperclip copies text to the clipboard.
10. except ImportError:
11.     pass  # If pyperclip is not installed, do nothing. It's no big deal.
12.
13.
14. def main():
15.     """Run the Spongetext program."""
16.     print('''sPoNgEcAsE, bY aL sWeIGaRt Al@iNvEnTwItHpYtHoN.cOm
17.
18. eNtEr YoUr MeSsAgE:''')
19.     spongetext = englishToSpongecase(input('> '))
20.     print()
21.     print(spongetext)
22.
23.     try:
24.         pyperclip.copy(spongetext)
25.         print('(cOpIed SpOnGeTexT to ClIpbOaRd.)')
26.     except:
27.         pass  # Do nothing if pyperclip wasn't installed.
28.
29.
30. def englishToSpongecase(message):
31.     """Return the spongetext form of the given string."""
32.     spongetext = ''
```

```
33.        useUpper = False
34.
35.        for character in message:
36.            if not character.isalpha():
37.                spongetext += character
38.                continue
39.
40.            if useUpper:
41.                spongetext += character.upper()
42.            else:
43.                spongetext += character.lower()
44.
45.            # Flip the case, 90% of the time.
46.            if random.randint(1, 100) <= 90:
47.                useUpper = not useUpper  # Flip the case.
48.        return spongetext
49.
50.
51. # If this program was run (instead of imported), run the game:
52. if __name__ == '__main__':
53.     main()
```

ExPloRiNg tHe PrOgRaM

Try to find the answers to the following questions. Experiment with some modifications to the code and rerun the program to see what effect the changes have.

1. What happens if you change `random.randint(1, 100)` on line 46 to `random.randint(80, 100)`?

2. What happens if you delete or comment out `useUpper = not useUpper` on line 47?

#73

SUDOKU PUZZLE

Sudoku is a popular puzzle game in newspapers and mobile apps. The Sudoku board is a 9 × 9 grid in which the player must place the digits 1 to 9 once, and only once, in each row, column, and 3 × 3 subgrid. The game begins with a few spaces already filled in with digits, called *givens*. A well-formed Sudoku puzzle will have only one possible valid solution.

The Program in Action

When you run *sudoku.py*, the output will look like this:

```
Sudoku Puzzle, by Al Sweigart al@inventwithpython.com
--snip--
  A B C   D E F   G H I
1 . . . | . . . | . . .
2 . 7 9 | . 5 . | 1 8 .
3 8 . . | . . . | . . 7
  ------+-------+------
4 . . 7 | 3 . 6 | 8 . .
5 4 5 . | 7 . 8 | . 9 6
6 . . 3 | 5 . 2 | 7 . .
  ------+-------+------
7 7 . . | . . . | . . 5
8 . 1 6 | . 3 . | 4 2 .
9 . . . | . . . | . . .

Enter a move, or RESET, NEW, UNDO, ORIGINAL, or QUIT:
(For example, a move looks like "B4 9".)
--snip--
```

How It Works

Objects of the SudokuGrid class are the data structures that represent the Sudoku grid. You can call their methods to make modifications to, or retrieve information about, the grid. For example, the makeMove() method places a number on the grid, the resetGrid() method restores the grid to its original state, and isSolved() returns True if all the solution's numbers have been placed on the grid.

The main part of the program, starting on line 141, uses a SudokuGrid object and its methods for this game, but you could also copy and paste this class into other Sudoku programs you create to reuse its functionality.

```
1. """Sudoku Puzzle, by Al Sweigart al@inventwithpython.com
2. The classic 9x9 number placement puzzle.
3. More info at https://en.wikipedia.org/wiki/Sudoku
4. View this code at https://nostarch.com/big-book-small-python-projects
5. Tags: large, game, object-oriented, puzzle"""
6.
7. import copy, random, sys
8.
9. # This game requires a sudokupuzzle.txt file that contains the puzzles.
10. # Download it from https://inventwithpython.com/sudokupuzzles.txt
11. # Here's a sample of the content in this file:
12. # ..3.2.6..9..3.5..1..18.64....81.29..7.......8..67.82....26.95..8..2.3..9..5.1.3..
13. # 2...8.3...6..7..84.3.5..2.9...1.54.8.........4.27.6...3.1..7.4.72..4..6...4.1...3
14. # ......9.7...42.18....7.5.261..9.4....5.....4....5.7..992.1.8...34.59...5.7......
15. # .3..5..4...8.1.5..46.....12.7.5.2.8....6.3....4.1.9.3.25.....98..1.2.6...8..6..2.
16.
```

```
17. # Set up the constants:
18. EMPTY_SPACE = '.'
19. GRID_LENGTH = 9
20. BOX_LENGTH = 3
21. FULL_GRID_SIZE = GRID_LENGTH * GRID_LENGTH
22.
23.
24. class SudokuGrid:
25.     def __init__(self, originalSetup):
26.         # originalSetup is a string of 81 characters for the puzzle
27.         # setup, with numbers and periods (for the blank spaces).
28.         # See https://inventwithpython.com/sudokupuzzles.txt
29.         self.originalSetup = originalSetup
30.
31.         # The state of the sudoku grid is represented by a dictionary
32.         # with (x, y) keys and values of the number (as a string) at
33.         # that space.
34.         self.grid = {}
35.         self.resetGrid()  # Set the grid state to its original setup.
36.         self.moves = []  # Tracks each move for the undo feature.
37.
38.     def resetGrid(self):
39.         """Reset the state of the grid, tracked by self.grid, to the
40.         state in self.originalSetup."""
41.         for x in range(1, GRID_LENGTH + 1):
42.             for y in range(1, GRID_LENGTH + 1):
43.                 self.grid[(x, y)] = EMPTY_SPACE
44.
45.         assert len(self.originalSetup) == FULL_GRID_SIZE
46.         i = 0  # i goes from 0 to 80
47.         y = 0  # y goes from 0 to 8
48.         while i < FULL_GRID_SIZE:
49.             for x in range(GRID_LENGTH):
50.                 self.grid[(x, y)] = self.originalSetup[i]
51.                 i += 1
52.             y += 1
53.
54.     def makeMove(self, column, row, number):
55.         """Place the number at the column (a letter from A to I) and row
56.         (an integer from 1 to 9) on the grid."""
57.         x = 'ABCDEFGHI'.find(column)  # Convert this to an integer.
58.         y = int(row) - 1
59.
60.         # Check if the move is being made on a "given" number:
61.         if self.originalSetup[y * GRID_LENGTH + x] != EMPTY_SPACE:
62.             return False
63.
64.         self.grid[(x, y)] = number  # Place this number on the grid.
65.
66.         # We need to store a separate copy of the dictionary object:
67.         self.moves.append(copy.copy(self.grid))
68.         return True
69.
70.     def undo(self):
71.         """Set the current grid state to the previous state in the
```

```
72.            self.moves list."""
73.            if self.moves == []:
74.                return  # No states in self.moves, so do nothing.
75.
76.            self.moves.pop()  # Remove the current state.
77.
78.            if self.moves == []:
79.                self.resetGrid()
80.            else:
81.                # set the grid to the last move.
82.                self.grid = copy.copy(self.moves[-1])
83.
84.        def display(self):
85.            """Display the current state of the grid on the screen."""
86.            print('  A B C   D E F   G H I')  # Display column labels.
87.            for y in range(GRID_LENGTH):
88.                for x in range(GRID_LENGTH):
89.                    if x == 0:
90.                        # Display row label:
91.                        print(str(y + 1) + '  ', end='')
92.
93.                    print(self.grid[(x, y)] + ' ', end='')
94.                    if x == 2 or x == 5:
95.                        # Display a vertical line:
96.                        print('| ', end='')
97.                print()  # Print a newline.
98.
99.                if y == 2 or y == 5:
100.                    # Display a horizontal line:
101.                    print('   ------+-------+------')
102.
103.        def _isCompleteSetOfNumbers(self, numbers):
104.            """Return True if numbers contains the digits 1 through 9."""
105.            return sorted(numbers) == list('123456789')
106.
107.        def isSolved(self):
108.            """Returns True if the current grid is in a solved state."""
109.            # Check each row:
110.            for row in range(GRID_LENGTH):
111.                rowNumbers = []
112.                for x in range(GRID_LENGTH):
113.                    number = self.grid[(x, row)]
114.                    rowNumbers.append(number)
115.                if not self._isCompleteSetOfNumbers(rowNumbers):
116.                    return False
117.
118.            # Check each column:
119.            for column in range(GRID_LENGTH):
120.                columnNumbers = []
121.                for y in range(GRID_LENGTH):
122.                    number = self.grid[(column, y)]
123.                    columnNumbers.append(number)
124.                if not self._isCompleteSetOfNumbers(columnNumbers):
125.                    return False
126.
```

```
127.          # Check each box:
128.          for boxx in (0, 3, 6):
129.              for boxy in (0, 3, 6):
130.                  boxNumbers = []
131.                  for x in range(BOX_LENGTH):
132.                      for y in range(BOX_LENGTH):
133.                          number = self.grid[(boxx + x, boxy + y)]
134.                          boxNumbers.append(number)
135.                  if not self._isCompleteSetOfNumbers(boxNumbers):
136.                      return False
137.
138.          return True
139.
140.
141. print('''Sudoku Puzzle, by Al Sweigart al@inventwithpython.com
142.
143. Sudoku is a number placement logic puzzle game. A Sudoku grid is a 9x9
144. grid of numbers. Try to place numbers in the grid such that every row,
145. column, and 3x3 box has the numbers 1 through 9 once and only once.
146.
147. For example, here is a starting Sudoku grid and its solved form:
148.
149.     5 3 . | . 7 . | . . .     5 3 4 | 6 7 8 | 9 1 2
150.     6 . . | 1 9 5 | . . .     6 7 2 | 1 9 5 | 3 4 8
151.     . 9 8 | . . . | . 6 .     1 9 8 | 3 4 2 | 5 6 7
152.     ------+-------+------     ------+-------+------
153.     8 . . | . 6 . | . . 3     8 5 9 | 7 6 1 | 4 2 3
154.     4 . . | 8 . 3 | . . 1 --> 4 2 6 | 8 5 3 | 7 9 1
155.     7 . . | . 2 . | . . 6     7 1 3 | 9 2 4 | 8 5 6
156.     ------+-------+------     ------+-------+------
157.     . 6 . | . . . | 2 8 .     9 6 1 | 5 3 7 | 2 8 4
158.     . . . | 4 1 9 | . . 5     2 8 7 | 4 1 9 | 6 3 5
159.     . . . | . 8 . | . 7 9     3 4 5 | 2 8 6 | 1 7 9
160. ''')
161. input('Press Enter to begin...')
162.
163.
164. # Load the sudokupuzzles.txt file:
165. with open('sudokupuzzles.txt') as puzzleFile:
166.     puzzles = puzzleFile.readlines()
167.
168. # Remove the newlines at the end of each puzzle:
169. for i, puzzle in enumerate(puzzles):
170.     puzzles[i] = puzzle.strip()
171.
172. grid = SudokuGrid(random.choice(puzzles))
173.
174. while True:  # Main game loop.
175.     grid.display()
176.
177.     # Check if the puzzle is solved.
178.     if grid.isSolved():
179.         print('Congratulations! You solved the puzzle!')
180.         print('Thanks for playing!')
181.         sys.exit()
```

```
182.
183.     # Get the player's action:
184.     while True:  # Keep asking until the player enters a valid action.
185.         print()  # Print a newline.
186.         print('Enter a move, or RESET, NEW, UNDO, ORIGINAL, or QUIT:')
187.         print('(For example, a move looks like "B4 9".)')
188.
189.         action = input('> ').upper().strip()
190.
191.         if len(action) > 0 and action[0] in ('R', 'N', 'U', 'O', 'Q'):
192.             # Player entered a valid action.
193.             break
194.
195.         if len(action.split()) == 2:
196.             space, number = action.split()
197.             if len(space) != 2:
198.                 continue
199.
200.             column, row = space
201.             if column not in list('ABCDEFGHI'):
202.                 print('There is no column', column)
203.                 continue
204.             if not row.isdecimal() or not (1 <= int(row) <= 9):
205.                 print('There is no row', row)
206.                 continue
207.             if not (1 <= int(number) <= 9):
208.                 print('Select a number from 1 to 9, not ', number)
209.                 continue
210.             break  # Player entered a valid move.
211.
212.     print()  # Print a newline.
213.
214.     if action.startswith('R'):
215.         # Reset the grid:
216.         grid.resetGrid()
217.         continue
218.
219.     if action.startswith('N'):
220.         # Get a new puzzle:
221.         grid = SudokuGrid(random.choice(puzzles))
222.         continue
223.
224.     if action.startswith('U'):
225.         # Undo the last move:
226.         grid.undo()
227.         continue
228.
229.     if action.startswith('O'):
230.         # View the original numbers:
231.         originalGrid = SudokuGrid(grid.originalSetup)
232.         print('The original grid looked like this:')
233.         originalGrid.display()
234.         input('Press Enter to continue...')
235.
236.     if action.startswith('Q'):
```

```
237.          # Quit the game.
238.          print('Thanks for playing!')
239.          sys.exit()
240.
241.      # Handle the move the player selected.
242.      if grid.makeMove(column, row, number) == False:
243.          print('You cannot overwrite the original grid\'s numbers.')
244.          print('Enter ORIGINAL to view the original grid.')
245.          input('Press Enter to continue...')
```

Exploring the Program

Try to find the answers to the following questions. Experiment with some modifications to the code and rerun the program to see what effect the changes have.

1. What error happens if you delete or rename the *sudokupuzzles.txt* file and run the program?

2. What happens if you change str(y + 1) on line 91 to str(y)?

3. What happens if you change if y == 2 or y == 5: on line 99 to if y == 1 or y == 6:?

#74

TEXT-TO-SPEECH TALKER

This program demonstrates the use of the pyttsx3 third-party module. Any message you enter will be spoken out loud by your operating system's text-to-speech capabilities. Although computer-generated speech is an incredibly complex branch of computer science, the pyttsx3 module provides an easy interface for it, making this small program suitable for beginners. Once you've learned how to use the module, you can add generated speech to your own programs.

More information about the pyttsx3 module can be found at *https://pypi.org/project/pyttsx3/*.

The Program in Action

When you run *texttospeechtalker.py*, the output will look like this:

```
Text To Speech Talker, by Al Sweigart al@inventwithpython.com
Text-to-speech using the pyttsx3 module, which in turn uses
the NSSpeechSynthesizer (on macOS), SAPI5 (on Windows), or
eSpeak (on Linux) speech engines.

Enter the text to speak, or QUIT to quit.
> Hello. My name is Guido van Robot.
<computer speaks text out loud>
> quit
Thanks for playing!
```

How It Works

This program is short because the pyttsx3 module handles all of the text-to-speech code. To use this module, install it by following the instructions in this book's introduction. Once you've done so, your Python script can import it with import pyttsx3 and call the pyttsc3.init() function. This returns an Engine object that represents the text-to-speech engine. This object has a say() method to which you can pass a string of text for the computer to speak when you run the runAndWait() method.

```
 1. """Text To Speech Talker, by Al Sweigart al@inventwithpython.com
 2. An example program using the text-to-speech features of the pyttsx3
 3. module.
 4. View this code at https://nostarch.com/big-book-small-python-projects
 5. Tags: tiny, beginner"""
 6.
 7. import sys
 8.
 9. try:
10.     import pyttsx3
11. except ImportError:
12.     print('The pyttsx3 module needs to be installed to run this')
13.     print('program. On Windows, open a Command Prompt and run:')
14.     print('pip install pyttsx3')
16.     print('On macOS and Linux, open a Terminal and run:')
16.     print('pip3 install pyttsx3')
17.     sys.exit()
18.
19. tts = pyttsx3.init()  # Initialize the TTS engine.
20.
21. print('Text To Speech Talker, by Al Sweigart al@inventwithpython.com')
22. print('Text-to-speech using the pyttsx3 module, which in turn uses')
23. print('the NSSpeechSynthesizer (on macOS), SAPI5 (on Windows), or')
24. print('eSpeak (on Linux) speech engines.')
25. print()
26. print('Enter the text to speak, or QUIT to quit.')
27. while True:
28.     text = input('> ')
```

```
29.
30.    if text.upper() == 'QUIT':
31.        print('Thanks for playing!')
32.        sys.exit()
33.
34.    tts.say(text)  # Add some text for the TTS engine to say.
35.    tts.runAndWait()  # Make the TTS engine say it.
```

Exploring the Program

This is a base program, so there aren't many options to customize it. Instead, consider what other programs of yours would benefit from text-to-speech.

#75

THREE-CARD MONTE

 Three-card monte is a common scam played on gullible tourists and other easy marks. Three playing cards, one of which is the "red lady" Queen of Hearts, are put face-down on a cardboard box. The dealer quickly rear-ranges the cards and then asks the mark to pick the Queen of Hearts. But the dealer can use all sorts of tricks to hide the card or otherwise cheat, guarantee-ing that the victim never wins. It's also common for the dealer to have shills in the crowd who secretly work with the dealer but pretend to win the game (to make the victim think they too could win) or purposefully lose badly (to make the victim think they could do much better).

This program shows the three cards and then quickly describes a series of swaps. At the end, it clears the screen, and the player must pick a card.

Can you keep up with the "red lady"? For the authentic three-card monte experience, you can enable the cheat feature, which causes the player to always lose, even if they select the correct card.

The Program in Action

When you run *threecardmonte.py*, the output will look like this:

```
Three-Card Monte, by Al Sweigart al@inventwithpython.com

Find the red lady (the Queen of Hearts)! Keep an eye on how
the cards move.

Here are the cards:
 ___   ___   ___
|J  | |Q  | |8  |
| ♦ | | ♥ | | ♣ |
|__J| |__Q| |__8|
Press Enter when you are ready to begin...
swapping left and middle...
swapping right and middle...
swapping middle and left...
swapping right and left...
swapping left and middle...
--snip--
<screen clears>
Which card has the Queen of Hearts? (LEFT MIDDLE RIGHT)
> middle

 ___   ___   ___
|Q  | |8  | |J  |
| ♥ | | ♣ | | ♦ |
|__Q| |__8| |__J|
You lost!
Thanks for playing, sucker!
```

How It Works

In this program, we use a (*rank, suit*) tuple to represent a playing card. The rank is a string representing the card number, such as '2', '10', 'Q', or 'K', and the suit is a string of either a heart, club, spade, or diamond emoji. Since you cannot enter the emoji character using your keyboard, we'll use the chr() function calls on lines 16 to 19 to produce them. The tuple ('9', '♦') represents the nine of diamonds.

Instead of printing these tuples directly, the displayCards() function on lines 28 to 43 interprets them and displays ASCII-art representations on the screen, like in Project 4, "Blackjack." The cards argument for this function is a list of the playing card tuples, allowing multiple cards to be displayed in a row.

```
1. """Three-Card Monte, by Al Sweigart al@inventwithpython.com
2. Find the Queen of Hearts after cards have been swapped around.
3. (In the real-life version, the scammer palms the Queen of Hearts so you
4. always lose.)
5. More info at https://en.wikipedia.org/wiki/Three-card_Monte
6. View this code at https://nostarch.com/big-book-small-python-projects
7. Tags: large, card game, game"""
8.
9. import random, time
10.
11. # Set up the constants:
12. NUM_SWAPS = 16   # (!) Try changing this to 30 or 100.
13. DELAY    = 0.8  # (!) Try changing this 2.0 or 0.0.
14.
15. # The card suit characters:
16. HEARTS   = chr(9829)  # Character 9829 is '♥'
17. DIAMONDS = chr(9830)  # Character 9830 is '♦'
18. SPADES   = chr(9824)  # Character 9824 is '♠'
19. CLUBS    = chr(9827)  # Character 9827 is '♣'
20. # A list of chr() codes is at https://inventwithpython.com/chr
21.
22. # The indexes of a 3-card list:
23. LEFT   = 0
24. MIDDLE = 1
25. RIGHT  = 2
26.
27.
28. def displayCards(cards):
29.     """Display the cards in "cards", which is a list of (rank, suit)
30.     tuples."""
31.     rows = ['', '', '', '', '']  # Stores the text to display.
32.
33.     for i, card in enumerate(cards):
34.         rank, suit = card  # The card is a tuple data structure.
35.         rows[0] += ' ___ '  # Print the top line of the card.
36.         rows[1] += '|{} | '.format(rank.ljust(2))
37.         rows[2] += '| {} | '.format(suit)
38.         rows[3] += '|_{}| '.format(rank.rjust(2, '_'))
39.
40.
41.     # Print each row on the screen:
42.     for i in range(5):
43.         print(rows[i])
44.
45.
46. def getRandomCard():
47.     """Returns a random card that is NOT the Queen of Hearts."""
48.     while True:  # Make cards until you get a non-Queen of Hearts.
49.         rank = random.choice(list('23456789JQKA') + ['10'])
50.         suit = random.choice([HEARTS, DIAMONDS, SPADES, CLUBS])
51.
52.         # Return the card as long as it's not the Queen of Hearts:
53.         if rank != 'Q' and suit != HEARTS:
54.             return (rank, suit)
```

```
55.
56.
57. print('Three-Card Monte, by Al Sweigart al@inventwithpython.com')
58. print()
59. print('Find the red lady (the Queen of Hearts)! Keep an eye on how')
60. print('the cards move.')
61. print()
62.
63. # Show the original arrangement:
64. cards = [('Q', HEARTS), getRandomCard(), getRandomCard()]
65. random.shuffle(cards)  # Put the Queen of Hearts in a random place.
66. print('Here are the cards:')
67. displayCards(cards)
68. input('Press Enter when you are ready to begin...')
69.
70. # Print the swaps:
71. for i in range(NUM_SWAPS):
72.     swap = random.choice(['l-m', 'm-r', 'l-r', 'm-l', 'r-m', 'r-l'])
73.
74.     if swap == 'l-m':
75.         print('swapping left and middle...')
76.         cards[LEFT], cards[MIDDLE] = cards[MIDDLE], cards[LEFT]
77.     elif swap == 'm-r':
78.         print('swapping middle and right...')
79.         cards[MIDDLE], cards[RIGHT] = cards[RIGHT], cards[MIDDLE]
80.     elif swap == 'l-r':
81.         print('swapping left and right...')
82.         cards[LEFT], cards[RIGHT] = cards[RIGHT], cards[LEFT]
83.     elif swap == 'm-l':
84.         print('swapping middle and left...')
85.         cards[MIDDLE], cards[LEFT] = cards[LEFT], cards[MIDDLE]
86.     elif swap == 'r-m':
87.         print('swapping right and middle...')
88.         cards[RIGHT], cards[MIDDLE] = cards[MIDDLE], cards[RIGHT]
89.     elif swap == 'r-l':
90.         print('swapping right and left...')
91.         cards[RIGHT], cards[LEFT] = cards[LEFT], cards[RIGHT]
92.
93.     time.sleep(DELAY)
94.
95. # Print several new lines to hide the swaps.
96. print('\n' * 60)
97.
98. # Ask the user to find the red lady:
99. while True:  # Keep asking until LEFT, MIDDLE, or RIGHT is entered.
100.     print('Which card has the Queen of Hearts? (LEFT MIDDLE RIGHT)')
101.     guess = input('> ').upper()
102.
103.     # Get the index in cards for the position that the player entered:
104.     if guess in ['LEFT', 'MIDDLE', 'RIGHT']:
105.         if guess == 'LEFT':
106.             guessIndex = 0
107.         elif guess == 'MIDDLE':
108.             guessIndex = 1
109.         elif guess == 'RIGHT':
```

```
110.            guessIndex = 2
111.        break
112.
113. # (!) Uncomment this code to make the player always lose:
114. #if cards[guessIndex] == ('Q', HEARTS):
115. #    # Player has won, so let's move the queen.
116. #    possibleNewIndexes = [0, 1, 2]
117. #    possibleNewIndexes.remove(guessIndex)  # Remove the queen's index.
118. #    newInd = random.choice(possibleNewIndexes)  # Choose a new index.
119. #    # Place the queen at the new index:
120. #    cards[guessIndex], cards[newInd] = cards[newInd], cards[guessIndex]
121.
122. displayCards(cards)  # Show all the cards.
123.
124. # Check if the player won:
125. if cards[guessIndex] == ('Q', HEARTS):
126.     print('You won!')
127.     print('Thanks for playing!')
128. else:
129.     print('You lost!')
130.     print('Thanks for playing, sucker!')
```

After entering the source code and running it a few times, try making experimental changes to it. The comments marked with (!) have suggestions for small changes you can make. On your own, you can also try to figure out how to do the following:

- Use the backspace-printing technique from Project 57, "Progress Bar," to display each swap message briefly and then print \b characters to erase it before printing the next one.
- Create a four-card monte game for added difficulty.

Exploring the Program

Try to find the answers to the following questions. Experiment with some modifications to the code and rerun the program to see what effect the changes have.

1. What happens if you change [('Q', HEARTS), getRandomCard(), getRandomCard()] on line 64 to [('Q', HEARTS), ('Q', HEARTS), ('Q', HEARTS)]?

2. What happens if you change list('23456789JQKA') on line 49 to list('ABCDEFGHIJK')?

3. What happens if you delete or comment out time.sleep(DELAY) on line 93?

#76

TIC-TAC-TOE

 Tic-tac-toe is a classic pencil-and-paper game played on a 3 × 3 grid. Players take turns placing their X or O marks, trying to get three in a row. Most games of tic-tac-toe end in a tie, but it is possible to outsmart your opponent if they're not careful.

The Program in Action

When you run *tictactoe.py*, the output will look like this:

```
Welcome to Tic-Tac-Toe!

        | |    1 2 3
       -+-+-
        | |    4 5 6
       -+-+-
        | |    7 8 9
What is X's move? (1-9)
> 1

       X| |    1 2 3
       -+-+-
        | |    4 5 6
       -+-+-
        | |    7 8 9
What is O's move? (1-9)
--snip--
       X|O|X   1 2 3
       -+-+-
       X|O|O   4 5 6
       -+-+-
       O|X|X   7 8 9
The game is a tie!
Thanks for playing!
```

How It Works

To represent tic-tac-toe boards in this program, we use a dictionary with keys '1' through '9' for the spaces on the board. The numbered spaces are arranged in the same way as a phone's keypad. The values in this dictionary are the string 'X' or 'O' for a player's mark and ' ' for an empty space.

```
 1. """Tic-Tac-Toe, by Al Sweigart al@inventwithpython.com
 2. The classic board game.
 3. View this code at https://nostarch.com/big-book-small-python-projects
 4. Tags: short, board game, game, two-player"""
 5.
 6. ALL_SPACES = ['1', '2', '3', '4', '5', '6', '7', '8', '9']
 7. X, O, BLANK = 'X', 'O', ' '   # Constants for string values.
 8.
 9.
10. def main():
11.     print('Welcome to Tic-Tac-Toe!')
12.     gameBoard = getBlankBoard()  # Create a TTT board dictionary.
13.     currentPlayer, nextPlayer = X, O  # X goes first, O goes next.
14.
15.     while True:  # Main game loop.
16.         # Display the board on the screen:
17.         print(getBoardStr(gameBoard))
```

```
18.
19.         # Keep asking the player until they enter a number 1-9:
20.         move = None
21.         while not isValidSpace(gameBoard, move):
22.             print('What is {}\'s move? (1-9)'.format(currentPlayer))
23.             move = input('> ')
24.         updateBoard(gameBoard, move, currentPlayer)  # Make the move.
25.
26.         # Check if the game is over:
27.         if isWinner(gameBoard, currentPlayer):  # Check for a winner.
28.             print(getBoardStr(gameBoard))
29.             print(currentPlayer + ' has won the game!')
30.             break
31.         elif isBoardFull(gameBoard):  # Check for a tie.
32.             print(getBoardStr(gameBoard))
33.             print('The game is a tie!')
34.             break
35.         # Switch turns to the next player:
36.         currentPlayer, nextPlayer = nextPlayer, currentPlayer
37.     print('Thanks for playing!')
38.
39.
40. def getBlankBoard():
41.     """Create a new, blank tic-tac-toe board."""
42.     # Map of space numbers: 1|2|3
43.     #                        -+-+-
44.     #                        4|5|6
45.     #                        -+-+-
46.     #                        7|8|9
47.     # Keys are 1 through 9, the values are X, O, or BLANK:
48.     board = {}
49.     for space in ALL_SPACES:
50.         board[space] = BLANK  # All spaces start as blank.
51.     return board
52.
53.
54. def getBoardStr(board):
55.     """Return a text-representation of the board."""
56.     return '''
57.       {}|{}|{}   1 2 3
58.       -+-+-
59.       {}|{}|{}   4 5 6
60.       -+-+-
61.       {}|{}|{}   7 8 9'''.format(board['1'], board['2'], board['3'],
62.                                  board['4'], board['5'], board['6'],
63.                                  board['7'], board['8'], board['9'])
64.
65. def isValidSpace(board, space):
66.     """Returns True if the space on the board is a valid space number
67.     and the space is blank."""
68.     return space in ALL_SPACES and board[space] == BLANK
69.
70.
71. def isWinner(board, player):
72.     """Return True if player is a winner on this TTTBoard."""
```

```
73.    # Shorter variable names used here for readability:
74.    b, p = board, player
75.    # Check for 3 marks across 3 rows, 3 columns, and 2 diagonals.
76.    return ((b['1'] == b['2'] == b['3'] == p) or   # Across top
77.            (b['4'] == b['5'] == b['6'] == p) or   # Across middle
78.            (b['7'] == b['8'] == b['9'] == p) or   # Across bottom
79.            (b['1'] == b['4'] == b['7'] == p) or   # Down left
80.            (b['2'] == b['5'] == b['8'] == p) or   # Down middle
81.            (b['3'] == b['6'] == b['9'] == p) or   # Down right
82.            (b['3'] == b['5'] == b['7'] == p) or   # Diagonal
83.            (b['1'] == b['5'] == b['9'] == p))     # Diagonal
84.
85. def isBoardFull(board):
86.    """Return True if every space on the board has been taken."""
87.    for space in ALL_SPACES:
88.        if board[space] == BLANK:
89.            return False  # If any space is blank, return False.
90.    return True  # No spaces are blank, so return True.
91.
92.
93. def updateBoard(board, space, mark):
94.    """Sets the space on the board to mark."""
95.    board[space] = mark
96.
97.
98. if __name__ == '__main__':
99.    main()  # Call main() if this module is run, but not when imported.
```

Exploring the Program

Try to find the answers to the following questions. Experiment with some modifications to the code and rerun the program to see what effect the changes have.

1. What happens if you change X, O, BLANK = 'X', 'O', ' ' on line 7 to X, O, BLANK = 'X', 'X', ' '?

2. What happens if you change board[space] = mark on line 95 to board[space] = X?

3. What happens if you change board[space] = BLANK on line 50 to board[space] = X?

#77

TOWER OF HANOI

The Tower of Hanoi is a stack-moving puzzle game that features three poles on which you can stack various-sized disks. The object of the game is to move one tower of disks to another pole. However, only one disk can be moved at a time, and larger disks cannot be placed on top of smaller ones. Figuring out a certain pattern will help you solve this puzzle. Can you discover it? (Hint: Try setting the TOTAL_DISKS variable to 3 or 4 to solve an easier version first.)

The Program in Action

When you run *towerofhanoi.py*, the output will look like this:

```
The Tower of Hanoi, by Al Sweigart al@inventwithpython.com

Move the tower of disks, one disk at a time, to another tower. Larger
disks cannot rest on top of a smaller disk.

More info at https://en.wikipedia.org/wiki/Tower_of_Hanoi

        ||            ||            ||
      @_1@            ||            ||
     @@_2@@           ||            ||
    @@@_3@@@          ||            ||
   @@@@_4@@@@         ||            ||
  @@@@@_5@@@@@        ||            ||
        A             B             C

Enter the letters of "from" and "to" towers, or QUIT.
(e.g. AB to moves a disk from tower A to tower B.)
> ab
        ||            ||            ||
        ||            ||            ||
     @@_2@@           ||            ||
    @@@_3@@@          ||            ||
   @@@@_4@@@@         ||            ||
  @@@@@_5@@@@@      @_1@            ||
        A             B             C

Enter the letters of "from" and "to" towers, or QUIT.
(e.g. AB to moves a disk from tower A to tower B.)
--snip--
```

How It Works

The data structure that represents a tower is a list of integers. Each integer is the size of the disk. The first integer in the list represents the bottom disk, and the last integer represents the top disk. For example, [5, 4, 2] would represent the following tower:

```
        ||
        ||
     @@_2@@
   @@@@_4@@@@
  @@@@@_5@@@@@
```

Python's append() and pop() list methods can add and remove values from the end of the list, respectively. Just as someList[0] and someList[1] allow us to access the first and second values in a list, Python lets us use negative indexes to access values from the end of the list using expressions like someList[-1] and someList[-2], which access the last and second-to-last values in a list, respectively. This is useful for finding the disk currently at the top of the tower.

```python
1. """The Tower of Hanoi, by Al Sweigart al@inventwithpython.com
2. A stack-moving puzzle game.
3. View this code at https://nostarch.com/big-book-small-python-projects
4. Tags: short, game, puzzle"""
5.
6. import copy
7. import sys
8.
9. TOTAL_DISKS = 5  # More disks means a more difficult puzzle.
10.
11. # Start with all disks on tower A:
12. COMPLETE_TOWER = list(range(TOTAL_DISKS, 0, -1))
13.
14.
15. def main():
16.     print("""The Tower of Hanoi, by Al Sweigart al@inventwithpython.com
17.
18. Move the tower of disks, one disk at a time, to another tower. Larger
19. disks cannot rest on top of a smaller disk.
20.
21. More info at https://en.wikipedia.org/wiki/Tower_of_Hanoi
22. """
23.     )
24.
25.     # Set up the towers. The end of the list is the top of the tower.
26.     towers = {'A': copy.copy(COMPLETE_TOWER), 'B': [], 'C': []}
27.
28.     while True:  # Run a single turn.
29.         # Display the towers and disks:
30.         displayTowers(towers)
31.
32.         # Ask the user for a move:
33.         fromTower, toTower = askForPlayerMove(towers)
34.
35.         # Move the top disk from fromTower to toTower:
36.         disk = towers[fromTower].pop()
37.         towers[toTower].append(disk)
38.
39.         # Check if the user has solved the puzzle:
40.         if COMPLETE_TOWER in (towers['B'], towers['C']):
41.             displayTowers(towers)  # Display the towers one last time.
42.             print('You have solved the puzzle! Well done!')
43.             sys.exit()
44.
45.
46. def askForPlayerMove(towers):
47.     """Asks the player for a move. Returns (fromTower, toTower)."""
48.
49.     while True:  # Keep asking player until they enter a valid move.
50.         print('Enter the letters of "from" and "to" towers, or QUIT.')
```

```
51.             print('(e.g. AB to moves a disk from tower A to tower B.)')
52.             response = input('> ').upper().strip()
53.
54.             if response == 'QUIT':
55.                 print('Thanks for playing!')
56.                 sys.exit()
57.
58.             # Make sure the user entered valid tower letters:
59.             if response not in ('AB', 'AC', 'BA', 'BC', 'CA', 'CB'):
60.                 print('Enter one of AB, AC, BA, BC, CA, or CB.')
61.                 continue  # Ask player again for their move.
62.
63.             # Syntactic sugar - Use more descriptive variable names:
64.             fromTower, toTower = response[0], response[1]
65.
66.             if len(towers[fromTower]) == 0:
67.                 # The "from" tower cannot be an empty tower:
68.                 print('You selected a tower with no disks.')
69.                 continue  # Ask player again for their move.
70.             elif len(towers[toTower]) == 0:
71.                 # Any disk can be moved onto an empty "to" tower:
72.                 return fromTower, toTower
73.             elif towers[toTower][-1] < towers[fromTower][-1]:
74.                 print('Can\'t put larger disks on top of smaller ones.')
75.                 continue  # Ask player again for their move.
76.             else:
77.                 # This is a valid move, so return the selected towers:
78.                 return fromTower, toTower
79.
80.
81. def displayTowers(towers):
82.     """Display the current state."""
83.
84.     # Display the three towers:
85.     for level in range(TOTAL_DISKS, -1, -1):
86.         for tower in (towers['A'], towers['B'], towers['C']):
87.             if level >= len(tower):
88.                 displayDisk(0)  # Display the bare pole with no disk.
89.             else:
90.                 displayDisk(tower[level])  # Display the disk.
91.         print()
92.
93.     # Display the tower labels A, B, and C.
94.     emptySpace = ' ' * (TOTAL_DISKS)
95.     print('{0} A{0}{0} B{0}{0} C\n'.format(emptySpace))
96.
97.
98. def displayDisk(width):
99.     """Display a disk of the given width. A width of 0 means no disk."""
100.     emptySpace = ' ' * (TOTAL_DISKS - width)
101.
102.     if width == 0:
103.         # Display a pole segment without a disk:
104.         print(emptySpace + '||' + emptySpace, end='')
105.     else:
```

```
106.        # Display the disk:
107.        disk = '@' * width
108.        numLabel = str(width).rjust(2, '_')
109.        print(emptySpace + disk + numLabel + disk + emptySpace, end='')
110.
111.
112. # If the program is run (instead of imported), run the game:
113. if __name__ == '__main__':
114.     main()
```

Exploring the Program

Try to find the answers to the following questions. Experiment with some modifications to the code and rerun the program to see what effect the changes have.

1. What happens if you delete or comment out lines 73, 74, and 75?
2. What happens if you change emptySpace = ' ' * (TOTAL_DISKS - width) on line 100 to emptySpace = ' '?
3. What happens if you change width == 0 on line 102 to width != 0?

#78

TRICK QUESTIONS

What does a yellow stone thrown into a blue pond become? Do they have a 4th of July in England? How can a doctor go 30 days without sleep? Whatever you think the answers to these trick questions are, you're probably wrong. The 54 questions in this program have been specifically crafted so that their answers are simple, obvious, and misleading. Finding the true answer will require some cleverness.

Copying the code from this book will spoil the fun, since you'll see the answers, so you might want to download and play this game from *https://inventwithpython.com/trickquestions.py* before looking at the source code.

The Program in Action

When you run *trickquestions.py*, the output will look like this:

```
Trick Questions, by Al Sweigart al@inventwithpython.com

Can you figure out the answers to these trick questions?
(Enter QUIT to quit at any time.)

Press Enter to begin...
--snip--
Question: 1
Score: 0 / 54
QUESTION: A 39 year old person was born on the 22nd of February. What year is
their birthday?
  ANSWER: 1981
Incorrect! The answer is: Their birthday is on February 22nd of every year.
Press Enter for the next question...
--snip--
Question: 2
Score: 0 / 54
QUESTION: If there are ten apples and you take away two, how many do you have?
  ANSWER: Eight
Incorrect! The answer is: Two.
Press Enter for the next question...
--snip--
```

How It Works

The QUESTIONS variable holds a list of dictionaries. Each dictionary represents a single trick question and has the keys 'question', 'answer', and 'accept'. The values for 'question' and 'answer' are strings the program displays when it poses the question to the player and reveals the answer, respectively. The value for the 'accept' key is a list of strings. If the player enters a response that contains any of these strings, it's accepted as correct. This allows the player to enter free-form text as their reply. The program is reasonably accurate in detecting when they've provided the correct answer.

```python
1. """Trick Questions, by Al Sweigart al@inventwithpython.com
2. A quiz of several trick questions.
3. View this code at https://nostarch.com/big-book-small-python-projects
4. Tags: large, humor"""
5.
6. import random, sys
7.
8. # QUESTIONS is a list of dictionaries, each dictionary represents a
9. # trick question and its answer. The dictionary has the keys 'question'
10. # (which holds the text of the question), 'answer' (which holds the text
11. # of the answer), and 'accept' (which holds a list of strings that, if
12. # the player's answer contains any of, they've answered correctly).
13. # (!) Try coming up with your own trick questions to add here:
14. QUESTIONS = [
```

```
15.  {'question': "How many times can you take 2 apples from a pile of 10 apples?",
16.   'answer': "Once. Then you have a pile of 8 apples.",
17.   'accept': ['once', 'one', '1']},
18.  {'question': 'What begins with "e" and ends with "e" but only has one letter in it?',
19.   'answer': "An envelope.",
20.   'accept': ['envelope']},
21.  {'question': "Is it possible to draw a square with three sides?",
22.   'answer': "Yes. All squares have three sides. They also have a fourth side.",
23.   'accept': ['yes']},
24.  {'question': "How many times can a piece of paper be folded in half by hand without
        unfolding?",
25.   'answer': "Once. Then you are folding it in quarters.",
26.   'accept': ['one', '1', 'once']},
27.  {'question': "What does a towel get as it dries?",
28.   'answer': "Wet.",
29.   'accept': ['wet']},
30.  {'question': "What does a towel get as it dries?",
31.   'answer': "Drier.",
32.   'accept': ['drier', 'dry']},
33.  {'question': "Imagine you are in a haunted house full of evil ghosts. What do you
        have to do to stay safe?",
34.   'answer': "Nothing. You're only imagining it.",
35.   'accept': ['nothing', 'stop']},
36.  {'question': "A taxi driver is going the wrong way down a one-way street. She passes
        ten cops but doesn't get a ticket. Why not?",
37.   'answer': "She was walking.",
38.   'accept': ['walk']},
39.  {'question': "What does a yellow stone thrown into a blue pond become?",
40.   'answer': "Wet.",
41.   'accept': ['wet']},
42.  {'question': "How many miles does must a cyclist bike to get to training?",
43.   'answer': "None. They're training as soon as they get on the bike.",
44.   'accept': ['none', 'zero', '0']},
45.  {'question': "What building do people want to leave as soon as they enter?",
46.   'answer': "An airport.",
47.   'accept': ['airport', 'bus', 'port', 'train', 'station', 'stop']},
48.  {'question': "If you're in the middle of a square house facing the west side with
        the south side to your left and the north side to your right, which side of the
        house are you next to?",
49.   'answer': "None. You're in the middle.",
50.   'accept': ['none', 'middle', 'not', 'any']},
51.  {'question': "How much dirt is in a hole 3 meters wide, 3 meters long, and 3 meters
        deep?",
52.   'answer': "There is no dirt in a hole.",
53.   'accept': ['no', 'none', 'zero']},
54.  {'question': "A girl mails a letter from America to Japan. How many miles did the
        stamp move?",
55.   'answer': "Zero. The stamp was in the same place on the envelope the whole time.",
56.   'accept': ['zero', '0', 'none', 'no']},
57.  {'question': "What was the highest mountain on Earth the day before Mount Everest
        was discovered?",
58.   'answer': "Mount Everest was still the highest mountain of Earth the day before it
        was discovered.",
59.   'accept': ['everest']},
60.  {'question': "How many fingers do most people have on their two hands?",
```

61.   'answer': "Eight. They also have two thumbs.",
62.   'accept': ['eight', '8']},
63.   {'question': "The 4th of July is a holiday in America. Do they have a 4th of July in England?",
64.   'answer': "Yes. All countries have a 4th of July on their calendar.",
65.   'accept': ['yes']},
66.   {'question': "Which letter of the alphabet makes honey?",
67.   'answer': "None. A bee is an insect, not a letter.",
68.   'accept': ['no', 'none', 'not']},
69.   {'question': "How can a doctor go 30 days without sleep?",
70.   'answer': "By sleeping at night.",
71.   'accept': ['night', 'evening']},
72.   {'question': "How many months have 28 days?",
73.   'answer': "12. All months have 28 days. Some have more days as well.",
74.   'accept': ['12', 'twelve', 'all']},
75.   {'question': "How many two cent stamps are in a dozen?",
76.   'answer': "A dozen.",
77.   'accept': ['12', 'twelve', 'dozen']},
78.   {'question': "Why is it illegal for a person living in North Dakota to be buried in South Dakota?",
79.   'answer': "Because it is illegal to bury someone alive.",
80.   'accept': ['alive', 'living', 'live']},
81.   {'question': "How many heads does a two-headed coin have?",
82.   'answer': "Zero. Coins are just circular pieces of metal. They don't have heads.",
83.   'accept': ['zero', 'none', 'no', '0']},
84.   {'question': "What kind of vehicle has four wheels and flies?",
85.   'answer': "A garbage truck.",
86.   'accept': ['garbage', 'dump', 'trash']},
87.   {'question': "What kind of vehicle has four wheels and flies?",
88.   'answer': "An airplane.",
89.   'accept': ['airplane', 'plane']},
90.   {'question': "What five-letter word becomes shorter by adding two letters?",
91.   'answer': "Short.",
92.   'accept': ['short']},
93.   {'question': "Gwen's mother has five daughters. Four are named Haha, Hehe, Hihi, and Hoho. What's the fifth daughter's name?",
94.   'answer': "Gwen.",
95.   'accept': ['gwen']},
96.   {'question': "How long is a fence if there are three fence posts each one meter apart?",
97.   'answer': "Two meters long.",
98.   'accept': ['2', 'two']},
99.   {'question': "How many legs does a dog have if you count its tail as a leg?",
100.   'answer': "Four. Calling a tail a leg doesn't make it one.",
101.   'accept': ['four', '4']},
102.   {'question': "How much more are 1976 pennies worth compared to 1975 pennies?",
103.   'answer': "One cent.",
104.   'accept': ['1', 'one']},
105.   {'question': "What two things can you never eat for breakfast?",
106.   'answer': "Lunch and dinner.",
107.   'accept': ['lunch', 'dinner', 'supper']},
108.   {'question': "How many birthdays does the average person have?",
109.   'answer': "One. You're only born once.",
110.   'accept': ['one', '1', 'once' 'born']},
111.   {'question': "Where was the United States Declaration of Independence signed?",
112.   'answer': "It was signed at the bottom.",

```
113.     'accept': ['bottom']},
114. {'question': "A person puts two walnuts in their pocket but only has one thing in
           their pocket five minutes later. What is it?",
115.     'answer': "A hole.",
116.     'accept': ['hole']},
117. {'question': "What did the sculptor make that no one could see?",
118.     'answer': "Noise.",
119.     'accept': ['noise']},
120. {'question': "If you drop a raw egg on a concrete floor, will it crack?",
121.     'answer': "No. Concrete is very hard to crack.",
122.     'accept': ['no']},
123. {'question': "If it takes ten people ten hours to build a fence, how many hours does
           it take five people to build it?",
124.     'answer': "Zero. It's already built.",
125.     'accept': ['zero', 'no', '0', 'already', 'built']},
126. {'question': "Which is heavier, 100 pounds of rocks or 100 pounds of feathers?",
127.     'answer': "Neither. They weigh the same.",
128.     'accept': ['neither', 'none', 'no', 'same', 'even', 'balance']},
129. {'question': "What do you have to do to survive being bitten by a poisonous snake?",
130.     'answer': "Nothing. Only venomous snakes are deadly.",
131.     'accept': ['nothing', 'anything']},
132. {'question': "What three consecutive days don't include Sunday, Wednesday, or
           Friday?",
133.     'answer': "Yesterday, today, and tomorrow.",
134.     'accept': ['yesterday', 'today', 'tomorrow']},
135. {'question': "If there are ten apples and you take away two, how many do you have?",
136.     'answer': "Two.",
137.     'accept': ['2', 'two']},
138. {'question': "A 39 year old person was born on the 22nd of February. What year is
           their birthday?",
139.     'answer': "Their birthday is on February 22nd of every year.",
140.     'accept': ['every', 'each']},
141. {'question': "How far can you walk in the woods?",
142.     'answer': "Halfway. Then you are walking out of the woods.",
143.     'accept': ['half', '1/2']},
144. {'question': "Can a man marry his widow's sister?",
145.     'answer': "No, because he's dead.",
146.     'accept': ['no']},
147. {'question': "What do you get if you divide one hundred by half?",
148.     'answer': "One hundred divided by half is two hundred. One hundred divided by two
           is fifty.",
149.     'accept': ['two', '200']},
150. {'question': "What do you call someone who always knows where their spouse is?",
151.     'answer': "A widow or widower.",
152.     'accept': ['widow', 'widower']},
153. {'question': "How can someone take a photo but not be a photographer?",
154.     'answer': "They can be a thief.",
155.     'accept': ['thief', 'steal', 'take', 'literal']},
156. {'question': "An electric train leaves the windy city of Chicago at 4pm on a Monday
           heading south at 100 kilometers per hour. Which way does the smoke blow from the
           smokestack?",
157.     'answer': "Electric trains don't have smokestacks.",
158.     'accept': ["don't", "doesn't", 'not', 'no', 'none']},
159. {'question': 'What is the only word that rhymes with "orange"?',
160.     'answer': "Orange.",
```

```
161.         'accept': ['orange']},
162.    {'question': "Who is the U.S. President if the U.S. Vice President dies?",
163.         'answer': "The current U.S. President.",
164.         'accept': ['president', 'current', 'already']},
165.    {'question': "A doctor gives you three pills with instructions to take one every
            half-hour. How long will the pills last?",
166.         'answer': "One hour.",
167.         'accept': ['1', 'one']},
168.    {'question': "Where is there an ocean with no water?",
169.         'answer': "On a map.",
170.         'accept': ['map']},
171.    {'question': "What is the size of a rhino but weighs nothing?",
172.         'answer': "A rhino's shadow.",
173.         'accept': ['shadow']},
174.    {'question': "The clerk at a butcher shop is exactly 177 centimeters tall.
            What do they weigh?",
175.         'answer': "The clerk weighs meat.",
176.         'accept': ['meat']}]
177.
178. CORRECT_TEXT = ['Correct!', 'That is right.', "You're right.",
179.                      'You got it.', 'Righto!']
180. INCORRECT_TEXT = ['Incorrect!', "Nope, that isn't it.", 'Nope.',
181.                      'Not quite.', 'You missed it.']
182.
183. print('''Trick Questions, by Al Sweigart al@inventwithpython.com
184.
185. Can you figure out the answers to these trick questions?
186. (Enter QUIT to quit at any time.)
187. ''')
188.
189. input('Press Enter to begin...')
190.
191. random.shuffle(QUESTIONS)
192. score = 0
193.
194. for questionNumber, qa in enumerate(QUESTIONS):  # Main program loop.
195.     print('\n' * 40)  # "Clear" the screen.
196.     print('Question:', questionNumber + 1)
197.     print('Score:', score, '/', len(QUESTIONS))
198.     print('QUESTION:', qa['question'])
199.     response = input('  ANSWER: ').lower()
200.
201.     if response == 'quit':
202.         print('Thanks for playing!')
203.         sys.exit()
204.
205.     correct = False
206.     for acceptanceWord in qa['accept']:
207.         if acceptanceWord in response:
208.             correct = True
209.
210.     if correct:
211.         text = random.choice(CORRECT_TEXT)
212.         print(text, qa['answer'])
213.         score += 1
```

```
214.       else:
215.           text = random.choice(INCORRECT_TEXT)
216.           print(text, 'The answer is:', qa['answer'])
217.       response = input('Press Enter for the next question...').lower()
218.
219.       if response == 'quit':
220.           print('Thanks for playing!')
221.           sys.exit()
222.
223. print("That's all the questions. Thanks for playing!")
```

After entering the source code and running it a few times, try making experimental changes to it. The comments marked with (!) have suggestions for small changes you can make.

Exploring the Program

This is a base program, so there aren't many options to customize it. Instead, consider other uses for a question-and-answer program format.

#79

TWENTY FORTY-EIGHT

Gabriele Cirulli, a web developer, invented the game 2048 in one weekend. It was inspired by Veewo Studios' 1024 game, which in turn was inspired by Threes!, a game by the development team Sirvo. In 2048, you must merge numbers on a 4 × 4 board to clear them from the screen. Two 2s merge into a 4, two 4s merge into an 8, and so on. The game adds a new 2 to the board on each merging. The objective is to reach 2048 before the entire board fills up.

The Program in Action

When you run *twentyfortyeight.py*, the output will look like this:

```
Twenty Forty-Eight, by Al Sweigart al@inventwithpython.com
--snip--
+-----+-----+-----+-----+
|     |     |     |     |
|     |     |  2  | 16  |
|     |     |     |     |
+-----+-----+-----+-----+
|     |     |     |     |
|     | 16  |  4  |  2  |
|     |     |     |     |
+-----+-----+-----+-----+
|     |     |     |     |
|  2  |     |  4  | 32  |
|     |     |     |     |
+-----+-----+-----+-----+
|     |     |     |     |
|     |     |     |  2  |
|     |     |     |     |
+-----+-----+-----+-----+

Score: 80
Enter move: (WASD or Q to quit)
--snip--
```

How It Works

This program implements its sliding behavior using "column" data structures, represented by lists of four strings: BLANK (a single-space string), '2', '4', '8', and so on. The first value in this list represents the bottom of the column, while the last represents the top. Numbers that combine in a column always slide downward, whether the player slides the tiles up, down, left, or right. Think of it as gravity pulling the tiles in these directions. For example, Figure 79-1 shows a board with tiles sliding to the right. We'll create four lists to represent the columns:

- ['2', '4', '8', ' ']
- [' ', ' ', ' ', '4']
- [' ', ' ', ' ', '2']
- [' ', ' ', ' ', ' ']

The combineTilesInColumn() function accepts one column list and returns another, with the matching numbers combined and shifted toward the bottom. The code that calls combineTilesInColumn() handles creating the column lists in the appropriate direction and updating the game board with the returned list.

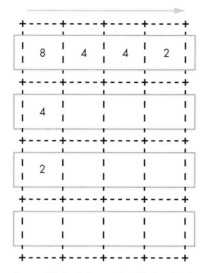

Figure 79-1: Columns (highlighted) when a game board is sliding to the right

```
1. """Twenty Forty-Eight, by Al Sweigart al@inventwithpython.com
2. A sliding tile game to combine exponentially-increasing numbers.
3. Inspired by Gabriele Cirulli's 2048, which is a clone of Veewo Studios'
4. 1024, which in turn is a clone of the Threes! game.
5. More info at https://en.wikipedia.org/wiki/2048_(video_game)
6. View this code at https://nostarch.com/big-book-small-python-projects
7. Tags: large, game, puzzle"""
8.
9. import random, sys
10.
11. # Set up the constants:
12. BLANK = ''  # A value that represents a blank space on the board.
13.
14.
15. def main():
16.     print('''Twenty Forty-Eight, by Al Sweigart al@inventwithpython.com
17.
18. Slide all the tiles on the board in one of four directions. Tiles with
19. like numbers will combine into larger-numbered tiles. A new 2 tile is
20. added to the board on each move. You win if you can create a 2048 tile.
21. You lose if the board fills up the tiles before then.''')
22.     input('Press Enter to begin...')
23.
24.     gameBoard = getNewBoard()
25.
26.     while True:  # Main game loop.
27.         drawBoard(gameBoard)
28.         print('Score:', getScore(gameBoard))
29.         playerMove = askForPlayerMove()
30.         gameBoard = makeMove(gameBoard, playerMove)
31.         addTwoToBoard(gameBoard)
32.
```

```
33.          if isFull(gameBoard):
34.              drawBoard(gameBoard)
35.              print('Game Over - Thanks for playing!')
36.              sys.exit()
37.
38.
39. def getNewBoard():
40.     """Returns a new data structure that represents a board.
41.
42.     It's a dictionary with keys of (x, y) tuples and values of the tile
43.     at that space. The tile is either a power-of-two integer or BLANK.
44.     The coordinates are laid out as:
45.        X0 1 2 3
46.        Y+-+-+-+-+
47.        0| | | | |
48.         +-+-+-+-+
49.        1| | | | |
50.         +-+-+-+-+
51.        2| | | | |
52.         +-+-+-+-+
53.        3| | | | |
54.         +-+-+-+-+"""
55.
56.     newBoard = {}  # Contains the board data structure to be returned.
57.     # Loop over every possible space and set all the tiles to blank:
58.     for x in range(4):
59.         for y in range(4):
60.             newBoard[(x, y)] = BLANK
61.
62.     # Pick two random spaces for the two starting 2s:
63.     startingTwosPlaced = 0  # The number of starting spaces picked.
64.     while startingTwosPlaced < 2:  # Repeat for duplicate spaces.
65.         randomSpace = (random.randint(0, 3), random.randint(0, 3))
66.         # Make sure the randomly selected space isn't already taken:
67.         if newBoard[randomSpace] == BLANK:
68.             newBoard[randomSpace] = 2
69.             startingTwosPlaced = startingTwosPlaced + 1
70.
71.     return newBoard
72.
73.
74. def drawBoard(board):
75.     """Draws the board data structure on the screen."""
76.
77.     # Go through each possible space left to right, top to bottom, and
78.     # create a list of what each space's label should be.
79.     labels = []  # A list of strings for the number/blank for that tile.
80.     for y in range(4):
81.         for x in range(4):
82.             tile = board[(x, y)]  # Get the tile at this space.
83.             # Make sure the label is 5 spaces long:
84.             labelForThisTile = str(tile).center(5)
85.             labels.append(labelForThisTile)
86.
87.     # The {} are replaced with the label for that tile:
```

```
88.    print("""
89. +-----+-----+-----+-----+
90. |     |     |     |     |
91. |{}|{}|{}|{}|
92. |     |     |     |     |
93. +-----+-----+-----+-----+
94. |     |     |     |     |
95. |{}|{}|{}|{}|
96. |     |     |     |     |
97. +-----+-----+-----+-----+
98. |     |     |     |     |
99. |{}|{}|{}|{}|
100. |     |     |     |     |
101. +-----+-----+-----+-----+
102. |     |     |     |     |
103. |{}|{}|{}|{}|
104. |     |     |     |     |
105. +-----+-----+-----+-----+
106. """.format(*labels))
107.
108.
109. def getScore(board):
110.     """Returns the sum of all the tiles on the board data structure."""
111.     score = 0
112.     # Loop over every space and add the tile to the score:
113.     for x in range(4):
114.         for y in range(4):
115.             # Only add non-blank tiles to the score:
116.             if board[(x, y)] != BLANK:
117.                 score = score + board[(x, y)]
118.     return score
119.
120.
121. def combineTilesInColumn(column):
122.     """The column is a list of four tile. Index 0 is the "bottom" of
123.     the column, and tiles are pulled "down" and combine if they are the
124.     same. For example, combineTilesInColumn([2, BLANK, 2, BLANK])
125.     returns [4, BLANK, BLANK, BLANK]."""
126.
127.     # Copy only the numbers (not blanks) from column to combinedTiles
128.     combinedTiles = []  # A list of the non-blank tiles in column.
129.     for i in range(4):
130.         if column[i] != BLANK:
131.             combinedTiles.append(column[i])
132.
133.     # Keep adding blanks until there are 4 tiles:
134.     while len(combinedTiles) < 4:
135.         combinedTiles.append(BLANK)
136.
137.     # Combine numbers if the one "above" it is the same, and double it.
138.     for i in range(3):  # Skip index 3: it's the topmost space.
139.         if combinedTiles[i] == combinedTiles[i + 1]:
140.             combinedTiles[i] *= 2  # Double the number in the tile.
141.             # Move the tiles above it down one space:
142.             for aboveIndex in range(i + 1, 3):
```

```
143.                      combinedTiles[aboveIndex] = combinedTiles[aboveIndex + 1]
144.                combinedTiles[3] = BLANK  # Topmost space is always BLANK.
145.        return combinedTiles
146.
147.
148. def makeMove(board, move):
149.        """Carries out the move on the board.
150.
151.        The move argument is either 'W', 'A', 'S', or 'D' and the function
152.        returns the resulting board data structure."""
153.
154.        # The board is split up into four columns, which are different
155.        # depending on the direction of the move:
156.        if move == 'W':
157.            allColumnsSpaces = [[(0, 0), (0, 1), (0, 2), (0, 3)],
158.                                [(1, 0), (1, 1), (1, 2), (1, 3)],
159.                                [(2, 0), (2, 1), (2, 2), (2, 3)],
160.                                [(3, 0), (3, 1), (3, 2), (3, 3)]]
161.        elif move == 'A':
162.            allColumnsSpaces = [[(0, 0), (1, 0), (2, 0), (3, 0)],
163.                                [(0, 1), (1, 1), (2, 1), (3, 1)],
164.                                [(0, 2), (1, 2), (2, 2), (3, 2)],
165.                                [(0, 3), (1, 3), (2, 3), (3, 3)]]
166.        elif move == 'S':
167.            allColumnsSpaces = [[(0, 3), (0, 2), (0, 1), (0, 0)],
168.                                [(1, 3), (1, 2), (1, 1), (1, 0)],
169.                                [(2, 3), (2, 2), (2, 1), (2, 0)],
170.                                [(3, 3), (3, 2), (3, 1), (3, 0)]]
171.        elif move == 'D':
172.            allColumnsSpaces = [[(3, 0), (2, 0), (1, 0), (0, 0)],
173.                                [(3, 1), (2, 1), (1, 1), (0, 1)],
174.                                [(3, 2), (2, 2), (1, 2), (0, 2)],
175.                                [(3, 3), (2, 3), (1, 3), (0, 3)]]
176.
177.        # The board data structure after making the move:
178.        boardAfterMove = {}
179.        for columnSpaces in allColumnsSpaces:  # Loop over all 4 columns.
180.            # Get the tiles of this column (The first tile is the "bottom"
181.            # of the column):
182.            firstTileSpace = columnSpaces[0]
183.            secondTileSpace = columnSpaces[1]
184.            thirdTileSpace = columnSpaces[2]
185.            fourthTileSpace = columnSpaces[3]
186.
187.            firstTile = board[firstTileSpace]
188.            secondTile = board[secondTileSpace]
189.            thirdTile = board[thirdTileSpace]
190.            fourthTile = board[fourthTileSpace]
191.
192.            # Form the column and combine the tiles in it:
193.            column = [firstTile, secondTile, thirdTile, fourthTile]
194.            combinedTilesColumn = combineTilesInColumn(column)
195.
196.            # Set up the new board data structure with the combined tiles:
197.            boardAfterMove[firstTileSpace] = combinedTilesColumn[0]
```

```python
198.            boardAfterMove[secondTileSpace] = combinedTilesColumn[1]
199.            boardAfterMove[thirdTileSpace] = combinedTilesColumn[2]
200.            boardAfterMove[fourthTileSpace] = combinedTilesColumn[3]
201.
202.     return boardAfterMove
203.
204.
205. def askForPlayerMove():
206.     """Asks the player for the direction of their next move (or quit).
207.
208.     Ensures they enter a valid move: either 'W', 'A', 'S' or 'D'."""
209.     print('Enter move: (WASD or Q to quit)')
210.     while True:  # Keep looping until they enter a valid move.
211.         move = input('> ').upper()
212.         if move == 'Q':
213.             # End the program:
214.             print('Thanks for playing!')
215.             sys.exit()
216.
217.         # Either return the valid move, or loop back and ask again:
218.         if move in ('W', 'A', 'S', 'D'):
219.             return move
220.         else:
221.             print('Enter one of "W", "A", "S", "D", or "Q".')
222.
223.
224. def addTwoToBoard(board):
225.     """Adds a new 2 tile randomly to the board."""
226.     while True:
227.         randomSpace = (random.randint(0, 3), random.randint(0, 3))
228.         if board[randomSpace] == BLANK:
229.             board[randomSpace] = 2
230.             return  # Return after finding one non-blank tile.
231.
232.
233. def isFull(board):
234.     """Returns True if the board data structure has no blanks."""
235.     # Loop over every space on the board:
236.     for x in range(4):
237.         for y in range(4):
238.             # If a space is blank, return False:
239.             if board[(x, y)] == BLANK:
240.                 return False
241.     return True  # No space is blank, so return True.
242.
243.
244. # If this program was run (instead of imported), run the game:
245. if __name__ == '__main__':
246.     try:
247.         main()
248.     except KeyboardInterrupt:
249.         sys.exit()  # When Ctrl-C is pressed, end the program.
```

Exploring the Program

Try to find the answers to the following questions. Experiment with some modifications to the code and rerun the program to see what effect the changes have.

1. What happens if you change return score on line 118 to return 9999?

2. What happens if you change board[randomSpace] = 2 on line 229 to board[randomSpace] = 256?

#80

VIGENÈRE CIPHER

 The Vigenère cipher, misattributed to 19th-century cryptographer Blaise de Vigenère (others had independently invented it earlier), was impossible to crack for hundreds of years. It is essentially the Caesar cipher, except it makes use of a multipart key. The so-called *Vigenère key* is a word, or even a random series of letters. Each letter represents a number by which to shift the letter in the message: *A* represents shifting a letter in the message by 0, *B* represents 1, *C* represents 2, and so on.

For example, if a Vigenère key is the word "CAT," the *C* represents a shift of 2, the *A* represents 0, and the *T* represents 19. The first letter of the message gets shifted by 2, the second letter by 0, and the third letter by 19. For the fourth letter, we repeat the key of 2.

This use of multiple Caesar cipher keys is what gives the Vigenère cipher its strength. The possible number of combinations is too big to brute force.

At the same time, the Vigenère cipher doesn't suffer from the frequency analysis weakness that can crack the simple substitution cipher. For centuries, the Vigenère cipher represented the state of the art in cryptography.

You'll notice many similarities between the code for the Vigenère and Caesar cipher programs. More info about the Vigenère cipher can be found at *https://en.wikipedia.org/wiki/Vigen%C3%A8re_cipher*. If you'd like to learn more about ciphers and code breaking, you can read my book *Cracking Codes with Python* (No Starch Press, 2018; *https://nostarch.com/crackingcodes/*).

The Program in Action

When you run *vigenere.py*, the output will look like this:

```
Vigenère Cipher, by Al Sweigart al@inventwithpython.com
The Vigenère cipher is a polyalphabetic substitution cipher that was
powerful enough to remain unbroken for centuries.
Do you want to (e)ncrypt or (d)ecrypt?
> e
Please specify the key to use.
It can be a word or any combination of letters:
> PIZZA
Enter the message to encrypt.
> Meet me by the rose bushes tonight.
Encrypted message:
Bmds mt jx sht znre qcrgeh bnmivps.
Full encrypted text copied to clipboard.
```

How It Works

Because the encryption and decryption processes are fairly similar, the translateMessage() function handles both of them. The encryptMessage() and decryptMessage() functions are merely *wrapper functions* for translateMessage(). In other words, they are functions that adjust their arguments, forward these to another function, and then return that function's return value. This program uses these wrapper functions so that they can be called in a manner similar to encryptMessage() and decryptMessage() in Project 66, "Simple Substitution Cipher." You can import these projects as modules in other programs to make use of their encryption code without having to copy and paste the code directly into your new program.

```
1. """Vigenère Cipher, by Al Sweigart al@inventwithpython.com
2. The Vigenère cipher is a polyalphabetic substitution cipher that was
3. powerful enough to remain unbroken for centuries.
4. More info at: https://en.wikipedia.org/wiki/Vigen%C3%A8re_cipher
5. View this code at https://nostarch.com/big-book-small-python-projects
6. Tags: short, cryptography, math"""
7.
8. try:
9.     import pyperclip  # pyperclip copies text to the clipboard.
```

```
10. except ImportError:
11.     pass  # If pyperclip is not installed, do nothing. It's no big deal.
12.
13. # Every possible symbol that can be encrypted/decrypted:
14. LETTERS = 'ABCDEFGHIJKLMNOPQRSTUVWXYZ'
15.
16.
17. def main():
18.     print('''Vigenère Cipher, by Al Sweigart al@inventwithpython.com
19. The Vigenère cipher is a polyalphabetic substitution cipher that was
20. powerful enough to remain unbroken for centuries.''')
21.
22.     # Let the user specify if they are encrypting or decrypting:
23.     while True:  # Keep asking until the user enters e or d.
24.         print('Do you want to (e)ncrypt or (d)ecrypt?')
25.         response = input('> ').lower()
26.         if response.startswith('e'):
27.             myMode = 'encrypt'
28.             break
29.         elif response.startswith('d'):
30.             myMode = 'decrypt'
31.             break
32.         print('Please enter the letter e or d.')
33.
34.     # Let the user specify the key to use:
35.     while True:  # Keep asking until the user enters a valid key.
36.         print('Please specify the key to use.')
37.         print('It can be a word or any combination of letters:')
38.         response = input('> ').upper()
39.         if response.isalpha():
40.             myKey = response
41.             break
42.
43.     # Let the user specify the message to encrypt/decrypt:
44.     print('Enter the message to {}.'.format(myMode))
45.     myMessage = input('> ')
46.
47.     # Perform the encryption/decryption:
48.     if myMode == 'encrypt':
49.         translated = encryptMessage(myMessage, myKey)
50.     elif myMode == 'decrypt':
51.         translated = decryptMessage(myMessage, myKey)
52.
53.     print('%sed message:' % (myMode.title()))
54.     print(translated)
55.
56.     try:
57.         pyperclip.copy(translated)
58.         print('Full %sed text copied to clipboard.' % (myMode))
59.     except:
60.         pass  # Do nothing if pyperclip wasn't installed.
61.
62.
63. def encryptMessage(message, key):
```

```
64.        """Encrypt the message using the key."""
65.        return translateMessage(message, key, 'encrypt')
66.
67.
68. def decryptMessage(message, key):
69.        """Decrypt the message using the key."""
70.        return translateMessage(message, key, 'decrypt')
71.
72.
73. def translateMessage(message, key, mode):
74.        """Encrypt or decrypt the message using the key."""
75.        translated = []  # Stores the encrypted/decrypted message string.
76.
77.        keyIndex = 0
78.        key = key.upper()
79.
80.        for symbol in message:  # Loop through each character in message.
81.            num = LETTERS.find(symbol.upper())
82.            if num != -1:  # -1 means symbol.upper() was not in LETTERS.
83.                if mode == 'encrypt':
84.                    # Add if encrypting:
85.                    num += LETTERS.find(key[keyIndex])
86.                elif mode == 'decrypt':
87.                    # Subtract if decrypting:
88.                    num -= LETTERS.find(key[keyIndex])
89.
90.                num %= len(LETTERS)  # Handle the potential wrap-around.
91.
92.                # Add the encrypted/decrypted symbol to translated.
93.                if symbol.isupper():
94.                    translated.append(LETTERS[num])
95.                elif symbol.islower():
96.                    translated.append(LETTERS[num].lower())
97.
98.                keyIndex += 1  # Move to the next letter in the key.
99.                if keyIndex == len(key):
100.                    keyIndex = 0
101.            else:
102.                # Just add the symbol without encrypting/decrypting:
103.                translated.append(symbol)
104.
105.        return ''.join(translated)
106.
107.
108. # If this program was run (instead of imported), run the program:
109. if __name__ == '__main__':
110.        main()
```

Exploring the Program

Try to find the answers to the following questions. Experiment with some modifications to the code and rerun the program to see what effect the changes have.

1. What happens when you encrypt with the key 'A'?
2. What error do you cause when you delete or comment out
   myKey = response on line 40?

#81

WATER BUCKET PUZZLE

 In this solitaire puzzle game, you must use three buckets (three-liter, five-liter, and eight-liter buckets) to collect exactly four liters of water in one of the buckets. Buckets can only be emptied, completely filled, or poured into another bucket. For example, you can fill the five-liter bucket and then pour its contents into the three-liter bucket, leaving you with a full three-liter bucket and two liters of water in the five-liter bucket.

With some effort, you should be able to solve the puzzle. But can you figure out how to solve it with the minimal number of moves?

The Program in Action

When you run *waterbucket.py*, the output will look like this:

```
Water Bucket Puzzle, by Al Sweigart al@inventwithpython.com

Try to get 4L of water into one of these
buckets:

8|      |
7|      |
6|      |
5|      |  5|      |
4|      |  4|      |
3|      |  3|      |  3|      |
2|      |  2|      |  2|      |
1|      |  1|      |  1|      |
 +------+   +------+   +------+
    8L        5L        3L

You can:
  (F)ill the bucket
  (E)mpty the bucket
  (P)our one bucket into another
  (Q)uit
> f
Select a bucket 8, 5, 3, or QUIT:
> 5

Try to get 4L of water into one of these
buckets:

8|      |
7|      |
6|      |
5|      |  5|WWWWWW|
4|      |  4|WWWWWW|
3|      |  3|WWWWWW|  3|      |
2|      |  2|WWWWWW|  2|      |
1|      |  1|WWWWWW|  1|      |
 +------+   +------+   +------+
    8L        5L        3L
--snip--
```

How It Works

The waterInBucket variable stores a dictionary that represents the state of the water buckets. The keys to this dictionary are the strings '8', '5', and '3' (representing the buckets), and their values are integers (representing the liters of water in that bucket).

Lines 48 to 59 use this dictionary to render the buckets and water on the screen. The waterDisplay list contains either 'WWWWWW' (representing water) or '   ' (representing air) and is passed to the format() string method. The first eight strings in the waterDisplay list fill the eight-liter bucket, the next five strings the five-liter bucket, and the final three strings the three-liter bucket.

```python
1. """Water Bucket Puzzle, by Al Sweigart al@inventwithpython.com
2. A water pouring puzzle.
3. More info: https://en.wikipedia.org/wiki/Water_pouring_puzzle
4. View this code at https://nostarch.com/big-book-small-python-projects
5. Tags: large, game, math, puzzle"""
6.
7. import sys
8.
9.
10. print('Water Bucket Puzzle, by Al Sweigart al@inventwithpython.com')
11.
12. GOAL = 4  # The exact amount of water to have in a bucket to win.
13. steps = 0  # Keep track of how many steps the player made to solve this.
14.
15. # The amount of water in each bucket:
16. waterInBucket = {'8': 0, '5': 0, '3': 0}
17.
18. while True:  # Main game loop.
19.     # Display the current state of the buckets:
20.     print()
21.     print('Try to get ' + str(GOAL) + 'L of water into one of these')
22.     print('buckets:')
23.
24.     waterDisplay = []  # Contains strings for water or empty space.
25.
26.     # Get the strings for the 8L bucket:
27.     for i in range(1, 9):
28.         if waterInBucket['8'] < i:
29.             waterDisplay.append('     ')  # Add empty space.
30.         else:
31.             waterDisplay.append('WWWWW')  # Add water.
32.
33.     # Get the strings for the 5L bucket:
34.     for i in range(1, 6):
35.         if waterInBucket['5'] < i:
36.             waterDisplay.append('     ')  # Add empty space.
37.         else:
38.             waterDisplay.append('WWWWW')  # Add water.
39.
40.     # Get the strings for the 3L bucket:
41.     for i in range(1, 4):
42.         if waterInBucket['3'] < i:
43.             waterDisplay.append('     ')  # Add empty space.
44.         else:
45.             waterDisplay.append('WWWWW')  # Add water.
46.
47.     # Display the buckets with the amount of water in each one:
48.     print('''
49. 8|{7}|
50. 7|{6}|
```

```
51.  6|{5}|
52.  5|{4}|   5|{12}|
53.  4|{3}|   4|{11}|
54.  3|{2}|   3|{10}|   3|{15}|
55.  2|{1}|   2|{9}|    2|{14}|
56.  1|{0}|   1|{8}|    1|{13}|
57.  +------+   +------+   +------+
58.     8L        5L        3L
59.  '''.format(*waterDisplay))
60.
61.      # Check if any of the buckets has the goal amount of water:
62.      for waterAmount in waterInBucket.values():
63.          if waterAmount == GOAL:
64.              print('Good job! You solved it in', steps, 'steps!')
65.              sys.exit()
66.
67.      # Let the player select an action to do with a bucket:
68.      print('You can:')
69.      print('  (F)ill the bucket')
70.      print('  (E)mpty the bucket')
71.      print('  (P)our one bucket into another')
72.      print('  (Q)uit')
73.
74.      while True:  # Keep asking until the player enters a valid action.
75.          move = input('> ').upper()
76.          if move == 'QUIT' or move == 'Q':
77.              print('Thanks for playing!')
78.              sys.exit()
79.
80.          if move in ('F', 'E', 'P'):
81.              break  # Player has selected a valid action.
82.          print('Enter F, E, P, or Q')
83.
84.      # Let the player select a bucket:
85.      while True:  # Keep asking until valid bucket entered.
86.          print('Select a bucket 8, 5, 3, or QUIT:')
87.          srcBucket = input('> ').upper()
88.
89.          if srcBucket == 'QUIT':
90.              print('Thanks for playing!')
91.              sys.exit()
92.
93.          if srcBucket in ('8', '5', '3'):
94.              break  # Player has selected a valid bucket.
95.
96.      # Carry out the selected action:
97.      if move == 'F':
98.          # Set the amount of water to the max size.
99.          srcBucketSize = int(srcBucket)
100.         waterInBucket[srcBucket] = srcBucketSize
101.         steps += 1
102.
103.     elif move == 'E':
104.         waterInBucket[srcBucket] = 0  # Set water amount to nothing.
105.         steps += 1
```

```
106.
107.     elif move == 'P':
108.         # Let the player select a bucket to pour into:
109.         while True:  # Keep asking until valid bucket entered.
110.             print('Select a bucket to pour into: 8, 5, or 3')
111.             dstBucket = input('> ').upper()
112.             if dstBucket in ('8', '5', '3'):
113.                 break  # Player has selected a valid bucket.
114.
115.         # Figure out the amount to pour:
116.         dstBucketSize = int(dstBucket)
117.         emptySpaceInDstBucket = dstBucketSize - waterInBucket[dstBucket]
118.         waterInSrcBucket = waterInBucket[srcBucket]
119.         amountToPour = min(emptySpaceInDstBucket, waterInSrcBucket)
120.
121.         # Pour out water from this bucket:
122.         waterInBucket[srcBucket] -= amountToPour
123.
124.         # Put the poured out water into the other bucket:
125.         waterInBucket[dstBucket] += amountToPour
126.         steps += 1
127.
128.     elif move == 'C':
129.         pass  # If the player selected Cancel, do nothing.
```

After entering the source code and running it a few times, try making experimental changes to it. On your own, you can also try to figure out how to do the following:

- Add variety by making the game configurable so you can specify any sizes for the three buckets and any amount for the goal quantity.
- Add a "hint" that examines the amount of water in each bucket and provides the next step to take. If the program can't figure out which action to take next, it can simply display "I don't know what you should do next. Maybe start over?"

Exploring the Program

Try to find the answers to the following questions. Experiment with some modifications to the code and rerun the program to see what effect the changes have.

1. What happens if you change waterInBucket[srcBucket] = 0 on line 104 to waterInBucket[srcBucket] = 1?

2. What happens if you change {'8': 0, '5': 0, '3': 0} on line 16 to {'8': 0, '5': 4, '3': 0}?

3. What happens if you change {'8': 0, '5': 0, '3': 0} on line 16 to {'8': 9, '5': 0, '3': 0}?

A

TAG INDEX

The projects in this book are marked with a set of tags that describe the type of program they are. The first tag indicates their size: tiny (1 to 63 lines), short (64 to 127 lines), large (128 to 255 lines), and extra-large (256 lines or more). The size tags are as follows:

tiny: #3 Bitmap Message, #7 Caesar Hacker, #12 Collatz Sequence, #14 Countdown, #15 Deep Cave, #16 Diamonds, #19 Digital Clock, #20 Digital Stream, #24 Factor Finder, #25 Fast Draw, #31 Guess the Number, #32 Gullible, #35 Hex Grid, #40 Leetspeak, #42 Magic Fortune Ball, #46 Million Dice Roll Statistics Simulator, #49 Multiplication Table, #50 Ninety-Nine Bottles, #52 Numeral Systems Counter, #56 Prime Numbers, #57 Progress Bar, #58 Rainbow, #60 Rock Paper Scissors (Always-Win Version), #61 ROT13 Cipher, #65 Shining Carpet, #67 Sine Message, #72 sPoNgEcAsE, #74 Text-To-Speech Talker

short: #1 Bagels, #2 Birthday Paradox, #5 Bouncing DVD Logo, #6 Caesar Cipher, #8 Calendar Maker, #10 Cho-Han, #13 Conway's Game of Life, #18 Dice Roller, #21 DNA Visualization, #26 Fibonacci, #29 Forest Fire Sim, #51 niNety nniinE BoOttels, #53 Periodic Table of the Elements, #54 Pig Latin, #55 Powerball Lottery, #59 Rock Paper Scissors, #64 Seven-Segment Display Module, #66 Simple Substitution Cipher, #69 Snail Race, #71 Sound Mimic, #76 Tic-Tac-Toe, #77 Tower of Hanoi, #80 Vigenère Cipher

large: #4 Blackjack, #9 Carrot in a Box, #11 Clickbait Headline Generator, #17 Dice Math, #22 Ducklings, #23 Etching Drawer, #28 Flooder, #30 Four in a Row, #33 Hacking Minigame, #34 Hangman and Guillotine, #36 Hourglass, #37 Hungry Robots, #39 Langton's Ant, #41 Lucky Stars, #43 Mancala, #44 Maze Runner 2D, #47 Mondrian Art Generator, #48 Monty Hall Problem, #62 Rotating Cube, #63 Royal Game of Ur, #68 Sliding Tile Puzzle, #70 Soroban Japanese Abacus, #73 Sudoku Puzzle, #75 Three-Card Monte, #78 Trick Questions, #79 Twenty Forty-Eight, #81 Water Bucket Puzzle

extra-large: #27 Fish Tank, #38 J'accuse!, #45 Maze Runner 3D

The remaining tags indicate the features of the program:

artistic: #3 Bitmap Message, #5 Bouncing DVD Logo, #13 Conway's Game of Life, #14 Countdown, #15 Deep Cave, #16 Diamonds, #17 Dice Math, #19 Digital Clock, #20 Digital Stream, #21 DNA Visualization, #22 Ducklings, #23 Etching Drawer, #27 Fish Tank, #33 Hacking Minigame, #35 Hex Grid, #36 Hourglass, #39 Langton's Ant, #45 Maze Runner 3D, #47 Mondrian Art Generator, #58 Rainbow, #62 Rotating Cube, #65 Shining Carpet, #67 Sine Message, #69 Snail Race, #70 Soroban Japanese Abacus

beginner: #3 Bitmap Message, #6 Caesar Cipher, #7 Caesar Hacker, #9 Carrot in a Box, #10 Cho-Han, #11 Clickbait Headline Generator, #12 Collatz Sequence, #15 Deep Cave, #16 Diamonds, #20 Digital Stream, #24 Factor Finder, #25 Fast Draw, #31 Guess the Number, #32 Gullible, #35 Hex Grid, #40 Leetspeak, #42 Magic Fortune Ball, #46 Million Dice Roll Statistics Simulator, #49 Multiplication Table, #50 Ninety-Nine Bottles, #58 Rainbow, #65 Shining Carpet, #69 Snail Race, #71 Sound Mimic, #72 sPoNgEcAsE, #74 Text-To-Speech Talker

bext: #5 Bouncing DVD Logo, #27 Fish Tank, #28 Flooder, #29 Forest Fire Sim, #36 Hourglass, #39 Langton's Ant, #47 Mondrian Art Generator, #58 Rainbow

board game: #30 Four in a Row, #43 Mancala, #63 Royal Game of Ur, #76 Tic-Tac-Toe

card game: #4 Blackjack, #75 Three-Card Monte

cryptography: #6 Caesar Cipher, #7 Caesar Hacker, #61 ROT13 Cipher, #66 Simple Substitution Cipher, #80 Vigenère Cipher

game: #1 Bagels, #4 Blackjack, #9 Carrot in a Box, #10 Cho-Han, #17 Dice Math, #25 Fast Draw, #28 Flooder, #30 Four in a Row, #31 Guess the Number, #33 Hacking Minigame, #34 Hangman and Guillotine, #37 Hungry Robots, #38 J'accuse!, #41 Lucky Stars, #43 Mancala, #44 Maze Runner 2D, #45 Maze Runner 3D, #48 Monty Hall Problem, #59 Rock Paper Scissors, #60 Rock Paper Scissors (Always-Win Version), #63 Royal Game of Ur, #68 Sliding Tile Puzzle, #69 Snail Race, #71 Sound Mimic, #73 Sudoku Puzzle, #75 Three-Card Monte, #76 Tic-Tac-Toe, #77 Tower of Hanoi Puzzle, #79 Twenty Forty-Eight, #81 Water Bucket Puzzle

humor: #11 Clickbait Headline Generator, #32 Gullible, #38 J'accuse!, #42 Magic Fortune Ball, #55 Powerball Lottery, #60 Rock Paper Scissors (Always-Win Version), #78 Trick Questions

math: #2 Birthday Paradox, #6 Caesar Cipher, #7 Caesar Hacker, #12 Collatz Sequence, #17 Dice Math, #24 Factor Finder, #26 Fibonacci, #46 Million Dice Roll Statistics Simulator, #48 Monty Hall Problem, #49 Multiplication Table, #52 Numeral Systems Counter, #56 Prime Numbers, #62 Rotating Cube, #66 Simple Substitution Cipher, #70 Soroban Japanese Abacus, #80 Vigenère Cipher, #81 Water Bucket Puzzle

maze: #44 Maze Runner 2D, #45 Maze Runner 3D

module: #57 Progress Bar, #64 Seven-Segment Display Module

multiplayer: #41 Lucky Stars, #69 Snail Race

object-oriented: #22 Ducklings, #73 Sudoku Puzzle

puzzle: #1 Bagels, #33 Hacking Minigame, #34 Hangman and Guillotine, #38 J'accuse!, #68 Sliding Tile Puzzle, #73 Sudoku Puzzle, #77 Tower of Hanoi Puzzle, #79 Twenty Forty-Eight, #81 Water Bucket Puzzle

science: #21 DNA Visualization, #53 Periodic Table of the Elements

scrolling: #15 Deep Cave, #20 Digital Stream, #21 DNA Visualization, #22 Ducklings, #50 Ninety-Nine Bottles, #51 niNety nniinE BoOttels, #56 Prime Numbers, #58 Rainbow

simulation: #2 Birthday Paradox, #13 Conway's Game of Life, #18 Dice Roller, #29 Forest Fire Sim, #36 Hourglass, #39 Langton's Ant, #46 Million Dice Roll Statistics Simulator, #48 Monty Hall Problem, #55 Powerball Lottery, #70 Soroban Japanese Abacus

two-player: #9 Carrot in a Box, #30 Four in a Row, #43 Mancala, #63 Royal Game of Ur, #76 Tic-Tac-Toe

word: #11 Clickbait Headline Generator, #34 Hangman and Guillotine, #40 Leetspeak, #51 niNety nniinE BoOttels, #54 Pig Latin, #72 sPoNgEcAsE

B

CHARACTER MAP

The `print()` function allows you to easily make any character you can type on the keyboard appear on the screen. However, there are many other characters you may like to display: the hearts, diamonds, clubs, and spades card suits; lines; shaded boxes; arrows; music notes; and so on. You can obtain string values of these characters by passing their numeric code, called a Unicode code point, to the `chr()` function. Text is stored on computers as a series of numbers, with each character represented by a different number. This appendix contains a list of such code points.

Using the chr() and ord() Functions

Python's built-in chr() function accepts an integer argument and returns a string of the number's character. The ord() function does the opposite: it accepts a string argument of a single character and returns the character's number. This number is the code point for the character in the Unicode standard.

For example, enter the following into the interactive shell:

```
>>> chr(65)
'A'
>>> ord('A')
65
>>> chr(66)
'B'
>>> chr(9829)
'♥'
```

Not all numbers are valid code points for printable characters. The terminal windows that show the text output of programs may be limited in which characters they can display. The font the terminal window uses also must support the character your program prints. The terminal window prints a Unicode replacement character, ◆, for any character it is unable to print.

Windows' terminal window has a far more limited range of characters it can display. This set is known as the Windows Glyph List 4, and it appears in this appendix and on Wikipedia at *https://en.wikipedia.org/wiki/Windows_Glyph_List_4*.

The code points for characters are often listed with a base-16 hexadecimal number, as opposed to the base-10 decimal numbers we are used to. Instead of the decimal digits 0 to 9, hexadecimal has the digits 0 to 9 and then continues with the letters A to F. Hexadecimal numbers are often written with a 0x prefix to denote that the number that follows is in hex.

You can convert a decimal integer value to a string of the hexadecimal number with the hex() function. You can convert a string of the hexadecimal number to a decimal integer with the int() function, passing 16 as the second argument. For example, enter the following into the interactive shell:

```
>>> hex(9)
'0x9'
>>> hex(10)
'0xa'
>>> hex(15)
'0xf'
>>> hex(16)
'0x10'
>>> hex(17)
'0x11'
>>> int('0x11', 16)
17
```

```
>>> int('11', 16)
17
```

When calling the chr() function, you must pass a decimal integer as the argument, not a hexadecimal string.

Table of Code Points

The following are all the Unicode code points in the set known as Windows Glyph List 4, which are the characters supported by the Windows terminal program, Command Prompt. Both macOS and Linux can display more characters than are in this list, but to keep your Python programs compatible, I recommend you stick to the characters in this table.

32 <space>	60 <	88 X	116 t
33 !	61 =	89 Y	117 u
34 "	62 >	90 Z	118 v
35 #	63 ?	91 [	119 w
36 $	64 @	92 \	120 x
37 %	65 A	93]	121 y
38 &	66 B	94 ^	122 z
39 '	67 C	95 _	123 {
40 (	68 D	96 `	124	
41)	69 E	97 a	125 }
42 *	70 F	98 b	126 ~
43 +	71 G	99 c	161 ¡
44 ,	72 H	100 d	162 ¢
45 -	73 I	101 e	163 £
46 .	74 J	102 f	164 ¤
47 /	75 K	103 g	165 ¥
48 0	76 L	104 h	166 ¦
49 1	77 M	105 i	167 §
50 2	78 N	106 j	168 ¨
51 3	79 O	107 k	169 ©
52 4	80 P	108 l	170 ª
53 5	81 Q	109 m	171 «
54 6	82 R	110 n	172 ¬
55 7	83 S	111 o	173 -
56 8	84 T	112 p	174 ®
57 9	85 U	113 q	175 ¯
58 :	86 V	114 r	176 °
59 ;	87 W	115 s	177 ±

178 ²	217 Ù	258 Ă	321 Ł
179 ³	218 Ú	259 ă	322 ł
180 ´	219 Û	260 Ą	323 Ń
181 µ	220 Ü	261 ą	324 ń
182 ¶	221 Ý	262 Ć	325 Ņ
183 ·	223 ß	263 ć	326 ņ
184 ¸	224 à	268 Č	327 Ň
185 ¹	225 á	269 č	328 ň
186 º	226 â	270 Ď	332 Ō
187 »	227 ã	271 ď	333 ō
188 ¼	228 ä	272 Đ	336 Ő
189 ½	229 å	273 đ	337 ő
190 ¾	230 æ	274 Ē	338 Œ
191 ¿	231 ç	275 ē	339 œ
192 À	232 è	278 Ė	340 Ŕ
193 Á	233 é	279 ė	341 ŕ
194 Â	234 ê	280 Ę	342 Ŗ
195 Ã	235 ë	281 ę	343 ŗ
196 Ä	236 ì	282 Ě	344 Ř
197 Å	237 í	283 ě	345 ř
198 Æ	238 î	286 Ğ	346 Ś
199 Ç	239 ï	287 ğ	347 ś
200 È	241 ñ	290 Ġ	350 Ş
201 É	242 ò	291 ġ	351 ş
202 Ê	243 ó	298 Ī	352 Š
203 Ë	244 ô	299 ī	353 š
204 Ì	245 õ	302 Į	354 Ţ
205 Í	246 ö	303 į	355 ţ
206 Î	247 ÷	304 İ	356 Ť
207 Ï	248 ø	305 ı	357 ť
209 Ñ	249 ù	310 Ķ	362 Ū
210 Ò	250 ú	311 ķ	363 ū
211 Ó	251 û	313 Ĺ	366 Ů
212 Ô	252 ü	314 ĺ	367 ů
213 Õ	253 ý	315 Ļ	368 Ű
214 Ö	255 ÿ	316 ļ	369 ű
215 ×	256 Ā	317 Ľ	370 Ų
216 Ø	257 ā	318 ľ	371 ų

376 Ÿ	926 Ξ	965 υ	1054 О
377 Ź	927 Ο	966 φ	1055 П
378 ź	928 Π	967 χ	1056 Р
379 Ż	929 Ρ	968 ψ	1057 С
380 ż	931 Σ	969 ω	1058 Т
381 Ž	932 Τ	970 ϊ	1059 У
382 ž	933 Υ	971 ϋ	1060 Ф
402 ƒ	934 Φ	972 ό	1061 Х
710 ˆ	935 Χ	973 ύ	1062 Ц
711 ˇ	936 Ψ	974 ώ	1063 Ч
728 ˘	937 Ω	1025 Ё	1064 Ш
729 ˙	938 Ϊ	1026 Ђ	1065 Щ
731 ˛	939 Ϋ	1027 Ѓ	1066 Ъ
732 ˜	940 ά	1028 Є	1067 Ы
733 ˝	941 έ	1029 Ѕ	1068 Ь
900 ΄	942 ή	1030 І	1069 Э
901 ΅	943 ί	1031 Ї	1070 Ю
902 Ά	944 ΰ	1032 Ј	1071 Я
904 Έ	945 α	1033 Љ	1072 а
905 Ή	946 β	1034 Њ	1073 б
906 Ί	947 γ	1035 Ћ	1074 в
908 Ό	948 δ	1036 Ќ	1075 г
910 Ύ	949 ε	1038 Ў	1076 д
911 Ώ	950 ζ	1039 Џ	1077 е
912 ΐ	951 η	1040 А	1078 ж
913 Α	952 θ	1041 Б	1079 з
914 Β	953 ι	1042 В	1080 и
915 Γ	954 κ	1043 Г	1081 й
916 Δ	955 λ	1044 Д	1082 к
917 Ε	956 μ	1045 Е	1083 л
918 Ζ	957 ν	1046 Ж	1084 м
919 Η	958 ξ	1047 З	1085 н
920 Θ	959 ο	1048 И	1086 о
921 Ι	960 π	1049 Й	1087 п
922 Κ	961 ρ	1050 К	1088 р
923 Λ	962 ς	1051 Л	1089 с
924 Μ	963 σ	1052 М	1090 т
925 Ν	964 τ	1053 Н	1091 у

1092 ф	8220 "	9516 ┬	9608 █
1093 x	8221 "	9524 ┴	9612 ▌
1094 ц	8222 „	9532 ┼	9616 ▐
1095 ч	8224 †	9552 ═	9617 ░
1096 ш	8225 ‡	9553 ║	9618 ▒
1097 щ	8226 •	9554 ╒	9619 ▓
1098 ъ	8230 …	9555 ╓	9632 ■
1099 ы	8240 ‰	9556 ╔	9633 □
1100 ь	8249 ‹	9557 ╕	9642 ▪
1101 э	8250 ›	9558 ╖	9643 ▫
1102 ю	8319 n	9559 ╗	9644 ▬
1103 я	8359 Pts	9560 ╘	9650 ▲
1105 ё	8364 €	9561 ╙	9658 ►
1106 ђ	8470 №	9562 ╚	9660 ▼
1107 ѓ	8482 ™	9563 ╛	9668 ◄
1108 є	8729 ·	9564 ╜	9674 ◊
1109 s	8730 √	9565 ╝	9675 ○
1110 i	8734 ∞	9566 ╞	9679 ●
1111 ï	8745 ∩	9567 ╟	9688 ◘
1112 j	8776 ≈	9568 ╠	9689 ◙
1113 љ	8801 ≡	9569 ╡	9702 ◦
1114 њ	8804 ≤	9570 ╢	9786 ☺
1115 ћ	8805 ≥	9571 ╣	9787 ☻
1116 ќ	8976 ⌐	9572 ╤	9788 ☼
1118 ў	8992 ⌠	9573 ╥	9792 ♀
1119 џ	8993 ⌡	9574 ╦	9794 ♂
1168 Ґ	9472 —	9575 ╧	9824 ♠
1169 ґ	9474 |	9576 ╨	9827 ♣
8211 –	9484 ┌	9577 ╩	9829 ♥
8212 —	9488 ┐	9578 ╪	9830 ♦
8213 ——	9492 └	9579 ╫	9834 ♪
8216 '	9496 ┘	9580 ╬	9835 ♫
8217 '	9500 ├	9600 ▀	
8218 ,	9508 ┤	9604 ▄	

The Big Book of Small Python Projects is set in New Baskerville, Futura, Dogma, and TheSansMono Condensed. The book was printed and bound by Sheridan Books, Inc. in Chelsea, Michigan.